PRAISE FOR FOUl

"You can't build a revenue house based on outbound selling without a solid foundation. *Founding Sales* helps founders, and other first time sellers, understand the basics that create that foundation and allows them to successfully scale."

—*Trish Bertuzzi, Founder of The Bridge Group & author of "The Sales Development Playbook"*

"Modern sales organizations succeed by a thoughtful, rigorous approach to the art and science of sales. *Founding Sales* introduces founders and other first time sellers to these concepts clearly and comprehensively."

—*Jeremey Donovan, SVP Sales Strategy and Operations at SalesLoft & author of "Leading Sales Development"*

"[My book] *Predictable Revenue* introduced the world to scalable outbound sales. But it won't work without a solid foundation. *Founding Sales* helps founders and other first-time sellers go from a dead stop to first gear in sales (the hardest part). Time after time first time founders and sellers try to sell and grow sales too fast, leading to failure. *Founding Sales* gets you started, building that foundation first so you're prepared to scale later."

—*Aaron Ross, Co-CEO at PredictableRevenue.com & author of "Predictable Revenue"*

For a searchable digital copy of *Founding Sales,* visit FoundingSales.com.

FOUNDING
SALES

The Early Stage Go-to-Market Handbook
Sales for founders (and others) in first time sales roles

PETER KAZANJY

Printed and Bound in the United States by Ingram/Lightning Source

Project Editing by Christina Bailly
Cover Design & Book Design by Tracy Moeller
Front Cover Photograph by Jeremy Bishop/Unsplash
Back Cover Photograph by Josiah Weiss/Unsplash

Library of Congress Control Number: 2020910086

ISBN: 978-1-7345051-1-5

Founding Sales is dedicated to my brother, Michael T. Kazanjy, and my son, Michael P. Kazanjy.

Contents

How a Product Marketing & Product Management Guy Ended Up a Sales Leader at a Public Company

WHAT INSPIRED THIS BOOK?

In Spring of 2010, our startup, Unvarnished, launched to a massive cataclysm of press coverage, venture capital interest, and general gnashing of teeth. As the world's first serious attempt at a community contributed reputation system for professionals, or a "Yelp for professionals", we were featured on the Today Show, covered by many national newspapers, and enjoyed traffic spikes that would be the envy of any newly launched startup.

By January of 2011, had we concluded that our concept was a failure, and we needed to try something new.

At the behest of our board members, Josh Kopelman and Phin Barnes of First Round Capital and Saar Gur of CRV, we started looking at other potential ways to solve the same problem (that is, hiring well is hard, and there is likely a data centric way to help with that).

And while our first concept was a failure, the next one wasn't.

In April 2011, we started building TalentBin, the earliest versions of which were centered around employee network-based referral recruiting products to help recruiters better pro-actively mine the networks of their existing staff to assist in recruiting for their hardest-to-fill openings.

Rather than sit in a cave, pretending we were building the next great thing before revealing it to the world, we were dead set on getting outside, and getting this in the hands of our intended customers as early as possible.

And that meant selling.

Unfortunately, we didn't have any sales professionals on the team. Or anyone with any sales experience, really. We had my co-founder, Jason, who started his career as a software engineer, before progressing to, variously, interaction design, then product management, then product management leadership, with a sprinkling of professional poker playing in between. And we had three engineers, who, while very smart and hardworking, weren't about to bang the phones all day every day plus we kind of needed them to focus on building and shipping the product.

It quickly became apparent that the sales piece would fall to me, and not because of my overwhelming qualification for the role—my background was as a product marketing and marketing generalist, with some product management for kicks. Rather, everyone else had things that only they could do, so I had better get my ass in gear.

What followed in the ensuing three years was a massive exercise in painful growth and learning as TalentBin went from hypothesis, to early minimum viable product, to strong product-market fit and sales scaling, to acquisition by Monster Worldwide in early 2014.

And for me, this meant a transition from a "generalist business founder", to TalentBin's first evangelical sales rep, trying to get someone, anyone, to use our product, for free, through summer and fall of 2011, to our first smiling and dialing account executive, asking for the sale with real money and a straight face, starting in fall 2011, to the first beginnings of sales management as I brought on our first Market Development Rep to fill my calendar in January 2012, and then haltingly adding account executives and market development reps through 2012, all the way through robust, repeatable, scalable B2B SAAS sales, with account management and customer success apparatuses, in 2013 into 2014. When it was all said and done, we had a team of ~20 sales and customer success staff, and were cranking along at a $6m/year run rate.

It was not without its misfires, train wrecks, and victories, individual and team. Most importantly, there were countless learnings to be discovered at each step of the process.

The goal of this book is to share those hard-won learnings with those who are beginning, midway, or even at the end of a similar journey, so that others could potentially avoid the misfires and train wrecks and just skip ahead to the victories—or in the very least minimize the misfires and train wrecks.

WHO IS THIS BOOK FOR?

Importantly, like any good sales conversation, first, we're going to qualify this opportunity. This book is specifically targeted for founders who find themselves at the point where they need to transition into a selling role. And not the "founders are always selling" chestnut you constantly hear, but actually turning their attention to revenue generating activities.

And not just any revenue generating activities, like monetizing your software with ads, or freemium $9.99 a month recurring revenues. Those are all fine on their own, but that's not our focus here. Rather, this book is specifically for founders who are leading organizations that have a B2B, direct sales model that involves sales professionals engaging in verbal, commercial conversations with buyers.

Moreover, many examples in this book will be targeted specifically to the realm of B2B SaaS software, and specifically as regards new, potentially innovative or disruptive offerings that are being brought to market for the first time. In short, direct sales of the sort a B2B SaaS software startup would engage in.

With that said, if you are looking to be a first time salesperson, transitioning in from another type of role, or fresh out of school, in an organization that meets those characteristics above, you will get value out of this book. Similarly, if you are a first time sales manager, either of the founder type, or a sales individual contributor who is transitioning into that role, again, in an organization who meets the criteria above, you will also get value from this book.

WHY DO I THINK I AM UNIQUELY QUALIFIED TO TELL THIS STORY?

Then there's the open question of why I am even qualified to be dispensing this sort of advice. Aside from the above existence proof of success—albeit not hundreds of millions of dollars in revenue—I believe that a book written for non-sales people becoming sales people requires the point of view of that very same non-sales guy who became a sales guy, then sales leader.

While I did not learn at the knees of more senior sales professionals, inside an existing organizational framework, say by starting as a Business Development Rep at Salesforce, before moving into a Junior Account Executive role, and progressing from there, I believe that this was actually a benefit, in that it compelled the derivation of many best practices, which both aids with strong internalization (when you derive the answer, it sticks with you much more robustly), and opens up opportunities for innovation as everything is "on the table" for questioning.

While this approach was time costly, and opportunity costly, in that I made many mistakes that likely would have been avoided by just cloning an existing reference architecture from a Salesforce or a SuccessFactors or a Box.net or an Oracle, I also was able to approach the craft of selling, and later, the scaling, operationalization, and management thereof, with the sort of fresh, child's eyes that, coupled with a product management and engineering mindset, beget new innovation, and adoption of the state of the art.

Which, as I have since become both a sales leader at a larger, legacy sales organization, and have become "the sales guru" that many startups and venture investors in my network come to for help, I think we ended up winning the tradeoff, in that we were able to innovate and adopt new, better approaches, cherry pick the best stuff from established sales orgs, and avoid any of the baggage that often accompanies calcified processes from sales organizations who, say, grew to scale in the 80s, 90s, or 00s.

WHO HELPED?

Lastly, by no means was this a solitary enterprise. On our sales team we celebrate what we liked to say was an "engineering mindset", and that we were "the product managers of our sales apparatus."

So chief among those who helped accelerate these learnings and overcome our errors were my sales staff, particularly Brad Snider, our first account executive, Rob Perez, our second account executive, whom we poached as an overlooked Sales Development Rep at LinkedIn, and Manny Ortega, who began as a particularly operations-minded Market Development Rep before transitioning more fully into a sales operations role before our acquisition. And on the customer success and enablement side, we went through a similar set of learnings spearheaded by our head of customer success, Adam Abeles.

The First Round Capital CEO community was also invaluable, in that I was able to glean learnings from Q&A from the likes of Angus Davis, CEO of Swipely, and sales automation typhoon, Sean Black, former head of sales for Trulia, and later CEO of Crunched, amongst others.

And then there were certainly other organizations that we poached approaches from heavily. LinkedIn, ironically, as a primary competitor, was a particular pace setter with regard to certain sales operations practices, from whom we heavily borrowed, not to mention the writings of Aaron Ross, whose Predictable Revenue was influential in the later architecture of our sales org as it went from being me and a sole market development rep, to scaling up to a larger market development apparatus. Lastly Eric Ries' The Lean Startup and Steve Blank's Four Steps to the Epiphany were both influential in the beginning of our product development and hypothesis construction—in fact, I consider Founding Sales a cultural descendant of both books.

HOW TO USE THIS BOOK

Importantly, this book is written in stages, in that your sales efforts, like your product development efforts, will typically take a stepwise path where subsequent stages build on the prior stages.

You can read through the entire book if you want—the table of contents has estimated reading times, and all in it shouldn't take more than a few hours. That said, usually you should only go as far as the stage that you're at—in that worrying about things like, say, Sales Hiring, before you even have your sales narrative, slides, or outreach collateral in place, is going to be a premature optimization, and likely a distraction.

The goal of this book is to be a resource you can come back to frequently, like a textbook, when you need to refresh yourself on something, or when you are about to enter a new stage of your sales maturity process, and need to prepare for what's coming next.

THE TWO STAGES OF YOUR SALES EFFORTS

While the entire early stage sales transformation involves massive learnings, these learnings will largely fall into two distinct buckets. First, "figuring it out" and then second, once figured out, "scaling it". This is related to the notion of "product-market fit", that Eric Ries, Steve Blank, and Marc Andreessen have made common-parlance in the software industry. The first is before substantial product-market fit, mainly. The second is after. Both require different sales approaches, and applying the approaches designed for the latter, while you're still in the first bucket, can be disastrous.

In the first epoch, it's a tight, iterative process where you're evangelically "selling" (there may not even be money involved) your solution (or, perhaps even "would-be solution", before you've even started building it) to would-be customers, and sorting out if indeed they have the pain that you're looking to address, how big that pain is, and what they'd be willing to pay to resolve it. This stage involves its own set of approaches, which, largely won't be very scalable, but will support those early learnings.

The second epoch comes only after you've passed the first (importantly, for reasons we'll discuss more in depth later). This is when you know your solution is viable, solves customer pain, for which they are willing to pay money, and now it's simply a question of scaling the number of humans who are doing the selling, and, by extension scaling all inputs and outputs associated with that activity. This book will be split accordingly, with the first part coming first.

And while much of what will be discussed in the coming pages will be largely prescriptive in nature, the goal will be to present the sections in a way to provide a framework for understanding and thought, to aid you in your own solutions. Yes, taking what has worked before, and adopting is wholesale will shorten your learning curve, but if you don't understand the underpinnings, there's always the risk of engaging in Cargo Cult sales activities, where you don't quite know why you're doing the thing you're doing, but it worked over there, so it must work over here, right?

Lastly, by no means is what follows the end all, be all of early stage direct sales. So if you can adopt an engineering mindset as regards your sales approach, and consider yourself the product manager of your go to market, stealing best practices where they make sense, rejecting that which is no longer applicable or doesn't fit, and building anew where needed.

Pre-Scaling When You're Just Starting Out

Evangelical Sales is Not Scaling Sales

When you're first starting out, there are many things you will do in your "sales" role that don't look anything like sales you see in the movies, at a large sales organization, and so forth.

The goal of the first section of this book will be to discuss what those stage-appropriate activities look like, to ensure that you actually get to the second part—scaling what works.

One hallmark of this section will be doing the activities yourself. A lot of time founders think that once they've built a product, they can "sprinkle some sales pros on it" and poof, it'll work. This is an incredibly destructive misconception, largely popularized by both founders and funders who don't actually know terribly much about sales, and are falsely pattern matching off of bad blog posts, movies, and sales books targeted for, and behaviors they've seen at, later stage organizations. This misconception has historically resulted in delayed, or never-reached product-market fit. Steve Blank talks about it substantially in his Four Steps to the Epiphany. Much like startups are not just littler versions of large organizations, startup sales is not a smaller version of large, established sales orgs.

There's an old saying that an organization can't really start scaling until they've fired their first VP of Sales. This conception falsely presents this as a failure of that VP of Sales. Rather, this is more a failure of the founders and funders in thinking that they could hand a sales professional, who's not a product manager, a nascent product, and magically she would be able to sell the hell out of it.

At this stage, your "sales" is in large part evangelical product management and product marketing, and this is why you, as a founder, need to be involved in it. There needs to be as little abstraction between the person crafting, and taking the message of your value proposition and probing its utility to would-be customers, and the people who are working on deciding what to build, what to build now versus later, and doing the actual building. Because the loop between articulation, presentation, listening, and building needs to be a tight one. If it can be the same person (no abstraction), then all the better, within the bounds of time constraints.

In the case of TalentBin, Jason Heidema, my co-founder, led our product efforts, and engineering management, as we were building TalentBin, but as he and I are largely symbiotically attached at the brain, it was very easy for me to come back to the office, and discuss where our product hypotheses were good, where we should double down, and where we were wasting engineering investment. One might argue that we could have done a better job of getting "outside the building," by me pulling Jason along more often, but we were able to get by with this approach, as long as one product-minded founder (me) was involved in the early sales processes.

Second, in addition to doing the actual work, yourself, a lot of that work will be activity that "doesn't scale." Like doing on-site sales visits for a product that will end up selling for less than $1,000 a year. The economics of that would never work at scale. Or manual implementation and professional services for early customers. Or manual lead generation via mindless copying and pasting from one tab of your browser to a spreadsheet in the other. Things like these are not scalable, but at this stage, it doesn't matter. Y Combinator's Paul Graham has popularized this notion with regards to consumer products, and it applies here as well. At this stage, this is largely an exercise in information gathering, and as such, is an investment exercise, as much as a revenue-generating exercise.

And while we've spoken above to the benefits founder-led early sales, and non-scalable activities, I want to take a second to flip it, and speaking specifically to the perils of premature professionalization and scale-mindedness of your sales apparatus.

Those who think they can just "sprinkle" some sales on it are going to be in for a very big surprise. You will likely hire that first Account Executive or VP of Sales, probably from an organization that builds something competitive to your offering, and maybe even the incumbent. For instance, had we embarked on this ill-advised path, we would have likely hired an Account Executive or Sales Manager from LinkedIn. Once hired, he will then call on some of his existing accounts, and secure some early pilots, or worse, maybe even bounce off the purchasing decision maker, and not be able to tell you why. He'll tell you what the customer said, but likely not what the customer meant. You won't be able to tell between pure sales failure and product failure. And all sorts of other unpleasant things.

This is because, with exceptions, sales professionals are not product managers or product marketers. They are in the business of taking a known-good solution, and taking it to market, in a repeatable scalable way. They're good at finding prospects that match a known-good persona. They're good at persuasively presenting a known-good solution that fits a known problem. They're good at having many concurrent customer conversations related to that known-good offering. They're good at enlarging deal size, sniffing out deal influencers, and handling objections. But you don't need that yet.

You need someone who can take a partially baked product, formulate a coherent narrative around it, present it, and then listen. And then iterate. You need evangelical sales, which is a mix of product management and product marketing. So hiring "one of those" from a mature organization with a known-good, scalably solid solution won't get you what you need. Save her resume for when you get to the second act, and are ready to scale, because she'll be awesome then. For now, you need someone who can take a partially baked product, formulate a coherent narrative around it, present it, and then iterate. You need evangelical sales, which is a mix of product management and product marketing. You need you.

Moreover, if you are unwilling to do these "unscalable" things to start, instead assuming that because Reference Org ABC doesn't do those things, you can't and shouldn't, you will encounter all manner of bad things. Instead of having information-rich transfer with your would-be customers, you'll be too focused on executing via telesales and miss critical insights. Or trying to intuit what customers mean based on their activity on your website. Or by buying lists of prospects that are poorly targeted rather than prospecting your own lists, you will waste your time and energy having bad conversations with irrelevant targets.

Another common anti-pattern founders in early stage go to markets fall into is simply not selling, full stop. That is, they falsely believe you can simply hang a shingle out for your offering, and magically customers will come and find you. And moreover, they'll simply buy without you having to talk to them! Even better! The myth of the "sales rep-less" go to market is a persistent, seductive, and nefarious myth in the technology industry that trips up many a founder, especially those who hear stories of how Dropbox or Twilio or whatever large successful company has no sales staff. Of course, when you search on LinkedIn in those organizations for sales staff, they are indeed crawling with them. But don't tell that to the founder who would love to tell himself the story that he doesn't have to learn how to sell!

A lot of this bad behavior is driven by misconceptions and misplaced expectations on the part of founders. For instance, they think they "can't do sales" because they've never done it before. Or that they're not "salesy." This is absolute bullshit. Sales acumen is not inborn. It's just another skill to be learned. And if you can't roll up your sleeves and learn a new skill set, then woe betide your startup, because startups are just one long chain of learning new things and solving new problems. Sales is no different. Just another problem to be solved. And if and when you make it to scaling mode, knowing the ins and outs of the sales individual contributor role will make you a better hirer, manager, and auditor of your growing sales force.

At the earliest stage of your go to market, your success will depend on an evangelical sales mindset, focused on rich, customer interaction and information gathering, and not being overly concerned about scale thinking, and "professionalization."

So roll up your sleeves, because this is your job now, tiger.

CHAPTER 1

Mindset Changes in First Time Sales Professionals

INTRODUCTION

One of the biggest things to adjust to when approaching sales for the first time is the often counterintuitive shift required to your mindset. This is especially true for founders with a background in non-sales disciplines like engineering, product management, finance, or even marketing.

I like to joke with new members of my team that doing sales changes neural pathways in your brain—but it's really not a joke. They end up agreeing with me a few months in. A lot of the behaviors required for sales success are a massive departure from the ones you've valued in your career to date, even from generally accepted ways of being in society. But while they may feel uncomfortable at first, they have led, time and time again, to sales success.

This isn't to say you need to run out and adopt all of these behaviors immediately, right out of the gate. My goal is simply to lay out a number of the sales mindsets that you will encounter. I want to validate, ahead of time, that when you do run into these, yes, you're seeing what you think you are, and you shouldn't be surprised. While a change, these new ways of thinking and interacting should be expected, and welcomed. And yes, if you can start driving yourself toward these attitudes in a proactive way, you will increase your success.

With that said, here are some of the mindset changes that will help you in the transition from founder to sales professional.

EMBRACE PLENTY, NOT SCARCITY

Generally speaking, we're taught that we should conserve resources. We're told not to waste things. We're all probably guilty of this—saving those extra MP3s in our iPhone's music app, or leaving that email in our inbox, telling ourselves that we're eventually going to get around to it. Don't throw away that half sandwich; you can keep it in the fridge for later.

Stop that, now. Reject a mindset of scarcity—and, hence, hoarding—and embrace a mindset of plenty. The thinking should be "Even if this one does not work out, there's a line of thousands standing behind it that I need to get to." So if a deal is stalling, if the customer doesn't have the budget, if it turns out an account is not a perfect fit, and so on, great, fine, close it out. On to the next. You'll get them the next time around.

The thing that is scarce in sales is time. To quote one of TalentBin's key early sales staff, Brad Snider, spending "good time with good opportunities" is paramount. And, by extension, that means not spending time on opportunities that aren't going to pan out. We'll talk more about this later as it relates to qualifying accounts, and there certainly is an art and science piece to judging whether an account is "worth it."

You should be ruthless with respect to truncating unproductive conversations with marginal opportunities, especially at the earliest of stages, when the world is a greenfield of untouched accounts in front of you.

If you do not, those marginal, crappy opportunities will cruft up your pipeline, hiding the golden opportunities on which you should be spending your time. It will be unclear which action you should take next on which account; the good will be hidden by the bad, reducing your ability to act at scale, and generally eroding your efficiency. Even if you do end up closing the marginal opp, a customer who is a bad target will consume more than their fair share of customer success resources, likely not achieve the best ROI, form a bad opinion of your solution, and tell others about it, before churning out themselves.

Spend good time with good opportunities. Let go of the marginal opps, knowing that you can get them later if they become more viable. There's plenty of opportunity here.

PUT ACTIVITY ABOVE ALL ELSE

Everyone's a fan of working "smarter, not harder" in the modern knowledge-worker economy. Well, sometimes you just have to grind. Sales, like recruiting, is all about activity and leverage. Generally speaking, activity in equals value out. There are certainly ways to ensure that your activity is high quality; you can also lever it with technology to get more in less time, and higher impact out of each unit of activity. We'll dig into that more later. But to quote Joseph Stalin (likely apocryphally), "quantity has a quality all its own," and internalizing that is key.

More time on the phone. More demos. More proposals sent. More emails sent. More dials. More keystrokes. All of the above is activity, and activity is the goal.

This is often in direct contravention to typical notions of "quality" work. Thinking deeply about the perfect response to that email. Spending five minutes to game out a call before you make it. Reading, and rereading, that email to understand every nuance. "Studying up" on the materials to make sure that your pitch is perfect.

No more. Just as you need to shift your mindset from scarcity to plenty, the reality is that in order to move opportunities down the pipeline and close deals, activity is job one. Jump first, prepare midair. Template all communication. Drive activity, and output will follow.

This is not to say that your activity should be crap, but simply that your mindset should be one of productivity. Ask yourself, "How can I do more of X [an input to the deal process] in a given time period?" And if you can figure out ways to systematize more quality, fantastic. This is an exercise in recognizing the point at which you reach diminishing returns on a given sales action, catching yourself, and moving on to the next. The thought should be "Why am I not on the phone?" or "Why am I not sending emails right now?" Your default should be activity, and lack of activity should be aberrant. This is why sales managers get skeeved out if their sales floors are quiet—a palpable lack of activity is a bad sign.

Don't read the entire email communication history with that prospect before you call him. Just call. It's probably going to go to voice mail anyway, and you just saved yourself five minutes of unnecessary preparation. One proofread is all that email needs. Send it, and then move on to the other fifty you have to send to your pipeline today.

Don't overthink. Just act.

BE DIRECT & GET DOWN TO BUSINESS

Society often gets along through polite obfuscation. Through indirection. Through politesse, and circuitousness. Not in sales land, friend.

Much of sales is about getting down to brass tacks. Do you have the problem I'm trying to solve? Are you in agreement that it needs a solution? Are you prepared to spend money to solve it?

In the pursuit of efficiently attacking your account, you, as a sales professional, have full license to be direct in asking these sorts of questions. In fact, you can go all the way up to directly stating to your prospect, with full confidence, that your solution and their problem are an excellent fit, and that they should buy X amount of your product to help their business. Asking for the sale is not optional, and it will quickly become second nature.

As Alec Baldwin states so entertainingly in that famous ABC scene in *Glengarry Glen Ross*, "A guy don't walk on the lot lest he wants to buy." People go to singles bars with very specific goals in mind. Your prospects would not bother being on the phone with you, taking your demo, if they didn't have some buying intent. It is imperative to respect their time and yours by being direct and getting to the heart of the matter.

BUILD MANY SHALLOW RELATIONSHIPS

For the first-time sales pro, the scale of person-to-person interaction is a massive adjustment. Think about how many distinct people you typically interact with in a given week. If you're like most professionals, it's likely a constellation of one or two dozen people with whom you have frequent, ongoing interactions that build over time, and with whom you have substantial history.

With sales, it's the opposite. If you're doing it right—see comments above about the importance of activity orientation—you're having dozens of net-new interactions a week, and maintaining a pipeline of anywhere from a few dozen to north of a hundred ongoing, concurrent conversations.

It's a substantial change of pace, and it also puts substantial stressors on you to be able to quickly build and maintain rapport with a new contact, while juggling key deal information, over the cycle of the sale. (Why do you think the weather and sports teams are the sales pro's best friends? Instant conversation topics.) It puts the onus on the sales pro to keep readily accessible details of these individuals, their organizations, and their pains, as well as general rapport notes—which, of course, is not possible for a normal human brain. It can be exhausting, and it can be taxing. That's why record keeping and CRM excellence (more on this later) are paramount.

This isn't to say that these relationships are fake, or that they're not valuable or meaningful. They just demand a different way of interacting with other professionals than what you're likely used to. To make the most of them, and manage them correctly, requires a change of mindset.

ASSUME THE SALE IS INEVITABLE & IT JUST MIGHT BE

Approach your sales conversations with the stance that the prospect will inevitably be a customer. This is more applicable when you are at the scaling stage, when it is now clear that the solution that you are presenting has product/market fit. But it can be helpful even at the earlier stages of your go-to-market period.

What do I mean by a mindset of "inevitability"? If you have indeed qualified an account as a good fit, then the mindset should look something like this—"This is going to happen. It makes sense for you. This solution is the future, and it will make you more successful now and going forward. So we can do it now or we can do it later, but it's going to happen, either with me or with a competitor of mine."

Here are a few helpful things come out of this mindset. First, it frames the conversation as "when" instead of "if." This naturally makes the conversation more consultative and focused around business needs—that is, "This solution exists to solve this problem, and we have validated that you have this problem, so clearly this solution makes sense. Let's figure out when and how it should be implemented." Second, it provides a confidence boost to the sales professional, related to the "expertness and fearlessness" we'll talk about next. Third, it sets the groundwork for an ongoing relationship with the prospect; even if they don't close this time through the funnel (and odds are, they won't), they will be prepped for the next pass. It will also reinforce your own record-keeping processes, since you'll know that recording these interactions will enable your future self the next time this prospect passes through the funnel.

It may feel odd to take on such a presumptuous mindset, and by no means is this a suggestion to be arrogant or off-putting in your dealings. But approaching each interaction with certainty will drive success in your conversations.

EXPECT TO WIN, BUT BE UNFAZED BY REJECTION

In most of your professional interactions, you probably achieve some semblance of your goal most of the time, largely because you wouldn't be engaged in the activity in question if you didn't think you had a reasonable expectation of success.

This is definitely not the case in sales. You're going to get shot down most of the time. And by "shot down," I mean that you will not close the deal on that particular pass through the pipeline. For whatever reason there won't be budget, the timing will be off, the prospect will be happy with their current tools, a competitor will win the deal, the prospect will just disappear, etc. It happens. Depending on your industry, and the point at which sales gets a prospect in the funnel, if yours is a new, innovative solution, a 20%–30% win rate is solid.

The mindset change required to contend with this is the ability to hold what are essentially two seemingly opposed ideas in your head at once. That is, you need to have and project full confidence that you're going to win the deal, but at the same time be unfazed when you do not. Being unfazed by rejection, and not internalizing it as a negative reflection on you or your offering, is key to maintaining the tempo and confidence required for sales success.

This is not to say that you should not learn from those losses; the reason for the loss should be recorded to benefit product iteration, and also for reference the next time you engage with the account. Be intellectually honest about where the loss came from. Was it timing? Did you get beaten by a competitor because you didn't follow up appropriately? Or because the product had a feature deficit? And make sure that the answer gets shared with others, so they don't have to learn the same hard lesson you did by eating a loss. But after honestly reviewing and recording the loss cause, put it aside and move on. You should still expect to win the next one.

RECORD EVERYTHING—BUT EFFICIENTLY

As an outcome of sales strategies we've already covered—the sheer magnitude of professional interactions you'll have and the importance of high activity—the reality is that you are going to "closed lost" most of your opportunities. For that reason, a mindset of constant record keeping is paramount for success.

Previously, you could perhaps rely on your own memory to recall what it is that you were working on, or what your last conversation with a given person had covered. No longer.

Instead, you need to admit to yourself that there's no way that you can retain all this information, not just day to day and week to week when dealing with your current pipeline, but month to month and quarter to quarter as you revisit and resurrect previously closed opportunities. On my sales teams, we call it "setting 'future you' up for success." That is, when you come back to look at this account in a week, month, or quarter, what information will you wish you had? Record that now while it's available, and make the ephemeral permanent.

And while your CRM will be the primary repository of this information, this mindset shift includes a variety of tactics (CRM excellence being one of them). For instance, in my sales teams, every person has a lab notebook to allow them to take notes during a call (especially during the discovery section), including size of opportunity, qualification details, and so on, to later be transferred to the CRM (not wholesale, but the salient points).

Of course, you don't need to transcribe each and every thing that a prospect says on the phone. However, you do need to adopt a mindset of persistently pursuing and checking off key pieces of information, in an efficient fashion.

Moreover, once you and your team have internalized this mindset, you can start looking for constant opportunities to use technology (email capture, call recording, presentation recording) to make the capture of this information automatic, and instantaneous.

BE EXPERT & AUTHORITATIVE. IT BEGETS FEARLESSNESS.

Modern sales is not about trying to sell snake oil to a "mark." Rather, sales professionals are the grease of the market. They seek out inefficiencies in the world, in the form of qualified prospects who have the business pain that the proposed solution resolves. Then they engage and consult with the prospect, and propose the implementation of the solution, to help fix that business pain.

As such, expertness in the vertical in which you are selling is an absolute requirement. You need to be a student of the game you are playing and, ideally, even more expert than the prospects to whom you are selling. This means absorbing as much information as possible about the field, the business processes that exist within it, the common organizational players, and the other solutions that already help with these business processes, or compete with yours.

This expertness will make you fearless in your interactions. It will help with your activity orientation, removing your desire to over-prep for conversations and empowering you to just call, just email, just act. It will help with your ability to be direct, to operate from a position of inevitability, and to quickly establish rapport by demonstrating authority.

But even before you achieve that level of expertness, you can adopt a mindset of fearlessness, confident that you have "enough" expertise to engage in any conversation. You'll find this manifesting in your real life, as it becomes easier and easier for you to strike up conversation with any random stranger on the bus or at the grocery store, knowing that you'll have no problem participating in whatever ensues. As with others of these mindsets, not only will you start seeing this one show up naturally, you can also push in that direction pro-actively. Compel yourself to talk to grocery store clerks, people in lines, or strangers at parties with no introductory context. You'll be exercising your fearlessness muscles.

MAKE YOURSELF AT HOME IN A GLASS HOUSE

The level of transparency in a well-instrumented sales organization is a massive change for most people. From win and loss notes and closing ratios to leaderboards and error checking, everything is right there, available for everyone to see.

If you are doing a good job, you will have all customer-facing interaction instrumented and recorded—every single email, every presentation, and every call—either in its entirety in the case of presentations and email, or in some partial capacity when it comes to calls and conversations. You should get comfortable with teammates jumping into those records and asking questions about why a call went this way or that way. Your creation of this transparent data is of paramount importance for the success of the organization, from both a go-to-market and a product-development standpoint.

Similarly, activity levels, or lack thereof, should be clearly documented and inescapable. If a rep spaced out today for some reason, the lack of calls and emails will be fully observable. And if your CRM is really well done, it will be observable down to the granularity of which hours of the day that rep was lagging.

So too with error checking. Again, if your CRM is well executed, you will have reporting that shows exactly which opportunities and accounts have been missing activity for a certain period of time, and are in danger. The only question that will remain is why you haven't hopped on top of that! In fact, your CRM reporting should yield valuable insights all the way down to every single closed-won and closed-lost opportunity. For every win, you can see the strategy that sold five seats instead of two. For every lost opportunity, you'll see what went wrong—budget, competition, a prospect not yet convinced of your solution's value, and so on. But you lose this insight without transparency.

And while this may sound frightening, it's actually extremely beneficial, both for the individual and, in aggregate, for the organization. It creates an environment of accountability and shared learning that drives a positive, self-reinforcing feedback loop. Your staff focuses because there's no way not to. There's no excuse to not work on high-priority items, because the errors are documented and visible. Flubs and failures are socialized so other staff won't crash on the same rocks, but also so they'll realize that failure is part of the game, and not to be feared. And that foments a culture of action orientation rather than loss aversion, because fear of failure is one of the biggest blocks on action. If you remove that fear, you remove that brake on activity. And when you transparently share wins alongside losses, your staff know that they're real, and not puffed up, and thus can take them as helpful guideposts for how they should execute.

Document all of your team's activity, and everyone can simply put forth their maximal effort without worrying what will be available to whom—because the answer is everything, to everyone.

REMEMBER, SALES IS ABOUT MATH

When people think about what is needed for sales success, they jump to a lot of "right brain" activities. Storytelling, persuasion, rapport building, and such. Socialization, drinking, and dinner. Shooting from the hip and making it up as you go. They don't consider, or at least not as much, that sales is something that involves lots of metrics, math, and reporting. Guess what? You can't escape math in sales either—especially if you want to have success at any amount of scale greater than a single rep.

All that instrumentation and recording that we talked about needs monitoring and analysis. Want to know how many emails to how many prospects are generally needed to get a demo on the board? You're going to need the relevant Salesforce reports for that. Or want to know how many opportunities are required to close a deal, and what each of those opportunities is worth? Better have your win rates instrumented and reported on. Did you want to understand if you can afford to hire a sales development rep to feed your calendar? You're going to need to know your average contract value. Did you want to know which of your sales reps are most efficient at converting opportunities into wins? You'll need to split those win rates by rep, and probably add a revenue component to your calculation too. The sales leader who struggles with Salesforce reporting and Excel pivot tables is going to have a rough time in a high-velocity, high-scale sales environment.

Sales in the movies may be about dinners, suits, and booze, and there's certainly still a steak-dinner component to it. But all of that activity is underpinned by a healthy helping of metrical excellence. You won't be able to avoid it, so you might as well start getting cozy with it.

MINDSETS THAT BUILD ON EACH OTHER

These certainly aren't the only mindset changes that you'll notice starting to take hold. However, they are the ones that are initially the most crucial for your transition from founder to sales professional. Moreover, as you may have seen as you read, these first mindset shifts have a complementary, multiplicative impact on each other. Success begets success.

For instance, if you record everything, you can be direct and "non-scarcity-minded," quickly identifying opportunities to spend your time on now. You'll be free to move on from imperfect opportunities, knowing that you can come back later to get them because you did a great job of recording the customer interaction and creating backstops for future engagement. All of which will raise your activity levels and efficiency.

Or if you expect to win, are unfazed by loss, and have adopted the mindset of expertise, it's easier to adopt a stance of inevitability. That, in turn, will help you be fearless and authoritative in your interactions, and more consultative, which will lead to higher close rates.

Or if you expect that you will have high volumes of shallow relationships, you will be prepared to be more direct and efficient in surfacing relevant business details. That will focus you on the importance of efficient record keeping, which will better empower your future self to pick these conversations back up if they do not close this time through the funnel.

And the permutations go on and on.

While you may encounter some of these mindset shifts before others, and while some may be easier for you to adopt than others, the important thing to internalize is that the universe of enterprise sales has its own "physics"—and you're subject to those rules now. Proactively identifying, embracing, and driving toward them will foreshorten your learning curve, and make you more successful in your efforts, faster.

CHAPTER 2

Baking Your Narrative
& Product Marketing Basics

INTRODUCTION

The first step on the road to a repeatable, scalable sales process is to build your narrative. That is, craft the "story" you will be presenting to your would-be customers, which will eventually take the form of slides, email templates, spoken messaging, website copy, videos and so forth. Because before you start creating those artifacts, you have to have the framework.

Your sales narrative will likely be a recasting of other content your organization may already have documented. For instance, if you already have concrete product narrative, posing customer pain and your proposed solution, then turning it into a customer-facing sales narrative should not be too hard.

"It's hard for small local businesses to acquire new customers. So we fix that by aggregating new customers with the help of compelling coupon offerings." —Groupon

"Salespeople have to keep track of lots of concurrent conversations, and end up dropping balls and losing revenue. So we make software that helps them avoid those errors and book more revenue." —Salesforce

There will be a circular feedback loop between the product narrative and your sales narrative as it meets the market and either fails, succeeds, or does a little of both. So this shouldn't be looked at as something set in stone, but rather as a hypothesis that will change over time. But you still have to have a coherent rough draft to start.

WHAT IS THE RIGHT FORMATION?

While there are a variety of ways to construct your customer-facing narrative, for early-stage, new-technology sales organizations, I'm a fan of the "problem-solution-specifics" narrative framing.

That is, identify the problem, who has it, how it is currently solved (or not), and why that's unsatisfactory, followed by what has changed to make this problem solvable in a new way, what that means for the problem in question, how your new solution works to solve this problem, and what the quantitative and qualitative proof points are that validate this line of argumentation. Those will be the core components of a sales narrative, along with potential additions, like competitive messaging (why is your proposed approach better than other proposed approaches?), and all manner of embellishments (like digging into the specifics and features of your solution).

If this sounds like a fundraising pitch, you shouldn't be surprised. A funding pitch typically has all of the same trappings, plus macroeconomic rollups of certain parts. For example, "How many people have the proposed problem and what are they willing to pay to solve it" would be a market-sizing exercise, which is not relevant to a customer-facing sales pitch but requires the same precursory information.

Framing your narrative in this way will also be helpful as you develop your marketing collateral, in that each part builds on the part before. Think of it as an inductive approach. If someone disagrees with your framing of the problem, great, it's the first thing you've discussed; you can focus on that (or end the interaction), rather than rehearsing other parts of your pitch that are not relevant. Or if the person you're talking to agrees that this problem exists, but not that he has it, again, great; you can save time by not pitching someone who doesn't care. Narrative framing nicely complements the efficiency mindset that should pervade sales, as covered previously in Chapter 1 on Sales Mindset Changes.

BUILDING A COHESIVE NARRATIVE

So let's walk through these individual components. Once you understand how to think about them—and have them mapped out—you can put it all together into a cohesive narrative.

What is The Problem?

You need to identify the business pain you're seeking to solve, as crisply as possible, so your audience can quickly evaluate whether what you're talking about is relevant to them.

For instance, in the case of TalentBin, "Technical recruiting is hard. It's hard to find software engineering talent that has the relevant skills, and even if you can find them, getting in contact with them is tough. And once you've found and contacted talent, keeping on top of all those conversations can be a huge time suck fraught with dropped balls, all leading to slower hire times and raised cost of hire."

Or in the case of, say, Groupon, it might be "Finding new customers for your local business is hard. With all the time you spend running day-to-day operations, who has time to figure out how to drive new business through the door? But if you don't grow your customer base to find new, repeat customers, how can you get off the hamster wheel and grow your business?"

Or in the case of Salesforce, it might be "B2B sales is hard. You're working on a million things at once, and it can be really easy to lose track of deals and let things fall through the cracks, which hurts your ability to reach your quota. And as a manager, it's hard to know if your teams are working on the right things, if their efforts are directed toward the highest-value opportunities, and how they're tracking against their goals. Which leads to under-performing teams and missed forecasts."

Or in the case of HubSpot, it might be "Being an online marketer is hard. Sales wants more leads. And there are so many things you could be spending your time on, but you're constantly pulled in lots of directions, many of them not particularly fruitful. Really, you just want an all-in-one solution that can help you do the right things, automatedly, and help you keep track of your success.

Or in the case of Zendesk, it might be "Being a support agent is hard. You have all these people running into issues with the product you're supporting and emailing you, needing help. You want to help them all, but with so many concurrent conversations happening, it can be hard to keep up, and keep balls from being dropped, which leads to unhappy customers who stop paying. Moreover, so many of the questions are the same, again and again, and answering those repetitive questions keeps you from helping the people who need more advanced guidance. As a support manager, you want to help your teams be as efficient as possible and not drop balls, so they can spend their time delighting customers, rather than typing out the same answer."

There may be particular nuances and levels to the problem in question. In the case of TalentBin, for example, more advanced sales conversations addressed discovery, contact, and management of recruiting conversations too. In the case of Salesforce, there's a distinction to be made between the problem individual reps have and the problem sales managers have. But at least identifying the baseline is key.

A good test of whether you've got it is to pose the problem statement to someone in the industry. You're in good shape if you say, "Have you encountered this?", and she not only says "yes", but can then proceed to have a deeper conversation about it.

Know, and be able to articulate, the problem you're addressing.

Who Has The Problem?

Equally important is identifying the person who has the problem. We've already touched on this a little bit, since the person with the problem will often pop up in the problem statement—they're somewhat hard to separate, and that's fine. But you should know the players who are navigating, or trying to manage, the business hassles you're tackling.

This is both so you have a strong sense of who you should be addressing with this narrative, and so that when you are addressing someone, they themselves can make the same evaluation. Are you talking to the right person, and do they want to listen to what you have to say?

In B2B software and sales, there is generally a specific person, or group of people, whose job it is to solve the problem you're proposing. Identifying them is the goal here. There can be more than one person, and generally as an organization gets larger what might have been the problem of one person, or a slice of a person, becomes the distributed problem of more people. The collective "business speak" for this is "stakeholders," but you want to focus on those who are purely responsible for solving the business pain. If the person in question can say, "Well, that's not really my job," then you know you have the wrong person. And you should understand the different players in your narrative.

You might say, "Well, the CEO is the one who has this problem, because the buck stops with her." But generally speaking, you want to be talking to the people who have specific functional responsibility for resolving the problem that you are addressing.

So in the case of TalentBin, for example, the people who have the problem being solved would be recruiters who are responsible for filling individual requisitions (ideally just the technical ones) and recruiting managers who are responsible for providing talent to the other parts of the business—like engineering managers and the VP of Engineering. But the people in those other parts of the business, while impacted by the problem, aren't precisely responsible for its solution (except in very small organizations where you don't yet have separation of responsibilities).

For, say, Zendesk, the most direct stakeholders would be the Head of Support or Customer Success and the individual customer service people who solve customer issues.

For a CRM solution, focused on rep efficiency and managerial insight, this would be a Manager, Director, or VP of Sales Operations, or, absent that, the sales leader who is most concerned about sales efficiency as supports revenue growth.

A good rule of thumb for targeting the right stakeholders is to look for the person who has control of the budgetary resources allotted to resolve the pain point you solve. Or, alternatively, the person who spends meaningful amounts of time (i.e., labor resources), day to day, resolving that pain point.

As organizations get larger, you see more specialization and focus with regard to who would be the owner of a given business pain, and thus ought to be the target of your message. For instance, in a small organization that has a single sales rep, with the CEO focused on sales performance, those would be the individuals to target for a sales automation solution. As an organization gets larger, you might have a Director of Sales managing six sales reps, and that Director of Sales would be your target. And as that organization get larger still, the pure responsibility for sales enablement and operation may be specifically split off into its own role, with titles like Sales Operations Manager, Director, and so forth, at which point, those people would be your best target.

Relatedly, and we'll get into this more when we talk about account qualification, just because there's someone at an organization who addresses your problem, that doesn't mean that the organization is necessarily qualified for your solution. An organization with a single customer service rep who is also the office manager, and is managed by the CEO, yes, has someone who addresses customer success issues. But the amount of time—and, by extension, budget—that is spent on those issues will be far below that of an organization with dozens of customer service people. Engaging with this smaller account would therefore be far less likely to be worth your time. Generally, having a crisp sense of the specific titles you are selling to will help lead to the right accounts, because accounts that don't have those titles in-house won't be qualified. We'll get into that more when we talk about prospecting.

What Are The Costs Associated With This Problem?

Understanding the costs associated with the problem you're addressing will help you frame an argument for why would-be customers should expend budget on your solution. Depending on your space, you might be looking at what it costs to solve a given problem—or what it will cost not to solve it. Either way, you'll want to calculate the return on investment (the mythical "ROI") associated with your solution.

Often, these are very clear costs. For instance, in datacenter solutions, like data storage, there's the issue of ever-expanding storage. That is, for every number of employees that are added to an organization, there will be a need to add more disk storage to support them—and this has a very distinct cost. So if your solution is focused on, say, storage de-duplication and virtualization, then you'll need to understand the cost of expanded storage.

Or for support software, you'd need to understand the cost of support personnel—each of whom can only handle so many tickets per workday—for a growing customer base.

Or for sales automation and CRM solutions, you'd need to understand the cost of adding more salespeople to get more revenue. Because reps can only handle a limited number of deals without software assistance, CRMs can reduce the number of reps a company needs per dollar of revenue, or, on the flip side, create more revenue per rep.

In cases like this—where the implementation of a given solution clearly and directly minimizes certain costs—you're dealing with what's known as "hard ROI."

Other times, the costs a solution addresses may be opportunity costs. For instance, consider the customer support example above. The flip side to the cost of additional support personnel is the opportunity cost of customers who stop being customers due to insufficient support. So while one problem companies need to consider is the cost of adding more personnel as they add new customers, they also need to consider whether these new customers may end up becoming former customers if they aren't sufficiently enabled or supported. The cost here would be the opportunity cost of those customers not renewing their licenses or purchasing more seats of the product being supported.

Or in the case of sales automation and efficiency software, an opportunity cost would be incremental deals missed in a given time frame due to insufficient rep efficiency. For instance, your solution might allow reps to do more in a given amount of time—if instead of closing eight deals of average deal value $8,000 every month, they can instead close ten deals, that's a 25% bump and $16,000 in incremental revenue per rep per month. In this case, you're identifying the opportunity cost of not employing your solution. These benefits can sometimes be harder to prove, in that other actions must occur in order to realize the promised benefit. As such, they are sometimes referred to as "soft ROI."

Lastly, there may be more directional costs and opportunity costs and benefits. These are often harder to quantify. For instance, information technology vendors often sell the value of "increased agility"—that is, that users will be able to more quickly execute projects for their internal customers and thus allow the businesses they support to capture opportunities better. That's great, but that's a pretty big domino rally of cause and effect and hypothesized impact to take to the bank, and another example of "soft ROI."

Once you have a sense of what these specific costs or opportunity costs are, it's an easy trick to simply scale them up or down based on the size of the potential customers you are looking to engage with. As you do, you will better understand the potential opportunity of sale for your organization, and the value of your solution for the prospect organization (which goes to qualification and, later, prospecting).

But at the very minimum, you need to understand the unit costs of the problems you're addressing, so you can position the value of solving them with your solution.

How Do People Currently Solve This Problem? Why Do Current Solutions Fail?

Knowing the current solution paths for your problem will be important, in that the thrust of your sales conversations will be to persuade your would-be customers that the means by which they currently solve the problem—or their continued non-solution of the problem—is insufficient for their business, and that they should be implementing your solution instead. You'll have a hard time driving that argument, or even identifying the current state of the world within a target organization, if you're not clear on the typical solution paths and their shortfalls.

No Solution

In high-technology, innovative solution sales, where your solution is brand-new, one of the most common answers to this question will be "we don't solve this problem." Your challenge, then, is to persuade prospective customers that it's worth solving—in that the current non-solution is costly, whether that means actual hard cost or softer opportunity cost. Hence the importance of understanding and being able to model the costs of non-solution.

Solution via Process

Organizations that already solve the problem via process are one step further along. For instance, in the case of TalentBin's customers, the problem that technical recruiters have is being able to discover and engage with software-engineering candidates that they can't find on traditional hiring services like LinkedIn or Monster. Some of the more advanced technical recruiters have implemented processes to use generic search engines like Google to manually browse and discover these engineering candidates on places like Twitter, GitHub, and Stack Overflow. They then use, again, standard email tooling to reach out to and follow up with those candidates. While there are tools being used in this situation, they're in service of a process that has been implemented to solve the root issue.

So, too, for sales organizations that don't have a robust CRM solution and associated reporting in place. In lieu of that reporting, the sales organization might use a process of status meetings or habitual cc'ing of sales management on ongoing deal conversations.

In these cases, you need to address the question of why that existing process is an inferior solution path. Often it comes down to the time cost associated with it and, beyond that, with the general frailty of process.

In the TalentBin case above, for example, the use of normal search engines in a manual process of candidate discovery is very time-consuming; while the outcomes could be valuable (a quality candidate hired), the time cost to get there may be substantial. Or a pertinent candidate may be missed, delaying the speed of hiring. In the example of the sales organization, the time cost of the reporting process keeps reps from spending their time on selling. Moreover, what's reported is self-reported, without an audit path—potentially allowing reps to provide information that makes them look good but actually diverges from the reality of their sales pipelines.

Solution via Service Providers

A step beyond organizations that have implemented processes to resolve their business pains would be those doing so with service providers. For instance, rather than subscribing to a media database like Cision to help their PR team keep tabs on relevant journalists, an organization might just have a PR firm on retainer. Or instead of solving their engineering-hiring problems with process or products, an organization might just work with a recruiting agency.

Solving a business pain with a professional service could be a totally viable solution for the organization in question, but it will have downsides. Cost will typically be one of those downsides, in that service providers need to make a margin for their businesses to be successful. For instance, in technical recruiting, a recruiting agency will typically make a fee of 25% of the first-year salary for an engineer that they place. If an engineer is making $150,000, that's a $37,500 fee—not a small amount. If an organization has recruiters in place, then a solution that provides them candidate access and engagement tools, like TalentBin, could help them hire the same quality of engineer, but at a dramatically reduced cost—the cost of the solution in question, plus the salary expense of the in-house recruiter.

Solution via Product

Lastly, we have the most advanced organizations, those that already are using products to solve the problem in question. These products won't necessarily be pure "competition"—they might simply be in the same general space as yours—but this introduces a larger concept that includes competition. That is, these organizations are using solutions that are competing for the budget and user time you want. But that is often a good sign when you are qualifying an account (more on this later), since the organization has sufficient conviction in the importance of the problem that they expend budget on tooling to solve it.

For instance, while TalentBin is a talent search engine with advanced recruiting CRM features, with pure competitors in the market, there are a variety of other solutions that organizations use to solve the business problem of engineering recruiting—job postings on a traditional job board, subscriptions to a traditional resume database, or the business solutions of professional networks like LinkedIn.

This is where things can get complicated, in that the more mature a space, the more variety or alternative solutions there may be—including those that are perhaps not pure market substitutes, but instead are complementary/co-operative solutions. I'm a fan of sales professionals being "students of the game." The more you know about these other solutions and their relative plusses and minuses, the better. But there will invariably be diminishing returns in knowing everything about every potential solution under the sun; having intimacy with at least the most common ones should suffice, so you're rarely surprised in a conversation.

Importantly, this isn't just about knowing who the players are, and their deficits. The only way you'll be able to build an authoritative narrative is if it is credible, and that means recognizing the strengths in existing solutions too—even if that's as simple as their low cost. For instance, while recruiting agencies may be costly, they're extremely useful if you need candidate flow immediately, or don't have in-house recruiter labor. Or while job postings may not be very helpful for hiring in verticals where candidate demand and supply is out of whack, that doesn't mean that job postings are fundamentally problematic; they are very helpful for hiring proactive, motivated job seekers, like sales or customer success staff.

Having a deep understanding of the myriad ways organizations resolve the problem you're addressing will position you well, so you can frame your solution's narrative in the larger context of the market.

What Has Changed That Enables a New Solution?

Typically in product innovation, and the associated selling of those products, something has "changed" that enables a new solution. It's important for you to understand the underpinnings of the change, because your narrative will need to explain it. In fact, that change will be crucial to how you frame the new opportunities that have opened up for your would-be customers.

For instance, in sales CRM, the rise of ubiquitous web access and browser technology provided an opportunity for Salesforce to create a SaaS offering that was far less clunky than traditional on-premise CRMs, accessible from any web-enabled client, and always up-to-date with the latest features.

Or in the recruiting world, the creation of LinkedIn as a "professional network," which was adopted by a segment of the populace, enabled recruiters to tap into a much broader set of potential employees than traditional job board resume databases offered.

Or the falling price of flash memory made it cost-effective to create datacenter storage appliances made purely of flash memory, with companies like Pure Storage helping organizations take advantage of this development.

Knowing what has changed will not only allow you to pose a credible narrative, but will also point to the trends you can expect in the market. Pay close attention to those trends and what they mean for your sales narrative—whether they support it or undermine it.

For instance, TalentBin takes advantage of the rise of "implicit professional activity" available on the web—for example, question-and-answer activity on places like Stack Overflow, professionally relevant tweets, and so on. This has been enabled by the creation of online communities and the growing availability of digitized "professional output" like patent databases, publications, and so forth. But to the extent that this trend is only increasing—as more and more software engineers make GitHub, Stack Overflow, Twitter, and so on part of their day-to-day professional world, for instance—then the "thing that has changed" will only continue to increase in momentum, further supporting TalentBin's approach and underscoring its sales narrative.

In other cases, these changes don't enable a new solution—they demand one. With the rise of the iPhone and other smartphones, for example, consumers now spend much more of their "online time" on their small mobile devices, rather than on desktop or laptop computers. As a result, time spent online shopping is following suit, putting pressure on existing e-commerce brands to produce mobile-first offerings. Those vendors are now responsive to companies promising solutions to this new problem, like mobile app development firms, software vendors that make existing e-commerce websites mobile-friendly, and so on. Again, a change precipitated the need, and thus the attractiveness of the solution.

How Does The New Solution Work?

Of course, if something has changed that enables a new means of attacking an existing problem, or creates a new problem to be solved, you're going to need to explain how your solution goes about addressing that change.

Conveniently, for most founders this should be pretty easy; they will generally have strong market and product intimacy. The more important thing, though, may be to have a good sense of how to easily and clearly explain your approach to prospects. Often a good way to do that is to compare your product to existing solutions that your prospect understands.

For Salesforce, this would be something like "It's like your traditional CRMs, but it takes advantage of the browser and the web to let you access your CRM whenever you want, wherever you are. And it's way less clunky, and always has the most up-to-date features."

Or for Groupon, it might be "We have acquired email lists of tens of thousands of would-be customers in a given geography, who we'll help you access by offering compelling coupon-like deals, once a day, that get them in your door."

The level of detail that you'll have to delve into will vary depending on the audience. But at a minimum, you'll have to be able to explain the nuts and bolts of how your new solution takes advantage of change to help resolve a problem.

QUALITATIVE/QUANTITATIVE PROOF OF A BETTER SOLUTION

As you can see, each part of the narrative builds on the part before. This will be true for every piece of marketing collateral you produce—messaging, email and web copy, slide decks, and so on. And once you've covered "this is what has changed" and "this is how we take advantage of that change," you'll naturally want to get to "and here's why we know our solution is better."

Because you are now intimate with the problem space, the costs associated with the problem, and the means by which the problem is typically solved, quantitative comparisons should be easy. You already know the general metrics by which existing solutions are measured. Take another look at how you answered "What are the costs associated with the problem?" Now it's time to present why your solution does a better job, as measured in the same language as existing solutions. Typically, it'll be as simple as "Our offering does more X" or "Our offering requires less Y." What that X and Y are will depend on the space, but that will typically be the formula.

So for the recruiting space, where TalentBin plays, key metrics are cost per hire, time to fill an open role, and quality of hire. Of course, each of those metrics involves a lot of moving parts. So while you'll want to be able to address the big picture, you'll have to address the constituent pieces too.

For instance, a recruiter or recruiting manager will typically look at candidate databases to determine how many of their target candidates they can find and then recruit, and whether the contact information for those candidates is readily available. In the case of a solution like TalentBin, the metrics that would be interesting to a recruiter are things like search-result counts for a given skill profile in a given geography. So when presenting to recruiters, we would make sure to present our search results for candidates with, say, Ruby, Java Script, and MySQL experience in the region they were recruiting out of; then we'd compare those search results to what came up on LinkedIn Recruiter or a job board's resume database. When the recruiter saw that we offered three, four, or ten times the number of results, it was pretty clear why our offering was superior.

You'll need to do this for each part of your offering's value proposition. For instance, search discovery is only part of the workflow that a recruiter engages in. Outreach is another. When assessing how a product can help with candidate outreach, recruiters might be interested, for example, in email-address availability and the speed with which they can execute their outreach. If you were selling to recruiters, then, you might start by noting the one hundred InMails per month that a recruiter gets through LinkedIn Recruiter, and the amount of time it would take to send those InMails without templating or mass-outreach functionality. Then you would present the volume of email outreach that could be achieved in the same amount of time using your solution.

This is also where you can do a good job of guiding the conversation, based on your deep understanding of the problem, market, and existing solutions. For instance, your competitors may try to cite metrics that don't matter. In the world of talent acquisition, that's often large numbers of resumes in a database. "We have two hundred million profiles!" That might be interesting, but what does it matter for a recruiter focused on physician assistants or iOS developers if there are only twelve possible candidates in those two hundred million profiles?

You can also spotlight qualitative differences between your solution and the competition, but this should be in supplement, where possible, to metric-based comparison. And ideally you should have metrical backing to support those qualitative differences. For instance, if you were presenting a mobile CRM offering that promised better usability than desktop CRMs (a qualitative claim), ideally you would have metrics to support those claims. Logins per day or data-quality metrics, for example, could help prove that as a result of this enhanced usability, actions that can be counted—and compared—are happening more or less often than with existing solutions.

Third-party validation is another means by which to present your offering's superiority and lend credibility to your claims. This would be things like customer counts, customer testimonials (which ideally feature the metrics and qualitative claims you've defined above), deeper case studies, press and analyst coverage (which we'll get into more later and ideally features large parts of your narrative, restated by the author), and so on. This isn't a core part of the narrative, per se, but rather a means by which to say "and this is who agrees."

There are all manner of ways to respond to "Okay, so how do you know your product's better?" Whichever you choose, though, having them at the ready is a requirement for your narrative.

PRICING

Pricing is a funny thing. It could be considered part of your narrative, or it could be considered part of your sales materials. In a way, it's the conclusion of the narrative arc for your solution—"And because of all this, you should pay us this for the right to access our solution." While pricing is something that is likely to change—usually going up as you gain more functionality, or getting more nuanced as you segment your solution—it's definitely something that you'll want to have nailed down, at least in an initial version, when you start having sales conversations.

First, I think it's important to charge, even at the outset. If you don't charge, people won't take you seriously or think hard about whether your solution provides them value. They also likely won't use the solution. It's no skin off their backs, and they're not paying for it, so why should they invest time in it? This isn't to say that you have to charge an arm and a leg. Or that you can't do a freemium approach, where there is a free initial period or volume of usage. And it doesn't mean that you can't have a set of "lighthouse customers" early on that pay for their license fees with engaged, ongoing, validated feedback. But you definitely should charge for your solution. Founders frequently kick the can down the road on this issue because they don't want to hear someone say no to them. But you're not doing yourself a favor by avoiding that moment. So figure out an initial price point, and then ask for it. Your solution provides real value to the customer (if it doesn't, bigger problem), and your engineers need to eat. So charge.

I like to approach pricing in an iterative capacity, biasing toward giving away more value than is captured—at least to start. The goal here being that, early on, you want to get customers in the product, using it and testing your value promises; if your solution is priced to perfection, it will likely hurt your close rates and make acquiring those customers more challenging at the margin. This doesn't mean that you'll stick with lowish pricing forever. Rather, as you progress, with each incremental conversation, you'll be getting more information about how the market reacts to your pricing. If you present your product for $100 per seat per month, and no one bats an eye, well, maybe next time make it $150! At TalentBin we started out asking for $99 a month just to test the water, then moved that to $199, $299, $399, and then $499 a month, with an annual contract, paid up front. But we pushed this up over time (not to mention, the product was getting better by leaps as we went).

Once you start to raise prices, don't worry about those early customers that you have at 20% or 50% of your eventual pricing; there are tens of thousands of other customers in the world that will pay full price. Just grandfather those existing folks in and thank them for their early votes of confidence. No reason to punish them for being early believers. In fact, this can be a means by which to get people to jump and buy now. "Well, it's five hundred a month right now, but as we add functionality, that may go up. Of course, if you buy now, you would be grandfathered in at that price."

Approaches to Pricing

In terms of taking early shots at pricing, there are a couple of ways to think about it. It's more art than science early on, and you'll typically blend a number of data points together. But these approaches can help you get started.

Existing Solutions Comparison

Since your solution is likely addressing an existing pain point in the market, a great place to look for guideposts on pricing is existing products. For instance, with TalentBin, we found strong comparators in the form of resume search databases like Dice.com's resume search, or quasi-social-network profile-search and CRM tools like LinkedIn Recruiter. Both are priced on a per-seat basis, with certain usage limits (profile views and message sends). As such, it was easy to position TalentBin on a per-seat basis for recruiters, because they were used to that. Even better, because LinkedIn charges up front for their annual contracts, that was the "default" in the minds of the customer base and something that we could take advantage of in our pricing.

By looking at existing solutions, you can also understand what the current market is used to paying for a set amount of "value." To go back to TalentBin as an example, when we started out, a seat of LinkedIn Recruiter was ~$8,000 a year for a technical recruiter focused on engineering hiring (~$5,000 for an agency recruiter); the product gave a certain amount of search recall for certain types of talent (i.e., "Ruby engineer in Dallas, Texas" might bring back four thousand results) and allowed one hundred InMail outreach messages a month. TalentBin, on the other hand, would give a recruiter between 2–5x the search recall, including candidates' direct email addresses, and unlimited outreach volume. So one could argue that for a recruiter focused purely on technical recruiting, TalentBin might be worth much more than LinkedIn Recruiter. Of course, TalentBin was just a small upstart when we were having our initial sales conversations, so this is an example of optimizing to provide more value to the customer than you take. Our pricing ended up being $6,000 per seat per year for most of the time before we were acquired. In this case, the goal was to engender in the prospect's thinking, "Wow, this smokes LinkedIn Recruiter for tech hiring, and it's twenty-five percent cheaper? I'll give it a shot."

Another compelling reason to look at how existing solutions are priced is that there is likely a rationale behind those pricing decisions, which you may not have figured out yet. Your solution is likely a better way of doing things via some sort of technical innovation; trying to do pricing innovation at the same time is often a distraction. One innovation at a time, please.

Take a second to think about what the comparators in the market might be for your solution and their pricing. If you don't know, go figure it out and use it to inform your thinking.

ROI & Value Pricing

Another, more advanced, way to do pricing is known as "ROI pricing." That is, determining the amount of value you expect to provide for the prospect and setting your price to capture some of that value. That's not to say that pricing would change on a customer-by-customer basis necessarily (that adds unnecessary complication). But it means that you would be aiming to provide a certain amount of value above and beyond the cost of your solution.

A great example of this is HIRABL, a company that makes recruiting agency revenue-acceleration tools. One of the things they do is help recruiting agencies identity "missed fees," where a client does not report that they hired a candidate submitted by the agency. Remember, agency fees are usually 10%–25% of a candidate's first-year salary, and as such can be between $10,000 and $30,000. Based on their massive dataset of submission data crossed with missed fee identification and missed fee capture, HIRABL knows that across the board there's typically one recoverable missed fee per five hundred candidate submissions. Because of this, they are able to price their solution based on the number of submissions that they will be monitoring for a recruiting agency, using an average fee of $15,000 and that 1 in 500 ratio, and have a very high confidence that their customers will get a 10x return on their investment. That is, if HIRABL is charging $20,000 to a recruiting agency for a year of monitoring, they know that the agency will recover around $200,000 of fees over the term of the contract. Some agencies may make out like gangbusters and get a 15x ROI on the solution, and others might only get 6x. Later we'll talk about recording these instances of captured value, but the idea here is to peg pricing in a way that correlates price with value.

You might be wondering, "Well, if you're going to do pricing directionally based on value capture, why not charge specifically based on the actual value captured?" In the case of HIRABL, for example, why not charge a percentage of actually recovered fees? While compelling in principle, the challenge there comes in reporting—that is, in instrumenting the actual value that was captured. And while you can architect your product to record ROI signifiers (i.e., marking a fee as "recovered"), this creates a situation where not only is the onus of usage taken off the shoulders of the customer, but there is also an incentive to hide captured value. Better to keep it simple and charge a known price, based on a defensible ROI model.

This sort of pricing can be challenging if you're too early to have a solid ROI case. First, this shows you how important it is to understand the dollars-and-cents value that you are providing to the customer, and to think about how you can actually prove the ROI case. (Can you do your own experiments at scale to see how your solution raises or lowers a key metric associated with a known value?) Second, this is why it may be most effective to use a mix of approaches—like blending pricing from existing solutions and your ROI proof understanding. For instance, if you know that your job-posting solution doubles the number of qualified applicants that show up for an engineering role based on your own experiments, maybe you charge 150% of the price of that other solution.

Value Alignment and Thresholding

Another approach to pricing is an extension of this ROI-based mindset—that is, aligning your pricing to the value provided to the prospect. For instance, this might be something like the model that Dropbox or Box use, where the more storage you use, the more it costs. Or you might approach it like Marketo, Eloqua, Act-On, or HubSpot, where the more contacts you are drip marketing to, the more the solution costs. This structure has the advantage of allowing a customer to "start small" (either with a small portion of their total demand or because their total demand just isn't that large, yet), and then grow—ensuring that the price you capture from them grows in step with the value they are deriving from the solution.

This is especially important if you're using a "trial" or freemium approach to selling your solution (more on trials and pilots later). You want to make sure that you can turn on the pricing at the point that the customer has gotten definite value. For instance, Yesware offers a free version of their product that allows users to track outbound emails. If you track above a certain number, though, they prevent you from tracking more that month. The idea being that if you're tracking a high number of outbound emails, you're likely a sales or recruiting professional and getting definite value from these tracking events. LinkedIn does something similar; if you use your free account to do more than a certain number of searches or view more than a certain number of profiles, they will prompt you to pay.

Related to this is the notion of "thresholding" of pricing. That is, can an organization, an individual within it, or a team within it just decide to purchase your solution within their budgetary constraints? (This is the beauty of SaaS delivered over the web.) If it's an individual, can they just buy it themselves because they grasp the value and how it can help them (Yesware)? If it's a team or a manager, is it under the threshold of their corporate purchasing card, and can they just expense it (Box, Slack)? If it's a department in an organization, is it under the amount of money they may have in their discretionary budget (i.e., TalentBin's $6,000 annual license fee often was). If you are mindful of these natural pricing breakpoints, you can help ease your entry into an account by slipping in under one of these thresholds. This isn't necessarily applicable to all solutions; it's hard to have a single team using an HR system designed for a whole organization, for example. But if you block an organization's ability to "just buy one to try it out," be aware that you are making your sales challenge harder.

With your solution, can you align value and threshold in a way that eases your entry into organizations, while at the same time positioning you well for growth?

Pricing to Perfection

We touched on this above, but you want to be careful about "pricing to perfection." That is, watch out for charging such a high price that all the stars have to align for the prospect to get a sufficient amount of value out of your solution to be satisfied—or, before then, for the prospect to even believe that they could get the requisite value. On the one hand, you don't want to give your product away, but pricing too high will work against you in a number of ways. First, it will hurt your win rates. A prospect can totally be on board with the pain you're solving and believe that you will solve it for them, but if you are charging so much that they don't believe that the ratio of pain solved to money paid is in balance, they won't buy. You'll see this in scenarios where the prospect has nodded in agreement with all of your pitches, only to seriously blanch when you get to a pricing conversation. It's a balance. You don't want prospects to say "Oh, that's easy, sure" when you tell them pricing, because then you're leaving money on the table. But if you're charging through the nose, and your win rates are suffering, reconsider. This is why it's often good to start low and raise pricing until you get to the point where you see it becoming a serious drag on closing conversations.

Too-high pricing also hurts your churn rate. If customers aren't getting sufficient value from your solution compared to the price, at the end of their term (whether a year or a month), they simply won't renew. So the onus is definitely on you to make sure they are using the product, and also deriving sufficient value from it—like HIRABL making sure that their clients are collecting missed fees that have been identified. (We'll talk about this more in the Implementation and Customer Success chapter.) But if you've priced to perfection, it will put substantial pressure on your product and your customer success apparatus to make sure value is delivered, lest the account churn out.

You can often see this proved out with low-priced products like Reputation. com that try to hook customers at $9.99 a month. Then they just make it difficult enough to cancel that it's never worth $9.99 of your time to try to do so, even though most users get zero value from it. Most of the people reading this will have enterprise and B2B solutions that actually provide value, but this example proves the point that the value provided and the price charged need to be in alignment, or else you'll see serious churn.

Segmenting

This is where founders can get into trouble. Like indexing off of mature companies' sales collateral, there's an impulse to index off of Box's, Slack's, or Salesforce's pricing pages. You see that they all have three options—and one marked "Most Popular!"—and feel that you need to have that too. Resist the urge. They've been doing this for years. They know which segments of customers care about which features and usage volumes. And they likely have a number of customer segments. You, on the other hand, probably don't have either. First, you should be focused on your ideal customer profile right now (which we'll discuss at length in Early Prospecting). You shouldn't be engaging in sales conversations with accounts that are substantially different from one another. So even if you knew the features and usage patterns that could be used to price discriminate, you shouldn't be talking about different prospect profiles to begin with. Second, you probably have no idea which features matter for which customers segments. So let's deal with it down the road! Not right now. Segmenting your solution can be a great approach later on to extract better pricing out of higher-end clients who are price insensitive. But early on, it's usually a distraction.

Pricing is an iterative process where you learn more about what parts of your product matter, and how much, over time. Like other sales materials, you shouldn't view it as "done," nor should you feel that it needs to be "perfect" before you start using it. But you do need to have it.

PUTTING IT ALL TOGETHER

Lastly, you have to put all these thoughts together. This doesn't mean that you have to take these constituent parts and write them into a page-long meditation, put it on a shelf, and never touch it again. Or that you need to have a holistic "messaging document" that you deliver verbatim. But it's good to have a concept of what the narrative looks like, summed up, all together. Again, the narrative actually exists separate from whatever medium you end up collateralizing it in, whether slides, video, messaging, and so on. Whatever collateral you use, though, you need to be able to tell a coherent story.

Test yourself by experimenting with an elevator pitch, or how you might explain your story to someone you met at a cocktail party who has intimacy with the space you're working in. This won't be a full treatise, but rather the first skeleton of your story. Then, based on your interaction with the listener, as they double click here or there, you can expand—because you're deeply familiar with the details that underlie the cursory overview.

Another great exercise is to try writing it down to see if you can incorporate all of the pieces we've covered. So what would this look like? Let's consider a couple of examples.

The TalentBin Narrative

What's the problem? Technical recruiting is really hard! Finding software-engineering talent that has the skills that your organization requires, and then engaging with them to get them to consider your organization, is a tough problem.

Who has the problem? What's the cost of not solving the problem? It's something that makes the lives of technical sourcers, recruiters, and recruiting managers rough, particularly because if they don't solve the problem, they may have to pay large sums of money to recruiting agencies—25% of a first-year salary of $125,000 or more. Otherwise they don't hire on schedule, and that impacts the ability of their organizations to ship software on time, and make revenue!

How is this currently solved? Why doesn't that work? Yes, you can use things like job boards or LinkedIn, but the problem is that unemployment is so low in software engineering that very few engineers are actively looking for jobs. And because most people don't really pay attention to LinkedIn or update their profiles, software-engineering profiles have a tendency not to exist, or to be missing the skill information that indicates that the engineer in question would be a good fit. Not to mention the fact that there are hundreds of thousands of recruiters on LinkedIn messaging every engineer they can find, and that creates tons of noise to cut through.

What has changed? But the good news is, the Internet has undergone some amazing changes of late to help make finding and engaging with these potential hires much easier and more effective. Because people are spending so much more time online, day in and out, on social sites like Twitter, Facebook, and Meetup and professional networks like GitHub and Stack Overflow—and because of the general move toward the digitization of work materials—there are reams and reams of information available. If properly leveraged, that material can help recruiters find talented individuals based on the activity they engage in online—for instance, tweeting about iOS development, being a member of an Android Meetup, participating in email lists about Java, and so on. (How does it work?) TalentBin scoops up all the information that individuals leave as digital fingerprints of their professional selves, analyzes it, and turns it into profiles for these individuals, with skill details and contact information. Then we let recruiters search and review the profiles and reach out to folks.

How do you know it's better? Because TalentBin makes use of these mountains of "implicit" professional activity, it solves the problem of finding individuals who are not searching for jobs, not present in job board resume databases, and undiscoverable on LinkedIn due to their thin profiles. For instance, for a typical search like "Ruby on Rails" in the San Francisco Bay Area, TalentBin returns 5x the number of results compared to LinkedIn Recruiter. Moreover, 60% of these profiles have personal email addresses, which are so, so much better for engaging candidates. Recruiter open, click, and response rates using TalentBin provided personal email addresses are 3x-5x better than generic InMail outreach. And while the raw statistics tell the story, the hundreds of customers TalentBin has amassed—who have hired thousands of technical staff with the solution—tell the story even better. Not to mention the awards, press, and analyst accolades TalentBin has won since entering the market.

And all of this is available to you for $6,000 per user, per year. That includes unlimited requisitions, searches, and profile views, and unlimited email sends. Compare this to $8,000 for a LinkedIn Recruiter account with inferior technical candidate search recall, capped at a hundred InMails a month. It's a total steal!

The Salesforce Narrative

What is the problem? Who has it? Being a B2B sales rep is tough! You have to manage dozens of concurrent conversations, follow up at the right time, and not drop any balls. So too with being a sales manager. You have to make sure that your team is engaging in high activity—but also the right activity—and keep track of potential issues, while forecasting how your revenue achievement will end up for the quarter.

What is the cost of the issue? And this is serious business. If a rep drops a ball, forgetting to follow up with a prospect at the right time or neglecting to send a proposal as promised, it can mean tens or hundreds of thousands of dollars of lost revenue. Moreover, from an efficiency standpoint, if reps aren't sufficiently productive, they're missing out on potential deals and conversations. And for sales managers, not being able to manage the activity levels of staff, identify weaknesses, and forecast accurately could mean leaving problems unaddressed, which can turn into hundreds of thousands of dollars of short fallen targets. And that could mean missed quarters and stock impacts. It's no joke.

How is this currently solved? For how important customer-relationship tracking and management is, it's amazing how poorly it's generally done. You have reps either living out of their email and calendars or using ancient, clunky contact managers like Act! or GoldMine, or last-generation CRMs made by Siebel that look like something out of Tron.

Why don't current solutions work? The problem with these approaches is that email and calendars are not designed for tracking customer relationships, and make it more likely for very costly balls to be dropped. Last-generation CRM systems require reps to be in front of their computers, dialed into a VPN. And even if they are, those systems are extremely clunky and hard to use—creating more time and bookkeeping overhead rather than actually enabling reps to sell more, faster.

What has changed? However, with the rise of the Internet, now the power of modern, usable, always-accessible CRM can be available to reps wherever they are, whenever.

How does it work? Salesforce provides a modern, next-generation CRM that is accessed through the browser, connecting reps to their important deal information quickly and easily. And because it's software delivered as a service, the latest and greatest innovations in rep-efficiency features are available to all users, all at once, rather than requiring IT to upgrade the on-premise CRM system. And because web technologies make for easy interoperability, Salesforce has a massive partner ecosystem of amazing add-on tools that offer all manner of efficiency benefits.

How do you know it's better? Because the software is available to reps wherever and whenever via a browser, and is much more usable, you get reps who are logging in and updating opportunities and pipelines as much as 3x–10x as often as on traditional systems. That not only reduces the potential for dropped balls—as you can see by the 20%–50% increase in win rates for reps who adopt Salesforce—but also makes for more accurate forecasts on a rep and sales manager basis. We've seen a 30%–50% reduction in missed forecasts for managers whose teams use Salesforce. All of which has resulted in Salesforce being the most lauded CRM solution on the market, consistently in Gartner's Magic Quadrant for CRM, and gaining tens of thousands of customers.

Bake That Narrative, and then Get Ready to Make Some Collateral

Once you've formed your narrative, you're going to be taking this core story and distributing it in different formats for easy consumption by interested parties. Generally this will take the form of sales collateral for prospects, but the same narrative will get recast for other interested parties too- press, analysts, partners, and even investors and acquirers.

But if you don't have that narrative nailed—if it's not coherent and persuasive—all the collateral in the world won't do you a bit of good. It'll just be shiny nonsense. Nail your narrative first.

Great, now you do it:

What is the problem?

Who has the problem?

What are the costs associated with the problem?

How do people currently solve this problem, and how do those solutions fall down?

What has changed enabling a new solution?

How does the new solution work?

How do you know it's better? (Quantitative, Qualitative)

Put that all together, then be sure you're armed with qualitative and quantitative proof that yours is a better solution. Finally, give some thought to your initial pricing structure, and you'll be ready to take your narrative out into the world.

CHAPTER 3

Sales Materials Basics:
What You Need to Sell & How to Build it

INTRODUCTION

Now that your narrative is baked, it is time to start building the materials that you will be using to communicate that narrative to your would-be customers. The goal of this chapter is to get you to the point where you have a solid set of materials that you can use to engage, pitch, and close your first set of customers.

While there's a galaxy's worth of different sales materials that you could create and use, we're focused on the very basics here. We're going to cover only the few you should start with—namely, slides for a sales presentation, email templates and phone scripts for prospecting and appointment setting, sales-demo scripting, and basic video content. It's a necessarily limited set of materials, but it will set you up for later success in creating more varied and more involved collateral items, as you'll start building a set of reusable assets for use across other tools.

A NOTE ON PRODUCTION VALUE & SPEED

Before we get started, I want to take a second to talk about a common misconception among new sales professionals, which can really hurt their efforts. Because their prior experience with sales comes from what they've seen in movies and the materials they've pulled off of mature organizations' websites, they believe that everything they produce has to be spit-shined and sparkly before it can get in front of a customer. That something has to be triple-checked and signed off on by everyone before they can present it. That it has to be reviewed by "legal." And so on.

While that may be true of larger organizations with slower-moving offerings (and even then, I don't buy it), this mindset is extremely damaging for an early-stage sales organization. When you are getting started, speed is key.

The shorter the feedback loop between hearing an objection from a customer and building a slide to combat that objection, the better. The less time between shipping an amazing new feature and recording a rough-around-the-edges video demo of it, the more appointments you will set. The faster you build a new slide documenting the feature and how it supports your value prop, or update your "why we matter" slide when a prestigious publication mentions you, the more mileage you will get. This is how you will win.

When there is a trade-off between "perfect" and "good enough to persuade the customer," opt for speed. Having 10 five-minute screencasts explaining each of your major features up on YouTube—recorded directly from your laptop while you speak into its microphone, complete with "ums," "uhs," and sneezes—will be more impactful for your efforts, to start, than one sparkling, pristine explainer video.

SALES PRESENTATIONS

With that out of the way, we're going to start with your sales presentation. For the more visually inclined, I have put together a presentation of this section on sales presentations print (Ha!), complete with lots of examples.

You'll note that we're starting with slides. While a killer demo and a great verbal description are no doubt important, and explainer videos are nifty, nothing works in a sales context like slides. They're visual, so you can mix in images, charts, and so on that underscore your point, alongside text that explains it. You can speak over them, live. You can send them to someone who missed the presentation. You can use them in prospecting, to send to someone who isn't sure they want to take a demo. You can record an overview video in which you talk over them. You can post them online to generate leads. You can screenshot one and email it to make a point. You can chop a deck down to a smaller mini-deck to make a more targeted point. You can remix slides to create presentations with different thrusts.

And importantly, a slide deck is what customers expect to see. It's the means by which they're used to consuming commercially oriented product information. This is not unlike how VCs are used to consuming would-be investment information via a "pitch deck." There are just certain patterns of information presentation and consumption that have become standards, and in the B2B enterprise sales world, the big daddy is your sales presentation.

Often technical founders have a tendency to think "no way, I should just do a demo." While a demo is important, it's not the whole story. It's a sub-chapter, and if you jump straight to it without ensuring the proper context is set, you'll injure your ability to communicate the value of your solution as a means by which to solve a problem your prospect has. A good presentation tees up a great demo.

So let's get started with what you should include in that deck.

Structuring Your Deck for Extensibility

As with all of your marketing and sales collateral, your slide deck will be an implementation of your sales narrative. And much like your sales narrative, it will pretty much always be a work in progress. The more you embrace this notion of "always shipping" marketing collateral, kind of like your product, the better off you will be. It will drive the correct behavior—that is, not thinking about a deck as being "done"—and remove the onus for a "perfect" deck. It will also compel you to think about your deck and other materials in an extensible fashion. As you build your sales deck right now, think about how you will build on top of this later.

At a bare minimum, you should structure your sales deck to correspond to the various steps in your sales narrative—that is, what is the problem, who has it, what are the associated costs of the problem, what are the existing solutions and their shortfalls, what has changed to enable a new solution, how does it work, is there qualitative/quantitative proof that yours is a superior solution, and how much does it cost.

The "minimum viable product" is literally a slide on each of those steps, with bullet points elucidating the elements of your narrative. Now, that wouldn't be very sexy—but remember, like your narrative, and your product itself, this will always be a work in progress, getting better and more involved with each iteration. So when you get to the point where you want to break, say, your solution slide from a single slide with four bullets on your product's value propositions into a series of individual slides on each value prop, great, go for it. But before you do that, using a single slide is just fine.

Something like this:

Happier purple squirrel hunting...

 Find candidates other recruiting organizations **can't find**.

 Get a full, **360 candidate view** to qualify and start the conversation.

 Reach out using all available communication vectors, that candidates actually respond to.

 Stay on top of the candidates you find with pipeline management, tasks, and automation.

TalentBin

As that bare-bones solution section evolves, it can be broken into "sub-chapters" by adding a single slide on each major value proposition. For instance, one of TalentBin's value props is "Scalable, impactful outreach that helps recruiters engage with candidates and drive them down the hiring funnel." The corresponding slide speaks to how TalentBin enables recruiters to:

1. Integrate their existing email systems with the product.

2. Use mail-merge templates to quickly send email through that integrated email system.

3. Leverage "open and click" tracking in those emails to see who's interacting with their messages and who's ignoring them.

4. Send up to thirty messages at once through a mass-mail system.

5. And implement drip marketing to would-be candidates with campaigns that send follow-up emails without any additional recruiter effort.

In the deck, this "sub-chapter" looked like this:

High Impact, Scalable Recruiting Outreach

Scalable, impactful outreach helps recruiters engage candidates, and drive them down the hiring funnel.

 Use your corporate Outlook or Gmail email directly in TalentBin.

 Smart mail-merge templates to speed custom outreach.

 Open and click-tracking shows which candidates are engaging.

 Mass-mail allows mail-merged outreach 30 candidates at a time.

 Drip-marketing executes candidate follow up emails, automatically.

TalentBin

Imagine doing this for your product's value propositions. Each slide should include the features that speak to a key selling point, bulleted out, perhaps with a small screenshot or icon signifying each. Now, rather than a single solution slide, you have a top-level overview and several additional, focused, slides with the next level of detail on each value prop. This evolution of the deck will allow you to speak to key features—or, if sent stand-alone, encourage the customer to review and understand how those features support your value proposition.

Then, later, when you want to go to the next level of detail, you can create a dedicated slide for each of the bullet points on those slides. To help the user buy into the value of key features, dedicate a slide to each one, with screenshots and subtitles that offer a more detailed explanation and supporting metrics. Of course, all the while, be sure to retain the summary versions of these sections; you'll want them later so you can choose the level of granularity you use in a given presentation and appropriately customize it for customers, press, analysts, investors, or what have you.

For instance, these are some of the slides we developed at TalentBin to highlight those "scalable recruiting outreach" features:

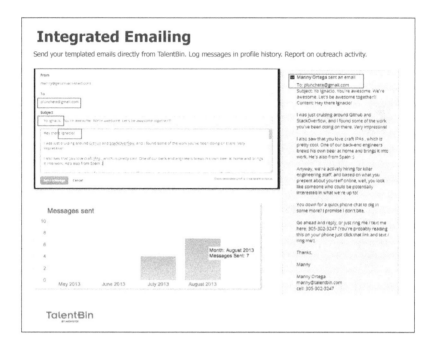

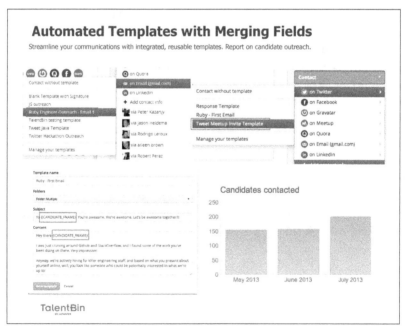

Mass Emailing

Send emails to up to 30 candidates at a time using TalentBin's mass email functionality.

Automated Follow Up

Candidate Drip Marketing sends automatic, pre-configured follow up messages to candidates, raising response rates.

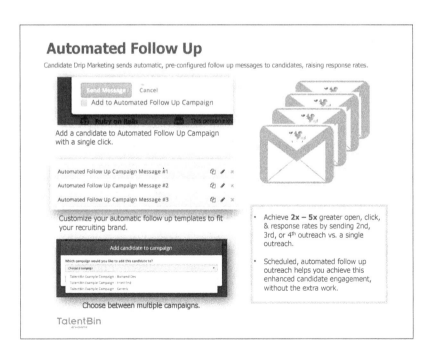

Add a candidate to Automated Follow Up Campaign with a single click.

Customize your automatic follow up templates to fit your recruiting brand.

Choose between multiple campaigns.

- Achieve **2x – 5x** greater open, click, & response rates by sending 2nd, 3rd, or 4th outreach vs. a single outreach.

- Scheduled, automated follow up outreach helps you achieve this enhanced candidate engagement, without the extra work.

How would you bucket your solution? What features would you drop into each bucket? And how would you describe the value of those features in a slide? Take a second to think about what this looks like for your product.

Now imagine this approach applied across the rest of your slide deck, not just in your "solution" section. Start with the minimum viable coverage of each piece of the narrative, and then build out as appropriate. A helpful metaphor is "zoom in, zoom out". Start at a higher level, and if you want to "zoom in" on a section, build more slides for it. But you can start at the broadest level and still be fine. The important thing is to have at least a coarse version of your end-to-end narrative that can handle those cases we talked about—speaking over the slides during an online presentation, sending them to someone, etc.

Production Value of Your Slides

On the note of starting with "minimum viable" and then embellishing as you go, let's talk about production value as it relates specifically to your sales deck. As with all things startup, it's important to not mistakenly believe you need to have "big company" materials before you get started. That is, even the starkest slides with no branding or shine, when loaded with impactful, persuasive content that presents a transformative, innovative product, will still close business. The most important thing is to never let some notion of "but it's not flashy enough" block your ability to create content (whether it's slides, videos, etc.). The goal is communication of business meaning, and that can be done with a minimal amount of flash. This isn't to say that you can't add the flash later, but it should never be viewed as a gate. Also, flash without a valid narrative is actually worse than nothing—you just look like an idiot with nothing to say who wastes people's time. I've seen plenty of these sales decks. Don't be that guy.

That said, there are some basics that, with minimal effort, can help boost your production value in support of your messaging. For instance, a simple slide template with background coloring, font theme coloring (that is, headline text of a certain color, smaller subtitle text of a different color, all correlated to your brand coloring), and your logo in a corner can do remarkably much to spruce things up. Conveniently, a lot of this stuff may already be built for fundraising materials. If you have a slide deck with a theme, logos, and so on that was used for raising money for the company, just steal that, and iterate on it. Be sure to include title slides in your template—that is, full-stop slides to define a new section of your presentation (even if that's just "Demo!" or "Appendix"). And as you progress, have a "templating" mindset. If you create a new type of slide—like one that shows images of features along with subtitles to support a value prop—make sure that you clone it as you're making new versions of that slide for other value props.

Lastly, a great way to "spiff up" your MVP slides is to find a designer on Upwork or similar, and have them give your slides and templates a glossy coat of polish, which you can now use on new slides. Again, this is after you've made them yourself, and to enable you to make higher production value slides going forward. Never should design be a blocker on you creating a new slide to explain a new feature, document an ROI proof, and so on.

The following are some examples of good template slides:

Title/Section Slide Template: Logo, spot for segment title.

Feature Slide Template: Headline, sub-headline, screenshots, subtitles, value prop call-outs.

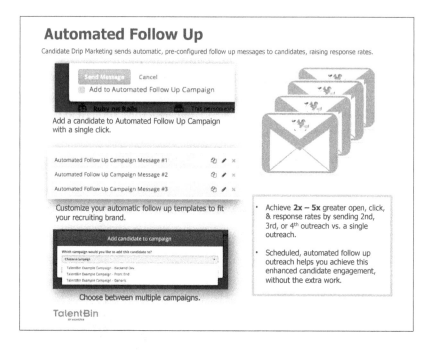

Overview Slide Template: Headline, sub-headline, bulleted list of concepts.

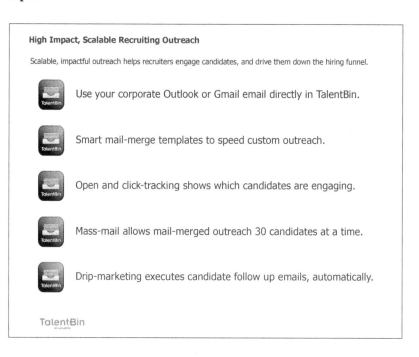

There are other pretty basic things you can do to help with your production value in a minimally viable way. Bullets that use your logo as an icon. Drop shadows on screenshots to make them pop out. You can use tools like Camtasia to take videos of certain use cases and make them into animated GIFs for inclusion in the deck—in effect adding mini demos to the relevant slides. Pay attention to information architecture too, by varying text size and formatting like bolding and italics to put emphasis on more important things, and diminish less important things (like subtitles on screenshots, footnotes, etc.).

But remember, the best production value in the world can't dress up a story that doesn't address the business pains of your audience and present how your solution is positioned to solve those pains. So nail that first.

Content Management and Deployment

As you create your deck—starting with the minimally viable slide-based version of your narrative, and then extending out as you embellish various sections—you're going to need to pay attention to "bootstrap content management." That is, as more and more content is produced, the best way I've found to manage it is in a single large slide deck that lives on the computer (or in a Dropbox/Google Drive folder) of the person responsible for its creation, editing, and extension. For instance, I started a "TalentBin Sales Master_tip_of_the_branch.pptx" file at the company's inception, then expanded and refactored it every step of the way.

That isn't to say that this is a deck you'll be presenting to customers—with all 120 slides, covering every possible angle of the product and market. It is simply the repository from which you'll produce sales-ready versions of the deck, or even press-centric versions, analyst-centric versions, etc. Every time I make edits, I like to fork off a copy of the deck and save it to whatever content-sharing mechanism my team is using (whether ClearSlide, or even just Google Drive, Dropbox, or SharePoint).

This way, nothing is ever destroyed, even as you extend and re-factor, and you'll still have a record of all prior slides, even if they've been dropped from the master as no longer necessary. And importantly, later, when you have dozens of sales reps using your materials, separating the master from a version that has been pushed out to "production" on ClearSlide is also important, so that you don't have others hacking at your canonical deck.

It's far from elegant, but until we have GitHub for PowerPoint, it's the best approach I've found. Building a master slide deck will ensure that you're not reinventing the wheel, and that the totality of slides that could be used to tell your sales story are always ready to be deployed or remixed.

Customization Mindset

A sales presentation is focused on identifying each customer's pain points (via discovery questions and pre-call planning) and presenting your offering as the solution to those pain points. Nothing does that better than using specific customer information in your sales presentation (and later, your demo) to help show that prospect exactly what your solution could do for them.

If your offering is web-based, then good examples of this could be screenshots of your solution dropped into screens of your prospect's website, or examples of their current pain points gathered from third-party data sources.

For instance, I've worked with a talented group of guys who run a startup called LifeGuides, which helps companies scalably create awesome employee-focused recruitment branding materials. They then make sure those materials rank high in Google search results for "working at *<your company name>*," and that those materials can be deployed in all manner of recruitment marketing tools. Their sales deck is set up such that they can drop in Google search results for "working at *<prospect company name>*" to demonstrate to the prospect what recruiting candidates see when Googling their company. And they have other slides set up to show what a prospect's career site could look like with LifeGuides-style content deployed.

All it takes is a little templating and some screenshotting to make a world of difference in how clearly you communicate your value to a prospect.

A Section-specific Slide Deck Notes

While you'll iterate your slide deck continually, in alignment with your sales narrative and feedback from the market, there are some particular things you should keep an eye out for in certain sections.

The Problem and Who Has It

Starting with the "problem" section is helpful to your sales deck in the same way it helped start off your larger sales narrative—if the person to whom you're presenting, when shown the problem your solution addresses, says, "Huh, I actually don't have that problem," then delightful! You've saved yourself and them the trouble of presenting a solution that doesn't fit their business pain.

Of course, even better if you didn't get all the way to the presentation before realizing that key piece of data (more on that in Prospecting and List Building). But better late than never to save your and your prospect's time.

This section of your deck is a great place to document not just the problem that you're seeking to resolve, but also other validators of that problem and its importance. This could be things like stats from industry analysts—e.g., for TalentBin, these slides address the extremely low unemployment rate of technical, creative, and healthcare talent—press clippings, and so forth. That way, you're not only further describing the problem, but showing that many others agree that it is a problem. For instance, this is a "problem statement" slide made when TalentBin was first getting into the healthcare space.

This slide documents the pain that recruiters trying to hire doctors and nurses have in a low-unemployment environment:

Healthcare employment continues to expand

- Healthcare employment **increased by 21,000 in June 2014**, about in line with the prior 12-month average gain of 18,000 per month.

- The unemployment rate within Healthcare & Social Assistance (super-sector i.e. Ambulatory Healthcare Services, Hospitals, and Nursing and Residential Care Facilities, etc.) **averaged 4% in the prior 12-months compared to 6.8% across the nation**.

- The Healthcare sector has some of the **nation's fastest expanding occupations** (i.e. registered nurses, home health aides, nursing assistants, licensed practical & licensed vocational nurses, and medical assistants).

TalentBin

This can be done via "anecdata" as well:

This is a good slide demonstrating the problem case that e-commerce providers face in the poor conversion rates of mobile shopping:

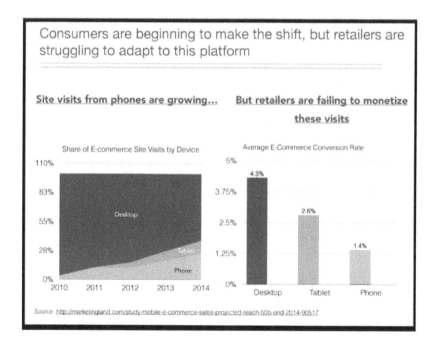

The Cost of the Problem

As with the problem section, the cost section is a great place to make the case not only that this problem exists for your target audience, but that it's a costly one that merits resolution. And as before, this is a good time to trot out validated metrics from studies, analysts, press, and so forth, and to generally cover the various ways that the problem in question is creating business issues for people like your prospect.

So, for a sales CRM solution, you might highlight the opportunity cost of lost deals on a per-rep basis. Or how increased sales rep efficiency can add additional deals per rep, per month, and that without proper CRM software, your organization is missing out on those deals. Or how missed forecasts injure the ability of an organization to plan properly, and can get a company into financial hot water. Or how, absent a robust CRM implementation, the crushing communication overhead of sales managers monitoring sales rep execution means that monitoring either isn't done, leading to bad sales outcomes, or occupies far too much time, sapping manager resources from things like program execution.

As you trot these out, it's best to append metrics to each, as possible, to allow for at least a directional notion of the actual dollars-and-cents cost of these problems, ideally in a way that can be applied to the business you're addressing. That might look like $X cost per rep, per month. Or $Y cost per manager, per month. Z deals per month not won, which, with your average contract value, would be $A per month in foregone revenue and, with your fifty sales reps, adds up to $50 x A per month in foregone revenue. Make it easy to understand the ongoing cost the prospect is encountering.

Existing Solutions and Their Challenges

Slides on existing solutions are a bit of a tightrope walk. On the one hand, it's typically a good idea to stay away from talking about the competition unless prospects bring it up themselves, so baking that into the core of your presentation can be dicey. However, in the case where existing solutions are pervasive—and if you're selling a new, upstart solution, there will generally be "market standards" that everyone is familiar with—then it can be good to address them directly. It helps you take control of framing how you're different from the existing solutions, what their shortcomings are, and how you surmount those.

At worst, if, for whatever reason, you find out from discovery questions that your prospect doesn't use these standard solutions, you can choose to skip over those slides.

At a minimum, this could be a single slide that groups the existing solutions into buckets so you can address how you are not like the things sitting on the page. Maybe with a headline identifying them, and a summary subtitle of their key issues. In the case of TalentBin, traditional solutions include job postings on boards like Monster.com or CareerBuilder, resume search in resume search databases from, again, traditional job boards, talent search in professional networks like LinkedIn, and, for corporate organizations, working with professional service providers like staffing agencies.

If there is a particular solution or set of solutions that the majority of your would-be customers will be comparing you to (or you would like to be compared to), then you can certainly dig into that specifically. In the case of TalentBin, for instance, as a passive-candidate search engine and recruiting CRM offering, we were an upstart competitor of LinkedIn, and their Talent Solutions offerings (namely, their flagship "LinkedIn Recruiter" product). More than 80 percent of the prospects that we spoke with likely had a LinkedIn Recruiter seat in house, maybe more, and that was actually a good thing. It demonstrated that the customer was already onboard with the notion of passive-candidate recruiting, and had a demonstrated willingness to spend money on it.

For that reason, we had a couple slides on the particular challenges of LinkedIn Recruiter as relates to technical, creative, and healthcare recruiting—pairing those categories with our particular value propositions of "Discovery," "Qualification," "Outreach," and "Pipeline Management." Take the challenges LinkedIn Recruiter has around discovery. Software engineering, design, and healthcare talent often does a poor job of even having LinkedIn profiles, and certainly of embellishing them with proper skill information. As such, those profiles can't be found by searching on LinkedIn Recruiter. This is a problem for recruiters, as demonstrated by the sparse results that come from a search for a particularly valuable skill or title like "iOS development" or "nurse anesthetists." Moreover, because of the hundreds of thousands of recruiters using LinkedIn Recruiter, outreach to candidates via InMail is a decreasingly effective means of engagement, as demonstrated by the number of InMails technical candidates get weekly, and declining response rates. These points, of course, correlate to the key value metrics that clients are familiar with (which is something you should have converged on in your narrative construction)—in this example, directed at technical and healthcare recruiters, those metrics include talent pool richness, contact information density, and candidate responsiveness.

Keeping that "extensibility" mindset, use your best judgment as to how much of this information you'd like to have in your primary presentation. The rest can go into the appendix.

The following are some examples of this from the TalentBin sales deck:

Characterizing the root cause of the challenges faced by the industry standard.

An existence proof of what this challenge looks like.

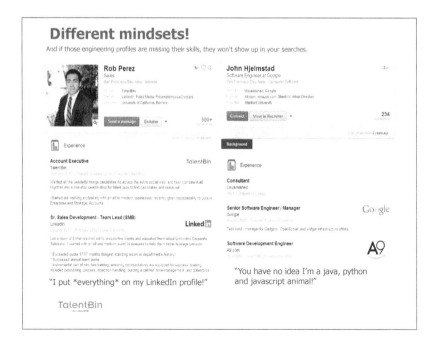

The extension of this challenge at scale.

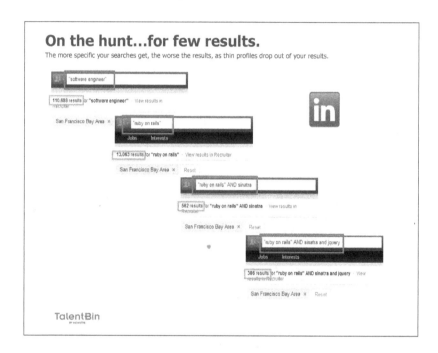

Further implications of this core challenge, and another set of challenges around outreach and candidate responsiveness (another value bucket that will resonate with customers):

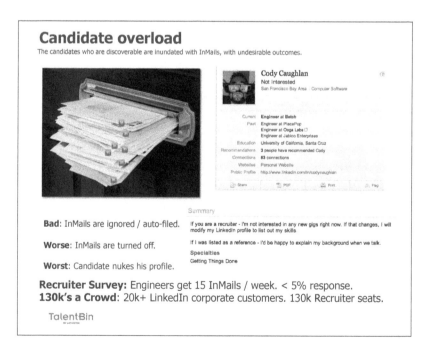

If you have multiple segments, you can speak to that too.

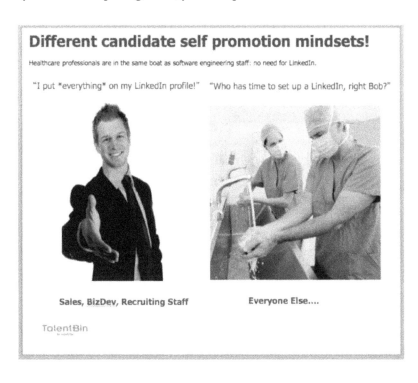

An even further extension of a common pain point that the client would recognize:

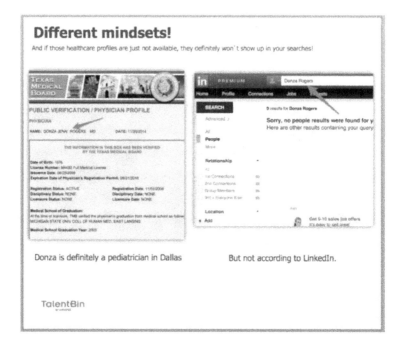

A summarization of these unit pains at a macro scale.

LinkedIn Healthcare Penetration

Comparisons of Bureau of Labors Statistics Totals vs. LinkedIn title search coverage.

Role	US Totals*	LinkedIn Totals**	LinkedIn Penetration
Nurse Practitioner	180k	71k	40%
Physician Assistant	84k	43k	52%
Registered Nurse	2.6m	320k	12.3%
Certified Registered Nurse Anesthetist	48k	17k	36%
Licensed Practical Nurse	738k	13k	13.6%
Speech Pathologist	134k	18k	13.4%
Occupational Therapist	113k	51k	45.2%
Physical Therapist	73k	95k	130%
Pediatrician	31k	11k	35%
Oncologist	15k	3.5k	23.6%
Cardiologist	27k	6.6k	24.7%
OBGYN	22k	7.6k	16%
Neurologist	21k	3.6k	30.2%
Orthopedic Surgeon	28k	3.4k	12.4%
Gastroenterologist	11k	1.7k	16%
Radiologist	43k	10.7	24.4%
Anesthesiologist	30k	11.6k	38%
Psychiatrist	25k	12.8k	51.5%

TalentBin   *Data from the Bureau of Labor Statistics   **US Geography Title" searches on LinkedIn. 11 10 14

There are a variety of ways to approach this, and varying levels to which you can dig into the challenges of existing solutions. But including at least some slides to frame your solution in contrast to existing solutions will be helpful in demonstrating why your product is so much better, and thus worth the investment.

What Has Changed

The worst sales meeting? It's the one where the client actually had no clue what was being discussed but, because he didn't want to admit that, just politely nodded along, committed to "follow up," and promptly disappeared. Of course he disappeared. He never understood what was going on.

I find that the best way to prevent this is to include a section in your deck on what has changed in the market, and how it impacts clients and created the opportunity for your solution. As you walk through it, with the help of a visual, you can check in on comprehension and agreement, and confirm that the prospect is actually, indeed, following along and building consensus.

For instance, the TalentBin deck looks at how the process of finding talent online has changed, plotted on a timeline. This allows a quick (not deep! This isn't a history lesson!) review of resume search and job postings, followed by profile search databases masquerading as professional social networks, and then talent search on the larger web. As you go through your version of this catch-up slide, you can make sure that the client is following you and is familiar with the market and the technology changes that have driven this new opportunity. If they are, fantastic! Applaud them for being students of the game, and move on. If they are not, dig in and make sure that they are on board with the required contextual information before progressing. Either way, you're guaranteed to avoid a scenario where prospects blindly nod along to your presentation while they do email on the other end, totally not buying into your argument.

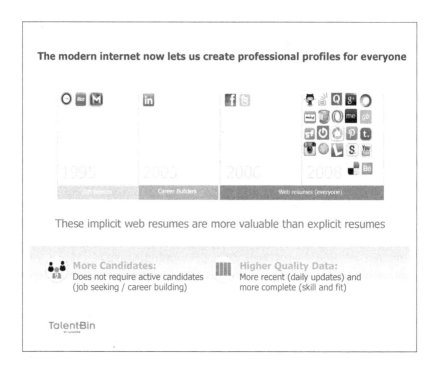

How Your Solution Works

We already looked at examples of these slides when we were discussing extensibility, so no need to do it again here. I do want to add one point though, I find it key to include a conceptual visualization of how your solution works—to clearly establish the correct understanding—even before you get into specific pain points and their associated solutions. For instance, in TalentBin's case, as so much flows from the aggregation of candidate profile data from across the web into a unified profile, it was very important to ensure that prospects comprehended how that process worked, or else they would have difficulty with the information that was built on this concept.

Another way to help structure this high-level understanding is in contrast to other solutions in the market. In TalentBin's case, as I mentioned, most recruiters are very well aware of LinkedIn's recruiting tools, especially LinkedIn Recruiter. Articulating that TalentBin is a recruiter-facing talent search engine and recruiting CRM like LinkedIn Recruiter, but where the database is the entire Internet, really hits home for clients.

And this is a "how it works" slide from the consumer finance company Affirm on how they work with e-commerce merchant partners, and how the payment flows work. Rather than hoping that the prospect understands the verbal articulation of how this payment flows this way and that, a nice diagram really nails the core concepts, so their sales staff can focus on the business value that then derives from this approach.

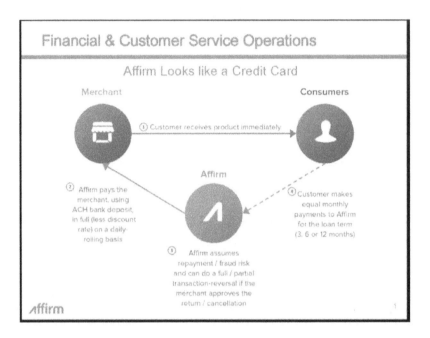

Quantitative/Qualitative Proof of a Better Solution

Once you've made the case that existing solutions have problems—and that there are real opportunity costs of not solving them—the next step is presenting proof of your superior solution. If you've done a good job, you'll make adoption of your solution look like a complete no-brainer by comparison. This should be done with both quantitative and qualitative means, but the overall goal is to answer one question, "Why you?"

When building this argument, I like to have proof of superiority bucketed by value proposition, the same way you likely bucketed pain points by value proposition. In your narrative, you keyed in on specific metrics that prospects track to gauge business success—this is where you can demonstrate how your solution impacts those relevant metrics.

This is also where you build your case for "why now?" The biggest challenge founders selling young products have is motivating any change at all. This is why you have to demonstrate a large cost or opportunity cost that the prospect is encountering every day that he doesn't adopt your solution. These slides are the ones that really bring this point home. You'll see below the crystallization of different types of opportunity cost related to TalentBin's features, but you can also imagine a rollup of these that succinctly states, "This is why this solution is so much better than what you're doing. It's a no-brainer to act on this now."

Quantitative Proof

Again, extensibility is key here. You can share the most basic proof of superiority for a set of key metrics in a single slide, or you can go deeper on each section. The goal is for customers to look at this information and agree that your solution, as measured along a particular value vector, is far superior to their status quo. You can achieve this with both granular and higher-level information. With TalentBin, for example, granular proof might be search-results superiority, contact-information density, and candidate responsiveness. Higher-level proof would be "rolled-up," bottom-line, return-on-investment data, like reduced time to hire, reduced cost per hire, and so on.

It's important that this information is presented clearly, as prospects are faced with a variety of potential solutions they could be implementing to various different problems in their business. One means by which prospects choose where to spend their time is by comparing potential return on investment—both money and time—between solutions. That is to say, you're not only competing against other solutions to the problem you solve, but also solutions to different problems your prospect faces. Quantitative proof demonstrating the large magnitude of benefits—whether increased revenue, more hires, better quality of hires, reduced costs—flowing from your solution ensures your solution goes to the front of the line of things to spend time on.

Here are some examples from the TalentBin deck.

Superior search results compared to industry standards:

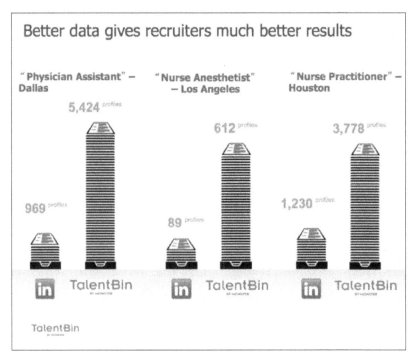

Profile availability compared to industry standards:

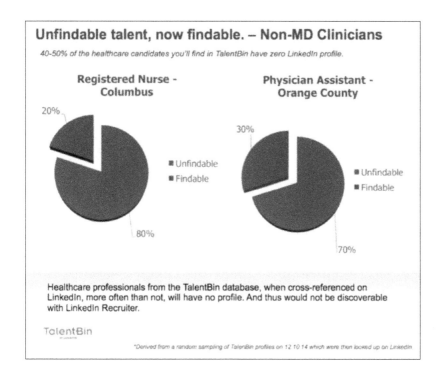

Enhanced candidate responsiveness via drip-marketing functionality (contrasted to opportunity cost of "one-and-done" candidate outreach):

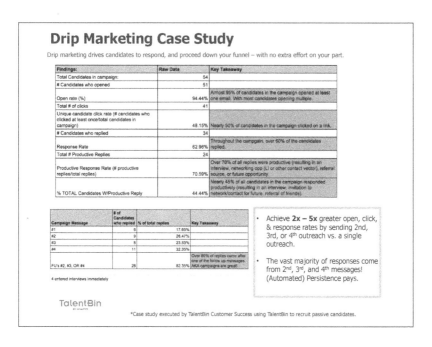

Enhanced candidate responsiveness via superior targeting and email content (contrasted to InMailing, generic messaging):

Targeted Outreach Case Study

Personal email addresses, professional activity, and personal interests make a profitable combination.

Initial Outreach

	Emails sent	Emails Opened	Open Rate %	Replies	Phone screens (replies w/interest)	Phone screens/total replies	Phone screen/total emails sent
Day 1	6	5	83.33%	4	2	50.00%	33.33%
Day 2	7	5	71.43%	1	1	100.00%	14.29%
Totals	13	10	76.92%	5	3	60.00%	23.08%

*note: 1 of the replies "not interested" was willing to refer friends. Not a total loss, the personalized message made him engage despite being happy with his recent job change

Follow Ups

	Emails Sent	Emails Opened	Open Rate %	Replies	Phone screens (replies w/interest)	Phone screens/total replies	Phone screen/total emails sent
FU#1 (9/9)	8	5	62.50%	0			

Results of phone screens:	Outcome	Notes
1 Evan	Received offer elsewhere, took it	If John had been more proactive, a month ago, would have gotten this candidate.
2 Dane	Submitted to client for interview (taking place 9/16)	Fee to be.
3 Larry	Was open to chat, but happy with current situation (awaiting further details from John)	Future fee.

60 minutes of work drove one in-process candidate, one future fee, a referral partner, and one missed fee because of slow adoption.

TalentBin

Recruiter time savings via automation (contrasted to time cost of "proper" recruiting follow-up behavior without automation):

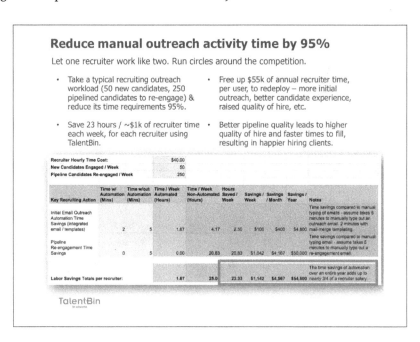

74 FOUNDING SALES

Recruiter Hourly Time Cost:		$40.00				
New Candidates Engaged / Week		50				
Pipeline Candidates Re-engaged / Week		250				

Key Recruiting Action	Time Savings Per Action (min)	Hours Saved / Week Week	Week	Month	Year	Notes
Candidate Discovery Time Savings	10	8.33	$333.33	$1,333.33	$16,000.00	Time savings compared to manual discovery via Google - assume takes 10 minutes per valid candidate discovered via Google.
Email Address Discovery Time Savings	5	4.17	$166.67	$666.67	$8,000.00	Time savings compared to manual discovery via Google - assume takes 5 minutes per email addresses search via Google.
Profile Data Aggregation - Qualification	5	4.17	$166.67	$666.67	$8,000.00	Time savings compared to manual discovery and review via Google - assume takes 5 minutes to do a semi-comprehensive review of a candidate's social footprint to qualify fit.
Profile Data Aggregation - Email Quality	5	4.17	$166.67	$666.67	$8,000.00	Time savings compared to manual discovery and review via Google - assume takes 5 minutes to do a semi-comprehensive review of a candidate's social footprint to elicit details for compelling outreach.
Initial Email Outreach Automation Time Savings (templates, mass mails)	5	4.17	$166.67	$666.67	$8,000.00	Time savings compared to manual typing of emails - assume takes 5 minutes to manually type out an outreach email.
Pipeline Re-engagement Time Savings	5	20.83	$833.33	$3,333.33	$40,000.00	Time savings compared to manual typing email - assume takes 5 minutes to manually type out a re-engagement email.
Labor Savings Totals per recruiter:		45.83	$1,833.33	$7,333.33	$88,000.00	

TalentBin

Prototypical customer hiring funnel driven by TalentBin best practices (contrasted to a LinkedIn InMail–driven funnel):

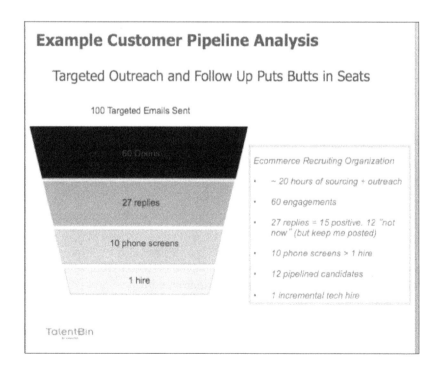

TalentBin

Qualitative Proof

While quantitative proof is usually the most impactful for B2B sales cycles, qualitative proof points can be helpful as well—and together, they make for an excellent one-two punch that hits both the left and right brain of your prospect. Traditionally these qualitative points come in the form of "customer success" materials. Like with quantitative proof points, they should correlate to your value proposition buckets, but can do so at a level of granularity that is up to you. The best way to do this is to have good relationships with some early customers and offer to write the testimonials for them; then all they have to do is approve them. The argument is that being made famous as a "thought leader" is the quid pro quo for them, in addition to helping out a nice early-stage founder. Also, it helps to have good schwag like hoodies or T-shirts to send them. Or, shoot, a $100 dinner gift certificate for them and their significant others.

Here is a Customer Success example of a "one-woman show," focused on time-savings benefits:

Here is a Customer Success example focused on the staffing vertical, specifically candidate discovery and contact-information density:

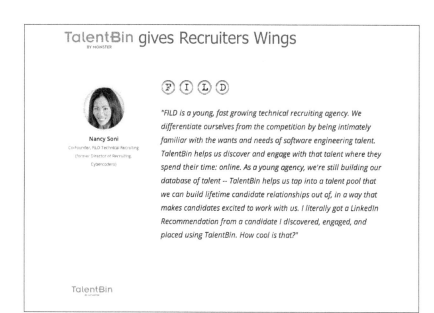

Company-centric Proof Points

You can also throw in company-centric signifiers of why your solution is superior—perhaps because it has been covered by third-party reputation providers, like press or analysts.

This example of a "why we are legit" slide is less about "aren't we hot" and instead says, "See, you will be in good company when you partner with us, and we will be around for the long term."

Many companies use a "logos" slide for this purpose. If you go that route, make sure to include examples of all the segments that you care about. In TalentBin's case that was small to large business, and both commercial enterprises and staffing agencies. The goal is for the prospect to look at that list and say, "Ah, I see others like me. And I see others whom I aspire to be." While you might be worried about getting permission to share this information with prospects, when you're very early, and trying to go from 5 to 50 to 100 customers, you have bigger issues. Just make the slide, share it in live presentations, but don't send it via email. Additionally, just bake publicity rights into your Master Service Agreement that customers agree to when they sign a contract. Most customers won't review your MSA in detail, and poof, you have publicity rights. If they end up unhappy after the fact when their PR organization realizes, you can always remove the logos. In the meantime, though, use the social proof as wind at your back, and ask forgiveness instead of permission.

Why This Will Be So Easy

While the monetary cost of your solution will of course be a topic of great interest to your prospect, so too will be the potential time cost required to implement it. Most of your prospects, especially the more sophisticated ones, will have experience being promised the moon, stars, and the sky by sales reps. But then when reality ensued, they were eventually faced with all kinds of delays and implementation headaches and so on, all of which blocked their ability to capture the promised return on investment. So they're going to want to know how do you make this easy? How do you make it such that they say "yes" and then magically everything proceeds from there?

These are some examples of slides that speak to this, giving comfort to the prospect that not only will this be easy at the start, but that there will be lots of support and engagement all throughout their relationship with you.

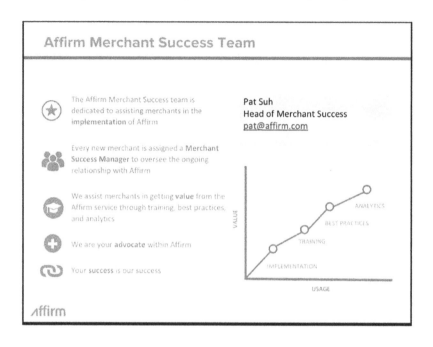

It can even be as simple as something like this:

Pricing

As you go through your presentation, if you have qualified well and are drawing customers along, gaining their agreement throughout, they're eventually going to want to talk financials. Having a slide that presents your solution's pricing, and any potential variations, helps here, and also helps for when you send your slides along later for reference by the client.

If you have a variety of permutations, but there is one that you want to push clients to, just present that one. You can always bring up the other ones at another juncture.

TalentBin Licensing Pricing:

Seat License	$6,000 / seat annual contract
Job Req Folders	Unlimited
Searches	Unlimited
Email Outreach	Unlimited
Customer Success Manager	Included
Team Training	Included
Saved Searches	Unlimited
Candidate Alerts	Unlimited
Support	5 x 8 email and phone

TalentBin

Appendices

One of the things you want to be mindful of when presenting is to not cover things that are unnecessary. For instance, if your solution integrates with a particular piece of software that only 10 percent of your customers use and you've decided to have a slide on it, don't include it in the main deck. Put it in the appendix. Have a specific slide comparing your solution and a competing one that doesn't need to be addressed with everyone? Don't bring up the competition unless asked. Put it in the appendix. When the customer says, "So, how do you compare to XYZ?"—boom, you can flip right to it. But it won't be in the main presentation to cruft things up and drain attention from your essential points.

As you execute more presentations, you will invariably find new cases that need their own appendix slides. I generally try to add an appendix slide anytime I have a question asked for a second time. It's a thirty-minute investment, and you know that at scale (doing dozens of these demos) you're going to hear that question a lot. Having a slide with the relevant messaging at the ready ensures that you nail that response, and impress the heck out of the prospect.

Deck for Presenting, Deck for Sending

When you're putting your deck together, remember that there's the one you present (along with an appendix that you pop into as necessary) and then there's the one that you'll send later. This is where content management and presentation solutions like ClearSlide can be helpful. You can have your "full-on" deck that you use for your live presentation, and an abridged version to send along after the fact.

When you're thinking about the one that you send, it can, and usually should, be a pretty heavily abridged version of your main presentation deck. A deck sent after the fact is not a substitute for incremental presentations to other stakeholders (more on this later in the chapter on pitching), but rather a reminder of the key topics that were covered. It can also be a teaser for other potential stakeholders with whom it gets shared, in the interest of driving further presentations. Moreover, sending your materials using something like DocSend or ClearSlide will allow you to see prospects' interaction with your materials, something that is helpful in distinguishing between those who have more commercial interest and intent than others. For instance, did they spend time on the pricing slide? Did they send it to a bunch of other people who reviewed it?

OUTREACH MATERIALS

Once you've got your deck nailed, the next step is going to be driving opportunities to present it to potential clients. And the precursor to that will be emails and phone calls. So having some basic templates there will be helpful.

Email Templates

A set of basic emails that handles inbound inquiries, and can be used for targeted outreach, is a key piece of your sales materials.

As with your deck, these emails will be medium-specific encapsulations of your narrative, whose end goal is to drive recipients to an online or offline presentation and demo. And as with your deck, these can start at the most basic and extend from there as your messaging gets more specific.

We'll start with the idea of outbound outreach. While inbound leads (that you heavily qualify) are the highest-quality source of potential deals, it's unlikely when you're first starting out that you'll have inbound demand of any merit before you start doing outbound.

Cold Outreach Emails

To start, you simply need a couple of outreach templates that you'll use to contact decision-makers to whom you want to present your solution. The benefit of prospecting (again, we'll get into this more in another chapter) is that you are able to select prospects that have the business pain characteristics that your solution addresses. (Remember the people and businesses we talked about when building your narrative? These are those folks.) So conveniently, when you're writing these templates, you can be very specific in assuming that readers have the pain points that you're solving and, moreover, talk to them plainly about their business pains and your solution.

As you read the following email templates, you should recognize parts of the master narrative—the problem and who has it (the recipient!), the differences between yours and existing solutions, and proof points of superiority. You'll note the subject lines are often customized. There's information in there to show the prospect that this message was specifically made for him or her—and include qualification information (e.g., "Hiring Ruby devs? That is NOT easy."). You'll also see that the templates include "click targets," hyperlinks pointing to pieces of collateral (I like YouTube demo videos in particular) that draw clicks from the prospect. These are important not just because they can provide more context and persuasion, but because, with the sort of email instrumentation you'll have implemented, they will allow you to see which prospects are clicking and thus demonstrating interest in what you have to say. And they don't have to be just text links. You can embed a screenshot of a slide or—one of my favorites—a thumbnail of a demo video that's hyperlinked to the source to drive click-through for more compelling information. Email templates should also include links to your website. This helps with the click-target question, but also allows the prospect to "see more" and potentially come inbound as a demo request through your inbound lead capture.

You'll also note that these sample templates are very specific about what the solution addresses, and take pains to demonstrate to the prospect that research was done to confirm that he or she has those business pains. In TalentBin's case, that's hiring technical talent. These emails don't talk about "social recruiting." They don't talk about "recruiting" in general. They don't talk about interviewing. They talk about the pain points of finding and recruiting technical talent, and potential solutions to those problems. And the messaging continually comes back to the prospect's point of view. Prospects don't care about you. They care about them. So as with your narrative and slides, prioritize the prospects' point of view; even as you present information about your solution, ground it in how it helps them.

The best templates do all of this in a plainspoken, dare I say fun, way that speaks to the prospect candidly, authoritatively, and as a peer. They avoid bullshit jargon-speak and unnecessarily "businessy" communication patterns. Same with over-involved designs; the templates should be 100 percent text, avoiding marketing images—with the exception of screenshots and slides, if you like. But avoid high-sheen logos and such. It makes your outreach look like a robot sent it, like there's no qualification behind it and it's therefore inapplicable spam rather than highly targeted consultative outreach. Don't let your emails get mistaken for that other crap.

Lastly, you'll notice that there are strong calls to action at the conclusion of each email, asking to set up a one-on-one interaction (whether via telepresence à la Join.me, ClearSlide, etc. or face-to-face). That is the ultimate goal of this outreach—to drive to a synchronous presentation and discussion of the prospect's business pains and your solution. A "demo," in the vernacular.

These are a couple examples of cold-outreach emails:

TEMPLATE: Short and sweet - quick pain documentation & ask

SUBJECT LINE: Hey {*First_Name*}! A magical solution to help with the pain of engineering hiring.

Hey {*First_Name*},

I hope you're having a great day! It's {*Sales Rep First Name*} at TalentBin, and I'm reaching out because I have something that can help make hiring all those Ruby, iOS, and Java roles I see on your career page waaaaay easier.

In short, we make really nifty technical recruiting software that:

1. Surfaces 3x as many technical candidates (e.g., "Ruby" or "iOS") as a LinkedIn recruiter search.

2. Gives you access to personal email addresses so candidates actually read your outreach.

3. And has all kinds of cool automation baked in to automate the annoying, repetitive parts of passive candidate technical recruiting (for example, our software can send dozens of outbound emails to dozens of candidates in the time it takes to send a single LinkedIn InMail!).

I would love to show you how we can help make you a technical recruiting superhero, the envy of all your coworkers, and your boss' personal favorite!

Do you have 20 minutes next week? What times work for you?

Feel free to reply to this email, or you can ring me directly at {*Sales_ Rep Biz_Phone*}.

Thanks,

{*Sales_Rep First_Name*}

TEMPLATE: A bit longer—quick pain documentation and ask

SUBJECT LINE: Hey {*First Name*}! The magical solution to your technical recruiting headaches.

Hey {*First_Name*},

I hope you're having a great day!

It's {*Sales Rep First Name*} at TalentBin, and I'm reaching out because I have something that can help make hiring all those Ruby, iOS, and Java roles I see on your career page way easier.

If you're like most technical recruiters we work with (we have thousands of customers), you're probably frustrated by the poor LinkedIn profiles of most developers, the fact that they don't respond to InMails, and that it all just takes way too much time. Super frustrating.

The good news is, TalentBin is designed specifically to reduce that time and drudgery via automation, so you can spend more of your time having great candidate conversations and selling them on working at {*Company Name*}. Which is what recruiting is all about, right?

You see, TalentBin is a talent search engine that helps recruiter find and reach out to fantastic technical talent based on the activity they demonstrate on places like Github, Stack Overflow, Twitter, Meetup, the

US Patent Database, and more. More here: https://www.youtube.com/watch?v=fClV97ONRyI

I would love to show you how we might be able to help you find qualified technical candidates for your open positions and hire more and better technical staff, faster, with less work on your part.

Do you have 20 minutes next week? What times work for you? Feel free to reply to this email, or you can ring me directly at {*Sales Rep Biz Phone*}.

Thanks,

{*Sales_Rep First_Name*}

TEMPLATE: A little Longer and sweeter—the basics of TalentBin.

SUBJECT LINE: Hey {*First Name*}! Meet TalentBin: the Talent Search Engine

Hey {*First_Name*},

I hope you're having a great day!

It's {*Sales_Rep First_Name*} at Monster, and I am looking to introduce you to our newest acquisition, a technical recruiting tool called TalentBin (http://www.talentbin.com). It's clear that {*Company_Name*} is hiring technical talent, and I'd love the opportunity to show you how TalentBin can make your life easier in that regard.

TalentBin has developed an amazing talent search engine used by recruiters to find software developers and other technical talent. See more in this helpful video here: https://www.youtube.com/watch?v=fClV97ONRyI

Facebook, Amazon, Microsoft, Salesforce, and hundreds of other companies have recruiters using TalentBin daily to search for and recruit these hard-to-find candidates.

We derive our candidate data by crawling the *entire Internet* and making it your technical-recruiting playground. That means we are capitalizing on the grand potential of the Internet by recording information from disparate web locations and constructing rich composite profiles. So all those software engineers with terrible or nonexistent LinkedIn profiles who don't respond to InMails? We have profiles for them based on what they do on GitHub, Stack Overflow, Twitter, Meetup, and more. And we have their personal email addresses.

These profiles span professional and personal interests, and they include personal email addresses!

Based on the open technical positions I see listed on your career site ({*CareerSiteLink*}), TalentBin should serve you well.

I'd love to show you how TalentBin can help you find qualified technical candidates for your open positions and hire more and better technical staff, faster, with less work on your part.

Do you have 20 minutes next week? What times work for you? Feel free to reply to this email, or you can ring me directly at {*Sales_ Rep Biz_Phone*}.

Thanks,

{*Sales Rep First Name*}

TEMPLATE: Quick Summary of TalentBin—focused on how it will save time.

SUBJECT LINE: Want to reach twice the technical candidates in half the time? TalentBin can help.

Hi there {*First Name*},

It's {*Sales Rep First Name*} here with Monster. I wanted to take a minute to introduce you to the newest addition to our ever-growing bag of recruiting tricks—TalentBin. If the information below is relevant to you, I would love to connect one-to-one to discuss further. I believe it will be a very helpful tool for you.

TalentBin has developed a search engine used by recruiters to find software developers and other technical talent.

Facebook, Amazon, Kelly IT, Robert Half, and hundreds of other companies and agencies have recruiters using TalentBin daily to search for these hard-to-find candidates.

Based on the open positions I see listed on your website, TalentBin should serve you well in your search!

Snapshot of some sweet features:

4–5x more technical candidates than LinkedIn Recruiter can identify

Millions of personal email addresses

Messaging templates and mass emailing capability (Send an email blast to up to 30 candidates at once in a single click.)

Email-open/link-click tracking (See when a candidate opens your emails.)

Gmail and Outlook integration (Send candidates emails from within TalentBin without having to bounce out to another window.)

CRM functionality (pipeline management & automation—no dropped balls)

...and some more cool/nerdy data stuff. :)

Quick explainer video (It's pretty funny. You *will* laugh.): https://www.youtube.com/watch?v=fClV97ONRyI

We'd love to show you how TalentBin can help you find and recruit qualified technical candidates for your open positions. Do you have 30 minutes next week? What times work for you?

Don't believe the subject line? Email me! I'd be happy to explain. Or you can ring me directly at {*Sales_Rep Biz_Phone*}.

Thanks,

{*Sales_Rep First_Name*}

Lastly, when you build these templates, you want to build them with a concept that they'll eventually be dripped out over time in a multi-week cadence. So think about how you can split your message into more than one email, as this has a number of benefits. For instance, your first email could be short and sweet to get attention with a big ROI metric callout, your next email could have fuller detail about major messaging buckets of your solution, and then incremental emails could "zoom in" on each of those messaging buckets. In TalentBin's case, that could have been a first general email, a follow up email that's focused on "superior candidate search results", a follow up email that's focused on "better qualification information through social activity", another on "better response rates through better contact information like personal emails", another on "automation and time savings with drip marketing", and then one on customer success stories. This is an example drip email series I wrote for a Sales Operations salon that I run, which all has the same call to action— "join this group"—but approaches it with different value propositions along the way.

Warm Outreach Emails

In Chapter 4 Early Prospecting, we discuss prospecting and we talk about how in your prospecting efforts when you identify an Account and the relevant decision-making contacts internally, you may be able to identify a professional contact of yours that is a LinkedIn connection of the target contact. Or at very least, works in the same organization as them. This can be a very effective means of engagement, but it takes a little bit of extra footwork than pure compelling argumentation, as there is a social component, and social graces, involved.

In this case, your initial outreach will be to the intermediary, asking them if they'd be willing to forward something along to the target. An email template detailing to them who you're trying to engage, why you think that they might know them (always authenticate this, because sometimes LinkedIn connections can mean not a lot!), why you want to engage the target in question, and why you think it would be valuable to the target. This is the part that tells the potential introducer whether it will be worth their time to assist you—as in, will they be a bringer of compelling information, or just helping an annoying gadfly? They are a lightweight gatekeeper who has split allegiances—some to you, and some to the other contact. So you want to show them how there is social benefit to them as an introducer—a great way here is to include some sort of specialness, like maybe it's a closed beta and no one else knows about it, and you prospected the target especially.

If they're willing to help you, send them an easy-to-forward email template with all the relevant information detailed in, customized to the target contact, along with the rationale as to why you thought they'd be really excited to hear more. Don't ask the introducer to email introduce you directly, as you want to other side to opt in to engaging rather than being dropped blindly into their lap.

And don't rely on the introducer to execute the outreach on their own, since she doesn't know much about your pitch and argument. You simply want her to be in charge of passing your message along, with commentary about why you're a great guy. This should have parts of your pitch in it, like the templates above, because it's going to be making your argument for you when your introducer forwards it along, and a call to action for the target to respond back to you directly if they're interested in hearing more. Send that to your introducer, making sure to instrument it with a email-tracking pixel (e.g., Yesware, Tout, HubSpot Sidekick, etc.), so you can see when your introducer forwards it, and it gets opened (or not). Set a reminder to yourself to follow up directly with the target if you don't hear back (once your introducer has sent this first thing along, they're out of the loop.) At this point, you can just treat the target like a standard cold outreach target, but with the added social context benefit of that initial warm introduction.

As with your slides, you should approach these email templates with an iterative mindset. As your solution extends, you'll extend them. In fact, as you add slides, you can often add a correlating outreach email, maybe even with a screenshot of the slide embedded! As you find permutations in your customer base, you can fork off templates that are specific to sub-genres of your customers. As with your slides, you should keep email templates in some sort of "source repository"—which can be as simple as a Google Document or, eventually, a more complicated content management system, like Yesware, SalesLoft, or some other email-prospecting tool.

Phone and Voice Mail Scripts

While targeted email outreach for appointment setting is one of the most scalable means by which to put your message in front of qualified prospects, you'll likely be getting on the phone—either dealing with inbound calls (perhaps engendered by your outbound emailing!) or doing out-and-out cold-calling.

While there's little chance that a phone call will directly follow a script, having at least some bulleting in place can be helpful to ensure that you're nailing your messaging points. Again, these should be a reformatting of your core narrative, designed to be delivered in thirty to ninety seconds. This is not the kind of phone script that you'll have when you get to 10+ sales reps; instead, it's some guideposts to help you when you get on the phone and are trying to drive to a demo.

Below are some appointment-setting phone scripts from a company named HIRABL, which makes revenue-acceleration products for recruiting agencies. These are for a product that helps agencies know when candidates that they have submitted to clients may have been hired, even though the client has not reported it.

TEMPLATE: Cold-Calling Scripts—HIRABL

Hi there!

This is {Name} at HIRABL. I wanted to reach out, because we've been helping staffing agencies like yours identify backdoor hires.

Are you familiar with backdoor hires, or have you had many at your agency?

<Yes, we are familiar with them, but we don't do much about it because we don't know how we'd go about it.>

Yeah, we hear that quite a bit. It sounds like a demo with our Account Director {Name} might make sense—do you have twenty minutes on {Day} or {Day}?

Hi there!

This is {Name} at HIRABL. How's your day going?

The reason I'm calling is that we develop software that notifies recruiters when clients hire their candidates and forget to tell them. Last year, we found over 4,200 missed fees across just 120 customers.

I'd love to set up a time for you to speak with our Account Director {Name}, because I think we can identify fees you have already earned.

Do you have twenty minutes on {Day} or {Day}?

And this is a more involved call script for TalentBin, which encapsulates more of the sales narrative than the succinct ones above. It is unlikely that all of the information in this script would be utilized in a given call, but having the information available to the caller can be helpful.

Hey there! It's {*Name*} from Monster.

<*Pleasantries. Weather. Sports team. Personal tidbit.*>

So, I'm calling because I know that {*Account_Name*} hires quite a few {*software engineering/design/healthcare*} professionals.

Monster recently acquired a company called TalentBin. Did you see that news?

<*Answer*>

Got it! So TalentBin develops tools used by recruiters to find {*software engineering/design/healthcare*} talent. And it does this by crawling the entire Internet for activity that those folks engage in.

Because these sorts of candidates are highly employed, recruiting them often requires a passive-candidate outreach approach.

But at the same time, because these folks tend to not spend time on professional social networks like LinkedIn, finding them there can be really problematic. Unlike recruiters and sales people, they just don't spend time there.

However, these sorts of professionals do spend time other places online, leaving trails of information about what they do professionally. TalentBin scoops up all of that information and makes it recruiter-ready.

As a result, TalentBin identifies more of these professionals than any other sourcing tool on the market. It makes it easy for you to reach them directly, by providing personal contact information, like personal email addresses, and social communication vectors like Twitter, Meetup, Facebook, and so on.

Pretty nifty, eh?

<*Answer*>

Yeah, what's more:

Technical example: For instance, in a given geography, say {*their geography—Dallas, New York, Paris, etc.*}, TalentBin will have five to ten times the number of Ruby, Java, .NET, iOS, and Android developers compared to LinkedIn, and will have oodles of personal email addresses for those candidates. This is because TalentBin has crawled GitHub, Stack Overflow, Meetup, Twitter, and many other sites where those engineers hang out.

Healthcare example: For instance, in a given geography, say {*their geography—Dallas, New York, Paris, etc.*}, TalentBin will have five to ten times the number of registered nurses, physician assistants, nurse practitioners, physicians (oncologists, orthopedists, etc.), and so on, thank LinkedIn. And it includes lots of direct phone numbers and other contact information for these candidates! This is because TalentBin has crawled every single healthcare license database where those professionals have to show up. So we literally have every healthcare professional in the United States in our database! How cool is that?

Lastly, TalentBin saves recruiters tons of time by automating a lot of the drudgery work involved in candidate sourcing and outreach. Features like integrated email, templating and mail merging, mass messaging, drip-marketing campaigns, and email-open and click tracking make our clients super efficient jet fighters! It's like a robot recruiter helper, freeing recruiters up to spend more time on higher-value activities, like closing candidates.

Which is why Monster bought the company! Because it is really impactful for our clients who hire these sorts of staff. Thousands of clients have signed up for TalentBin, including big names such as Amazon, IBM, Kelly Services, Manpower, and more.

Because of {*Account_Name's*} current hiring characteristics, I feel that this is something that would be very impactful to your business. I would love to set up a walk-through demo for your team with myself and my TalentBin product specialist colleague to dig in more.

Are you available {*Day*} or {*Day*} next week for a thirty-minute demo? I promise it will be worth your time.

When we built this script, we also included some reaction permutations to help guide the next steps of the call:

Client is interested—Book demo.

Great! What are some times that work for you next week? I have avail-ability at {*Time Block*} on {*Day*}, {*Time Block*} on {*Day*}, and {*Time Block*} on {*Day*}.

Great. I'll send a meeting invite to block your calendar with the online meeting room information. We'll do a screen share and walk through some slides and the product. Looking forward to it!

Client asks follow-up question—Defer and drive to demo.

That's a great question! Usually that's the sort of thing we like to get into in a brief presentation and demo with one of the TalentBin product specialists, who are the pros when it comes to explaining every feature. It's usually thirty minutes and focuses specifically on your business pains and where TalentBin can help.

It's very educational, and well worth the time.

Are you available {*Day*} or {*Day*} next week for a thirty-minute demo? I promise it will be worth it.

Client says, "I'm not interested."—Deflect and articulate value. Drive to demo.

{*Name*}, I wouldn't be on the phone with you right now if I didn't strongly think that this could help {*Account_Name*} hire more people, faster, with less cost and less work on the part of your recruiters. [In the case of an agency, "And ultimately make {*Account_Name*} more money."]

I promise you that this sort of technology is going to be industry stan-dard. By deferring consideration of it, you're putting your business and your ability as a recruiter at a disadvantage.

Client asks, "Is it free/does it cost money?"—Defer and drive to demo.

It is not free, but it's extremely powerful and provides a strong return on investment. It's not uncommon for TalentBin to drive an additional engineering hire per month.

But usually that's the sort of thing we like to get into in a brief presentation and demo with one of the TalentBin product specialists. It's usually thirty minutes and focuses specifically on your business pains and where TalentBin can help solve them.

It's very educational, and well worth the time.

Are you available {*Day*} or {*Day*} next week for a thirty-minute demo? I promise it will be worth it.

Client says, "No, I'm really not interested."—Articulate that you're going to follow up, and aren't going away. (More here: http://kazanjy. svbtle.com/pitching-the-inevitable**)**

Okay, I understand that while this is relevant to your business, it sounds like the timing is not right just this instant.

However, I am convinced that TalentBin is something that will help your business be more successful. So I'm going to send some video examples of the massive time savings and ROI that TalentBin can provide for {*Account_Name*}, and I'll make sure to touch base in a month or so to update you on what's new. [From there, follow up by email with materials as defined in Email Templates.]

Client asks, "Is this like {*Competitor*}?"—Deflect and drive to demo.

Oh! You're familiar with {*Competitor_Name*}. TalentBin is similar, but is actually the original pioneer in the industry, with the richest functionality, the best data sources, and the most automation. Which is why TalentBin has won the most industry acclaim and awards! Given your familiarity with the space, it seems like a demo would be very helpful for you to further complete your knowledge.

Are you available {*Day*} or {*Day*} next week for a thirty-minute demo? I promise it will be worth it.

Next, we have some example voice mail scripts to elicit callbacks. As covered in the appointment-setting chapter, voice mails should generally be paired with emails; while listening to a voice mail can be easy (especially in the age of transcription to email), prospects will rarely return messages. Better to think of them as audio emails. However, an email that is paired with a voice mail that has piqued a prospect's interest is ripe for a reply.

Follow-Up Voice Mail

Hey there! It's {*Name*} from Monster again.

I wanted to follow up on my previous message regarding TalentBin by Monster, the talent search engine.

On paper, it seems like your company would be a great fit for our tool, given your {*technical/healthcare/design/finance*} hiring needs, and I just want to chat for a quick minute to see if scheduling you for a live web demo would make sense.

Once again, it's {*Name*} calling from TalentBin, {*Phone Number*}, that's {*Phone Number*}. I look forward to speaking with you soon.

Customer Proof Voice Mail

Hey there! This is {*Name*} from TalentBin.

I'm reaching out because our company makes amazing technical talent search software, and it looks like your organization loves to hire amazing software engineers.

We're super popular with awesome technical recruiting organizations like Facebook, Amazon, Groupon, Microsoft, and hundreds of others. So we're legit.

I'd love to connect with you on what we're up to and how it can help you guys with your engineering hiring needs.

Hit me back at {*Phone_Number*}, that's {*Phone_Number*} . I look forward to chatting with you soon! Thanks!

DEMO SCRIPTS

We'll talk more about the actual process of giving a combined sales presentation and demo in Chapter 7: Pitching, but before we get into the blocking and tackling of presentation and demo, it's good to have a concept of the content you'll want to demonstrate when your prospects agree to a formal sales presentation. As with the other materials discussed, this should be done with a mind toward your narrative. And because a live demo will typically come after you've shared some initial slides from your sales deck, follow the framing you presented in your deck. Your demo will reiterate much of it, but with much better context, customization, and visuality.

What is that framing? Well, as with your sales deck, it's the bucketing of key use cases and the features that enable them. Ideally, you should already have those use cases identified, as they are likely referred to in your sales deck. But think about the combination of most common, most important, and most impressive use cases your solution enables. Then rank them, such that you start with the most important and most compelling ones—because you never know when a demo will have to end early! Beyond that, I like to think of a demo as telling the story of how your solution is used, again starting with major pain points.

Customization

We've already looked at customizing sales presentation content for a given prospect, but your demo is where this sort of thing can really be done in earnest. In fact, as you're developing your product, think of ways you can make it easier to demonstrate using prospect content—it could be something as simple as ensuring that a prospect name and logo can be quickly embedded, or as complicated as making it easy to import customer data to use in a live demo. But the purpose of the demo is not to be a cold rehash of the features that you may have just touched on in your sales presentation. Rather, it's an opportunity to demonstrate the potential value the product could provide to the prospect, richly, before their eyes. More customization will raise close rates and shorten deal cycles. Both things you want!

The simplest version of this customization is knowing the prospect's business context—either from prior research or from discovery questions at the beginning of your call—and using that to guide the demo. At TalentBin, that meant making sure that our sales reps knew the technical- and design-hiring requirements for prospects they were talking to, which was easily divined by looking at those prospects' career web pages ahead of time. That way, the TalentBin rep could easily say, "I know by looking at your careers page that you're hiring some iOS developers in Philadelphia. I would love to show you how TalentBin could help with that." Consider this in contrast to something that is non-contextual, like "How about we show you what this looks like for recruiting for Java developers in San Francisco?"— when the prospect doesn't recruit for Java, and definitely isn't based in San Francisco. What are the key pieces of information you could use to modify your demo and make it more impactful to the prospect? Which can be sniffed out ahead of time, and which need to be elicited from the prospect?

If your demo is non-contextual and not tied directly to the business realities of the prospect, it will always smell like you're running the demo to make the product perform at its peak attractiveness, rather than showing how it will work when used by the client. You can avoid that by focusing on the prospect's business context first and foremost. It will make your materials more believable than other vendor demos they see and raise the trust factor. It also helps to do this research yourself. Because if you simply ask clients what they want to do, they may not know, or may ask to go in the wrong direction. Again, with TalentBin, the worst approach would have been to ask, "What's a role you're having a hard time filling?" Because the client would likely simply bring up their current most difficult role.

Better instead to focus on the roles that the client has the most hires for, for instance, because that's the larger pain point.

A more evolved version of demo customization is a demo that actually includes user data. A great example of that is how HIRABL (the company that makes revenue-acceleration products for recruiting agencies) runs their demos. A week ahead of the demo call, the prospect sends HIRABL candidate submission data from the CRM system they use to track hires. HIRABL then runs their "missed hire" analysis in a new instance of their SaaS software spun up for the prospect. When it comes time for the demo, they execute a lightweight presentation so the prospect understands the general mental model of the problem, solution, value, and such, and then they turn to all the missed fees that HIRABL has identified for that prospect. That's a pretty killer demo! "So, we found what looks like around twenty-five missed fees from your last two years of submission data. You make about twenty thousand per placement. Would you like to purchase the product so you can get cracking on collecting that four hundred thousand dollars of missed fees? We would just give you access to this instance right here. It's ready to go." The answer is usually "Yes!"

Candidate submission records imported
6,340 candidates
608 companies
Submissions analyzed from till Apr 2015

14,913

Submissions worth monitoring
1,097 submissions less than 6 months old (7.36%)
2,247 submissions less than 12 months old (15.07%)
3,453 submissions less than 18 months old (23.15%)
On average 204 submission per month

3,453

Online profiles reviewed
165,834 matching profiles identified
809 max number of profiles per candidate
26 average number of profiles per candidate

161,660

Missed revenue opportunities
4 in the last 6 months (15 in total)
0 in the last 6 to 12 months (10 in total)
0 in the last 12 to 18 months (13 in total)
2 older than 18 months (65 in total)

6
(105 in total)

Estimated fee opportunity

~$90,000
(Using average fee of $15,000)

Obviously the latter case is far more advanced, and by no means should you say, "Well, we don't have the ability to hyper-customize a demo environment, so we can't start selling." Not at all. However, when you work with product management, providing feedback on features you'd want to see in the product, remember that there are features that will make selling easier via a more customized demo. And even if those features don't necessarily provide post-purchase value to customers, they can still be very valuable from a revenue-generation standpoint, in that they raise close rates and bring in more money!

Example Demo Script

What did a demo script look like at TalentBin? Well, of course, it correlated to our core sales narrative, and was built around the "Search, Qualify, Reach Out, Automate" framing we presented in our sales deck. You can check out how we handled those first two buckets below (and if you want to see the whole script, you'll find it in the Appendix.). It starts with one of the most important use cases for our audience of recruiters, and then progresses from there in the way a recruiter would move from discovery of a new candidate to qualification of that candidate to outreach—a full life cycle of what recruiters do so often in their day-to-day workflow. Also note that it's broken up to allow for pauses and discussion with the client.

As you read through it, imagine what it would look like to walk prospects through all the ways TalentBin fits into their day-to-day, and solves their pains at each step, while screen sharing the product. And think about what your demo would look like! What are the natural work flows that your prospect works through on a daily basis? How does your solution fit into them and make them better, faster, stronger?

Search

Enhanced candidate discovery was TalentBin's first value proposition, and one of the most easily comprehended by prospects. This section was where we touched on the importance of being able to discover engineering candidates who were previously undiscoverable in traditional recruiting databases, or at least super hard to find requiring far too much manual effort.

We knew nothing would capture the attention of a technical recruiter like showing them the potential candidates they could find and engage using our solution—especially as compared to standard databases—so that is where we started.

"Well I saw from your company's career site that you need to hire some Ruby engineering staff there in the Dallas area, so let's search for some.

Here's how we build a search for people who know Ruby in the Dallas area. We can do it manually, or we can use our new Job Req Translator that automatically pulls out the relevant terms in your job posting.

I actually grabbed this posting before the call, so let's paste that in there. See how easy that is?

Now, we can save that search for later use since we're going to come back to this. Also by saving that search, you'll now get recommended candidate emails from those searches every few days. But let's expand this some to see the total number of potential candidates for this role in Dallas.

Excellent! Well it looks like we have around eight thousand results there. That's promising, since LinkedIn only has around eleven hundred for that same query. Very nice! So that's like seven times the number—I'm betting there's a pretty hefty load of people in these search results who have zero LinkedIn profiles.

And of course, the way that you'd do this previously was to manually browse through GitHub, or Stack Overflow, or Twitter—it might take you five minutes per valid candidate. This way they're already ready for you to review. And tons of them aren't on LinkedIn being accosted by every other recruiter with a LinkedIn Recruiter seat!"

Showing off scaled search results for desired skills in the prospect's region:

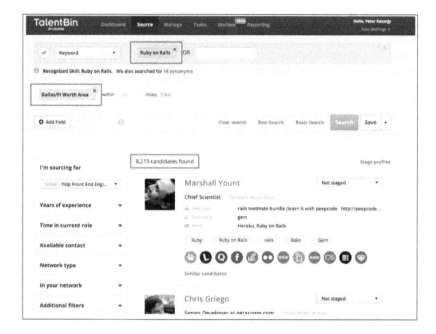

Qualify

This is where we would cover why having access to all of this aggregated professional activity was fantastic for qualifying that a candidate had the characteristics recruiters were looking for. Moreover, we looked at how using that contextual information, both professional and personal, in outreach could dramatically impact response rates and recruiter efficiency.

"Okay, let's start looking at some of these profiles. You can see that we show a preview on the search page that includes the relevant information for the skill that was searched for, along with the various social profiles that we have identified and crawled for the candidate. If you want to, you can also tag these folks as 'interesting' or 'not interesting' for later bulk processing.

But for now, let's check out an individual. Natalie looks interesting.

Showing off search results and preview information:

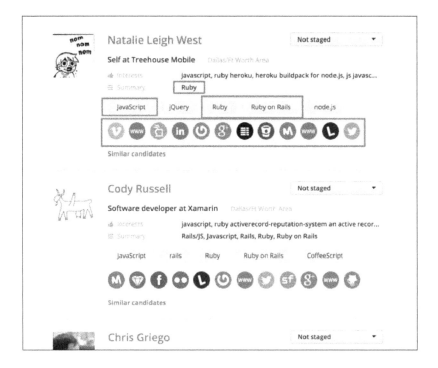

Profile View

Understanding that a candidate "fits the bill" and is at least worth reaching out to is a core recruiting workflow. Whether basing their decision on a resume or a LinkedIn profile, recruiters are used to doing that. So showing them how they could do that with a TalentBin profile, but with data aggregated from all over the web, was important.

"Let's click into her profile. Now you can see that we've aggregated all of her various web profiles. See, here's her GitHub, Stack Overflow, Meetup, Twitter, LinkedIn, and Facebook, and we even have her Lanyrd social conference profile. Nice.

If you ever wanted to go to those sites, you can just click on these like this. However, the big idea here is to aggregate that activity so you don't have to do that."

Showing off Natalie's various web profiles and how they've been aggregated:

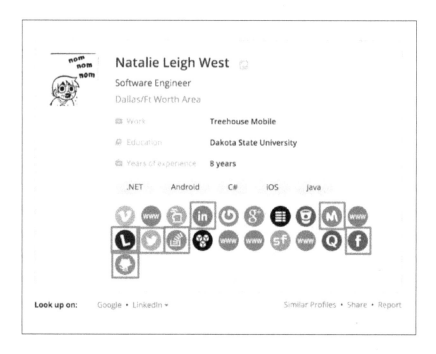

Interest Details

Understanding "why" a given candidate has the relevant professional skill is also important for recruiters. Often they spend time cross-correlating resume claims with sources of professional activity on the web. Moreover, they know that using contextual information in outreach is a valuable way to raise responsiveness, but often takes too long to do in a scalable fashion manually.

"So let's look at how we know that Natalie has 'Ruby' relevance. Okay, see down here on her profile, we've got her 'interest viewer' section, and if we click on 'Ruby' there we see that, wow, Natalie is really into Ruby! She's following a number of Ruby repositories on GitHub. She has it in her Twitter biography. She's a member of a couple Ruby Meetups, and she has answered some Ruby questions on Stack Overflow. Nice! Looks like Natalie is really into Ruby.

The problem is that historically this is the sort of thing you'd have to spend five minutes clicking all over the web to determine. Nice that these interest details are right here so you can check them out, and maybe even share them with the hiring manager.

Let's go check out Natalie LinkedIn profile. Whoops! That link is dead! Probably because she deleted her LinkedIn profile. But we've got it! We can see that she's got a bunch of other interests in technologies that are relevant to us—Ruby first and foremost—so she looks like a live one!"

Navigating around and showing off the Skills viewer:

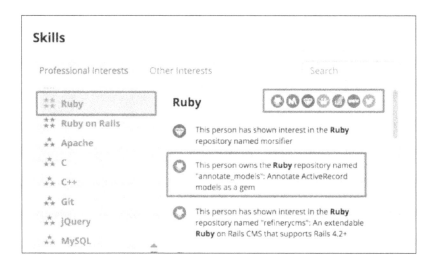

From here, we would cover the key remaining buckets, "Reach Out" and "Automate." We continued to follow the recruiter's natural workflow—using a real-world candidate that matched that prospect's hiring needs—and highlight features that would boost efficiency at every step. Importantly, we would tie parts of the demo to prior elements, making sure to create a holistic understanding of how the product would impact the entirety of the recruiter's workflow for the better.

In TalentBin's case, the product was fairly evolved, so there was quite a bit of bucketing, and a good amount of ground to cover. But that doesn't mean that this has to be the case with your demo. The goal is to connect the known pain points to the solution and its benefits, step by step, so your prospects can truly see how it fits into their workflow and makes their lives better. You know you're doing it well when prospects are saying things like "That's awesome" or "You have no idea how much this will help me with XYZ."

Think about the right way to go about demoing your offering. Is there a natural workflow to walk the user through? Is there a chronology? Are there specific key use cases that correlate to the value that you're providing that you would want to start with? Think about the "story" of your product in the hands of the person you're presenting it to, or the person that reports to her. What things will they care about, and what will make them better, faster, stronger, smarter, and more successful? Focus on those things, and you'll be in a good spot.

So that's demo basics and how you should be thinking about your demo script as you approach prospects!

VIDEO MATERIALS

I'm a big fan of video to help accelerate appointment setting in early-stage sales. Internet video is a fantastic tool; it's highly accessible and provides for a richness of communication that far outstrips email templates or even visual exhibits. And thanks to mobile phones with fast data plans, video collateral can be watched anywhere, at the moment it shows up in a prospect's email inbox or Twitter feed. As such, having a one-, two-, all the way up to five-minute overview of your offering to share with would-be prospects is extremely helpful.

MVP Overview Video

It's important to note that the goal here is not to sell the product. Rather, as with your email templates and phone scripts, the goal of these videos is to sell the prospect on the next step—getting on the phone for discovery, presentation, and a demo. And as with your slides and email templates, your video overview does not have to be perfect. It just has to exist. One of the easiest ways to create a viable overview video is to put together a highly shortened sales presentation and demo and record it on your laptop, while you narrate.

For instance, when TalentBin was extending its go-to-market from exclusively technical and design recruiting to include the healthcare vertical as well, we of course created a newly refreshed pitch deck focused on the realities of the healthcare recruiting market, and how TalentBin fit in there. Then I recorded a brief overview pitch that included the basics. Just use Camtasia or Snagit or QuickTime to record your screen while you speak over your slides, and give a lightweight demo (as appropriate). It's helpful to know the keystrokes to pause the recording in case you need to cough, or you stumble and need to pause and regain your footing.

You can see that video here: https://drive.google.com/file/d/0ByAYCl_pIY-jWQ1VzdHhOWGRWQzQ/view?usp=sharing

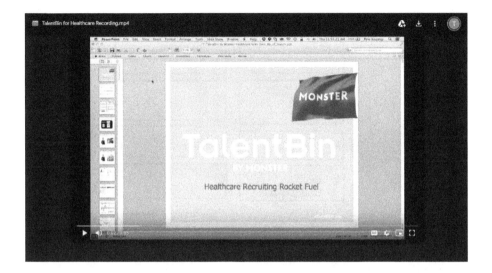

I prefer YouTube as a means of deploying videos for a variety of reasons. First, YouTube is mobile friendly. So much email is read initially on iPhone/Android nowadays, so if you include a link to a video, you want it to actually play when the prospect clicks through. Second, YouTube is a trusted URL. If the link in your email is clearly from YouTube, the prospect knows what's on the other end! A video! On YouTube! That place where delightful videos live!

There are other benefits as well, but they're mainly secondary. YouTube itself has lots of traffic and does a good job of cross-marketing video content based on title, description, tags, and such. So someone watching a related video can discover yours. For that reason, make sure you title your video well, and include a rich description and good tags. And in that description, add a link back to your website so that people can get from the video page to your website, and into your lead capture form! YouTube also has a great Google search engine optimization rank. Often when someone searches for your brand, Google will pepper in videos from YouTube—so make sure they're your videos. Lastly, because YouTube is the biggest video-sharing site around, your prospects are used to dealing with it. They know how to grab the hyperlink and email or text message it to their colleagues. Or post it to Facebook and Twitter. Or embed it with an embed code somewhere. Previously it was popular to use Vimeo because of better replay quality, but

YouTube has largely caught up on this front. For all the other reasons above, I highly recommend posting all your marketing videos on YouTube.

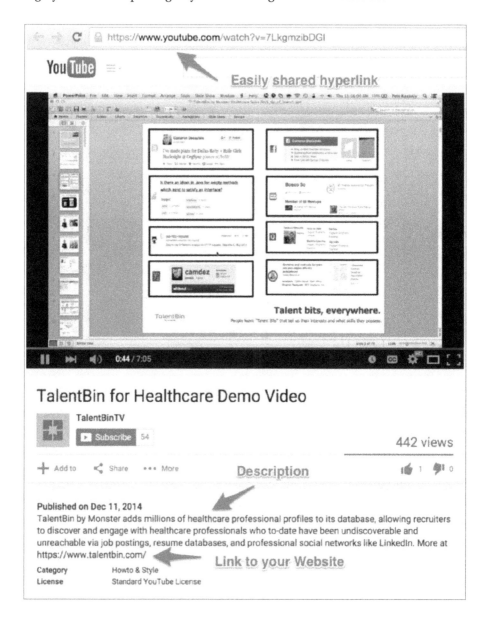

Again, note that the production value on that healthcare video is not the greatest. There are times when I stumble on my words or "um" and "uh" more than I would like. However, this is a perfectly viable recording to send to thousands of potential customers who have the business pain that TalentBin for Healthcare addresses. If your prospects have the pain point you're addressing, and the pain point is actually one that people care about, they'll get over a couple "ums" and "uhs" and instead focus on the fact that your solution fixes their problem! (If they don't have that pain point, you're prospecting wrong. More on that in the next chapter. And if they have the pain point, but it's not a substantial one, that's a product management problem, not a sales one!)

Additional Examples of MVP Overview Videos:

Immediately mobile sales email and CRM MVP demo: **https://vimeo. com/128302141**

Explainer Videos

There's a more advanced cousin of the video overview known as an "explainer video." This is typically a more abstract presentation of the sales narrative, oftentimes animated and voiced-over and made with a higher level of production value. I find that these videos are very helpful both as a first explanation for prospects who show up on your website and as an excellent piece of collateral to deploy via prospecting email. (Note that there were links to videos in some of the appointment-setting email templates above.) You can use your explainer video for outreach beyond email too, deploying it, for example, on monitors at events and conferences.

Typically these explainers work really hard to be shorter than two minutes in length—in large part because their primary use is on a website, and you don't necessarily have a lot of time to grab the attention of the visitor. But even though you see these things all over the place, and they are valuable, they don't have to be your first piece of video collateral. In fact, because they tend to be a bit of a project, especially if you want to do them with a professional third party, they can end up getting delayed over time. Don't fall into that trap. Get something going ahead of your explainer—remember, something is better than nothing—even as you work on your delightful, pixel-perfect masterpiece!

At TalentBin, my co-founder Jason and I worked our butts off on our first explainer video: https://www.youtube.com/watch?v=Jvjpj88f-LU

We finalized the last edits with the vendor, Epipheo, while we were driving a Ford Excursion from San Francisco to Las Vegas for the HR Tech Convention. It turned out great, and we used a variation of it for the ensuing four years. But! Even before we had that spiffy explainer, we had a variety of hacked-together pieces of video collateral that we used to land face-to-face meetings with our first few dozen customers. Videos like this one, which started out with very low production value, to this enhanced version that includes some custom artwork. The funny thing about both of these is that they talk about an initial feature set that was soon eclipsed by a much larger product narrative. But we would have had a much harder time getting those first couple dozen customers with our early product narrative if I hadn't had videos to send to local recruiting leaders in San Francisco. And if we hadn't been able to get those first few customers, we would never have had the opportunity to expand our product narrative to web-wide talent search. So don't gate a "good enough" video on perfection.

Additional Examples of Explainer Videos:

Textio explainer: https://vimeo.com/125538264 (This one was actually done by hand by the team—a really clever way of doing it with text!)

HIRABL explainer: https://vimeo.com/117674976 (created in conjunction with Simple Story Videos: http://simplestoryvideos.com/)

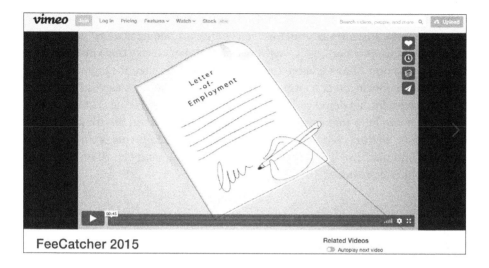

Lawn Love explainer: https://www.youtube.com/watch?v=rA4-6iArq1g

OTHER TYPES OF COLLATERAL

As you might imagine, there is a whole universe of other types of marketing collateral that you can invest in. PDFs! Webinars! Infographics! Blog listicles! Content marketing! Oh my! What we've covered are the basics that you should get going before you start in on anything else. This isn't to say that you can't start selling if you don't have a video overview. But it will make it easier for you to set appointments if you can embed one in your email templates. And you don't need to have a formal demo script in place before you start taking customer meetings. But it can help make them more effective. You should be thinking about collateral as "features" in your go-to-market—each one involves time, energy, and cost, and that should be weighed against how frequently it will be used, and the value its use provides.

One-off Requests

Often you will get a request from a prospect for some sort of collateral that you don't have. "Do you have a one-pager overview on this?" "Do you have customer success stories?" Most of the time you should think about the "question under the question" (more on this in objection handling). Consider whether an existing piece of collateral already handles their request before running off and manufacturing something new. Often that will be the case, so you can simply reply, "You're looking for what others who have used the product have said about it? Great! We have a number of testimonials on slides near the end of this deck I'm attaching!" or "The first ten slides of this attached deck give a great overview for anyone you'd like to share it with. Oh, and this video overview is quite helpful too."

On Demand Collateral

The one place where one-off collateral makes sense is when it is highly customized to the prospect. I'll say it once again, customization of marketing materials—whether a live demo or something that is recorded and repeatedly consumed—is very powerful. On-demand collateral to respond to prospect requests, or even to anticipate them, can accelerate sales conversations dramatically. One of the best ways to accomplish this is screenshotting and screen capturing. For instance, at TalentBin, our market development reps would often take screenshots/screen captures of search results to send to prospects.

For example: "Hi there, Jeff! I know you're hiring for iOS developers in Boston. Check out these search results from TalentBin, and compare that to what you'll find on LinkedIn. See that it's 4x? I'd love to show you more about how this can help your recruiting team out!" That context and relevancy was far more impactful than generic collateral, and the customization took all of sixty seconds.

Or account executives would do one-off five-minute Jing recordings of a certain search, creating a walk-through that was hyper-specific to client needs, maybe both covering comparative search counts and digging into profile data and contact information. The recording only took five minutes to do, could be shared with a hyperlink, and, importantly, could be shared across the entire prospect recruiting team—maybe twenty people or more. Five-minute investment, potentially massive impact.

What would this look like for your offering? What is the customized screenshot that you could send to prospects to make them sit up and pay attention? What is the customized five-minute walk-through that your prospects need to convince their CFOs that this is worth taking a look at?

Equipped with a smart deck, irresistible outreach templates, a prospect-focused demo, and a burgeoning video library, you should have no problem getting into the market and starting to sell. Each asset will require iteration as you learn from your prospects, but the important thing is that you have a full quiver of the basics you need to close your first few dozen customers. Next, we'll discuss how to find the folks you'll target for that selling!

CHAPTER 4

Early Prospecting:
Finding Your First Customers

INTRODUCTION

Now that you have your materials pulled together and are ready to engage with some prospects, you need some prospects to engage with! And that means prospecting, going out and looking for some relevant potential customers. Later on we'll be talking about how to do this at scale, and we'll also be covering how to get prospects to come to you—what's known as "inbound marketing," which has been heavily popularized by folks like HubSpot.

Those more advanced forms of customer acquisition can be challenging for early-stage startups. Your customers may not realize that there is a solution to their business pain—or that they even have the pain in question. And if that's the case, it can be tough to drive them inbound to you, at least to start.

Which is why, for now, your goal is to proactively find 50–100 potential clients that have the distinct pain point that your solution resolves, and to get the product in front of them for a commercial conversation about their business pains and how your solution can potentially help. Rest assured, we will definitely be iterating this approach, and you will learn things from your initial set of "supposed prospects" that help you tune your definition of whom you should actually be selling to. But this is your first shot.

IDEAL CUSTOMER PROFILE: WHAT DOES YOUR PROSPECT LOOK LIKE?

One of the biggest issues founders and first-time salespeople have is trying to sell to people who don't have the problem their solution solves. Instead they prioritize other characteristics, "availability" being the biggest temptress, when identifying prospects. You see this when founders sell to their incubator-mates or people they know from prior companies, or even their friends and family.

The whole purpose of B2B product development is to identify a business pain in the market and build a product or service that resolves that business pain. And the purpose of B2B sales is to identify companies and individuals that have that business pain, propose the product as a means by which to resolve it, and eventually come to a mutually beneficial agreement to exchange money for that product—which then resolves the business pain, as promised. That is how it's supposed to work.

The opposite of this approach is trying to sell your solution to anything with a heartbeat, regardless of whether or not they or their company has the pain point the solution resolves. It's approaches like this that give sales a slimy name. But what's worse (aside from peeing in the pool for all the other people who are doing B2B sales, and just generally irritating people), it's actually terrible for your business. All you have in B2B sales is your time. And when you spend your time on prospects who don't need your product, they won't close. So you're spending your scarce time (and salary expense, and runway) on prospects who are unlikely to buy. Think about that. Your goal in sales is to scalably acquire customers and revenue. So spending time on people who won't close is the equivalent of setting revenue on fire.

Running the numbers quickly, you see how bad this can be. Imagine you're aimless in your outreach targeting and qualification because your ideal customer profile is undefined or sloppy. Maybe you do twenty demos for people who don't have your pain point. Maybe each of those demos requires, on average, thirty minutes of prep, an hour of execution, and another thirty minutes of follow-up immediately after the fact. To say nothing of further down-funnel follow-up, chasing the opportunity. That's a full week of your time flushed down the drain, where it will never turn into revenue. You could have spent that time selling to people who might actually buy. Or working on your sales materials. Or doing a better job servicing your existing customers and making sure they are successful.

Even worse, if you do somehow magically convince a bad prospect to buy (because of your extreme charisma and perfect hair), they won't get value out of your offering because they don't have the pain (or a sufficient amount of the pain) your solution alleviates. That supposed "good trade" we talked about above will actually be a bum deal. And the customer will not be happy. They won't buy more and more of your product. They won't renew your product (they'll "churn out" in SaaS talk). They'll tell their friends. But even worse than that, they may try to be "helpful," and in the process actually hurt you. They'll offer you feedback on how to make the offering better for them—but they're not who the product is designed for. They'll try to give you a second chance, and in the process they'll consume all of your customer success and support time and resources (which, at this early stage, is probably you). And when they do, they'll be stealing those resources from customers who actually will get value from and might buy more of your product.

It's a disaster.

The impulse to prioritize prospects you know, even if they may not have a need for your solution, is understandable. If you've never done sales before, you're not used to the potential rejection associated with approaching people you don't know and engaging them in a commercial conversation. We touched on this in Sales Mindset Changes. The directness that sales demands is foreign and feels frightening, maybe even presumptuous and unwelcome. And it's so easy to get in touch with people you already know. How could this approach not be better than engaging people who don't know you from Adam? This apprehension goes back to the age-old vision of sales guy as slickster—trying to shove product onto someone who doesn't necessarily need it—and probably a fair amount of bad sales experiences you've had yourself. But you need to change your mindset and start seeing yourself as "bringer of solutions to those who have a problem." Prospecting is about finding those who have your problem.

Think about it this way, if my window is broken and a repairman knocks on my door, do I care that I don't know him? Or that he knocked unsolicited? No! He can fix my window! Even better if I didn't realize it was broken. I'm just venting air-conditioning and heat into the world. And leaving my house open to wildlife and potential intruders. This guy is my savior!

Conversely, I can be great friends with a window repairman. Went to college together. Same fraternity. But if I don't have a broken window, regardless of how great our friendship, is it a useful commercial conversation for me or him? I might be his kid's godfather, and might buy anyway, but am I going to get value? Tell others about how great my repair job was? No way.

Targeting based on relationship rather than need is ineffective and a waste of time.

So let's avoid it! The absolute best way to stop selling to people who don't have your pain point is to be able to identify, based on some number of key characteristics, accounts and contacts who do have your pain point. Prospecting is about finding those people in a repeatable fashion. By knowing your ideal customer profile, you'll be able to identify more prospects in the wild. And then scalably engage them and present your product as the solution to their problem. Additionally, you'll be able to easily "qualify" prospects that come to you—whether through your website's lead capture form or referral by a friend, or even at a cocktail party. If they fit that ideal customer profile, great! Run with it. And if they don't, also great! Don't spend any time on it. Instead, spend that time on something more useful—like finding and supporting customers that do match that profile. Or going to the gym. Or taking a nap. Anything other than selling to someone who is not qualified!

You'll know you've nailed your ideal customer profile when you're discussing what your company does with a friend, and she says something along the lines of "Oh, that sounds interesting, I could use it"—but instead of immediately selling her on it, you pause and take a step back. You ask her a couple quick questions that determine if, yes, she actually could use it, or if you should reply with "We're not really set up to do that yet, but maybe in the future! If you have friends that need X, Y, and Z, though, we'd definitely be relevant to them." You just saved yourself from potentially destroying hours of your time, you did your friend a solid by being respectful of her time, you underscored your trustworthiness by being candid, and you set up a word-of-mouth helper. Wins all around!

SO WHO DOES HAVE MY PAIN POINT?

Remember your sales narrative? Which in turn was based on hypotheses about how your offering solves the pain points of potential customers? Parts of your ideal customer profile were defined in there. But now, instead of expressing this in a narrative format, you want to boil it down to abstracted characteristics. You want to get to the point that you can rattle off a set of metadata characteristics that describe the relative level of attractiveness of a prospect.

For instance, in TalentBin's case, this would be something like "This account has five technical recruiters and twenty open technical hires, including iOS, Java, and Android roles, and uses LinkedIn Recruiter." What are the characteristics in there? First, we have the existence of technical recruiters—without at least one recruiter or sourcer to actively use the tool, customers are unlikely to have success. Passive-candidate recruiting is too time-consuming and challenging to be done "on the side" by an HR generalist or a hiring manager. In this case, the fact that there are five recruiters indicates that this is a juicier looking account, where there is an opportunity to sell up to five seats of TalentBin. And when it comes to business pain, there's a lot—twenty engineering hires is a tall order. Even better, iOS, Java, and Android roles are the kind that TalentBin does particularly well at compared to LinkedIn (versus, say, .NET or C#). Lastly, if we can figure out whether the account has multiple seats of LinkedIn Recruiter—a market alternative to TalentBin—we'll know how much they're willing to spend on passive-recruiting tooling to make those five recruiters more effective. If they all have seats, for example, we know that there's around $50k of budget already allocated for LinkedIn Recruiter, which we can take a bite of.

In the case of Immediately, makers of a really cool sales-focused mobile email client and CRM tool for Gmail and Salesforce, it might look something like this— "This account uses Gmail, Salesforce, and Marketo. They have fifty sales reps scattered across the United States, selling software that costs on average $50k. And it looks like the Vice President of Sales has a Sales Operations Manager reporting to her." What are the characteristics Immediately is looking for? Well, as of 2015, the software needs Gmail and Salesforce to work. So if an organization doesn't use Salesforce and Gmail, the conversation is dead in the water. Those are required characteristics. This account also uses Marketo, which indicates a level of sophistication within the sales and marketing organization, and a willingness to pay for expensive tooling that accelerates revenue acquisition. There are fifty reps, each of whom represents a potential user, so this seems like a potentially valuable opportunity. Moreover, because the reps are spread all over the United States—rather than co-located in a single area, indicating a call center—it would seem that these are outside sales reps. And outside sales reps are less frequently in front of a laptop, which makes a compelling sales-first mobile email client and CRM all the more important for them. Beyond that, the software this prospect sells is expensive; incremental wins are very valuable to them. A solution like Immediately, which helps reps handle more deals and avoid dropped balls while mobile, is all the more important when each of those potential dropped balls represents $50k of revenue. Lastly, because someone is managing sales operations, we know there is someone who is specifically charged with making those fifty sales reps more effective, and for maintaining a clean and effective CRM. He will likely be very interested in something that not only makes those reps more effective, but also helps him with the pain point of getting fifty distributed professionals to enter information into the CRM to help with data cleanliness, forecasting, and so forth.

Take a quick second to think about what your qualifying characteristics could look like.

The shared pattern here is a set of characteristics that indicate potential demand for your solution on the part of the account in question. Some of these characteristics will be outwardly identifiable, while others will be more difficult to identify before engaging with an account. The latter are things that will have to be surfaced via what's known as "discovery"—essentially asking questions about the prospect's business to better understand their pain points (or lack thereof). More on that at a later juncture. But just know that even if you can't sniff out all of your ideal customer characteristics for a given prospect ahead of time, that doesn't mean you're out of luck. It's a rare situation where all of those characteristics are outwardly visible—but we'll do our best to find them!

Importantly, while we'll be talking about a number of tools that support this prospecting effort below, over time, tools may change, but the core concepts of identifying prospects based on their outward facing characteristics remains the same and is the key to success here.

Finding Outwardly Available Data

When it comes to looking for potential accounts, you can start with people or you can start with companies, and you should figure out what the right approach is for your solution. You'll look in different places for this information depending on whether you're talking about contacts (people) or accounts (companies), and depending on the kind of characteristics you're assessing.

For account sourcing based on people who work for a given organization, it's really tough to beat LinkedIn—specifically their premium talent solutions. Much of the time, prospect identification will hinge on job title, and LinkedIn is pretty much the best place to find that information. Before LinkedIn, resume databases and contact databases like Salesforce's Data.com and Dun & Bradstreet were the go-tos, but they all suffer from being out-of-date and incomplete. Right now, LinkedIn is your best bet. There are industries whose professionals are less likely to be on LinkedIn, and that can present more of a challenge; in those cases, you may have to revert to more traditional sources. But for the purposes of finding 50–100 prospects, I would be very surprised if LinkedIn didn't handle this for you.

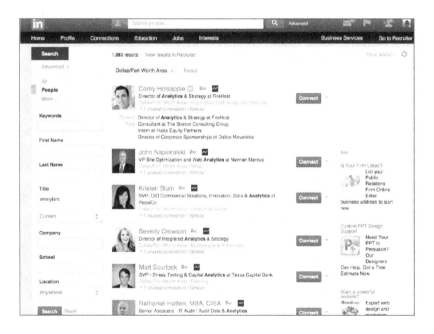

Do you sell an analytics tool that only someone with a title that includes "analytics" would use? LinkedIn is helpful for identifying those people, and thus the companies they work for.

Remember, though, that when you think about your ideal customer profile, you should be thinking about the organization you're selling to. While you may approach account sourcing by looking for the job titles you need, you shouldn't be focused on targeting a particular person or people just yet. Unless you are in a situation where there is literally no difference between the individual and the organization that is purchasing the solution (an organization of one, or an individual within a larger organization buying the solution on his own), your ideal customer is still an account. That account will certainly include key people (e.g., recruiters, sales reps, sales ops staff, data scientists, whatever), and you will eventually be seeking out the right point of contact, or multiple points of contact and decision-makers, to engage with. But your customer profile is the description of an organization.

As for account sourcing based on the characteristics of the company itself, because companies have a tendency to stick around longer than individuals stay in a specific role, information latency is less of an issue. LinkedIn is still a great resource here, in that you can find accounts based on the number of people in a specific role at those organizations. But there are a host of other providers as well. More traditional ones include Dun & Bradstreet, Hoover's, and Salesforce's Data.com, which are well suited to account sourcing based on size, geography, and industry, with DiscoverOrg and ZoomInfo being more modern variants of these. For small-business account sourcing, Yelp can be a great place to go looking for local businesses, bucketed by industry, along with contact information (but generally lacking the specific point of contact you would seek to engage with). Other helpful data sources for small and local businesses include Radius and InfoUSA's Salesgenie. A pure Google Maps search can work here as well. You can often use products you compete with for account sourcing too. For instance, if you're selling into restaurants, OpenTable's index is a great way to find restaurants that care about revenue management, and GrubHub and Seamless are great places to find restaurants that care about delivery. If you're selling into doctors' offices, Healthgrades, Doximity, and even state license databases are good places to look.

Moreover, some of these data sources can tell you if the prospect is paying for technology and services. The profile of a small business that is paying for Yelp business services looks visually different than one for a business that's not, showing you that they're paying for the service. And willingness to pay for marketing services can be a helpful signifier in prioritizing a given business as a prospect.

For example, a search on Yelp for dentists yields 16,000 dentists in Orange County to target:

With Google Maps, we find auto repair shops in San Francisco to target:

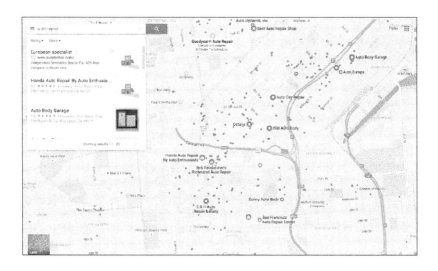

More modern account-sourcing services reveal the technologies that run on an organization's website, which can be indicative of their business pains and willingness to pay for solutions. An organization that has a Salesforce Web-to-Lead form on its home page clearly pays for CRM and could be a fit for a solution that extends Salesforce, or replaces it. An organization that runs Optimizely on its website might be a target for a solution that makes better A/B testing software. BuiltWith, Datanyze, Datafox, SimilarWeb, HGData, and Wappalyzer are examples of this type of account-sourcing service. There are also those that rely on self-reported information, like DiscoverOrg, Siftery, and RainKing, which can be helpful if the technology that is installed isn't visible to web crawling. And then there are services like Spiceworks that provides free network-monitoring software, and allows marketers access to see which accounts use what type of solutions for marketing purposes.

For example, using Datanyze to find accounts that use Salesforce and Gmail, in the sweet spot of 100–250 staff, we get:

You can also use hiring information for account sourcing. This is most directly applicable when your solution is also hiring-related. For instance, the number of open hires listed on an organization's website would be a good leading demand indicator for a SaaS solution that reduces time to onboard new employees, or a leading indicator of willingness to pay for recruitment-branding services like LifeGuides or Glassdoor. The type of open roles can also be revealing. If an organization is hiring for engineering staff, that indicates demand for a recruiting agency or candidate database that focuses on engineering. You can even tell if they're a current customer of companies that provide these solutions. For instance, if you're looking at Indeed, Glassdoor, Monster, or LinkedIn for hiring information, you can often see if the prospect has a paid account or just the free version based on the appearance of the company's profile.

Because Twitter has a "featured" review, and a list of "Jobs You May Like," you know that they pay for Glassdoor:

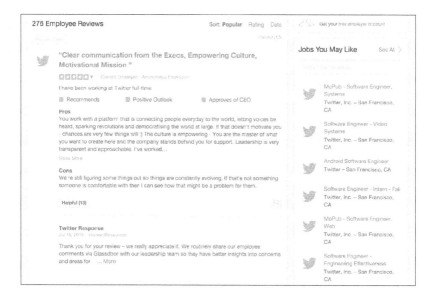

And thanks to their Careers page, we also know that Yelp is hiring a lot of engineers:

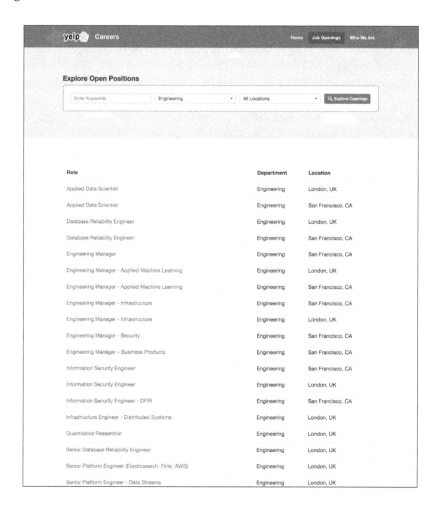

The kinds of people an organization has hired in the past can also be helpful. Even if an organization is not currently hiring for data scientists, if they previously had a posting up for that role, it's likely an organization that employs data scientists. So if you sell a solution that makes data scientists more successful and efficient, you know, at a minimum, that the account likely has data scientists in-house, and might be interested in your solution. Providers of hiring information include services like WANTED Analytics, or even just job boards like Indeed, Monster, Glassdoor, and LinkedIn.

There are 861 Companies hiring "data scientists" in the United States per WANTED Analytics:

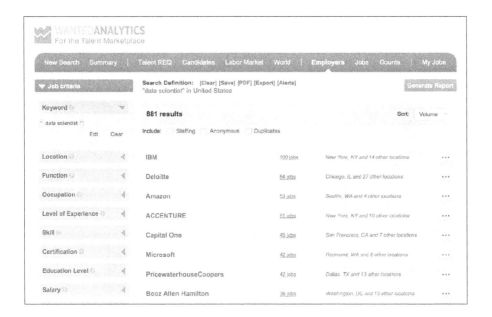

If you sell to organizations that employ data scientists, these accounts would be good ones to address.

While these services will often be able to show you the single piece of information that you're looking for—like whether an organization uses Salesforce or not—other times you can use them for finding information that is correlated with the actual demand signifier you're looking for. For example, organizations often replace the default Salesforce lead capture form with specialized marketing automation lead capture forms from Marketo or Eloqua. While the existence of a Marketo form on an organization's website isn't 100 percent correlated with Salesforce use, it's usually a pretty good leading indicator, and it shows that the company is willing to pay for a more evolved solution.

Remember, you aren't wedded to one data source when you're fleshing out ideal customer accounts and contacts. For instance, if you were Immediately, makers of that really cool sales-focused mobile email client and CRM tool, you might use BuiltWith or Datanyze to find organizations that use Salesforce and Gmail. Then, if you wanted to know how many salespeople there are in each of those organizations, you might run a title search on LinkedIn for "Account" or "Sales" (catching people with titles like Account Executive, Sales Consultant, Sales Director, Account Manager, etc.) to get that demand magnitude information. And that's before you would turn to finding the individual contacts you would like to engage, which are likely to be on LinkedIn.

We can see there are around a dozen recruiters at New Relic—so say we sourced New Relic as an account based on their Glassdoor company page, and wanted to see how many potential users there were, we now know they have a goodly amount of recruiters:

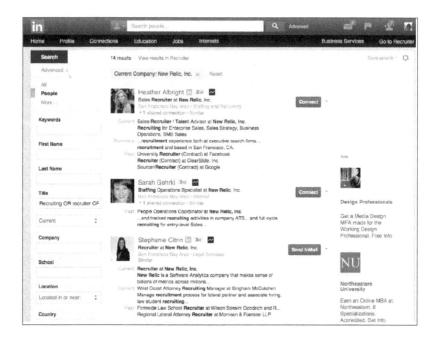

However, while you might use multiple data sources to flesh out the demand characteristics of accounts that you've already found, using multiple sources to drive sourcing is typically a bad idea. If you can reliably find promising new accounts with a specific source (e.g., Datanyze or LinkedIn or Yelp), and there is a good quantity of them, you're kidding yourself if you are trying to get much more out of other sources, at least to start. Usually this is a sign of prospecting ADHD more than anything else. Feel free to iterate and see if there is a more effective tool for account sourcing, but don't pretend that prospecting across things like Twitter and Meetup and Facebook is actually anything more than poor discipline.

Finally, a cautionary note. There are also lots of marketing list providers, but I typically take a pretty dim view of those. They're generally extremely out-of-date compared to information on LinkedIn, and they're generally poorly modeled. That is, they typically include very sparse metadata outside of name, title, contact information, and lightweight company geography, size, and industry information. So your targeting will be poor. Moreover, you don't want to waste your time calling numbers that go to nowhere and emailing email addresses that no longer exist. And for now, since you're just looking to get your first hundred targets, you can do it manually. Not to mention that manual prospecting is a very good exercise to go through to get a more concrete sense of what these accounts and individuals look like. As you go, you may discover that a characteristic you thought was important actually isn't, or discover another characteristic that is even more important for sourcing or qualifying potential prospects. So stay away from lists.

Getting Data That Isn't Outwardly Discoverable

Just because a given characteristic isn't outwardly discoverable doesn't mean that you shouldn't include it in your ideal customer profile. It could still be extremely important in determining whether or not your solution is relevant for a prospect. For instance, with TalentBin, whether an organization used passive-candidate recruiting databases, like LinkedIn Recruiter, was a fantastic indicator of whether TalentBin could help them with their recruiting efforts. The problem was, that information was not publicly available. There were correlating pieces of information. If an organization paid for a premium LinkedIn Company Page, or had job postings on LinkedIn's job search engine (by paying for a "job slot"), and also had recruiters in-house, they usually had one or more LinkedIn Recruiter seats. Still, we couldn't definitively identify this characteristic from publicly available information—but it was an important one to include in our ideal customer profile.

So, if a characteristic isn't identifiable, how will you ever be able to get the information you need? Well, you'll have to ask. That means when prospects come inbound through your lead capture forms, or you're on the phone with them, you'll have to specifically ask them if they have these characteristics. And if you can't proactively identify prospects that have these hidden characteristics, how can you scalably attract them? That's where things like content and inbound marketing come into play. More on that later. For now, for identifying a hundred potential targets, direct prospecting, coupled with discovery questions when key characteristics aren't readily observable, will be your approach.

Rolling Up The Demand Signifiers

When you think about your ideal customer profile, you should be thinking about not just the minimum requirements for product/prospect fit, but also the magnitude of demand that prospect may have. This helps for a couple of reasons. First, knowing the size of an account's demand can help with understanding how much of your solution you can potentially sell them, so you can focus on accounts that might buy lots of your solution. It can also help you understand the magnitude of their business pain and, as such, how motivated they will be to pay for your solution. It can also help you prioritize various opportunities, so you can spend your time on those with higher pain. (We'll talk about small versus medium versus large accounts in a bit—but more pain usually means more money.) You will eventually be able to converge on a "customer attractiveness" scoring algorithm that will help you (and later, your sales staff) judge the relative attractiveness of a prospect.

For instance, with TalentBin, the score would be based on any combination of the following—number of recruiters, volume of engineering hiring, passive-candidate recruiting acumen, and ability to pay. So an account that has a single recruiter in-house, but ten open iOS and Android engineering requisitions, and that just recently raised $5 million might be as attractive as an account with four recruiters, all sharing a LinkedIn Recruiter seat, and only a couple of engineering reqs. And both would pale in comparison to an account with three recruiters—and three LinkedIn Recruiter accounts—fifteen open engineering reqs, and a history of doing manual sourcing on GitHub and Twitter. Note that all of these accounts have the minimum viable criteria that we set at TalentBin—at least one recruiter and at least three open engineering roles. Think about what this looks like for your ideal customer. What factors will you consider? Perhaps it's number of field sales reps or how bad the company's Glassdoor reviews are or its volume of e-commerce sales—and how will you weigh them in combination?

ACCOUNT SOURCING: PUTTING IT INTO PRACTICE

Now that we have discussed the various places where you could go and look for accounts, let's get very specific about doing this in practice, shooting for that goal of 50–100 targets.

Prospect Data Management

Later we'll get into CRM and where to house your list of accounts and contacts to attack, but my recommendation at this stage is to just use a Google Sheet as your initial repository of prospects. This doesn't mean that you'll use this spreadsheet as your CRM (though you probably could for this limited scale of engagement), but you do want a place to house the structured prospect data. This is a rough example of a spreadsheet template you could use, with both "role-specific" prospecting and "hiring-specific" prospecting: https://docs.google.com/spreadsheets/d/1fmi04yO_5AvqgopTCCukWq5mbInLdZR25FXF_yCYYpI/edit?usp=sharing

You will note that there are typically distinct columns for pieces of information that we might eventually want to query on, or use in a mail merge campaign. For instance, for a company like LifeGuides, the makers of awesome recruitment-branding solutions, it would be useful to have a target prospect's Glassdoor information, as Glassdoor is a big indicator of recruitment-branding business pain and spend. So in this case, we'd not only capture their Glassdoor star rating (our messaging might change if their score is low versus high), but also the Glassdoor profile link, and maybe a link to a particularly bad review. Not only is this good for future reference (before you got on a call with a prospect, you'd want to check it out), it would also be useful in an initial outreach email.

So if you'd done a good job of structuring that metadata, you'd be able to send awesome mail merges like:

SUBJECT LINE: Hi {*First_Name*}! We can help {*Company_Name*} with that {*Star_Average*} Glassdoor average!

Hi there, {*First_Name*}! I saw that, like many companies out there, your Glassdoor ratings ({*Star_Average*}) are probably not where you would love them to be. And like a lot of companies, you have reviews that are probably not representative of the true employee experience at {*Company_Name*}. This one was a good example: {*Review_Link*}. Those are never fun.

The good news is that we've been working on something to help you tell your authentic employment experience story. And tell it in a way that isn't held hostage by an organization that wants to charge you to influence those reviews. And we can help you take back the top Google search results for "working at {*Company_Name*}." (Have you looked at that query lately? Glassdoor is in the first few results. Here's a {*Link*} to it.)

You can see an overview video of how we help out with that here: {*Video_Link*}.

Would you be interested in hearing more? We'd love to show you how TalentBin can help you find and recruit qualified technical candidates for your open positions. Do you have 30 minutes next week? What times work for you?

Don't believe the subject line? Email me! I'd be happy to explain. Or you can ring me directly at {*Sales Rep Biz Phone*}.

Thanks,

{*Sales Rep First Name*}

How great an outreach email is that compared to your typical mail-merged crap? Furthermore, you can see why creating your own custom prospect list is so much better than buying ready-made marketing lists. The better your own prospect metadata, the better your appeals to prospects can be, which leads to higher demo rates.

Diligently capturing those pieces of metadata in the prospecting process not only ensures you're targeting relevant accounts, with the right points of contact, it also puts you in a strong position to leverage automation when you start your outreach process.

Rabbits, Deer, or Elephants?

While you know to target accounts that have the business pain your solution is built to solve, there are varying levels of this business pain. Moreover, you also need to consider an organization's ability to react to a potential new solution to that pain. The traditional way that this is described is in terms of "hunting" various size animals. Whether it's "minnows," "dolphins," and "whales," or "rabbits," "deer," and "elephants," the point is that you will encounter accounts of varying sizes and magnitude of business pain. And while it might seem attractive to go elephant hunting, given that those deals could be potentially the largest, you'll want to think twice there. Large organizations have existing legacy systems and workflow and are less reactive; even if you do end up closing them, you may have trouble onboarding them and supporting them effectively. And if a single elephant ends up being a disproportionate amount of your revenue, you may end up beholden to them to build features that they demand. You might end up a professional services company for this particular elephant. The elephant might fall and crush you just as you're doing your victory dance.

Similarly, rabbits might seem attractive, in that you can get buy-in from a senior decision-maker quickly, and there won't be a lot of legacy process they need to modify to adopt your solution. Unfortunately, the size of their deals may not be much to write home about. And the lack of business process may mean that they aren't all that good at doing the thing your solution enables, which means that they're more likely to churn out.

Targeting "deer" is usually a good initial approach. They're large enough to have a goodly amount of the business pain—sufficient to entertain a new solution—and likely have business processes that can ingest new technologies. But they're small enough that they can make purchasing decisions quickly, and their existing business systems are probably not so entrenched that adopting a new solution would require substantial change management.

That said, you certainly want accounts that trend larger—bigger deer, let's say! With TalentBin, this might be a ~100-person organization with three recruiters and twenty open engineering requisitions. That would be far more attractive than a similarly sized organization with only three open engineering hiring requisitions. Or for Immediately, this might be a fifty-person company with ten field sales reps, selling software with an average contract value of $100k, as compared to maybe a hundred-person company that has thirty inside sales reps, selling software with an average contract value of $10k. In these examples, all the accounts might be considered "deer," but we want to target the most attractive ones to enhance our chances of winning.

Geography

To start, I find it most effective to look for accounts in your own geography. Even if the potential deal sizes for your solution are such that they will require an inside sales approach, being in the same time zone, and even being able to go on-site to visit potential customers, will be very helpful. Unless your solution is extremely specialized, or you are based somewhere with few potential accounts, you should certainly be able to find 50–100 juicy "deer" that meet your ideal customer profile. And if you can't, that might indicate that you should think about relocating to somewhere with more economic activity to help your chances of success.

Account First? Contact First?

When it comes to finding potential accounts, as noted above, you can start with people or you can start with the company, and you should figure out what the right approach is for your solution. Then, once you've started with one data source, you'll likely move to the other type—from company-centric to people-centric research, or vice versa—to flesh out more information about the account.

There will typically be a most efficient way of doing this, and it's usually the result of what your qualifying characteristics are, and how easy they are to find from existing data sources. With TalentBin, we started by using LinkedIn to find technical recruiters—because if an account didn't have any recruiters, it was a nonstarter. Once we found technical recruiters, this lead us to the organizations that employed them, whose current technical hiring demand we would then seek to understand. This meant we would flip to company-specific data sources to flesh out more account information. But if you're Immediately, the sales-focused mobile email client and CRM tool, you know that without Salesforce and Gmail your product is a nonstarter. So finding sales operations and sales leadership prospects whose organizations run on Microsoft Dynamics (a competing CRM to Salesforce) and Exchange isn't all that helpful. As such, you would probably start by using Datanyze or BuiltWith to find companies that match the required software characteristics, before pivoting to LinkedIn to sniff out how many sales reps they employ, whether those are inside reps or outside reps, and which relevant sales leadership or sales operations staff the Immediately sales team might seek to engage.

People-centric Sourcing

If you've decided that the best way to target accounts is based on the presence of people with a certain title (e.g., "Data Scientist"), as discussed above, LinkedIn is probably the right place to start.

Do a title search for the relevant title, constrain it to the relevant geography, and then use LinkedIn's search faceting to constrain to the appropriate size of company you'd like to target.

I'm using LinkedIn's Recruiter Lite in the screenshot below, but a number of their products let you achieve this type of query:

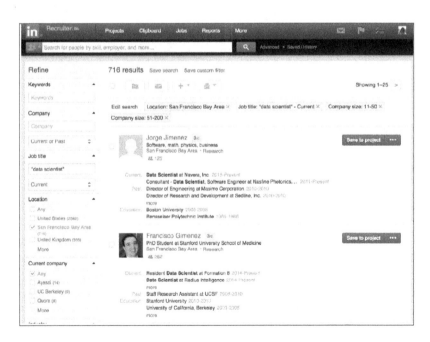

In this example, there are ~716 results for a query of the current title "Data Scientist" in the San Francisco Bay Area where the contact's company size falls into either the 11–50 or 51–200 buckets. Of course, that doesn't mean there are ~700 accounts for us to target, but rather 700-odd potential users for our solution.

In terms of low-hanging fruit, the "Current Company" facet will show you which companies have the most employees with the title in question. Of course, you'll only get a handful of companies, but those are probably great accounts to target. They're smallish, and have a ton of potential users of your solution!

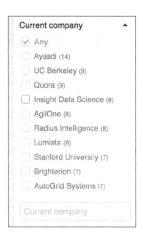

Beyond those accounts that show up in the "Current company" facet, the next step would be to walk through the rest of the profiles, capturing the relevant account names (e.g., Navera, Twitter, Dropbox, etc.). Again, remember that we may not actually be selling to the Data Scientists in question—they are simply potential users. Later we will be figuring out exactly who at the organization we would like to target with our outreach. For now, the goal is simply to capture the account that we want to target, along with demand signifiers that we touched on above—for instance, number of Data Scientists, size of sales staff, size of organization, and so on.

Company-centric Sourcing

As noted above, you can also use company-specific metadata to help find accounts that could be a good fit for your solution.

Say we were HIRABL, a company that sells revenue acceleration products for staffing agencies. In their case, prospecting by "company type" (industry) could be helpful. LinkedIn is great for this purpose too. We could go to LinkedIn's Company search function, select for Industry "Staffing and Recruiting," choose a Company Size in the "deer" range we discussed above, and constrain to the San Francisco Bay Area, because we want proximity to our initial accounts in the event we can go on-site.

This is what that search looks like:

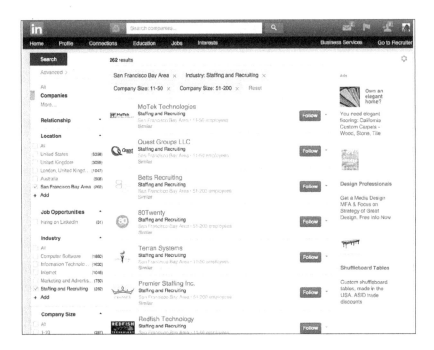

So we have a good 200+ of these targets, and we can now pull a selection of them into our prospect spreadsheet, and then start appending the relevant demand signifiers on top of that. In HIRABL's case, key signifiers include number of recruiters and the type of candidates the agency places (higher-value professionals being better, as HIRABL helps recover missed fees from high-value placements).

If you were doing this for a set of targets for your solution, what would be the right way of going about it? Would you look for accounts by starting with people or company metadata? What data source would be the most relevant to you?

POINT(S)-OF-CONTACT DISCOVERY: WHO WILL BE EXCITED ABOUT YOUR SOLUTION?

Now that you know how to find promising accounts, either by company-centric or people-centric demand signifiers, your next question is "Who should I be engaging at this company, and how can I reach them?" That is, you want to find the right point of contact—ideally, the relevant decision-maker for the account. Note that this is different than people-centric sourcing of accounts. In that case, you were looking for potential users of your solution, like data scientists or field sales reps, at the account in question. That doesn't necessarily mean that those data scientists or sales reps are the correct points of contact to sell to. This goes back to your sales narrative. You want to target and engage the person who is responsible for solving the pain your solution resolves, and who has the decision-making authority, and budgetary control, to resolve that pain. You may also choose to involve people who would be users of the solution, but that is more for the purposes of marketing to them to build a groundswell of support and help convince the decision-maker in question.

How can you identify these decision-makers? Conveniently, it's often their title that gives it away. By extension, you can use LinkedIn (or Data.com, or others) to search for those titles, constrained to a given account. You should be paying attention to what these titles look like as you are prospecting, and you'll eventually converge on the right set. If you're selling a recruiting solution, perhaps it's the VP of Talent, Director of Recruiting, or Recruiting Manager. Or if you're selling an e-commerce solution, it might be the Chief Marketing Officer, Digital Marketing Manager, and so on. If you sell sales tooling, it could be the VP of Sales, Chief Revenue Officer, VP of Sales Operations, Director of Sales Effectiveness, or Sales Operations Manager. The right title can vary based on stage—an early-stage company is less likely to have a Sales Operations Manager, so the responsibilities of sales operations might fall to the VP of Sales.

As such, I typically like to take the approach of "cascading" points of contact. If an account has a VP of Sales, a Director of Sales Operations, and a Sales Operations Manager, I prefer to grab all of them as potential points of contact. This can be even more scaled at a later juncture—perhaps you'll grab not just all the decision-makers, but potentially all the users too, for later engagement via drip email marketing. LinkedIn is very helpful for finding these individuals. Just do a Boolean title search, like "("account" OR "sales" OR "sales operations") AND ("Director" OR "Vice" OR "VP")," which will return people that have any of the words in the first set plus any of the words in the second. That will give you a good list to start with. Then look more deeply at each profile to figure out which person, or group of people, you really want to target.

If I thought that Zendesk were a good account to target for a sales enablement or acceleration solution, I would go looking in these contacts, which were uncovered by the search referenced above:

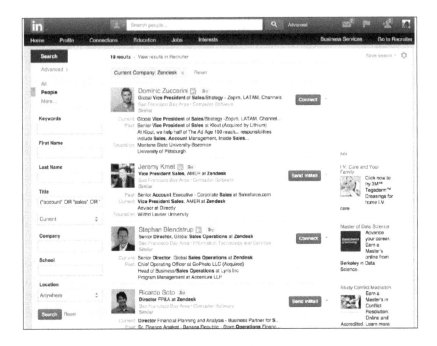

There's a concept of "complementary" decision-makers as well, who are typically internal customers of the primary decision-maker you're seeking to target. That is, while the VP of Talent is the person responsible for solving the business pain of "hiring more engineers," it is the VP of Engineering, or CTO, that has the downstream business pain of "ship more software." Or even though it might be the Director of Sales Operations who is responsible for making sales reps more effective, ultimately it falls to the VP of Sales to generate more revenue. That CTO or VP of Sales definitely has a stake in solving the business pain you're looking to address. Sometimes you can target these complementary decision-makers, with the intent of being referred to the appropriate primary decision-maker. You might even engage with these complementary decision-makers to make the case for your solution and, having convinced them, join forces with them to convince their colleagues, together.

Of course, you can take this logic to its end point and say, "Well, the CEO or founder of the company is the one who is ultimately responsible for all of these problems, so maybe I'll just go to her." There is a bit of truth to this. In fact, another fantastic sales-learning resource is the book Predictable Revenue by Aaron Ross and Marylou Tyler, which advocates what they term "Cold-Calling 2.0." The upshot of this idea is that CEOs or other very senior staff are highly identifiable, attuned to receiving ROI-based arguments about budgetary spend, and used to delegating investigation to subordinates. So if you just target the CEO or founder of a firm with an email that delineates your product's potential value to the organization in a crisp, dollars-and-cents fashion, and ask to be directed to the relevant delegate, the thinking goes that the CEO can refer you—and now you have tacit executive sponsorship, plus the name of the correct decision-maker. If it works, that sounds great. But this approach can be good and bad. It certainly made sense in the pre-LinkedIn world, when the proactive discovery of relevant decision-makers was much tougher. But the risk of this approach is that these individuals get amazing volumes of email and often have a delegate, like an executive assistant, assisting with email triage and ensuring that your outreach gets deleted promptly. So there are downsides.

I am a bigger fan of first determining who is most likely to be the decision-maker, and the individual most excited about solving this business pain, and appealing to her directly. If this doesn't work, then you can potentially cascade back to her internal customer (her complementary decision-maker), like the CEO. This is a more advanced form of prospecting and outbound lead generation, so for our initial purposes here, I would constrain to targeting the relevant decision-maker.

There's the opposite approach as well, in the form of "bottom up" prospecting. In this approach, you target the individual users of your solution—the sales reps, recruiters, data scientists, engineers, etc. The goal of this approach is to convince them of the validity of your solution and how it will improve their lives by making their jobs easier, making them more money, making them better at their jobs, etc. From there, you can enlist them in making the case to their management, who ultimately control the budget that would be used to purchase your solution. Again, this is another more advanced form of prospecting, and is something to consider when you're looking to scale your prospecting and lead-gen efforts, which we'll discuss more later. Some great examples of this approach are actually products that lend themselves to individual or team usage, where the "free" version of the product is really just a form of lead generation—the registration for which is used as a signifier to sell into an account. Box, Yammer, Slack, Yesware, and others are good examples of this; all, eventually, end in an enterprise sale to a relevant decision-maker. For now, though, we're going to skip this.

One piece of information that can be very helpful when engaging these prospect decision-makers is to see if you potentially have an "in" to them. That is, if you're using a professional network like LinkedIn, or any of its premium tools, you can see if you have a shared LinkedIn connection with the decision-maker in question. This is not the same as selecting the accounts you're going to target based on who you know. In this case, we know the account has the business pain we're trying to solve, and have identified the person(s) who should care most about this, and only then are we seeing if there's a potential "warm intro" into that person. This can be in the form of someone who is directly connected to both of you (look on LinkedIn and Facebook—you'd be amazed who you want to college with that is friends with them), or the broader version, where you can see if anyone you know is connected to the organization. That is, say you're trying to engage the head of Sales Operations, and you don't have an "in" there. But you happen to be LinkedIn connected to the VP of Marketing, or an engineering manager. They likely know the other person, and even if they don't, they can still forward along your outreach materials (more on this in the next chapter) with their commentary on how you're a good guy, and worth paying attention to. Mark these "ins" up in your CRM or a column in your prospecting list, e.g., "Potential Intros".

Once you've decided which individuals, or set of individuals, you want to target, it's time to find contact information so you can actually engage them. This will typically entail email addresses, and potentially phone numbers. Later, when you have market development staff, switchboards will be helpful for cold-calling, and you may do some of that yourself here. However, email addresses are typically the most beneficial, in that they allow for better automation via templating and lightweight drip marketing (more on this later), instrumentation via open and click tracking, and prospect progress tracking. So we'll focus on email outreach to start.

Later we'll discuss how you can use offshore resources via work marketplaces like Upwork to assist with this, but in the short term, finding emails yourself is good practice to get really intimate with how available these email addresses actually are in your vertical. If it turns out that it is nearly impossible to surface the email addresses of decision-makers in your market, you'll have to reconsider parts of your go-to-market. Much better to know that information earlier than later! One of the best ways to surface email addresses is to just search around. Depending on the decision-maker in question, you may find a fairly substantial digital footprint. So simply Googling for their name and "email address" can sometimes provide a hit. Looking for personal websites or LinkedIn profiles can be helpful. If you're selling to sales people or recruiters, they tend to include their email addresses and potentially desk and mobile phones on their LinkedIn profiles, so prospects and candidates can contact them easily. Let's make use of that! This can extend to personal email addresses as well. Some people are concerned about outreach to personal email addresses. I find that concern overblown. If you are doing a good job of pre-qualifying, and have excellent outreach materials that document why you're engaging prospects and how your solution will make their lives better, that information is still relevant delivered to a personal Gmail address. And they actually might have less email traffic in that inbox, anyway!

If you aren't able to find an email address via searching around, the next approach is email address formation. (Sometimes breathlessly called "hacking." Lol.) The nice thing about corporate email addresses is that they typically follow a given pattern, whether first.last@domain.com or flast@domain.com or whatever. Once you sort out what that pattern is, which can often be done by searching around for other people's email addresses from that company, all you need is your prospect's first and last name to form his email address. Services that help validate email addresses, like Rapportive or FullContact for Gmail, can be especially helpful. When you enter the correctly formed email address, social profile links will populate in those plugins, showing you that you "got it."

Who wants to sell sales tools to New Relic?

This approach can be a little manual, but there are some tools that help accelerate the process. Folks like Datanyze, Data.com, and SalesLoft can help; they've logged those patterns for a large number of companies, and streamlined the export of prospect name, title, and email address information from places like LinkedIn directly into a CSV or your CRM. And there are a handful of products that help you permute email addresses quickly and validate them against social APIs. Just to be helpful, here is a Google Sheet that includes some quick and dirty logic to take a first name, last name, and known company email address domain and spit out all the relevant permutations. Then take those, drop them into Gmail or Outlook, and quickly mouse over them to determine which one returns a "hit" in social lookup tools!

Who wants to sell technology to Home Depot?

Well, Matt's got a helpfully formed email address for us.

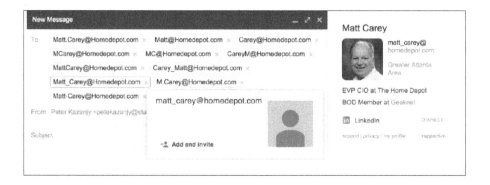

Lastly there are a host of modern prospecting tools that can assist you in finding email addresses tied to a given LinkedIn profile. Lusha and LeadIQ are two popular ones that make finding an email address associated with a LinkedIn profile as easy as clicking a button.

While email addresses are the piece of contact information you're going to want to start with, phone numbers also have a place—either personal or desk line, potentially discoverable through LinkedIn or sources like Data.com, or just the main direct switchboard line for the company. The latter is typically very easy to find just by Googling for "*<company_name>* contact," which will usually resolve to the company's contact information page. Later, as you bring on market development resources and do more substantial cold-calling, switchboard lines will be more important. Capturing them at this stage is also useful, so make sure to do that as you're building your initial list.

Phone numbers are particularly important for local businesses, which are typically an exception to our email-before-phone rule; the acquisition of email addresses for those decision-makers may be more challenging. For local business go-to-markets like Yelp, Groupon, GrubHub, Redbeacon, and more, acquiring phone numbers in order to reach out via direct dial is key.

And while grabbing this data once is the way you start out, over time, it will get more and more out of date, as decision makers move from company to company. While this is something not to be concerned about to start, later on something that refreshes those records automatically, like a LeadGenius, or otherwise, can be helpful to make sure that those contacts are always fresh.

Now Let's Get Going

At this point, you should have a targeted list of 50–100 prospect accounts—all of which represent the demand characteristics of your ideal customer profile, are in your local geography, and are in the sweet spot of company size—along with one or more potential contacts to engage at the prospect company, and their basic profile data (name, title, and so on).

Now it's time to go hunting! You've got your sales narrative, you've got various materials encapsulating it, and now you have a rich list of prospects for whom your narrative should resonate. So go sell.

CHAPTER 5

Prospect Outreach & Demo Appointment Setting

INTRODUCTION

Now that you've got your list of highly targeted potential accounts, and associated points of contact, it's time to tackle the business of actually selling. You were probably wondering when we'd get around to that! Up until this point, we've mainly been dealing with tooling to enable you to sell. But as covered in the Sales Mindset Changes chapter, the best tooling in the world is useless without the actual activity of emailing, calling, presenting, demoing, and closing. That's where the true work of "selling" is done, and because of this, it's often the scariest to people who have never done it before. They believe deep down, secretly, that planning and planning, building more and more tools, can shield them from potential rejection. But experienced salespeople know, in the words of the great American philosopher Mike Tyson, that "everyone has a plan until they get punched in the mouth." Sure, getting punched in the mouth is no fun, but you can't win if you don't get in the ring. Let's smile and get ready!

What we'll cover in the following chapters will prepare you for the various motions of selling, from appointment setting to "pitching" via sales presentation and product demonstration, all the way through closing and pipeline management. Note, though, that simply reading about these actions isn't enough, and you should not expect to be naturally comfortable with, and excellent at, any of them.

It will take practice and many repetitions before you have your pitch nailed and are eminently comfortable with all the objections prospects will throw at you. But this is totally to be expected, and the best way to get to that point is to just start!

STAGES OF THE SALES CYCLE

I like to think of the sales cycle bucketed into several major stages. First, there's "outreach and engagement," where you're engaging a prospect account with the goal of setting an appointment. Next comes "pitching," where you begin a commercial conversation with a prospect with the goal of eliciting more information about the particulars of their situation and persuading them that your solution fits their pain. And the stages continue all the way to "closing," getting the prospect to sign on the line that is dotted, and the associated pipeline management. Each stage has it own set of actions, and it own goals, which we'll cover in depth.

Importantly, you will be the one taking all of these actions. This is another place where early-stage founders get tripped up. They hope that they can just "hire a sales guy" who will figure this all out. Go to Costco, buy a bin of sales dust. Sprinkle some sales dust on product. Poof! IPO. This is simply not the case. Sales professionals are adept at taking a proven product to market with a proven message and a proven set of materials—with minimal variation. They are not there to prove those things out on their own. The selling you will be engaged in is what is known as "evangelical sales," a mix of product management, product marketing, and sales. In evangelical sales, there is a tight feedback loop between your interactions with the prospect and modifications of both the selling materials (product marketing) and even the features of the product itself (product management). It will be an iterative approach, with a number of false starts. But that tight feedback loop is indispensable in tuning your go-to-market in a way that allows you to start winning customers and, later, to package your approach in a way that can be replicated by an army of sales professionals. But the only way you'll get there later is by doing it yourself now.

In this chapter, we're going to touch on the first part of that cycle, "outreach and engagement," with the goal of getting appointments on your calendar. A little later, we'll cover the mechanics of presenting to a prospect, demoing, and then working the deal as it moves down the funnel. Both are important, in that if you don't do the first, you won't have the opportunity for the second. And even if you're somehow amazing at closing business from the first step, if you aren't able to reliably fill the top of your funnel, you'll struggle to acquire the number of customers you'd prefer. A .500 batter who only gets a single at-bat a game isn't nearly as productive as one who has three or four a game. So let's make sure you're getting those at-bats.

SETTING YOURSELF UP FOR SUCCESS

As noted above, there is a particular tempo to enterprise sales' distinct stages. In this first stage, the goal is to set up a commercial conversation about the prospect's business pains and how your solution could potentially solve them, a.k.a. a "pitch" or "demo." The goal at this stage is not to sell the solution. You're simply "selling" a conversation—the opportunity to learn more, and tell more. The same way that the goal of a first date is not to get married, but rather to get to a second date (assuming there is a potential fit!). You try to get married on the first date, it's gonna be an awkward scene. Same with sales.

As a non-sales person approaching this, you have an advantage of sorts over pure sales professionals seeking to set appointments. That is, because your offering is early stage, and you are not a salesperson, you can often approach these conversations as "research" or "customer development"—trying to understand pain points, and how they are currently solved. There is a balance here, as it is important to make sure that these conversations always remain in the realm of the commercial; you don't want prospects thinking this conversation has nothing to do with addressing their business pains and potentially solving them, for a price. But because you're the founder, CTO, CEO, or what have you, you can use that to your advantage, and in doing so reduce the friction of getting these meetings on the calendar.

Management and Early CRM

Given the activity-centric nature of sales, you're going to have many balls in the air concurrently. As noted in the Sales Mindset Changes chapter, this is a new experience for most professionals. And while you may be used to being able to keep all your open items and projects "in your head," this is extraordinarily challenging to do in sales. Every potential conversation, every conversation that is in flight, and all previous interactions are simply too much for someone to remember at once. Yes, yes, I'm sure you're very smart and clever, but there's no way you can keep it all straight in your head. And if you can, you're not dealing with enough prospects concurrently! This is why modern sales organizations rely on customer relationship management (CRM) software to handle this issue—not only to help reps keep track of things, but to support management functions too, like activity reporting, win-rate tracking, and even financial reporting on how many deals are happening.

For a sole founder, I'm split on the necessity of using a full-blown CRM to start. As someone who is extremely persnickety about these things, but also now quite adept at Salesforce CRM (the industry's CRM of choice), I would always use Salesforce. It's the default sales system of record (a distant second being Microsoft Dynamics), but with the power and extensibility of the tool comes a fair level of complexity and configuration requirements. For someone just starting out, it could be overkill. Given the small scale of your initial set of prospects, you could potentially get by with a Google Sheet, where each prospect is represented by a row, with a column for various pieces of deal-state metadata (as we talked about in the Prospecting chapter). A middle ground would be to use a "beginner CRM," like a Pipedrive, Close.io, Insightly, or SalesforceIQ (formerly RelateIQ, now owned by Salesforce). While not as powerful as Salesforce, and lacking the broad partner ecosystem of third-party tools, these products can be helpful in providing more structure around tracking who you've engaged with, who you haven't yet, and who is in what state. Regardless of whatever claims are made by marketing teams, the purpose of the CRM is to help you keep straight who you've talked to, and to capture those communications (via email or notes from calls).

However, you should know that none of those beginner CRMs will scale for the longer term. Eventually, you'll end up on Salesforce.com; it's just a question of when it will happen. How's that for a nice market position to be in, eh? Maybe you'll get your solution there eventually.

Materials and Personalization

We touched on materials in the previous chapter, but to recap, you'll need your set of prospects, the relevant pieces of metadata about their demand indicators that you researched (e.g., number of recruiters, number of open jobs, site traffic, etc.), a set of outreach emails with supporting collateral (i.e., video demos), ideally split up into a series of emails that can be dripped out over time, and your phone script.

The more you can demonstrate prior research and personalization, the better response you'll have from would-be prospects, who are used to irrelevant and poorly researched blanket outreach from crappy sales staff. By pulling relevant pieces of metadata into separate data fields for each of your prospects, you can get the best of both worlds—the automation leverage of mail-merged and drip-marketed email outreach along with extremely customized demand indicators and messaging. Other ways you can make your outreach more impactful include screenshots or little demo videos (Jing is great for this) that are customized for the prospect in question. Shoot, as you record that lightweight video, you can even speak over it like you're talking to your prospect—a form of "video voice mail/email" if you will. Who doesn't like it when someone makes them a personalized love letter?

EMAILING

Email is your friend. It is an extremely powerful means of directed outreach toward prospects, when done correctly. It has the benefit of a strong ecosystem of automation and instrumentation tools, benefiting from over a decade of innovation in the space. And it is especially powerful in conjunction with calling and voice mail delivery. But be careful. When done incorrectly, it can make you look like you have no idea what you're doing and poison potential client relationships. Bad emails are one of the main reasons why sales gets a bad name. So let's make sure to do it right, okay?

As covered in the previous chapters Sales Materials and Prospecting, you should have both a set of prospects (who have been pre-qualified) and their email addresses, along with a set of email templates that characterize why you think they have the business pain your solution solves, describe what you think you can do about it, and conclude with a call to action to engage in a one-to-one commercial conversation—the mythical "demo" we seek to arrange.

One email probably won't be enough to get the appointment on the calendar. As much as we'd like to think our words are magical and our arguments breathtakingly compelling, it's probably going to take more than one shot to gain a response from the prospect. Which is why we have more than one email template! People don't want to read a book dropped in their inbox (he says, while writing a book). Rather, they want quick snippets of information, hyper-targeted to them, providing them insight and value. You can achieve this through personalization, but also by breaking up your messaging into multiple distinct emails. We talked about this in the Sales Materials chapter, but splitting up the buckets of your narrative into separate, short emails, constrained to "one thought," can be a very effective way to "drip" messaging about the pain you're addressing. With this approach, you can demonstrate that you sniffed out that the prospect has that pain, and that the reason you're emailing is to verify this, help them solve it, and be a hero. It's hard to do that in a single monolithic email. Think of it as akin to what flash sale sites like One Kings Lane, Gilt, and Groupon figured out with their daily emails—delivering targeted, relevant content, one bit at a time, over time, is a great way to drive a prospect to eventual conversion.

The key, of course, is to ensure that you're not showing up in the prospect's inbox like a carnival barker, with exclamation points every sentence, bombastic claims, and all sorts of HTML layout elements. Yuck. Instead, using conversational, calm, text-based messaging, demonstrate your focus on their challenges. These emails should have the tone and candor of a message from one CEO to another (even if it's actually from a founder to the "CEO" of a function within the target organization). Moreover, small, lightweight, chunked emails help you take advantage of modern email marketing tooling, like lightweight drip marketing, which we'll tackle in a bit.

And as touched on in the prospecting and materials chapter, if you are able to determine a potential warm intro that is a connection (either via a social network, or just working in the same org), there is a somewhat different protocol there, but which still relies on high quality templates and outreach that make a compelling argument to the target. It just happens that you have someone adding a reputation layer of "he's a good guy and wouldn't steer you wrong" on top of your argument to the target contact.

Manual Email and Instrumentation

The most basic email outreach will be through your standard email client, whether Gmail or Outlook. This is the most laborious form of email outreach, and is fine to start, but at a minimum should involve email instrumentation via open and click tracking of the sort Yesware, Tout, and Sidekick by HubSpot provide. These tools embed a small, transparent pixel in each of your outbound emails, invisible to the recipient but which their email client (whether Gmail, Outlook, or mobile email) loads from a remote server on open. The result is that those tools know when your prospect opens that email, and can share that information with you. So too with links in your emails. These solutions will "rewrite" the hyperlinks in question, creating tracking hyperlinks unique to that specific email. So when the recipient of that email clicks on a link, routing through that tracked hyperlink on their way to the eventual target (i.e., your YouTube video), again, Yesware or Tout or whoever will see this action, and can share it with you. Yes, it feels like the NSA. Get over it. It'll help you close.

This is why I was jumping up and down about "click targets" in the Sales Materials chapter. The more juicy hyperlinks (like links to video thumbnails or to infographics or whatever. I haven't experimented with animated GIFs, but really want to.) are sitting in that email, enticing a click, the better. We care about this activity, because it shows that the prospect is interested in what you have to say. The more opens and clicks, potentially the more interest. If a prospect forwards your email to his team, and all of sudden you start seeing opens and clicks from different geographical locations (based on the IP addresses of the devices loading that pixel or clicking that link), even better! If he receives the email one day, opens and clicks on it, doesn't respond, and then two days later opens it again (which Yesware sees, again, as the email client loads that pixel again), it shows you that he's still thinking about what you had to say. He has a crush on your email. Fantastic! This tells us it's a prime time to email him again. Or call him, which we'll talk about more in a second.

This sort of email instrumentation is where there are benefits to lightweight CRMs like SalesforceIQ or Close.io, or SDR tools like SalesLoft and Outreach, which typically integrate Gmail or Exchange into the CRM. These products allow not only for easy templating (Yesware and company typically also have templating functionality), but also for open and click tracking that is baked right in (and they also record the outreach that has occurred).

Mass Mail and Drip Marketing

Nowadays, manually sent, instrumented email is table stakes. The next generation of email technology comes in the form of mass mailing and drip marketing. Brand-new Tesla versus mid-2000s Camaro. In drip marketing, which was pioneered via solutions like Marketo and Eloqua, individual email messages are dripped out to recipients over time, delivering snippets of messaging piecemeal and "nurturing" prospects, eventually driving them to conversion. Of course, this is relevant to sales as well as marketing, and so a number of software providers have stood up "lightweight drip marketing" solutions to assist sales staff. The notion of following up with prospects with whom you're trying to set an appointment is a sales best practice, but historically, it's been time-consuming to have to not only remember to do so, but then manually go back to the thread in question, reply to it, and drop in new messaging. These modern drip-marketing solutions do this for you, with fresh content, so you'll never have to send a dumb-as-nails "Just following up on this..." And these solutions are smart enough that when prospects responds to you, they drop out of the drip.

These tools can be utilized a few different ways. The most basic is mass mailing with automated follow-ups. In this approach, you can load up a set of prospects and their relevant metadata, typically in the form of an excel or CSV file, which will then be fed through a series of templates that turn that data into customize outreach emails via mail merge fields. The results can be as basic as the crappy mass mails that you're used to receiving and likely never respond to, or these can be thoughtful and advanced, making use of the demand signifier metadata that we talked about in the Prospecting chapter—like the number of potential users in-house, a calculation of how much time or money is being wasted based on some ROI metric you've calculated, or links to parts of each prospect's website. The latter requires smart prospecting and templating, but will make your outreach that much more fruitful. The former makes you look stupid and irritates your prospects, so don't do it. No one likes the guy who drives his Tesla into a wall.

An even more advanced approach involves a first outreach email that is heavily manually personalized—in addition to having basic merge fields like {!NAME}, {!COMPANY}, {!NUMBER_RECRUITERS}, {!CRM_TYPE}, {!NUMBER_PAGEVIEWS}, or what have you, you might include screenshots or custom recordings as discussed above. Or some sort of opening pleasantry that indicates a real human looked to see that they went to the University of Alabama, and that, wow, the Crimson Tide look particularly fearsome this year, and boy, what is up with Nick Saban's hair? Or all of the above. In studies, the drip-marketing vendor Outreach has seen response rates for "human-customized" emails go as high as 12% for an initial outreach, as compared to 5% for a baseline of totally unpersonalized outreach. I like to call this a "single-serving drip-marketing campaign" (is that a pour-over campaign?), where you can invest five minutes up front to knock an email out of the park.

While this level of customization executed for each in a series of messages would be overkill and totally inefficient, drip-marketing tooling lets you leverage that initial investment each time the system replies. Even if the prospect doesn't respond, the incremental drip emails will reply to that same email thread. That will give you the benefit of increased open rates, as prospects are more likely to open replies (believing that they are already participating in the thread). Moreover, as your excellently written and targeted messages show up to the prospect, she will be able to easily scroll up to the top of the thread, or look down at the quoted prior emails, to see the background, along with your initial customized outreach. In effect, your incremental emails are driving the prospect to read that first email (and, of course, the ensuing ones). So your initial five-minute investment gets leveraged at each step of the drip program. (Different vendors have this implemented differently, so make sure to double-check—Outreach in particular focuses on this approach.)

In the graph below, you can see the responsiveness over time in drip campaigns featuring varying levels of personalization (and compared to a "one-and-done" email outreach—ugh, the horror). Human-personalized initial outreach, when levered across a seven-email drip campaign, results in 30% more responses than a drip campaign with only heavy auto-personalization, and nearly 50% more responses than a drip campaign with a lightly customized first email. And 15x the responses of the one-and-done approach. If you're thinking, "Wow, it's kind of a no-brainer to adopt this approach, Pete," you're thinking about it correctly.

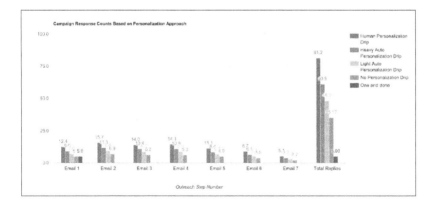

Here's that same data represented another way. Check out the differences in response counts for a 100-person campaign based on different personalization approaches:

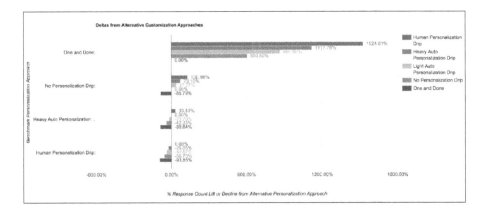

A last point about customization and context relates to "social context." In the age of LinkedIn, Facebook, and Twitter, it's fairly easy to get instantaneous context that can help demonstrate to the prospect that you've done a good job qualifying her (above and beyond the business pain context that we've already talked about). That context builds rapport, and raises the likelihood of setting the appointment. This can mean looking at things like a prospect's prior companies (did she work somewhere you worked before?), your shared LinkedIn or Facebook connections (is there someone you both know that you can use to break the ice?), or her Twitter profile (can you refer to something she tweeted recently that is fun or interesting?). This is why I like prospecting staff to grab prospects' LinkedIn profile URLs for quick and easy reference. Nick Saban's hair, a tweet about how bad the Giants are sucking, or a prospect's post about looking forward to a margarita after work—all are fair game and will help drive responses.

From a timing perspective, be thoughtful about when you want these email campaigns to fire. People get a lot of email these days, especially decision-makers who are desirable targets for many solution providers. So in addition to being awesome and personalized, your content needs to show up at a time that makes sense. Typically this means avoiding Monday mornings, when prospects will have big fat inboxes full of stuff to quickly triage. Target times when your email may be looked at as "infotainment"—10am on a Tuesday, when they have likely cleared out those inboxes, or 6am or 7am, when it might be the first thing they see on their phones while riding the bus, or even after office hours, like 7pm or 8pm. Essentially, think about low-traffic times when your email will stand out as the delightful diamond of commercial wisdom that it is!

There are a number of solutions that provide this functionality with variations on the theme. Outreach, Salesloft, PersistIQ, MixMax, Sendbloom, and others are all focused primarily on this lightweight drip-marketing functionality, while Yesware and Touthave some partial functionality in this regard, but aren't as developed. I highly recommend making use of one of these solutions to raise the volume of targeted, relevant outreach that you are able to execute as a single person—it's like having your own personal robot Market Development Rep before you staff that role.

Before we leave this section, a note on drip marketing and "spam." A lot of non-sales staff see this sort of thing and think, "My goodness, that sounds like spam!" They can be forgiven for this attitude, given that they've probably received large amounts of bullshit, untargeted outreach from crappy salespeople in their time. But that doesn't mean that you should forego a perfectly good tool because someone else has used it poorly. As noted in our Prospecting chapter, if you have done a good job of targeting prospects who are very likely to have the business pain you resolve, they will welcome your outreach. If your messaging is clear, straightforward, non-bombastic, and focused on them—with each communication adding value to their lives by teaching them something they didn't know, or offering a way of solving a problem that's been frustrating them—your outreach will be welcomed with open arms.

As a matter of fact, as seen above, the highest response rate to cold outreach emails, based on data from an Outreach study, is to the second email in your drip campaign (18% compared to 12% for first outreach). Response rates then hold steady (17%, 17%, 13%) through the fifth outreach, at which point they start to decline. In fact, by adding an "Okay, I'm breaking up with you" type email to the end of your drip campaign, you can actually prompt prospects to act. That is, they're used to sales reps continuing to follow up ad infinitum, so they feel that they always have the option to respond to you later. If you specifically say, "I'm not going to email you anymore, but I have conviction that this is relevant to you and will make you more successful in what you do," it can force a prospect to actually consider your arguments and, ideally, respond. These approaches work so well because prospects are simply used to terrible, irrelevant, one-and-done outreach from sales reps. They ignore the first outreach—but by sending a second, third, and fourth, and by making sure that those messages are relevant, you can sprint past all those other terrible sales staff.

But the onus is on you to do the work up front to make sure that your prospecting has been sound, your messaging is relevant to those well-prospected contacts, and you've structured your prospecting data in a way to make great use of sales technologies. It's not the tool that makes it spam. It's the person using it wrong that does.

CALLING

Cold-calling is the epitome of everything that scares first-time sales staff. While not face-to-face exactly, it's a synchronous interaction with the very person who can reject your solution, which, of course, your own personal worth is pretty heavily tied to. Why would I possibly want to put myself in a situation where someone could stomp on my product and, by extension, me?

For a lot of reasons, actually. Because synchronous verbal communication, miraculously, is a really rich way of communicating and gathering information. It's almost like it might be one of the linchpins of the last few hundred thousand years of human evolution!

The trick to calling on your prospects, unsurprisingly, is similar to the trick to engendering email responsiveness—make sure that your solution is relevant to their situation, get your point across with clear and concise messaging, and demonstrate that you are concerned about their situation with a customized, prospect-centric approach.

So let's shed that fear of cold-calling right now. Yes, it will take some getting used to. But remember, you're calling highly qualified contacts who have the problem you solve, and you're seeking to help them solve that problem. Who wouldn't welcome that?

Attempting Contact

Call Timing

The success of your phone outreach will often be contingent on the times at which you call. Connect rates can vary substantially depending on the day-in, day-out tempo of your prospects, so being in tune with this is helpful. For instance, if you're calling on white-collar office workers (say you're a recruiting or sales solution and are calling on Directors of Sales Operations or VPs of Talent Acquisition), then your better bets are going to be early in the morning, just as people are getting into the office, or at the end of the day. Middle of the day is tougher because people are away from their desks, in meetings, and going to or coming from lunch. Another trick can be particularly late calling. If you want to avoid gatekeepers, and get directly to a senior executive, often they are still around at 6pm or 7pm, when executive assistants have gone home.

If you're calling on small businesses, these times may be totally different. For instance, if you sell to restaurants, calling in the middle of service is a great way to piss off your potential customer! Figure out when your decision-maker's day begins (maybe it's 9am or 10am if they serve lunch, or maybe it's the 2pm or 3pm doldrums between lunch and dinner service). Because all of your customers (assuming they conform to a similar profile) will likely share this cyclicality, when you get to the point of calling against customers in multiple time zones, you can prioritize the ones whose time zone is within the raised connect-rate interval, and follow the "10am hour" as it moves from eastern to central to mountain to Pacific time. Think about what the right "day cycle" timing is and target your calling then. Otherwise the proportion of your calls that result in connects will suffer.

Context-Sensitive Timing

As discussed earlier, email instrumentation via Yesware, Tout, Outreach, and others can be particularly helpful in making your calling more effective by showing you which of your prospects have been engaging with your outreach, so you can focus your calling efforts on them.

For instance, if a drip-marketing email fires on a Tuesday at 10am, you can prioritize your Wednesday morning calling based on who opened and clicked links in that email. At a minimum, those who opened and clicked will have context for your call, and they will likely be more receptive to your messaging.

Even better are calls and follow-up emails that happen in immediate response to opens and clicks. If you're at your machine, and you see that a prospect just opened your email, give them a quick call. It does wonders for connect rates. This is where mobile sales email tools like Immediately can be especially helpful, in that you can see who has opened your email even if you're away from your computer, and call them right away.

Point-of-Contact Discovery

Calling can be particularly useful when it's not possible to get ahold of the email address of the most relevant point of contact for a given account, or if a specific point of contact wasn't readily discoverable. (SMBs, like local restaurants, auto repair shops, etc., often fall into this category.) But when calling on these types of businesses, without a specific point of contact, the first step of your engagement will likely be to locate that decision-maker, as he may not be the one answering the phone. This adds a wrinkle to the messaging in your phone scripting; now you need to sell this intermediary, this gatekeeper, on why it's a good idea for him to share the name of the decision-maker in question. Your best approach here is to use very, very simple statements of the value of your product, so someone who isn't necessarily invested with authority can quickly parse them and realize, "Hey, it's probably a good thing if I let Bob know about this." (For example, if you're Groupon, you might say, "Hi there! I'd like to be in touch with the owner, because I'd like to discuss how Groupon can make him twenty thousand dollars in one day. Who's the right person to talk to?") The goal is to make it clear to the gatekeeper that by helping you engage with the right person, he will be looked upon as a hero by the eventual decision-maker, likely his superior—and that if he doesn't, that same superior will be upset to have missed this opportunity.

Unfortunately, doing decision-maker discovery via calling can be a game of cat and mouse (even if you're Groupon!), which is why the prospecting approaches we've discussed are so helpful in shortening this exercise. And this is why solutions attacking the SMB market (like Groupon, Yelp, FreshBooks, etc.), where decision-maker identification (or even account sourcing) can be a challenge, will often rely on inbound marketing approaches of the sort HubSpot has heavily popularized. However, if there are no better ways to do so, you can call into these accounts, and seek to piece together who the relevant contact might be by asking who makes decisions about technology investment (even just getting a name is the first step), when she's typically in the office, and if you can get her email address or direct phone number. You might be wondering who would give out that sort of contact information, but you'd be amazed what you can get by just asking. Especially in conjunction with a solid gatekeeper pitch (like the Groupon example above) that convinces the person on the other end that she'll be a hero for bringing your solution to the fore (or potentially in the doghouse if she doesn't). No one wants to be responsible for barring a valuable solution, so gatekeepers are often happy passing you off so you can engage directly.

Gatekeepers and Directories

If you make contact with a gatekeeper, and you already know which point of contact you're seeking to engage, a different set of approaches is required. In this case, you're likely calling into the main switchboard. If there's a dial-by-name directory, you may be in luck and able to go straight to the desk line. Of course, there's a challenge there too—who answers their desk line nowadays? However, if you are able to get to the desk line, you may be able to connect to the target point of contact or, at worst, leave a voice mail. More on this later.

If there isn't a dial-by-name directory, and a human gatekeeper receives those switchboard calls, he's likely pretty used to receiving calls from sales professionals. In that case, it's good to just ask for the point of contact by name: "Hi there! Can you connect me to Frank?" If the organization is small enough that there is only one Frank, using just the first name will sometimes pass muster. "Ah, he knows Frank." In larger orgs, it may be more of a challenge, as you'd have to specify first and last name, which does away with that approach. That's fine. If the gatekeeper wants to guard the gate, that's his prerogative. And honestly, that's what he's there for—to make sure that decision-maker time is guarded for things that are actually relevant. Conveniently, you're only calling to discuss something that is relevant, so truth is on your side. It's just a question of making that clear. You'll likely get "Is he expecting your call?" Lying won't benefit you, nor will being unpleasant to gatekeepers. They deal with pushy sales reps (who may have done poor prospecting and be approaching with an irrelevant pitch) all day long, so you can really differentiate yourself by being pleasant, cheerful, and respectful. Plus, it's good karma. Deliver the gatekeeper the same shortened pitch about why your offering is relevant to Frank ("Twenty thousand in a single day. Sounds great, right? I want to get ten minutes on Frank's calendar to discuss."), and why he'll be a hero for letting you through. If he's not biting, you can always ask to leave Frank a voice mail, which the gatekeeper will typically be happy to facilitate (he doesn't like shooting you down, either). If he's willing to put you through (with or without a pitch), it's also good to ask for the direct number for future reference: "Hey, can I get Frank's direct line in case I get disconnected, so I don't have to bother you again? Thanks!"

Voice Mails

Generally speaking, when you call, you're probably not going to connect with the person you're seeking to engage, which can feel pretty inefficient. That's why calling is often more like verbal email (via voice mail) than anything else. In the Sales Materials chapter, we spoke to voice mail templates. Short and sweet and loaded with personalization related to the research you've done on the prospect, the magnitude of business pain you think they have, the potential benefit of talking with you, and the fact that you're the founder of the company, seeking to learn. Of course you should leave your contact information, though it's not going to be super common for prospects to return your call. Returning calls is a huge pain compared to just hitting "reply" in an email, which, again, makes voice mail behave more like audio email than anything else. Speaking of which, it's more and more common for folks to have their work voice mail set up in a way that forwards an audio message (and maybe even a transcription) to their email. So think about your voice mail being consumed in that format.

There are other sneaky approaches to voice mail, like not actually leaving much context, and instead saying something along the lines of "Hey, Frank, this is Pete. Call me back. 650-892-4475." Or even skeezier, "Hey, this is Pete returning your call. Call me back at 650-892-4475." (That last one is like adding a fake "Re:" prefix on emails, to trick the prospect into thinking he's already participating in a back-and-forth). While this sort of thing can be employed by market development staff, it's a little more advanced than you probably need to implement. Instead, the straightforward voice mail, patterned after your outreach emails, is probably your best bet. And importantly, always use voice mail in conjunction with email; if your voice mail is well formed, and well delivered, it may inspire your prospect to simply hit "reply" on the email that came in at the same time.

Live Messages

Lastly, there may be occasions when the gatekeeper offers to take down a "live message" for the point of contact—that is, write down your information and share it with Frank. This is typically not a great idea, in that the transmission of information here will end up looking like a kindergarten game of "telephone." Of course, you don't want to tell the gatekeeper that you have little confidence that he'll be able to pass along your message appropriately. A good approach is to instead frame it as a benefit to him for you to present the message yourself. Something along the lines of "That's so nice of you! It's kind of involved. Would you be open to sharing Frank's email address with me so I can just send it to him directly?" If that fails, often the gatekeeper will be willing to share his own email address as an intermediary, which you can then email with an amazing, super personalized first-outreach email (instrumented with Yesware, etc. so you can see when Frank opens it). Of course, if you have Frank's email address already, this isn't necessary; instead, it's a better idea to ask to be passed along to his voice mail. Or, you can try for the best of both worlds: "You know, it's kind of involved. How about this: Just note that Pete called and wants to discuss how to make your business twenty thousand dollars in a day—here's my phone number—and that the details are in his voice mail. And then you can patch me through to his voice mail. That saves you a bunch of scribbling." Or something to this effect.

Making Contact

Because live-connect rates are so low, it can often come as a surprise when you actually reach your prospect. Like, "Whoa! Why did you pick up the phone?!" In this context, you have about thirty seconds to sell her on an appointment, using the framework you put in place in your phone script. The most important thing to remember is that you're not selling the product on this call. You're selling the opportunity to spend a limited amount of time to understand the prospect's pains better, help her learn something new and valuable, and potentially solve a big issue she has. You would like to get on her calendar for ten to twenty minutes in the near future.

If you've been doing a good job with your email-based outreach, ideally the person on the other end of the phone has context on who you are and what it is you're up to. However, by no means can you rely on that to be the case. These folks get a lot of emails, and it's likely that yours—regardless of how well personalized and excellently and concisely written—have been going straight to their archives.

Once you deliver your scripted pitch, typically the response will fall into one of three buckets: success, outright rejection, and something in the middle, involving various types of objections—that is, not an outright rejection, but not agreement either.

Success

If your excellent prospecting research, coupled with compelling phone messaging, piques the prospect's interest and she agrees to a follow-up call at a more convenient time, you've won. That was the immediate goal, and you did it. High five!

However, in your excitement, don't forget to get all the info you need before you get off the phone. First and foremost is calendar availability. Don't rely on scheduling over email; this is a rookie error—being so excited (or scared) that you pull a "Great, I'll email you some times that could work!" That turns into email hell, and you just blew that demo you set. Instead, the approach should be "Wonderful! Are you in front of your calendar? I have availability on Thursday and Friday morning, if that could work for you. It would be best for us to block thirty minutes of time. Excellent, I'll send you a meeting invite for that time with the relevant details in it. Make sure you accept it when it comes through so I know that time works and the appointment gets on your calendar. Thanks so much. I'm excited to talk more about this with you!" Make sure that you're not setting the appointment too far in advance; anything over a week out heavily degrades attendance rates. Usually a good time frame is a couple days out; that raises the likelihood that the prospect will have an opening, but reduces the lag in which excitement can temper, lowering attendance rates.

Beyond calendaring, this is also the opportunity to get an email address, direct phone, mobile phone, or other pieces of contact information that you might need. (This is not the time for full discovery, though. We'll get into that in the "pitching" chapter.) If you didn't yet have the prospect's email address, you'll definitely need it to send a meeting invite, and it's also useful for sending a reminder email ahead of the meeting. And if the prospect doesn't make the meeting, you're going to want to have a direct phone number to call and remind her, or to follow up after the fact and get the meeting back on the calendar.

Lastly, this is an opportunity to potentially involve others in the call beyond the individual point of contact you're addressing. Again, you should be targeting the relevant decision-maker that you sniffed out during prospecting, but oftentimes if you have sufficiently excited the decision-maker you can pull in potential users, or influencers. For instance, if you connected with the VP of Sales and she's excited to learn more, but you know that there's a Sales Operations Lead and a couple of Sales Managers at the company, you could ask if the decision-maker would like them included in the call. If so, gather their contact information, primarily email, to put them on the meeting invite.

Hot Transfers

In rarer cases, the prospect may actually want to do the demo then and there: "Well, I have time right now. How about now?" If you were surprised to connect to your prospect, this one will probably really knock you off kilter! In sales land, this is known as a "hot transfer," and it's both fairly rare and a two-edged sword. On the one hand, it's great that the prospect is so interested in what you're doing and how you've described it that she's open to spending thirty minutes with you then and there, and you certainly don't want to say no to her on that count! On the other hand, you likely didn't do all the pre-call planning that you would ahead of a scheduled demo, so your level of personalization and preparation may be wanting. But this doesn't mean that you should do deep pre-call planning ahead of each cold call, thinking that you might end up in a hot transfer situation. No way! Most of the time you're not going to connect, so all that prep time would be hugely wasted. Rather, the approach I like here is to proceed with the hot transfer demo, but treat this as a "demo lite." Use the time to do your relevant discovery, and to offer a preview of what a fuller meeting might be, as a means by which to "sell" a full demo for which you're able to better prepare. Set that expectation ahead of time by noting what you would typically do for a full demo (more on that later), and what you're going to do here. In this manner, you can capitalize on the prospect's immediate interest and availability, while lessening the impact of the preparation deficit.

Rejection

If you follow the prospecting and messaging instruction we've already covered, the amount of out-and-out rejection you encounter shouldn't be terribly high. Prospects don't like to completely close the door on something, but rather prefer the "not now" approach to forestalling decision-making (even if it's the tiny decision of putting a meeting on the calendar!).

If you are seeing a bunch of out-and-out rejection, you may not be getting your point across, you may be targeting prospects poorly, or some other issue. In that case, listen for patterns of objection in your interactions that can help you proactively avoid these rejections. For instance, at TalentBin, recruiters and heads of talent were so used to being cold-called by agency recruiters that whenever they heard something with the word "talent" in it, they immediately thought "agency recruiter, reject." We got to the point where we might start a call with "I'm not calling from a recruiting agency, so let's just get that out of the way up front!", which had the added benefit of adding some disarming humor to the call. If you are commonly hearing a standard type of rejection, see if you can take a similar proactive approach.

With that said, you will certainly encounter rejection when you catch someone on a bad day and they're not interested in hearing anything. But there are ways of turning those interactions to your advantage to "win the call"—that is, make progress in pushing the prospect down the path to becoming a customer, even if it's the littlest step.

Firstly, you shouldn't take rejections as "never," but rather as "not now." If you think about every massive company out there, the Salesforces, LinkedIns, and others, there were thousands of prospects who rejected initial outreach and eventually became happy customers. When you encounter out-and-out aggressive rejection, treat it as an opportunity to make sure your goal is understood and give the prospect another chance to soften: "Okay, I understand. It sounds like this is something that might not be a priority right now. My only goal was to seek to understand your business pain (good to specify it, like "how your technical hiring efforts are going" or "how your organization currently handles backdoor hires and missed fees") and see how we can help with a fifteen-minute scheduled call. I know that you weren't expecting my call, but are you sure you wouldn't be open to a conversation at a more appropriate time?" If this gambit doesn't work, then it's fine to retreat to fight another day, typically in the form of "I understand. While I'm confident that we may be able to help your organization be more effective, we can table this for now. It will be my responsibility to be in touch at a more appropriate time." This is probably in stark contrast to what you want to do, which is say, "Fine! Continue living in the dark ages and wasting time and money on the dumb way you're currently doing things." Yeah. Don't do that, regardless of how satisfying it might feel.

This approach achieves a couple things. First, while you acquiesce to the prospect's request to disengage, you're doing it on your terms, stating your conviction that this is something that is highly likely to be relevant and helpful to him, and you provide him an "out" in the event he changes his tune. Further, you're characterizing this as something that is inevitable. That is, "I'm not going to give up. I believe this is relevant to you, so you're going to have to evaluate this on the merits, rather than dismissing it out of hand." This characterization of inevitability—"I'll be back" in the words our friend Arnold—sets the prospect up to be more attuned to your future emails and calls.

After disengaging from the call, you should absolutely send a follow-up email. It should be a subtle variation of your initial outreach messaging, crossed with some of the conciliatory messaging you used in your call retreat (templated, of course—"Rejected Call Template" sounds like a good title to me!). Thank them for their time and characterize why you thought your solution was relevant, with metrics supporting what you think it could do for the organization. Then close with a call to action to get something on the calendar (you're still selling the demo at this point, even though you retreated from the call), along with a statement echoing that you look forward to being in touch in the future. Following up with the prospect like this gives him an opportunity to marinate on what you spoke about on the phone, and take that "out" you gave him to actually get something on the calendar. You'd be amazed how many people who seemed hell-bent on getting off the phone change their tune, and decide that they'd like to get on that demo after all, when delivered this sort of follow-up. It's not luck. It's that your call cut through the noise, followed by a little bit of footwork to capitalize on the focus you engendered.

Objection

The vast majority of your interactions will fall in between the extremes of success and outright rejection. And typically they will involve objections to setting an appointment. Your job here is to handle those objections—to help the prospect understand why his concern, while valid, is unfounded in this case—and drive to setting the appointment. The last thing you should do in the face of objections is comply, and disengage, as tempting as it may be to get out of an awkward, conflicted situation. This is just where the fun begins! In fact, rather than problematic, objections are great. They mean that your prospect is engaged, and at least thinking about the problem you're addressing. They're giving you a chance to make a better case. Every time the prospect raises an objection, it's an opportunity to ask more questions and engage in a better conversation about their situation, and where your solution can potentially help.

The problem with preparing you for these objections is that they're going to be specific to your solution's space. Sales-productivity solutions will have different objections from recruitment-branding solutions, which will even have different objections from passive-candidate recruiting solutions. So you'll just have to discover them as you go. But, importantly, you need to make sure that you are recording the objections you hear, and your responses to them. That will ensure that as you encounter them more in the future, you are able to handle them with ease—and later, when you hire staff to help parallelize your efforts, you'll already have done the hard work for them.

With that said, there are some standard objections that people will use to try to get off the phone with you. If you're prepared for them, you'll be better positioned to get that meeting on the calendar.

"Call Me Later."

This is typically a gambit to get off the phone without having to actually tell you "no." Variants are things like "Can you call me in a quarter?" The problem with this is that if you comply, when it comes time to call the prospect in a quarter, what do you think his response will be? That's right. "Call me in a quarter." You can guess where this ends up. Now extend this across other prospects with this objection. Your end game becomes no demos, ever.

So rather than complying immediately, it's better to flip it around on him. "I'd be happy to do that. But if possible, maybe we could spend thirty seconds right now to make sure that this is relevant to you. And if it's not, in a quarter, I won't unnecessarily bug you, and you won't have to deal with irrelevant outreach. Great, right?" Then proceed with some lightweight discovery and qualification questions. Given that you've done a good job prospecting, and you know this prospect's pain points, you should be able to build a good case quickly for getting a demo on the calendar.

The key to this interaction is a small negotiation trade-off. Instead of getting off the phone immediately, you held out the carrot of never having to hear from you again, which the prospect "bought" by giving you thirty seconds. And then it's on you to blow him away with your research and messaging.

"I Don't Have the Budget."

This is tricky. We talked about demand-characteristic qualification in the Prospecting chapter, but we haven't talked about budget qualification yet; we'll do that more when we discuss discovery questions and pitching. The short of it is that it's a good thing to know that a prospect has money to spend on a solution and knows what the process is for procuring that solution. If an organization truly has no ability to pay for things, it's not a good use of time to pitch them, which is why budget is the B in the "BANT" qualification framework (budget, authority, need, timeline).

With that said, it's highly unlikely that the speaker of this objection is actually saying, "We don't spend money on solutions." Rather, this is a variation of "Call me later," and should be heard as "We may or may not have budget right now, but I'm saying that I don't have money to spend on the thing you want me to spend it on." The best way to handle this is with a response along the lines of "That's not a problem, because I really just want to understand more about your organization's way of <your problem space here>. If it turns out we're relevant, there will be time to talk about that later. Based on what I saw about your <signifier of demand>, I am confident that a ten-minute conversation will definitely be worth your time! Can we schedule something for Thursday?"

"Just Send Me Some Information."

This is another version of "I just want to get off the phone, but I'll throw you a bone by pretending you can send me information and I'll read it." The problem with this, of course, is that there is no commitment to actually consume the information you send. It is very likely it will go in the digital round file.

The right way to approach this, as with the "call me in a quarter" objection, is to capitalize on the fact that you're on the phone right now. Something along the lines of "I'm totally happy to do that. But if I do, I'm going to do a bang-up job, and it'll take me thirty minutes to put together something very personalized to you. I don't want to do that if our solution is not relevant. Can I take thirty seconds to explain what we do, and ask some questions to make sure this is a relevant conversation? That way if it's not, I won't be in your inbox chasing you and asking about information that wasn't even helpful." Again, you're trading the prospect time right now for the promise of avoiding pestering later—coupled with a guilt component of "Do you really want to waste my time? That's not nice." If you've already explained what you do and how it's relevant, you've qualified the prospect beyond a shadow of a doubt, and they still say, "Just send me some information," take the approach of selling the demo. Try something like "Well, I'm happy to do that. But honestly, given that I know this is relevant to you, a scheduled demo will really be a much better way of making sure you're fully informed. I promise that you'll learn things that are very relevant to <the thing they do>." This way, you're taking the request for "more information" and saying, "No problem! The best way for you to get the information you seek is on a synchronous, concurrent demo." Pair that with a promise of downside prevention—a promise that the prospect will not only get the information she just stated she wanted, but will also become a more competent professional. Who doesn't want to become better at their job?

"Oh, We Already Use <*The Competition*>."

The great thing about this objection is that the speaker is admitting that she has the problem that your solution addresses, and moreover, that she spends money to solve it. Fantastic! She just partially qualified herself. First, congratulate her on being a student of the game and clued in. Then, all you have to do is succinctly demonstrate why it's worth the time to look at your solution as a substantially better way to solve her problem.

So, for instance, if someone said to a TalentBin rep, "We already use LinkedIn Recruiter for our technical recruiting search and outreach," the rep might respond with "That's great! LinkedIn Recruiter has historically been the benchmark for passive technical recruiting. The good news is that TalentBin can help you find ten times the number of candidates in your area, complete with their personal email addresses, and with no limits on email outreach, unlike InMail. Sounds pretty helpful, right? I'd love to get twenty minutes on the calendar to show you how TalentBin is like LinkedIn Recruiter, with rocket boosters attached."

"Do You Have <X, Y, or Z Feature>?"

In this situation, the prospect starts to get deep into features and what your product has or doesn't have. This is actually a really great place to be, if you handle it correctly. It's not that the prospect is objecting to your solution, per se, it's just that he's blocking your ability to get a formal appointment on the calendar. This is kind of like an abortive "hot transfer" as discussed above, where instead of hearing the whole pitch, having his mental model set correctly, and going through proper discovery questions, the prospect is attempting to have "demo by a thousands cuts."

The best way to handle this is to "assumptively close" on setting the appointment, as he's partially admitted his interest in and familiarity with the problem and solution. Something like "These are fantastic questions, and show you really know the space inside and out. Typically folks find it more efficient and get a lot more out of putting twenty minutes on the calendar at a set time. Do you have twenty minutes on Thursday or Friday where we could slot that in?"

"How Much Does It Cost?"

The good thing about prospects asking about cost is that they are admitting that they have the problem, understand to some extent how your solution fits in, and are trying to get a sense of whether the cost fits the pain. The problem, though, is that there's still a huge information asymmetry here—you don't yet clearly know the magnitude of the prospect's pain (because you haven't asked your discovery questions), and the prospect isn't anywhere close to understanding all the ways in which your solution can help address this pain. So if you immediately jump to pricing—say, $10,000 a year—she has very little information with which to make a judgment about whether the value the solution provides is worth more (ideally far more) than the price. So you can end up in situations where the prospect responds, "Whoa, that's way too much." But let's say you're HIRABL, and your solution finds contingency recruiting fees worth $30,000 a pop. A customer passing on a solution that could make them $100,000 for just a $10,000 investment would be a tragedy, but you'd be amazed how common this is as a result of cost objections getting in the way.

The best way to avoid this is to not fall into that trap to begin with. Instead, parry the question and drive to a demo with something like "While the solution does have a cost, it's really contingent on a variety of factors, associated with how much value a given customer would get out of it. Typically people find it most effective to schedule a twenty-minute demo so we can get a better sense of whether the solution is relevant and how helpful it could be to your business. Do you have twenty minutes this Thursday or Friday for that conversation?"

"I Can't Make That Decision."

This objection can indicate one of two things, and it's important to resolve which. That is, is this person actually the relevant point of contact, and trying to dismiss you? Or is she truly not the relevant contact, and you need to find the correct one (and potentially refactor how you're doing prospecting if you're calling on the wrong people)? The challenge is that these two things can look the same if you don't ask the right questions.

The way to sort this out is to assume that the account does have the pain you're solving, but that this person could indeed be the wrong point of contact. Drive to sorting out who you should be talking to with something like "Got it! Well, it sounds like this is relevant to <company name>, but that you might be the wrong person to talk to about it. I tried to use LinkedIn to figure out who would be the most relevant contact, but I guess I got it wrong. Which of your colleagues should I be engaging instead?"

You can potentially refer to the person's supposed manager—for instance, if you're Immediately, the sales-first mobile email and CRM client, and you're talking to a Director of Sales Operations, you might refer to the VP of Sales, to whom the contact you're talking to likely reports. Or potentially the CFO. Or shoot, maybe even the CEO. This tactic helps indicate where you're going to go next if they don't tell you, so they might as well be straight. If that person is indeed the right point of contact, and you sound like you're going to show up on the CEO's doorstep saying, "Jeff said that he's not the right one to discuss this, so I'm here to talk to you," that's probably not going to look great for Jeff. So he might as well own up that he's the right point of contact. And now you're in the same situation as the "I don't have budget" objection, where it's less an issue of "not possible" and more a question of "is the timing right?"

If it's the second case, and you're actually targeting the wrong person, the contact you're talking to doesn't have much reason to obscure who the relevant contact would be. And, again, by indicating who you'll be targeting next, you create a poor best alternative to him giving you the correct name—that is, if you show up on the CEO's or CFO's or VP of Sales's doorstep indicating that Jeff sent you, and she's not the right person, well, the CEO, CFO, or VP of Sales will probably not be too stoked. So better for Jeff to just be straight with you and point you in the right direction. At this point, Jeff is acting like a gatekeeper, and you should simply employ the tactics described above to help him understand how beneficial passing you along to the right point of contact will be. Make Jeff look like a hero for bringing your solution to the fore!

SETTING UP THE APPOINTMENT

Meeting Invites

Once you have an appointment time and contact information, you need to send the relevant details for the meeting. For very early-stage customer conversations (like your first dozen customers), I'm a fan of going to visit the individual in person. As discussed in the Prospecting chapter, this is why initially targeting accounts in your own geography is helpful, even if the price point of your solution means that your scaled go-to-market will likely be via inside sales. If an in-person meeting is not tenable, you'll need a means of digital presentation. ClearSlide and join. me are good for this, as we'll discuss more later.

Whether the meeting will be digital or in person, all of the relevant coordinates need to be included in the meeting invite you send to the prospect. You absolutely must send a calendar meeting invite. You cannot rely on the prospect to put the relevant details on his calendar, and this is a convenient way to both put the meeting on his calendar and deliver the pertinent meeting details. Put the location details (whether online or offline) in the location section of the meeting invite, in addition to the description section (yes, repeat them)—something like "Online meeting via join.me. Click this link to join: *http://www.join.me/*

yourusername." Be sure to put a brief agenda in the description section, after the duplicate location coordinates. Lastly, make sure to include a rich title description that reminds both the prospect and you of the goal of the meeting, like "Twitter & TalentBin Online Demo" or "HIRABL & Robert Half In-Person Demo."

Also consider including "teaser" material, like a demo video hyperlink, in the body of the meeting invite. This will help prospects get excited about attending, but shouldn't give them enough information that they feel it can stand in for the actual demo.

Finally, make sure to invite all the relevant participants who were surfaced in your call. This is a good example:

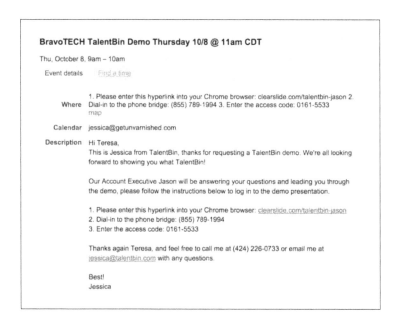

Time Blocking

After sending the relevant meeting invite to the prospect, make sure to block fifteen to thirty minutes on your own calendar both immediately before and after the appointment to ensure you have proper time to prepare and to follow up. If you don't, there's a risk that those slots may get calendared over, and you'll find yourself double-booked when you should be executing activities in support of your meeting. We'll discuss preparation activities in more depth later, but you want to make sure that you have the time to treat every appointment with the seriousness it deserves. You would be amazed by the lack of preparation some reps exhibit in approaching meetings that not only represent tens to hundreds of thousands of dollars of potential revenue but, moreover, are the culmination of hours of appointment-setting activities. At TalentBin, we used to call demos "five-thousand-dollar bills," because with our average contract value and win rate, each demo represented $5,000. This joking terminology helped focus the appropriate amount of attention on the importance of preparation, execution, and follow-up. Lastly, if you're going to be traveling to the meeting, make sure you block appropriate travel time so you get there with plenty of time to spare.

Remindering

Part of appointment setting is making sure that people actually show up to the meeting. This is more of an issue with digital meetings, because the individual needs to "come" to your join.me or ClearSlide room. And while attendance is somewhat helped by traveling to the prospect, the worst-case scenario can still happen if the prospect is double-booked. You wasted travel time and weren't able to complete the appointment. The solution to both of these outcomes is to sufficiently remind the prospect with a good amount of time. You can do this in the meeting invite by setting reminders; I like fifteen minutes ahead of the meeting. Setting one further out than that can be dangerous, because calendar-sent reminders are typically read by prospects as "This is happening right now"; if you set a reminder too early, or set multiple reminders, you can end up with prospects showing up multiple hours early. And unhappy about it. So using calendar-based notifications as anything other than immediate reminders can be a crapshoot. A better approach is email-based reminders. Use something like Yesware or Boomerang's "Send Later" functionality to stage a reminder email to send early in the morning of the meeting in question. You just have to make sure that if the meeting ends up being moved, you go into your "Scheduled Emails" and modify the date for the staged email.

Aside from ensuring that prospects show up, reminder emails are also another opportunity to set expectations, especially for a first call. Something like, "Hey, Sarah. Looking forward to speaking with you and going over TalentBin. I understand that when we reached out to you to schedule this call, you had expressed specific interest in learning more about boosting candidate response rates and managing existing candidates. I will cover these in depth with you." This not only provides guidance on what's going to be covered (so the prospect doesn't go rogue on you), but also is an opportunity to tease the content.

CADENCING: PUTTING IT ALL TOGETHER

It's a rare situation where your first email or first call results in a prospect getting back to you and agreeing to an appointment. Instead, you'll need to implement a series of outreach actions targeting your prospects, typically alternating between emails, calls, and voice mails. In sales, this interleaving of outreach actions over time is known as a "cadence."

You can of course implement this yourself via your lightweight Google Sheet CRM, or in a more formal fashion through an actual CRM. Or, if you want to get really crazy, there is a set of solutions that are designed specifically to orchestrate this outreach cadence—two primary players being Outreach and SalesLoft. Both have pricing that accommodates an individual inexpensively and can help you be much more efficient in your appointment-setting workflow.

Regardless of whether you're doing it yourself or using an orchestration system, typically you want to alternate emailing and calling. For instance, that might be an initial email and call on day one, followed by a call on day two, and then maybe a call and a voice mail on day three. From there, you might skip a day, and then email on day five, followed by an "I'm breaking up with you" email on day seven. By no means is this a cut-and-dried approach—you could decide to do calls with follow-up emails every other day, or some other permutation, if it works for you. To some extent, this will be related to how much content you have to share. If you have a lot of great things to say about your solution, and you have lots of video snippets you can add to consecutive emails, your cadence could potentially be longer and perhaps more frequent.

In addition to pure time-based cadencing, you can involve contextual data into this process as well. That is, part of your cadence could be reviewing the previous day's opens and clicks and prioritizing those prospects for calls. Or it could mean breaking out of your cadence to immediately call a prospect who opened an email when you see the alert. Or it could mean sending an immediate follow-up email to a prospect who just opened one of your emails. All of this contextual activity can raise connect rates and appointment-close rates by focusing on prospects who are already thinking about your solution.

Whatever strategy you employ, it is important to realize that multiple touch points, and a system that requires you to work through them, are core to being successful here. Having a cadence compels you to do the actual wood chopping to connect to your prospects, where you will have a chance to book them for an appointment.

REFERRAL PROSPECTING

With the advent of social networks like LinkedIn and Facebook, it has become far easier to understand who someone knows, and thus, could potentially refer you to, than ever before. This can be helpful for prospecting, and reduce friction for getting your foot in the door to set an appointment. Doing this at small scale can be a great way to initially supercharge your pipeline, but it will eventually run out of steam, in that you, your team, your investors, and so on will eventually run dry. So while it can't be a long term solution necessarily, it can help early on.

Connection Discovery

First, note that referral prospecting is not about selling to anyone who will take a meeting because they know someone in your organization. Rather, it is about using relationships within your organization to more easily access accounts that you know are qualified and have the pain your solution solves. So just be clear on which direction the causality runs here.

That said, there are two ways you do this. One is with contact connections and the other is with account connections. In the first case, you look at the target

How to do this? We will discuss a more manual process first, before talking about ways to do this in a more automated, scalable way. First, LinkedIn and Facebook connect with everyone in your organization, your investors, and your advisors. This will make it such that when you look at a prospect's LinkedIn or Facebook profile, you'll be able to see if any of your organization's stakeholders are shared connections.

Once this is done, visit the LinkedIn profile of decision maker prospects you identified in your prospecting exercises. If you want to just test this out, start with 100 decision makers, like Directors of Talent or VPs of Sales or CFOs or whatever the decision-maker is for your solution, and see which of your organization's stakeholders are joint connections. Note which of those stakeholders are potential referrers, as we'll be using it later.

Once you've done this, reach out to each of those joint connection via email, ask them if they would be open to connecting you with the target in question, specifically noting who I want to get in contact with, why it will be valuable to that target (that is, not a waste of their time), and lastly noting to the potential referrer that if they're willing to connect you, you'll send an introduction request email with full context to forward along. If a given shared connection is indicated for more than one target contact, aggregate all the targets together to note to them all at once who you'd like their help engaging with.

The other, more exhaustive, way you can do this is to sit together with each of these stakeholders, and together manually go through their LinkedIn networks. This can take an hour or two, but will invariably be worth it. This approach is particularly helpful in that you can be more thorough than the approach above—however it requires a stakeholder to sit with you, so can be more friction, but it can be worth it—and while you're going through their connections you can look for titles that are attractive, even if it's not a "VP of Talent", which would be your ideal contact, if instead they know a "Recruiter" or "Recruiting Manager" at the target company, that can be better than nothing, and, failing that, you can look for senior staff who work at a target company, even if they're not in the right part of the org.

That is, to use our recruiting example again, even if a staffer or advisor isn't connected to a single "VP of Talent" or "Director of Recruiting", he might be connected to a peer of that contact in the target organization. So look for titles like "VP" or "Director" at organizations that would be qualified. As you're going through contacts together, you may be able to quite easily identify some of these target organizations by name, but even if you can't, just log the LinkedIn profile of the relevant contact, and you can go back and qualify their organization after the fact. The goal of this session with your colleague is to quickly identify relevant contacts that they would be willing to introduce you to—you can do other legwork later.

When I say log these profiles as you're going, it doesn't have to be complicated. Just stand up a Google Spreadsheet and while you sit with your referrer, just copy and paste the LinkedIn URLs into cells for you to later prioritize and go through—typically it can be easier just have them log into LinkedIn on your laptop and you can drive, and all they have to say is "Yeah, that person's great" or "No, I don't know her well."

Contact Outreach

After this session is done, go back through the relevant contacts, and qualify their orgs to ensure that they'd be a fit for your solution. Again, we don't want to be introduced to organizations that don't have the pain we solve—it will be a waste of our time, and theirs. Once we have that list, you're going to send the referring stakeholder an introduction request email for each of the target contacts. That is, we're going to make it as easy as possible for them to just forward something along with their compliments. We're not going to rely on them to act or come up with messaging, or anything like that. We want this to be as low friction as possible.

This email should include a subject like "Intro to <target contact's name>?" and within the email should detail why you want to get introduced to them, and how it will be valuable to them. Specifically, you should characterize why you know their organization is qualified for your solution, and a terse statement of the clear value it would provide and the problems it would solve for their organization. So not dissimilar to the outreach emails above where we characterize the research we've done. But in this case, we're making it easy for our referrer to just hit "forward" and pass the outreach along, or just CC you into the thread, along with their comments as to why you're a worthwhile and trustworthy person to connect with. That is, our goal is simply to use our referrer as a reputation provider—they are validating that we are legit, and approving the statements we make in our introduction request email.

When you send the introduction request along, use something like Yesware or other email tracking services to put a tracking pixel into the email. This way you can see if indeed the email was forwarded along, by seeing how many unique IP addresses opened the email.

If your referrer CC's you into the email thread, be ready to quickly put them to BCC, and send a thoughtful quick request for a call, ideally providing a set of times and dates a week out or so, or, if the target is a peer of your ultimate target—i.e., this is a case where the target is the Director of Customer success, and you want a referral into the Head of Recruiting— quickly note that, and who that ultimate target person is (you should have sniffed that out ahead of time, and potentially could have noted that in your intro request). But speed is of the essence, in that you want to look like you're on top of things.

If you don't hear back from the target of your intro request, all is not lost. I typically recommend that you go directly at the target contact, using the same email thread, and take another shot at convincing them you're worth take a call with. Use the same email thread because it will have the reputation value of your referrer being willing to introduce you. But after that point, good to move on to another contact.

Typically it's a nice touch to hook up your referrer with a gift card for taking the time to go through all of her contacts with you. Then if you end up closing a deal based on her referral, well, then maybe add another gift card on top of the original!

The above is a more manual way of going about this, but if you want to get more scalable, you can use software like Teamable to consolidate all the contacts of your staff, advisor, investors, and so forth into a unified database that you can query for titles and company names, and will reduce friction in the email outreach part of this process. Given that these referral deals can move very quickly if properly executed, the return on investment on dedicated software to facilitate it can be very compelling.

INBOUND LEAD CAPTURE & RESPONSE PREVIEW

The last thing I want to cover on appointment setting is the basics of inbound lead capture and response. We'll get into this in more depth in the following chapter, but want to touch on a number of key points, briefly.

As a result of your outbound appointment-setting activity, invariably you will generate what is known as "inbound" interest. That is, people will read your emails and click on the links to your website to learn more. They'll listen to your voice mail, open Google, and search for your solution. And if your website, along with your primary outreach materials, does a good job convincing them it's worth engaging, you'll want to make sure that you can take advantage of that and easily allow them to become "inbound leads."

The basic requirement for capturing these leads is a means by which someone on your website can get in touch to express interest and engage with you. We'll talk more about lead capture forms in the next chapter, but to start this can be as simple as a big button that says "Request a demo," with a mailto: hyperlink to send an email to <sales@yourcompany.com>. If you want to get more involved, maybe even utilize the "subject" and "content" tags to pre-fill some information like "Demo Request for <Product Name>," so the prospect doesn't have to write anything. The more advanced version can be a Google Form linked from that button. Seriously, this doesn't need to be rocket surgery to start. You want prospects to be on that page, say, "Huh, yeah, this does sound good. I would like to learn more. <Click>," and be on their way.

The next step is making sure you know someone's trying to get in touch with you. An easy version of this is an email notification that is generated from whatever form or mailto setup you choose. The notifications should show up somewhere you know you'll be able to check on a fairly frequent basis. I like email notifications that are automatically foldered, such that when I pop into my email, I can see if that folder has gone bold with a little unread number count next to it.

Lastly, the most important thing about inbound leads is that you need to respond to them fast. We'll talk about qualification of inbound leads later, but even ahead of that, it's critical to respond to inbound leads as quickly as they come in. Don't let them wait around—they're excited now. At a minimum, you need to start the conversation immediately. Otherwise you're not capitalizing on all that hard work you did garnering their interest. Grab ahold of it, and set the appointment!

In summary, business-to-business sales are very rarely a "one-call close" situation. Regardless of what you may have seen in Boiler Room. Rather, it's a stepwise process that starts with identification, and then progresses to selling the prospect on a more formal evaluation. Appointment setting is the way to make that happen. Use thoughtful, methodical outreach strategies, and you will be putting appointments on your own calendar like a machine, teeing yourself to slam them shut come demo time.

CHAPTER 6

Early Inbound Lead Capture & Response

INTRODUCTION

I don't want to get too deep into inbound marketing, because when you're very early in your go-to-market, it's usually pretty unlikely that people will know who you are, what you do, or that they need you. This is the challenge with selling innovative solutions early on—if no one knows they have the problem you solve, or that there is a solution like yours that can solve that problem, they're not going to be Googling for you, or stumbling across your site.

Creating content, like blog posts, tweets, infographics, and such, and making sure that they are well SEO'd to engender inbound leads at scale, is what is known as "inbound marketing." This is a more advanced form of lead generation that we'll get into in a later chapter, as it's typically not appropriate for a very early-stage go-to-market. (You'd be producing a bunch of content for people who aren't looking for it...). There can be exceptions where you're attacking an existing market for cheaper—kind of like Hubspot took the power of marketing automation like Marketo and Eloqua, and brought it to the SMB and mid-market. But I find that these are often the exception, especially when we're talking about acquiring your first 100 customers.

When you do get more advanced, there are lots of resources to assist with this, not least Mark Roberge's book, The Sales Acceleration Formula, chronicling analytics-driven sales powered by a robust inbound marketing machine. It's no surprise that this come from the former Chief Revenue Officer at Hubspot, the company that has done some of the most impressive work at popularizing inbound marketing as a practice.

However, at this early stage, even though you won't be focused on manufacturing content for inbound marketing at scale, you will still need a minimum viable inbound lead capture process to capitalize on your outbound appointment-setting activity. Why? Well, if your content and messaging are well executed, your outreach will actually end up driving people back to your website, where, if they are convinced by the messaging there, they could easily request a demo. I like to call this "outbound inbound," and leads generated that way are some of the best inbound leads you can get—you know that you are only targeting qualified accounts, so inbound leads originating from your prospecting lists are bound to be strong.

Standard inbound leads, on the other hand, are a two-edged sword. On the one hand, they're fantastic because they have a lot of "intent." That is, prospects are requesting a demo because they're convinced that they are interested by what you are doing, and are actively asking you to sell to them. What could be better than that? Well, the downside of inbound leads is that it's the requester who is making this assessment, and he might not be super informed as to what makes someone qualified for your solution. So while he's excited to talk to you, you might not be excited to talk to him.

INBOUND LEAD QUALIFICATION

As we discussed when we covered qualification in the Prospecting chapter, you want to be focused on potential customers that have all the characteristics required to have success with your solution—namely the business pain points that you solve and the staff who would use your solution. If they don't meet those criteria, you don't really want to spend your time talking to them. Even if they end up buying, they're not going to have success and they're not going to be happy. Not with your solution, and not with you for selling it to them when you should have known better. Much better for you to instead funnel them away—giving them a good experience even when you're saying, "We don't make sense for you"—then spend your time giving relevant inbound leads a fantastic experience. Qualification is something you'll want to keep in mind at every step, from how you set up your lead capture forms to the questions you ask once you get those leads on the phone.

INBOUND LEAD CAPTURE FORMS

First, you need a means by which to capture these inbound leads in a structured format. In the previous chapter, we talked about setting up a *<sales@yourcompa-nyname.com>* inbox as an early solution. And that can work to start—it's definitely much better than nothing. But it also makes for a really difficult time of capturing the relevant demand signifiers in a helpful way. So as soon as you're able, swap that email link out for a big fat "Request Demo" call to action on your home page (ideally following the user down the page), and then point that button at some sort of form that lets you capture structured data. Don't make it subtle. If someone shows up on your home page and is eager to talk to you, make it damn easy. Check out some examples of how to do this.

It's pretty clear what you need to do if you want a demo of HIRABL:

Textio uses a "free trial" concept that acts as the primary call to action (but which routes through a lead data capture form):

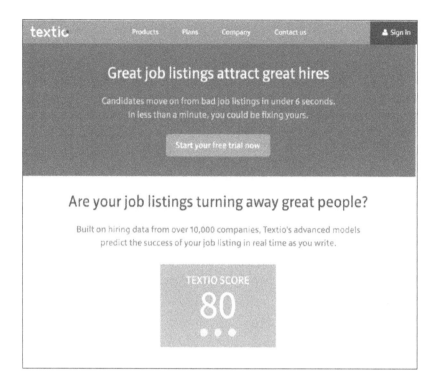

Your form tool, to start, could be something simple built with Google Forms, Wufoo, Typeform, or what have you. They're all pretty much the same, and all you want to do is allow the prospect to express interest in a structured way. Make sure the form works on mobile, as that's where a lot of your email outreach will be read. Often CRMs' lead capture forms (like Salesforce's Web-to-Lead) will include a feature that routes those leads directly into lead objects in the CRM, and can even provide a prospect-facing response email and a notification email to alert you to a new inbound lead.

What information do you want to capture? Resist the temptation to go crazy here. The biggest thing you're trying to capture is qualification information and a means by which to get in touch with the person. Honestly, the minimum minimum could be a work email address and phone number, if you believe that you can garner all of the relevant qualification data from a company website or LinkedIn with just the name of the company (from the email domain, duh).

That said, that level of minimalism might be a little weird given that most prospects are used to providing name and company, so I typically recommend first name, last name, company name, title (this quartet helps you understand who you're talking to); email address and phone number (this provides you the means by which to get into contact—and remember, these leads are asking you to get in touch, so you should definitely ask them for their phone numbers); and then the minimum viable demand signifiers that you can't get on your own.

For instance, at TalentBin, we didn't ask how many recruiters our inbound requesters had at their organizations, because that was trivial to find on LinkedIn—and every incremental field is a chance for leads to abandon the form. But we did ask how many software engineering roles they were looking to fill in the next six months, since we couldn't find that on our own and that hiring demand was required for an account to get value out of TalentBin. Think about what the minimum qualification signifiers are for your solution, and which ones aren't observable in the world and thus need to be asked. Check out some examples of demo request forms.

HIRABL asks for the type of ATS/CRM that a recruiting agency uses:

Textio can get all the demand signifiers they need from looking at company career pages (though they really should ask for phone number):

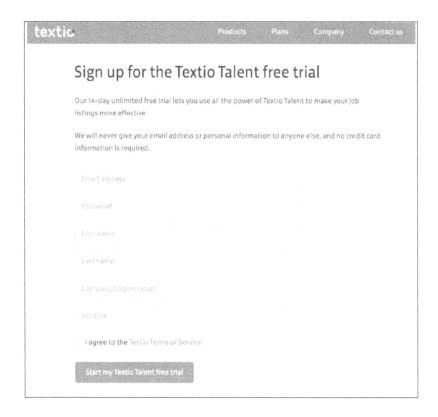

Immediately probably could find out how many salespeople a given account has worldwide on their own using LinkedIn, so they don't really need to ask that. But knowing the email system and CRM system the lead runs is important for their qualification process, so it's good they ask for it:

REQUEST A DEMO

Fill in the form bellow to request private demo for your company.

First Name *:

Last Name *:

Company E-mail *:

Company Name *

Phone Number *:

Number of Sales People (Worldwide) *:

How did you find us?

What CRM system does your organization use?

What email provider does your company run on?

Any other comments?

Fields marked with (*) are required.

SEND REQUEST

Once you have a form set up, in addition to adding those "Request Demo" calls to action on your home page (and other relevant pages on your website), you should make sure it's merchandised in your outreach emails, as well. That is, in most of those emails, you likely have a direct call to action like "just go ahead and respond to get something scheduled," but putting a link to your demo request form in your footer is a good addition.

Lastly, there are folks who like to get in touch the old fashioned way, and for them that means a phone number. You might think that putting a phone number (even if it's just for your cell phone) might lead to unwanted things like vendors calling you, or unqualified leads calling you and wasting your time. I assure you, your bigger problem is people not caring about you, rather than there being too much inbound. Instead, consider the decision-maker who is interested in getting a response really quickly, and used to doing business on the phone (do you sell to sales people? To recruiters? They're frequently verbal people, not text people.) staring at your demo request form, dozens of which they've filled out so many times before with nary a response. Plus, typing is hard. And so she closes the tab instead of requesting that demo, because you didn't populate a number. Populating a phone number somewhere on that demo request form gets you that demo. And make sure that phone number has a voicemail box that is checked for when it isn't monitored is a good thing to have. If you do get to a point where there's too much irrelevant inbound, and it's legitimately a waste of your time (I'd be shocked), you can always take it down later.

INBOUND LEAD RESPONSE

Once you have an inbound lead data capture form in place, the next question is—what do you do with these leads as they come in?

First, the most important thing is to respond to inbound leads as quickly as possible. This is something that organizations screw up constantly, thinking that because someone is asking to talk, they're happy to do it now, later, tomorrow, next week. This is completely false. Instead, what you have is a prospect who passed the threshold of sufficient interest in your solution and has made herself available right now. The key thing to understand is the "right now" component—as in, this can change because other priorities pop up, she finds another solution to her problem (how do you think she found you? She's actively trying to solve this problem), or a myriad of other reasons.

The pace at which this interest falls off is incredibly rapid. As surfaced in research done by MIT Sloan and InsideSales.com, there is a 100x drop-off in contact rates between leads that are contacted within five minutes of submitting a lead form and thirty minutes. And it's a 10x drop-off just between five minutes and ten minutes. As you can tell, responding to a qualified lead quickly is pretty darn important.

Of course, the challenge here, if it's just you, is that you're probably doing other things that keep you from checking your email every five minutes! And even if you're not, checking your email every five minutes sounds like a great way to get nothing else done (though later, you'll have a Market Development Rep who focuses just on this). That said, you should certainly make sure that your lead generation form provider can at a minimum send a new-lead notification to an email address of your choosing, including the information that was provided by the prospect. Especially phone number, so you can call her right away from wherever you are!

But the reality is that you may not always be able to instantly respond to those inbound leads. One way to help with this is an auto-response email coupled with a form completion "thank you" that includes that phone number we referred to above, directing leads who'd like to talk to someone quickly to call (a Google Voice number is great for this, as it can be redirected to any number). With this approach, you can increase your chance of an inbound call which, even if you're not able to answer, shows more commitment on the part of the prospect, while letting prospects know you will be in touch.

A more recent approach to inbound capture and response is the rise of chat interfaces. Companies like Drift and Intercom have offerings that allow you to have a pop up on your homepage or product page, which can then amount to a "form fill", but via a chat interface. The problem with this historically is that you need a human to staff this chat interface, and if you're at the point where you don't have enough inbound volume to merit that, you can mis-set expectation with the prospect when the chat window says "Hey, how can I help?" the prospect answers, and then there's no response. More modern versions of this, again, like Drift, can follow somewhat of a "mad libs" approach and ask the prospect questions, and then catalog the answers—kind of like a demo request form, one question at a time.

LIGHTWEIGHT DISCOVERY

Ideally, because you called the inbound lead back so quickly (right?), you can get him on the phone. But although I know you're excited about getting him on the calendar for a demo as quickly as possible, first you need to make sure he's qualified. If you go back to your ideal customer profile, you'll recall the demand signifiers that indicate a prospect has the pain points your solution solves. Now is the time to ensure that this inbound lead definitely has those characteristics. Of course, because you set up your inbound lead capture form in a way that captures these signifiers, this is more about verifying the information, and potentially digging in a bit more. Moreover, you should be figuring out what other folks should be on a call. This is where "size of prize" comes into play—if the organization has many other potential users of your product, maybe you could get them all on a demo together? Or while you have this champion-to-be on the phone, figure out who would be involved in a purchasing decision—is he the person who would pull that trigger, or should you think about involving the boss in this case? These are all valid things to consider, which we'll talk about more when we cover "discovery" in the Pitching chapter.

If, for whatever reason, it turns out that the individual and his organization aren't qualified, it's completely fine to let them know that this isn't relevant to them. Of course, be sure to differentiate between a truly unqualified account and a qualified account for which this is simply an unqualified contact. Qualify the account, not the lead. By no means should you think that because someone came inbound you are obligated to do a demo for him. Rather, you are being respectful of his time, and preventing him from having broken expectations at a later juncture when it finally surfaces that your solution isn't a fit. Worst, of course, would be if he ended up buying your product under a mistaken understanding of what it does and proceeded to feel cheated, all while soaking up your support resources and complaining to his colleagues about it. Let's avoid all that drama right now, okay? If you're respectful and candid about not wasting prospects' time, while making it clear who your solution would be relevant to, you have the chance to convert helpful brand ambassadors who will tell their colleagues about you.

This happened frequently at TalentBin, where our technical recruiting customers were so stoked on the product (and our delightfully designed swag!) that they often bragged to nontechnical recruiting colleagues about the solution—which is great. This is what you want. But those unqualified folks would then end up coming inbound as leads. As such it was very important that our inbound market development staff could qualify them. Rather than just putting a meeting on the calendar, they would pivot around the individual to figure out if she might simply be an unqualified contact at a qualified organization—and in that case, work with this contact to loop in more qualified contacts from that same organization. Or, alternatively, if the entire organization was unqualified. (For TalentBin, that means a company with no technical, healthcare, or finance hiring. For HIRABL, that's a staffing agency that doesn't do contingency recruiting. What's your version?)

FOLLOW-UP ON INBOUND LEADS

If, unfortunately, you weren't able to connect the first time you called that inbound lead back, all is not lost. Just as with your pure outbound efforts, even inbound appointment setting takes persistence. In fact, the second thing that people screw up about inbound leads is giving up on them too soon. Again, our friends at InsideSales.com and MIT Sloan figured out that each incremental attempt you make to reach out to an inbound lead adds another 15% chance of contacting them, falling off substantially after the sixth attempt. But after six attempts, you should have had roughly an aggregate 90% chance of making contact. So don't give up! Remember, they asked for it, so you have nothing to fear.

While you're trying to make contact, definitely make sure to leave voice mails and use your inbound lead response email template to let the prospect know that you're doing your best to reach him. But while persistence is good, you do need to move on after a half-dozen attempts or so. There are plenty of fish in the sea, and we need you spending your time fishing. Along the way, just make sure to log your activity in your CRM (or, if you're still in that Google Sheet, the new row you created for this inbound lead) to keep track of who's in process, and how many times you've attempted to contact them.

Lastly, not every inbound lead needs a call. If an inbound lead comes in, and the information that is provided makes it pretty darn clear it's unlikely to be qualified, a better approach can be to send what's known as a "hard qualifier" email. This would include who the product is intended for, and why you think it might not be relevant for that lead, plus an ask to clarify if your thinking is wrong.

For instance, something like:

SUBJECT LINE: Hey {*First_Name*}! Here's the magical solution to your recruiting headaches.

Hi there!

Thanks for your interest in HIRABL! I had an opportunity to check {*Company_Name*} out, and it looks like your recruiting team primarily does temp staffing, as opposed to contingency permanent placement. Is that right?

The reason I ask is because HIRABL is used by staffing agencies to monitor candidate submissions to avoid what are known as "backdoor hires"—when a client hires one of your submittals but doesn't let you know, so you potentially miss out on a fee. We find that 1 in 300 permanent placement submits ends up being a backdoor hire. So it's potentially tens of thousands of dollars in missed fees. Yikes! More here in this little video: https://youtu.be/QihH8WuJj0c.

If I'm mistaken and this sounds like it would be relevant to {*Company_ Name*}, then by all means let's get a demo scheduled for you.

Please let me know what you think!

Best,

Pete

This way, if you have a hunch that an account might not be qualified, you can send information over to help them disqualify themselves (while providing some nice marketing messaging in case they want to share it with their buddy who is qualified), saving you both time. Or, if your hunch was wrong, they'll reply letting you know as much, and you can get on your way to scheduling the meeting.

While scaled inbound marketing should likely not be a focus for you this early in your go-to-market, there are some basics that will help make sure you are capitalizing on the inbound interest generated by your outbound activity. Moreover, as you start getting early word of mouth from prospects you've demo'd, you'll already have a handy system for turning that inbound interest into appointments on the calendar, waiting to be pitched. Which we're going to talk about next!

CHAPTER 7

Pitching:
Preparation, Presentation,
Demos & Objections

INTRODUCTION

You've been probably thinking this whole time, "Pete, when do we get down to the actual selling, man?" Now is the time, friend. So far we've covered getting your story straight, documenting it well with relevant sales materials, finding accounts and contacts who will care about it, and then getting demos on their calendars. All of which, of course, is "selling." But now we're going to talk about the mechanics of executing your sales presentation and demo and closing business.

And like the topics we've covered before, it's best to think of the process of selling as having distinct substages, each of which you'll want to step through. Boil your sale down into those individual motions, and it won't feel as monolithic and insurmountable. Rather, it's just a case of going down a checklist, diligently checking things off as you go, and landing, at the end, in a big pile of revenue!

THE GOAL OF PITCHING

At bottom, pitching is the process of commercial persuasion, ending in a sale. Appointment setting was about persuading the prospect that this solution could potentially help with her business pains. Pitching is about persuading her, and other stakeholders in her organization, not only that they have this business pain, but that it is of large enough magnitude that it must be solved, that your solution will indeed solve it, and that they will be able to capture value—"return on investment" in the nomenclature—by implementing your solution.

Moreover, pitching is about persuading the prospect that she needs to deal with this now, rather than later. That the opportunity cost of holding off is too high to bear. And that notwithstanding the various pains facing her organization—and there are always many things that can be fixed—it's worth the money and time to implement your solution, ahead of all those other things.

This isn't to say that it'll be a one-shot deal, known as a "one-call close." You might see those occasionally, but it's pretty unlikely at the beginning of this process. And the more complicated your solution, the less likely they will be. This exercise in "organizational persuasion" may take a number of steps, a number of meetings, likely involving multiple people within the target organization. But the goal is still the same—to get the ball, now in play, across the line. And there's another related goal—if it is clear that the deal is not going to close, at least not this time around, you want to own that and stop spending time on something that won't yield a return.

NEW-TECHNOLOGY SALES PERSUASION FORMULA

One way I like to think about this is in terms of a formula—the potential value to the organization crossed with the level of value comprehension the prospect has achieved (did they "get it"?) crossed with the extent to which they believe they will achieve the promised value. Prospects will typically apply a risk discount—that is, they'll discount what they believe your solution is worth based on their incredulity that they'll achieve all the promised value.

You can visualize the formula like this:

Potential Value x Value Comprehension x Belief = Likelihood and Magnitude of Sale

Your goal is to maximize these terms. You can maximize the potential value to the organization by targeting those accounts that have the greatest need for your solution. You can maximize comprehension of that value through effective presentation, materials, and tooling. And you can maximize believability via proof points, demonstrations of the product, customization of those demos, and even proof of concept and pilots.

There is no way you will be able to maximize each of these terms in every deal. But if you focus on organizations with high levels of business pain, and do a good job ensuring comprehension, you may be able to surmount skepticism. As in

"Wow, based on what I see here, we can potentially save fifty thousand dollars a month by implementing this solution. Even if we only see half of that savings, that's still awesome."

Keep this mental model front of mind, and it will help you push each of those levers higher in your pitching process.

INSIDE OR OUTSIDE SALES?

The decision to sell a solution in person, face-to-face with the decision-maker in a conference room, or over the phone with presentation and screen-sharing software is typically based on the complexity of the solution crossed with average deal size.

That is, the number of meetings that you can have in person in a given day is far lower than the number of digital presentations you can do, just by virtue of transit times. A field sales rep getting two in-person presentations done in a day is pretty good, and three would be really pushing it. An inside sales rep who presents via phone and screen share, on the other hand, could easily do five or six 45-minute presentations a day and still have ample time for follow-up and pipeline maintenance.

Given that revenue is simply the number of opportunities attacked multiplied by your win rate (what proportion of opportunities result in a sale) multiplied by the average deal size, generally speaking, more opportunities attacked is a good thing. But that is often balanced by the higher win rate you can see from face-to-face interaction, as well as the increased comprehension, believability, and trust that it engenders. Also, some solutions are so involved and mission-critical that in-person is really the only way to go about it.

So for now, to begin with—and regardless of what you think the optimal approach to selling your solution would be at scale—it's pretty much always going to be better to sell in person. Even if that means only one or two meetings a day to start, don't worry about it. The increased fidelity of communication, the increased insights you'll get from a lively face-to-face exchange, and the increased trust engendered will overwhelm the efficiency gained by digital presentation. This is why when we talked about prospecting early customers, we focused on those in your geographical vicinity.

This doesn't mean that you shouldn't present to qualified accounts that you're unable to reach in person. If an amazing opportunity shows up in your inbound demo request form, by all means, engage that opportunity digitally (no, don't fly there, necessarily) as you would any qualified opportunity. It simply means that from a prioritization standpoint, you should be targeting accounts close to home, to enjoy the benefits of on-site presentation.

On the topic of travel, while you'll generally want to stick local or use digital presentation tools, there may be situations, likely after you've booked your first few customers, where it makes sense to fly to a prospect's location and execute an on-site sales presentation. This is usually best done in batches, so if you're traveling somewhere, line up meetings with other prime targets in the city in question. Typically, these meetings become an initial opportunity to "put a face to a name," and incremental presentations and meetings happen digitally, building off the comprehension and trust built in that first face-to-face exercise.

Later on, when you get to scale, it may be totally appropriate for all of your sales to be done inside, via telepresence. That is, once you've nailed your pitch and materials—and you're sure your team can do an amazing job of communicating value, backed by ROI studies and existing customers that make those claims believable—you can take advantage of the efficiency of digitally hosting five, six, or more meetings a day. Or, it may turn out that your solution is sufficiently complex, with a sufficiently high price tag, that most sales will be done on-site. Or you may have a blend, where smaller customers are addressed via telepresence, in light of their lower deal sizes, while larger customers, with larger potential sales, are handled on-site. But to start, aim for pitching on-site.

PRE-CALL PLANNING

Did you know your presentation starts before you even get on the call or show up at the prospect's office? Just as professional athletes use scouting reports and watch previous game recordings to maximize their performance on game day, the best sales staff rigorously prep for their demos and presentations to ensure they make the most out of them.

If you consider the time and energy that went into putting the demo in question on the calendar, you might think, "How could you not prep for something like that?" Well, you'd be shocked by the preparation laziness demonstrated by a lot of sales staff. Don't be that guy. You or your market development rep helper spent hundreds of dollars of salary expense to get this demo on the calendar. Don't set that work on fire. Further, this is about raising your win rate and making the most of this opportunity. What's your average contract value? $20,000? If proper preparation can raise your win rate from 15% to 25%, well, you just made $2,000 with fifteen minutes of preparatory work. Pre-call planning is not optional.

Note that presentation preparation is not the same as prepping for cold calling—which is usually a waste of time. Because connect rates on cold calls are fairly low, spending five minutes to get all the context about an account into your head before you dial means that you're just reducing the number of calls that you can make, for no particular benefit. However, because hold rates on demos should be

80% or higher, you know there's at least an 80% chance you're going to be having a serious commercial conversation that could result in $20,000 (or whatever your ACV is). It's worth the time investment.

Calendar Management

The best way to make sure you don't skip pre-call planning is to put it on the calendar. When you send a meeting invite to a prospect for the presentation, put an additional fifteen-minute block on your own calendar just ahead of the meeting. This way you won't accidentally put another meeting back to back with your presentation, jamming future-you up, and you'll have a calendar reminder to make sure you do your pre-call planning.

If you're doing outside sales, you'll typically need to block that time on your calendar for travel time, as well. Importantly, you want to book the travel time to precede your pre-call planning. That is, whatever the travel time will be, book that on your calendar so that you arrive thirty minutes ahead of your designated appointment. It will most certainly take five to ten minutes for you to check in with reception, reception to contact your prospect, and the prospect to pick you up at reception. Target checking in with reception fifteen minutes before your appointment, and arrive at your destination fifteen minutes before that to adequately prep for your meeting so everything is fresh in your head.

The goal of pre-call planning is to ensure that you have readily accessible, ideally in your brain, all the relevant information that you sniffed out ahead of time, and a list of "known unknowns" for you to figure out during "discovery," the first part of your presentation. Much of this information you'll remember from your prospecting activities, like outward signifiers of demand, relevant points of contact and influencers, and so forth. The goal is to stack the information advantage in your favor, so you know which questions to ask, and which to skip. And if the prospect tries to introduce information that isn't 100% true, you'll know. It's your job to control the call, and more information makes that more achievable.

Take another look at the Prospecting chapter for greater detail on how to gather this information. To refresh your memory, these are the different types of information you'll want to make sure you have front and center before you hop onto your demo.

Pain Points & the "Size of the Prize"

These are the outwardly identifiable characteristics that indicated that the prospect had a need for your solution. For TalentBin, this could be open technical hires. For Immediately, it could be number of field sales reps needing a sales-centric mobile email and CRM client. And for Textio, it could be number of open job postings that need to be optimized. Knowing these pain signifiers will help you with your proactive ROI understanding. If you're HIRABL, the staffing agency revenue-acceleration company, and you know that your solutions on average add $10,000 per recruiter per year in added revenue, then knowing how many recruiters there are in the agency you're going to talk to (thirty! fifty! more!) will help you proactively position that benefit in your presentation.

You'll also want to know how much you can potentially sell, known as "size of prize." That is, you shouldn't be trying to sell just one seat of your solution, or some other minimum amount. Rather, you need to know how much of your solution the organization could potentially consume. This might be correlated to the potential number of users, like the number of sales reps or recruiters or support reps, etc., or some other characteristic specific to your prospect.

This doesn't mean you're going to eat the whole apple in one bite. In fact, selling a young solution across an entire organization—like selling one hundred seats of TalentBin to a recruiting organization when we were a ten-person company—can be a dicey proposition. However, knowing how much could be sold, so you can properly guide the conversation, is a benefit. For example, "Well, I know you have ten recruiters, and from what I saw, Jeff, Suzy, and Julie are the ones that focus on technical hiring, so perhaps three seats would be appropriate." Having this information available can help you determine what would be a "good" outcome from a first-sale standpoint.

A quick LinkedIn search shows fourteen recruiters at New Relic. Maybe we can sell them five seats to start?

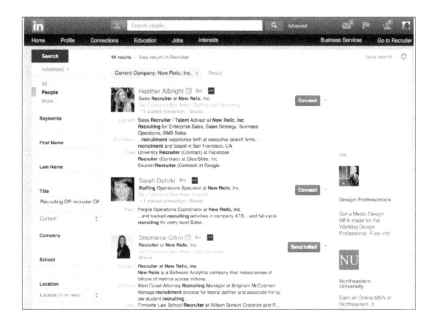

Complementary Products, Competitive Products & The Capacity to Pay

You'll also want to go into your pitch knowing the sort of products the organization has in the mix. Take another look at the Prospecting chapter for how to use tools like Datanyze and BuiltWith to determine the technologies running on an organization's website, and where else to look to determine whether they're paying for premium services. By understanding this ahead of time, you'll get a sense of how the organization currently solves the problem your solution addresses, and if they pay money to do it. And if you are able to sniff out a directly competitive product, not only will you know that the organization cares enough about the problem to spend money on it, you'll be prepared to explain why your solution is better, faster, and stronger than the one that they're currently using.

Lastly, understanding an organization's funding situation can help with the question of "capacity to pay." If an organization has raised $100 million in funding in the last few months, that money was raised to execute. To hire engineers, buy advertising, or what have you. Same with public companies—if they're growing their revenue and have a strong balance sheet, they will be more open to solutions that make the business better, compared to an organization that is not only loss making, but perhaps in decline (as measured by revenue growth).

Potential Users

Use LinkedIn to make sure you know who the potential users of your solution would be. You'll already have done this to determine "size of prize," but it will also help if you are speaking with a decision-maker different from the end user. Knowing your potential users can help if you get into discussions about who would be the most relevant person to use or even evaluate the solution. For instance, TalentBin needed to be careful that an inattentive decision-maker didn't ask a nontechnical recruiter to take a demo to evaluate our solution.

Stakeholders & Influencers

Ideally your demo is with the relevant decision-maker, but that doesn't mean there aren't other stakeholders in the problem your solution solves—the decision-maker's boss, for example, or her internal customers. Or if somehow you entered through one of those internal customers, you'll want to know whom you ultimately need to talk to after that first meeting. Same is true if you are entering through a level below the decision-maker.

Not only will this allow you to demonstrate organizational mastery and diligence, but it provides a "credible threat" (not stated, but mildly implied) that you have awareness of other people in the organization, and likely would not have any issue getting access to them. So, if you're Immediately, and you're talking to a Sales Operations decision-maker, it's helpful to know who the VP of Sales is (say, Christina), as she's ultimately on the hook for the organization's revenue achievement and personally stands to make more money with increased revenues. As in, "And you can imagine how happy Christina will be knowing that the field reps you work with will be closing more business in less time because they're not stuck in coffee shops updating Salesforce!"

Of course, this goes all the way up to the CEO, who has an interest in the downstream impacts of your solution. For instance, if you're talking about a solution to assist with sales hiring, you know that private and public organizations are valued at a multiple of their revenues. So faster sales hiring, with better hires, and faster onboarding can get an organization to higher revenue levels faster—which could allow a private organization to raise their next round of funding at a higher valuation. Or if the organization is public with, say, a price-to-earnings ratio of fifteen, and your ROI analysis indicates that your solution will save them $1 million a year, you're looking at adding $15 million of market capitalization to the organization through the implementation of your solution. Now, depending on the size of the company, this strategy may be more or less relevant. But at a medium or smaller organization, say five hundred people or fewer, this is certainly something a CEO would be interested in. Knowing who that is, so you can demonstrate to your point of contact why they would care and how you could potentially deliver that message, will make your case stronger.

Same if you are entering the account a level below your intended decision-maker target. Characterizing to that staffer that you're well aware of who the relevant decision-maker is changes his calculus when it comes to next steps. That is, you can indicate that the staffer has an opportunity to be the bringer of innovation and excellence to his boss—or, if he chooses not to, that you'll likely just engage directly with the decision-maker, potentially making the staffer look like someone who missed an opportunity. As in "You can imagine how excited Kieran will be knowing that she can save each of her recruiters ten hours a week. You'll be a hero!" In this case, your point of contact can help you with Kieran, or look to be behind the eight ball. It's clear to me which one sounds better!

Customization Information

As we discussed in the Sales Materials chapter, the ability to personalize your presentation and demo for the prospect is paramount. So if there is additional information that you need to gather in order to customize your presentation, do so. For TalentBin, this could mean looking at the prospect's careers site to see which technical openings you'd want to focus your demo on. So rather than asking

"What roles are you having a hard time filling?" the question is instead "I saw you're hiring for an iOS developer. That would be a good one for me to use to show you how TalentBin works. Does that work?" Better control.

Or if you're LifeGuides, and want to show how you can help with a problematic Glassdoor presence, you might want to take a screenshot of that Glassdoor page and some choice negative reviews. Or if you're Affirm, use Google Chrome's Developer Tools to drop a "Pay with Affirm" call to action into your e-commerce prospect's product detail page.

Look at how nice that financing call to action looks there! I bet it raises conversion rates!

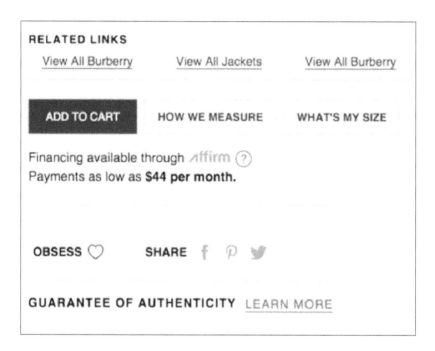

Conversational Guides/Icebreakers

Lastly, while business pain and stakeholder research is paramount from a nuts-and-bolts standpoint, you'll want to take time to gather conversational guides, icebreakers, and rapport-building information for the first couple minutes of your call. If you think blathering about the weather is going to get this done, you're really missing out. That's the limp fallback of someone who doesn't do his research ahead of time. This is especially important for phone sales. In face-to-face meetings, it's somehow easier to establish rapport. You have to be intentional about it on the phone, though, so selecting a piece of information you're going to key off of is all the more important.

LinkedIn is fantastic for a couple of reasons. First, you can see if you share any contacts with the prospect that you want to surface proactively. If it's an existing customer of yours, excellent! You should certainly bring that up. "I saw on LinkedIn that you know Jeff from Dropbox. He's a customer of ours. Great guy!" But this could be former colleagues or classmates of yours too—most shared contacts are a good opportunity to build rapport—unless the shared contact has a poor opinion of you. In that case, skip this! (Or be prepared for your words to get back to that contact!)

You can also see where else your prospect has worked. Perhaps you overlapped at a prior organization? And, of course, you can check out her educational background, which can be helpful if it's college football season. Even if she's not into that sort of thing, if you're dealing with an Ohio State, Alabama, University of Texas, or USC alum, she'll probably be at least secondarily aware, and it makes you look thoughtful. You can also check out geography to see where she's based (not all points of contact are based in the same location as the organization's headquarters). This can be helpful for local sports teams ("Wow, that Patriots-Steelers game was something, huh?") or, at worst, local weather ("Wow, you guys have been hammered by that blizzard, huh?").

Further, as LinkedIn has pushed users to surface personal interests on their profiles, you can often see if the prospect is into yoga, rock climbing, whatever. Sometimes she'll have a concurrent "Current" role for a side project, like the small business she also owns or a nonprofit organization on whose board she sits. All are potentially excellent topics for icebreaking. Beyond LinkedIn, many prospects will have active Twitter accounts, and they're often a valuable source of recent interests. (Following your prospects on Twitter is a great strategy, in general, and we'll talk about it more later.)

On the topic of rapport building, stay away from politics, religion, and so on. Even if the prospect is tweeting her head off about this political candidate or that one, it's just too dicey. You can find something else to establish rapport with if you try.

Known Unknowns

While you'll be able to nail down a lot of great information about your prospect ahead of time with fifteen minutes of work, you likely won't be able to find everything you need. This is perfectly fine, as the first part of your sales presentation will be focused on "discovery" and surfacing this information. However, as you do your pre-call planning and research, you'll want to note exactly what you weren't able to find ahead of time, so that you can make sure to ask the right questions during discovery.

As you do many of these presentations, your approach will evolve and you'll eventually form a pre-call planning checklist, along with a discovery question checklist. When you do, capture this information in your CRM. You'll be having dozens of these presentations, and when you go to follow up with the prospect, much of the pre-call research is reusable. Capturing it in its distilled form saves you time. Better yet, you'll be creating a piece of tooling for the sales reps you eventually hire to scale your activities.

Stated Pitch Goal

Once you have all of this information, you should be able to form a plan and establish your goal for the call. If you're talking to the right decision-maker, and it's clear that the account has tons of need for your solution and spends lots of money on analogous products, maybe that goal is to win consideration of a purchase. If you're talking to someone who is likely not the end practitioner, but is an internal customer and potential sponsor, perhaps the goal is to convince him of the benefit of your solution and partner with him to drive to a second call with the ultimate decision-maker. If you're coming in below the decision-maker level, maybe it's to drive to a secondary call with the decision-maker and the rest of the staffer's team. Whatever the goal, make sure you know what it is. Don't worry, your call will certainly diverge from plan! But identifying your polestar will help you drive toward it, even as things go sideways.

Pre-Call Attitude

Beyond gathering information and establishing your goal for the call, there's also the matter of just getting "in the zone." That is, a large part of selling is projecting confidence in your solution and your recommendations to the prospect. So prepare yourself accordingly. Stand, walk around, do jumping jacks (probably not in the prospect's lobby, if you're on-site!), and get yourself in a positive, and active, frame of mind. I have a standing desk, but even if you don't, take sales calls standing. You will project more authority and be quicker on your feet.

PITCH MATERIALS & CONCEPTS

Let's talk about where the rubber meets the road—the actual pitch we've been diligently lining up and preparing for!

Tools and Materials

Depending on the location of your pitch, the tooling you'll employ will change. However, just as you've been intentional with respect to your materials and preparations, so too you will be with your tooling.

If you're pitching on-site, don't assume that your prospect will have everything you need to present. Moreover, any hiccups will come out of your behind. The prospect will just remember an awkward, crappy meeting, even if it was his bad Internet that caused the demo failure or his dysfunctional projector that kept blinking out. Things will invariably go wrong, so plan for it.

It sounds obvious, but you'll want to make sure you have a laptop, loaded with your sales deck and demo materials, with which to present, and all the relevant connectors needed to connect your laptop to a projector. (This is another reason why showing up early is great. Projectors seem to be designed to derail the beginning of pitches!) I like to keep them in a little mesh bag in my backpack so there's no frantic digging required. Or, if it's just you and a prospect, present off your laptop screen, with the two of you looking at it side by side. Less risk, more intimate.

Recently, it's become fashionable to connect to large flat-panel displays via Apple's AirPlay. As far as I know, unless you download extra software to your Windows machine, you need an Apple laptop to AirPlay to one of these screens. So if you have an Apple machine, figure out AirPlay. And if you don't, think about adding that third-party software. Beyond knowing how to use existing projectors, bringing your own mini projector can be excellent as well. It isn't very costly, and you'll be 100% confident that you can project at a moment's notice.

Bringing your own source of Internet access can shortcut issues associated with office WiFi access—you'd be amazed how hard it can be to track those passwords down, eating fifteen minutes of your demo time. Just flip on your personal hotspot or pair your phone, and you're on your way. All of this makes you look super prepared and awesome, like the kind of person the prospect would like to be in business with. Lastly, make sure you have a lab notebook to take notes in. (Perhaps you already have your pre-call planning results in it for reference!) You'll be using your machine to present, so you won't be able to take notes with it. And you'll want to make sure you're diligently recording everything you cover in the discovery part of your conversation.

If you're presenting digitally, tooling is more straightforward. First, you need software that allows you to share your screen so you can show your slides and demo. One great, cheap option is join.me. Showpad is a little more involved and expensive, but integrates well with Salesforce. DocSend is a lightweight screen-share and document-sharing system that is a happy medium. All of these allow prospects to immediately see your screen without having to download any software—something that was always a huge pain with WebEx and GoToMeeting. If you use those last two, prospects invariably won't have the most recent version, or won't have the ability to administer and install software on their machine, and you'll spend the first ten minutes of your call trying to get the software installed. It's just a total disaster. I haven't personally used Google Hangouts or Skype for face-to-face digital sales communication, which is something I find potentially interesting from a rapport-building standpoint. Whatever software you choose, you want to optimize for ease of use, so the prospect can just hit the hyperlink that was included in the meeting invite and reminder email you sent them and, poof, be seeing your screen and hearing your voice.

You'll also want some sort of earbuds or headset for your phone. You'll be using your hands to mouse, type, or take notes, so occupying one with a handset is silly. And speakerphone makes for a crappy user experience for the prospect, so don't do that. You're going to be on the phone a lot—I like to buy a half dozen Apple earbuds so I know I'll have one in a pinch, even as I lose them. (You will.) As with on-site pitches, you'll want your lab notebook with your pre-call planning notes, ready to record the information (typing it while on the phone never seems to work for me).

We covered the construction of your sales materials back in a Chapter 3, but the primary materials you'll need for your pitch are your sales deck and your demo script (which you already memorized, in broad strokes!). Make sure you have an "offline proof" version of your demo. That is, you should have pre-populated in your browser (assuming that's where the demo takes place) the key screens that would allow you to give a good demo, even if something happened to your Internet connectivity.

Pitch Format

I find that the best pitches follow a consistent format. Specifically, they start with quick pleasantries, move into discovery, feature a slide-based presentation followed by a live demo, touch on success proof points, and conclude with pricing and commercial discussion. This format is important because it allows you to build the best case for your solution. You start with pleasantries to build rapport and set the tone for the prospect to share information with you and be receptive to your arguments. Discovery gives you the information you need to make an ROI argument to the prospect. (Or, if it turns out that she doesn't have the pain point that your organization solves, you can end the call and save both of you time!) Next, you use slides and visuals to make sure the prospect has the proper mental model for understanding the sales narrative you're delivering, and to prepare her to understand the features you demo. All of which builds up to a compelling argument for spending money on the solution.

One of the biggest things you'll converge on as you start selling is whether you'll be able to do discovery and presentation together or have to separate them. As you increase your volume of demos, one way to be more efficient with your time is to split your full presentation and demo from initial discovery by having a dedicated discovery call, often known as a "disco call" (what a delightful abbreviation!). The benefit of this approach is that it is often easier to get someone to agree to an initial fifteen-minute phone call than a thirty-, forty-five-, or even sixty-minute presentation and demo. In this mode, your discovery call helps you get better information about the prospect, but also lets you "sell" the full demo, as appropriate. Further, if your discovery questions reveal that the prospect is unqualified, you can conclude the call quickly. There isn't an onus to "make it worth their time" because you had them block thirty or sixty minutes.

The necessity of splitting your pitch often depends on how long your demo needs to be to characterize the solution's important functionality. If your solution is straight to the point, and can be demo'd in ten minutes, then the coordination costs of a ten-minute discovery call at one point in time and another ten-minute demo aren't worth it. You'll be adding fragility to your appointment setting, as there's about a 10%–20% chance that each meeting will be missed and thus rescheduled. So do them together. Moreover, as discussed in the Prospecting chapter, if the signifiers of a qualified customer are readily discoverable ahead of time via online research, you dramatically reduce the amount of time needed for discovery, as you can be surer that the prospect is qualified.

As you start, even if your solution is complex, it's probably best not to separate your pitch into two meetings. At least for your first few dozen demos, having more time to have a richer conversation is better, plus you're ideally on-site anyway.

Who Are You Talking To?

When you're approaching your pitch, you should be mindful of who you're talking to and, as such, what you should be emphasizing. We talked about this a bit in the "stated goal" part of pre-call planning—different types of people are going to be more receptive to different messages.

A friend of mine, Skip Miller, author of a number of sales books, crystallized this in three distinct "personas" set out for his sales reps. He even gave them national names to help differentiate them, and to remind reps to speak the right "language" when engaging. Each persona—individual users, first-line managers, and second-line/CXO managers—will speak quite differently. Your job is to learn, and develop messages in, all three languages.

First up are end users. They are going to care about making their jobs easier, pleasing their internal customers, making themselves look good to their managers, and setting themselves up for career progress. These contacts will be less concerned about ROI arguments, because it's not really their money. Some may care, but they'll be more focused on how your solution impacts them. Maybe your product helps them get a promotion or a better job somewhere else, for example. So when it comes to an email-automation solution for sales, Sales Development Reps are going to care about how it removes annoying repetitive email activity for them, helps them set more demos (because that makes them more money!), and maybe gives them a shiny new toy that they can brag about to their friends. They'll probably care less about how it accelerates top-line revenue for the organization.

Next you have first-line managers. They're going to be more interested in the ROI arguments you bring to the table. They'll be mindful of the impact your solution has on their commitments to internal customers. They'll probably also be responsible for a budget, including payroll for their team, so they'll be more attuned to arguments about making staff more efficient, producing more value for their internal customers, and facilitating staff adoption. While they're likely former individual contributors, and thus will probably enjoy understanding how various features work, they're going to care more about the business impact of your solution. So for TalentBin's email automation functionality—which helps recruiters send drip-marketing emails to candidates, raising response rates and the number of phone screens a given recruiter can set in a given time interval—the manager will care most about the fact that this means he can reduce his spending on candidate flow, he won't have to hire another sourcer at $65,000 a year just yet, his existing staff will be happy to lose some of their job's drudgery, and the VP of Engineering will be happy with the increased candidate volume.

Lastly, there's the second-level managers or CXOs. They're going to be responsive to arguments that drive top-line business value for the entire organization. For instance, if your solution speeds onboarding of new salespeople, so they can become fully productive quickly, the CEO will care because more salespeople adding more revenue literally raises the value of the company. And that's the CEO's job. The CFO, who's concerned about cash flow, will care that this reduces the salary expense new sales hires consume before they become productive, thereby helping the cash position of the company. These are not things a line recruiter or sales rep or data scientist will likely care about; they're not even things a first-line manager will frequently consider. But they're definitely things that a CXO/VP thinks about.

This isn't to say that a single argument will be sufficient. You will very likely have multiple meetings with each of these different types of folks, so make sure you're speaking the right language each time. Even more fun is when you have people who speak different value languages in the same meeting. That's some serious advanced action right there. But as long as you understand what each person cares about, and have that in mind when explaining features and benefits, you'll do well.

PITCH INTRODUCTION

Rapport Building & Opening Chitchat

Now is the time when you deploy those nuggets of information you surfaced ahead of time and do some hyper-charged rapport building. The goal of this part of the pitch is to form a bridge of shared experience that raises trust levels.

Importantly, though, you need to have a plan for transitioning things "down to business." That is, there's a certain amount of time, two or three minutes, that you can spend on this sort of thing before it starts to wear thin. Not to mention, you're eating into the time that was budgeted for the rest of your pitch. A great way to do this is to move from less to more professional topics as you go. It's nice to talk about the Red Sox if the prospect is from Boston, but you'll want to switch it up to "How long have you been recruiting?" or remark on professional components of his role as a segue to the commercial discussion at hand. "Well that's great. I'm glad we got to talk about that stuff! So..." And then begin.

Discovery

Discovery is where you take the time to ask questions of prospects to both qualify them and set yourself up for a more productive pitch. It's also the thing that first-time salespeople screw up the worst. Eager to hop into their pitch, instead of digging into the prospect's business realities, they just start firing from the hip—and miss a huge opportunity to tailor the conversation to the prospect's pains. Or, worse, they waste time and energy presenting to someone who isn't even qualified. Discovery is an extremely important part of the pitching process, and you should allocate the first five or ten minutes of your presentation to it (depending on the total time your presentation and demo take).

It's best to set this up at the beginning of your pitch, and characterize it as a benefit to the prospect. Something like "I like to start with some questions so I have a better idea of how your team goes about its day to day, and so I can do a better job of focusing on things you'll get more value out of."

There are a variety of qualification frameworks that sales folks will often refer to, each with its own helpful acronym. There's the classic "BANT," which stands for "budget, authority, need, timeline." As in, the prospect isn't qualified unless he has those four things—budget to pay for a solution, authority to command that budget, need for the solution, and a timeline as to when he wants to solve this pain. "ANUM" is another one I like, standing for "authority, need, urgency, money." And I recently came across "ChAMP," or "challenges, authority, money, prioritization."

You're probably seeing a pattern here. During the discovery process, you want to make sure that the prospect has the problem you're solving, but that's not necessarily sufficient. You also want to know that he does indeed have a process by which he considers and purchases technology to solve problems. You want to know who the person is, or group of people are, who makes these purchasing decisions. And you want to know the level of urgency with which they want to solve this problem. Discovery is how you figure this out (to start).

The problem with strict "letter of the law" qualification when you're selling an early-stage product is that oftentimes, you're having a conversation with someone who had no idea that this solution existed. If he didn't even know that it existed, probably pretty hard to have a set budget for it, right? And probably pretty hard to have a timeline. This is why some of the other qualification frameworks I mentioned focus on how big the problem is, and how much urgency there is around solving it (i.e., even though our early prospects didn't know that Internet talent search engines like TalentBin existed, they certainly knew that technical hiring was a big challenge for them, and one that they were eager to solve).

In the Prospecting chapter we discussed how, thanks to the magic of the Internet, you can often uncover discovery information ahead of interacting with prospects, and even use that information to engage them. Depending on how much of this information you are able to gather for a particular prospect, you could be pretty well informed ahead of your pitch. But you'll still want to validate that information to make sure that it's accurate and also, importantly, to ensure that the prospect knows that you know it. You're diligent and have done your homework, so set the tone for the conversation—you have good informational backing for the argument that your solution is likely a fit.

Moreover, because you have this information, you'll be able to position your discovery questions in a "leading" way, focusing on the part of the prospect's business pain that is aligned with your solution. For instance, if you're the guys from LifeGuides, makers of recruiting brand software, and you're talking to someone whose company has a 2.5-star Glassdoor rating, rather than asking, "Are you familiar with Glassdoor?" the question would be "You're probably aware that your company has a 2.5-star rating on Glassdoor. Do you find it frustrating that negative employee content is crowding out the employer story you'd like to tell?" Or you might try "When I Googled 'working at <your company>,' that Glassdoor page was the top result. Do you find it frustrating that they own that top result and hijack candidates who are looking for you?"

Or if you're Immediately, makers of an awesome sales-centric mobile email and CRM client, and you've determined that the prospect likely has primarily outside-based sales reps (based on the geographic distribution of their sales reps' LinkedIn profiles), instead of asking, "Do you have outside sales reps?" you might instead say, "Based on what I saw on LinkedIn, you have sales reps in the Bay Area, Chicago, New York, and Dallas. That's quite the outside team! Do you find that, like with most outside sales teams, they have a tendency to do a poor job of logging meetings and activities in the CRM because they're not at a desk?"

Lastly, as with your other sales materials, your discovery questions will be a work in progress. But even while in progress, they should be documented. Make sure they are saved as a living list in a Google Doc that you can refer to (and, later, hand to the reps that you hire).

The goal of all of this is to have the information you need for a productive pitch and down-funnel process. Or, if the account lacks important qualification criteria (like no pain, little urgency, or no ability to pay), discovery will enable you to helpfully truncate the conversation, respecting the time of the prospect and, most importantly, keeping you from burning your time on something that will never turn into a sale.

Pain and Urgency

The most important thing to converge on is whether the prospect has the actual business pain that your solution is seeking to solve. If she doesn't, this is going to be a useless conversation. Having done that, you can seek to discover the magnitude of that pain and if she has tried to solve it previously, along with how successful those attempts have been. All of this will give you a nuanced understanding of the prospect's business situation as relates to your solution.

As an example, take TalentBin's discovery process. We would of course start by asking what sort of technical roles an organization was hiring for, and how many. So this might have been something like "I saw a few technical roles on your careers site, but over the next twelve months, what software engineering headcount do you think you'll be hiring for? And what proportion of your hires do you think this will be?" Once we had an answer, we'd get into pain associated with the organization's current means of solving this problem, as in "When you think about how you currently do technical hiring, would you consider it easy?" (A leading question. No one is going to call his or her job easy!) Once the prospect had responded to that, we would then cascade further: "Do you find job postings insufficient to get the sort of software engineer applicant flow that you want? Have you had to do passive-candidate recruiting and outreach, for instance via LinkedIn?" If she answered no to this, then we knew the organization may not even have the pain we solved, and we'd have an uphill battle. If she answered yes, we'd cascade further, into problems that we knew many prospects were likely to have. For instance, "Interesting. Are you like most of the folks I talk to, struggling to get the level of responsiveness to LinkedIn outreach that you'd like? Is it a lot of time for not a lot of response? Right, well, many folks don't check their LinkedIn messages. Do you try to fix this by searching out personal email addresses so you can have a direct messaging path with better responsiveness? Yeah, I don't blame you. Who has the time?" or "Very nice. Yeah, it's kind of a lot of time, huh? But it can be worth it, because the response rates are so much higher." The idea is to keep cascading down the prospect's pain—its size and urgency, how it's currently solved, and the downsides of those approaches (sounds like your sales narrative, right?!)—all while recording this information in your handy dandy lab notebook.

You'll also want to touch on the downstream business implications of not solving this pain point. For instance, if you're Textio, the service for job-posting text optimization that is particularly helpful for raising the number of female and people-of-color applicants, it might be something like "Why is diversity hiring so important to you? What will happen if you aren't able to hit your diversity hiring goals?" To which the answer might be "Well, the CEO has publicly committed to these goals, so I'll kinda be in a lot of trouble [nervous chuckle]!"

Lastly, you'll want to try to tie your discovery questions to the features you've built to solve those pain points. So, for LifeGuides, not only would that be asking questions about Google search results and Glassdoor average ratings, but it might also be things like "It seems you're concerned about getting your employer branding story told. Have you thought about interviewing or recording video of your employees talking about their jobs? Yeah, it is a lot of work. It's no wonder you haven't gotten around to it." LifeGuides makes it extremely easy for employees to use their laptop webcams to record testimonials about what it's like working at a company, so they remove that time cost. Or "I saw that you guys have a careers Twitter handle and a premium LinkedIn company page—that's great, it shows that you're ahead of the pack! How do you find content to distribute on there? Yeah, it is a struggle to constantly find new things to publish that present the recruiting brand voice. I get it." LifeGuides makes recruiting brand content production easy, and high volume, so you're teasing out the pain associated with needing large amounts of recruiting brand content to share. You should think about doing the same with the features your team has built, by targeting discovery questions to validate the existence of the business pain those features intend to solve.

Team, Authority, and Commercials

Assuming that your discovery questions about business pain and urgency point to a worthwhile opportunity, next you need to understand the ins and outs of how this particular organization goes about purchasing things to solve business pain. Start with the people who would be using your solution. Do they exist in the organization? If not, it's going to be hard for your solution to get used! How many are there? Do people on the team have particular specialties?

Then it comes down to authority and commercials. Who is the person—or group of people— that makes decisions about buying solutions for the organization, or this particular slice of it? Have they done it before? Do they know what this process is? Is there a formal evaluation period for this sort of thing ("We buy all our tools in November and December for the year ahead.")? Or is there discretionary budget that can be utilized outside of typical budget cycles? This is why it's particularly good to cover other common solutions in the "pain and urgency" section of your pitch—if a prospect has spent money on solving this problem before, they clearly have a process for doing so.

Though it may feel weird to directly ask about this sort of thing, it's very important to do. It's great if an organization has business pain, but if they are unable to spend money on anything, let alone your solution, you're pissing your time away. And if your point of contact can't make purchasing decisions, that's fine—but you need to sort out who can, so you can make the case to the person with decision-making authority.

While the main goal of discovery is to qualify the prospect, you'll find yourself uncovering other valuable information. For instance, you'll start to get a sense of the general maturity level of the organization and their ability to solve the problems your solution addresses. You'll understand how forthcoming your point of contact is, and how readily he shares information. You'll even start settling into a better back-and-forth communication pattern, which is what you want the rest of your presentation, and the rest of your pipeline journey, to look like. And beyond all that, you'll benefit from demonstrating your commitment to making the conversation about the prospect's needs and business realities.

PRESENTATION, DEMO, & ASKING FOR THE SALE

Once you've completed discovery, you'll move from the part of the conversation where you are primarily consuming information to one where you are both consuming information and communicating it. Note that I didn't say that you'll be moving from listening to talking. If you are doing it right, you will still be consuming lots of information, asking lots of questions, and eliciting lots of feedback. However, you will be doing this while communicating your sales narrative, as documented in your slides, presentation, and demo scripting.

Overarching Guidelines

Before we talk about specific parts of your presentation and demo, some notes on things that will make you successful in your approach (and which may be different than prior presentations you've likely done).

Repetition

For many people, it's a big change to adjust to the amount of repetition that goes on in sales presentations. As writers and communicators, we typically worry about saying the same thing more than once, for fear of being boring or insulting the intelligence of the audience. In a sales presentation, repetition is your friend. You need to appreciate how new the topic you're covering is for your audience. You deal with the topic all the time, but they don't. It's critical to keep coming back to the key points that you want to get across, which typically correlate to the big messaging buckets in your sales narrative.

You can see what I mean in the TalentBin demo script we've already looked at. In brief, the key is that repeating the major points you want your prospects to take away—and constantly connecting various parts of your pitch, including pain point slides, solution slides, proof-of-value slides, and demonstrated features, back to those key points—will ensure that they stick.

Validation of Attention and Understanding

If the goal of the presentation is the communication of information that drives a prospect toward a commercial transaction, it's probably pretty important to know that the information is being consumed! How do you do this? Validate that your prospects are paying attention, and validate that they're understanding.

How do you validate attention? If you're face-to-face, look! Is your prospect looking at you or what you're projecting? Or are they on their phone or laptop? If the latter, you have to get their attention before you proceed, because otherwise you'll just be talking past them. On the phone this can be more of a challenge, in that you can't see what the prospect is doing. Tools like ClearSlide can tell you if the browser tab showing your presentation on prospects' computers is front-most, but even that's kind of weak. Instead, you have to ask things like "Can you see this right here on this slide?" to validate that they're following along.

Across the board, the best way to confirm that someone is paying attention, to regain attention if you've lost it, and to validate understanding is to ask questions. So after you make a point, ask something to make sure that the prospect has comprehended it—that will confirm whether she was paying attention and whether they actually "got it." The most basic question is "Does that make sense?" But the problem there is that prospects don't want to look dumb, so this often invites a standard "uh-huh" response, regardless of whether they are following along.

This is a bad outcome. You desperately want prospects to tell you if they're not following along so you can fix it quickly! One approach I use is proactively giving permission to say, "I'm not understanding." For instance, when presenting a slide for TalentBin on the growth of new specialty social networks like GitHub, Stack Overflow, Meetup, Behance, and so forth, I would ask, "Have you heard of some of these before?" to validate understanding. But to prevent prospects from saying yes even if they hadn't, I would say something like "It's okay if you haven't. Many are fairly new, and I didn't even know about them before we started TalentBin!"

or "It's okay if you haven't. These are pretty dorky specialty sites!" By doing this, you give prospects permission to not know, and ensure that they aren't too embarrassed to communicate their lack of understanding to you.

Another approach is to ask a specific question that requires a specific answer, ideally correlated to the pain point, solution, proof point, or feature being discussed. For instance, if you were Immediately, and discussing the challenges of field sales reps documenting customer-facing interactions, rather than saying, "Does that make sense?" the better approach would be something like "Do you find your field reps have this same issue?" Or if you were pitching TalentBin, and demonstrating a feature that showcases the benefits of automated email follow-up and drip marketing, you might ask, "Can you see how this sort of automation would reduce the amount of manual follow-up required to increase candidate response rates?" In this case, you can see that I am killing two birds with one stone—I am both trying to validate understanding of the feature and, by asking a leading question, seeking to elicit the prospect's agreement with one of my core points about TalentBin (another example of repetition).

Lastly, you can do open-ended questions as well, like "Do you have any questions for me so far?" and allowing the prospect to bring up anything that has been bothering them. By giving permission to do so, without judgment, you allow them to surface potential objections or concerns. Sometimes it takes real work to validate understanding, especially if you're selling over the phone and not face-to-face. But you absolutely must do it. Otherwise you might as well be talking into an empty room.

Rolling Discovery

One thing you may have noticed in the preceding section is that the questions used to validate attention and comprehension often sound a bit like discovery questions—or at least shortened versions of them. This is not a coincidence. In fact, as you proceed along your presentation, you can implement a form of "rolling discovery," where you learn more and more about the prospect's pain points, existing solutions, and so on, right at the moment that you're talking about a particular topic. For instance, if you're presenting pain point slides, you might ask if the prospect encounters those challenges. At TalentBin, when we were talking about poor LinkedIn InMail response rates, we'd ask, "Do you find your response rates aren't as good as you'd like?" and "Have you ever tried to find personal email addresses to help fix that?" Of course, if you already asked and got the answers to these questions in discovery, don't re-ask the question—take the opportunity to cite the prospect's response (repetition!). For example, "As you said earlier, you guys have the common issue of poor LinkedIn InMail response rates."

This sort of "rolling discovery" lets you get into discovery questions that are correlated to the specific pain point, solution statement, or feature that you're covering right there, which helps with comprehension. It also helps you out if you forgot a question in your discovery section. And if you have a lot of discovery questions you'd like to ask, this lets you distribute them, rather than stacking up a ten-minute interrogation at the beginning of the call!

Relatedly, you want to make sure that you're making use of the information that you surfaced through your discovery questions. This will allow you to make your pitch more impactful by correlating the things you are talking about to business realities at the prospect's organization. For instance, say we're pitching TalentBin, and the prospect tells us they'd love to send recruiting outreach to personal email addresses, but doesn't have the time to find those addresses. When we get to the part of the demo where we are showing off that TalentBin has millions of personal email addresses tied to candidate profiles, we'll relate that to the prospect's own words. By making good use of discovery information, we can demonstrate how our solution fixes a problem the prospect said they have, via a solution they already told us they know is the right one. Twofer!

Building Agreement

Extending from repetition and comprehension is the notion of building agreement. That is, at every opportunity, you want to elicit agreement from your prospect that their worldview is aligning with the one that you're espousing. If you do this well all along, at the conclusion of your pitch the sale should be a no-brainer! At that point, the prospect has agreed with you the whole time, about the pains they feel, the fact that existing solutions are not getting the job done, that it's important to solve this problem now, and that the solution you're proposing definitely does so. Now let's just sign a contract!

How do you achieve this consensus? As with validating comprehension, the best strategy is to ask for agreement at every point where it makes sense—to "score points." You can do this with leading questions that get the prospect to surface his agreement, or, just as important, his disagreement. Every time you can get the prospect to say that yes, they share that pain point, that yes, it is substantial across their organization, that yes, they've tried that other approach to fix it, and that yes, this specific feature looks like it fits that specific pain point well, you're building agreement. You're building a groundswell of alignment that leads inexorably to the prospect purchasing your solution.

Pacing and Pausing

By the time you've done a dozen or so of these pitches, you're going to have it pretty nailed. And when you know something well, you have a tendency to speed up your delivery. Even before that point, nervousness also tends to compel faster delivery.

Resist this. In pursuit of comprehension and agreement, you need to make sure that your delivery is methodical. Deliberate pacing will ensure that words aren't missed and that your prospect has the best chance to comprehend what you're saying and how it relates to what's on the screen or projector. Further, pausing here and there to allow for questions, and to proactively test for comprehension, ensures that there are opportunities for the prospect to "catch their breath" and clarify, if needed.

This becomes all the more important if you are delivering the pitch via phone. Because the prospect doesn't have the benefit of facial and gesture-based information, enunciation and conservative pacing will be all the more important. But even face-to-face, you want to make sure your presentation pacing is deliberate, and includes frequent breaks.

Customization and Curation

We've discussed personalization of your pitch at length in the Sales Material chapter, and in Pre-Call Planning, but now is when you put it to use. Because of your diligent prospecting, planning, and discovery, you are at peak understanding of the account's business context. So use it! The worst thing possible would be running through a canned presentation despite all that additional information—instead, put it to work for you.

You should feel empowered to completely drop whole slides out of your presentation, or to skip over features in your demo, that you don't think will appeal to the audience. You only have a certain amount of time in which to make your case—you should be spending those minutes on the topics that have the highest chance to resonate. This also means doubling down on pain points, value propositions, and features that will be particularly meaningful to the prospect.

So if you were pitching TalentBin to someone who was already very well aware of GitHub and Stack Overflow, and had previously used a competing talent search tool but canceled it, you would focus on substantially different things than if you were pitching to a prospect who was completely new to Internet talent search. For instance, you would probably quickly gloss over the "Here's how the Internet has changed to allow for finding technical talent" section, because the prospect knows the landscape already. And you'd probably speed through how TalentBin aggregates social network web profiles, since, again, he likely already knows that from prior experience. However, you would likely focus more on the differentiators between the former solution they were using and TalentBin. That is, you would change your pitch to focus on the things that were likely to matter.

Micro-Contract Creation and Execution

It's crucial during the pitching and down-funnel process that you have a good handle on where things stand. That is, is this deal still heading toward success? Has a potential block arisen that needs to be handled? Or has the prospect decided that there's no way he's moving forward? The reason knowing where you stand is so important is so you don't spend time on opportunities that are dead in the water. As we've previously discussed, your most important resource in sales is your time. There are likely thousands and thousands of potential prospects for your solution, but you only have forty (or sixty!) hours in your week.

A great way to facilitate being on the same page is what are known as "micro-contracts" between you and the prospect. That is, before you do something with the prospect (e.g., ask discovery questions, present slides, demo), you articulate what you want to do and why and ask if they are in agreement that it is the correct next step. This is a tool espoused in Sandler Sales Methodology, called "upfront contracts" there. You likely used it when setting the appointment, when you characterized the agenda and gained the prospect's agreement to attend, but it extends to the pitch, and even beyond. As you progress through your pitch and your demo, and through incremental demos, negotiations, and implementation, setting clear expectations with the prospect will help keep things moving and prevent getting stuck.

For instance, if after your initial demo it appears that the solution is a good fit, but there is a need to involve another decision-maker, then you should "contract" for that next meeting. That is, say, "It seems to me that you believe this solution can help your organization solve <the problem that you're focused on>, and that you believe it would be a good fit. But in order to progress, we need to involve Tonya so she can validate the conclusion we have come to. Is that right? If so, let's get another presentation on the calendar for you, her, and me. Do you have your calendar and her's available to you?"

If the prospect was genuinely interested in proceeding, then great—you get that meeting on the calendar right then and there. If for whatever reason the prospect was fudging a little bit, and there is another wrinkle (as in, they have no budget), it will surface. And that will be a huge benefit to you. The contract that the prospect wouldn't make keeps you from wasting your time chasing "Tonya" around. It gives you clarity.

If you do make the contract, restate it at the start of that next meeting to establish continuity of the deal in flight: "Tonya, Jeff and I met last week to discuss {*Your_Company*}'s challenges in {*business_pain*}. Based on the outcome of our conversation, Jeff and I believe that this is a very worthwhile investment for your organization, and stands to provide a lot of value. But it is my understanding that we need to share this case with you, so you can validate our conclusion, before we progress to a commercial agreement. And that is the purpose of this call today. Does that align with your expectations?"

At any point in the sales process, if you uphold your side of one of these micro-contracts, but the prospect diverges from his commitment, it is an early warning system. And you'll be justified in stating your concern: "I'm confused. We agreed that you believed this solution made sense for your organization, and is well positioned to help you save $X per year. Our next step was to meet with your CFO to help her validate your conclusion. But two of those meetings have been canceled at the last minute. Can you confirm for me that this is something that is a priority, and that you believe is important for your organization?"

Through continual creation and execution of micro-contracts, you can make sure that you are being effective with your time, and always on the same page with the prospect.

Presentation

Now that we've covered some overarching principles for your pitch, let's talk about its chronology. Some people think that a pitch should only be done in-product and jump straight to that. I feel it's important to set the correct "mental model," so that prospects are well primed to get the most out of the conversation. That is, I like to start by getting them into the mindset of the problem that we solve, and how our solution is poised to help, and only then move into showing how the product actually works.

What we are not doing is running through a slew of features and screenshots, where the prospect sits back and just listens. A "show and tell" (or better, a "show up and throw up") presentation, and later demo, is a recipe for an unengaged prospect who is not actively considering your commercial argument, nor seriously thinking about business pain and how your solution solves it. Instead of reeling off feature after feature in a one-way information deluge, you want to use the tone you set in your discovery conversation and cultivate a rich back-and-forth conversation with the prospect.

The best way to make sure that this happens, again, is to be explicit about it. Something along the lines of "Okay! Thank you so much for sharing all that great information with me. It's really going to make this a productive conversation. So, based on what you've shared with me, I think that what we're up to is definitely relevant to what you guys at <company> are doing as related to <whatever it is that you solve>. What I'd like to do next is share some slides that help set the tone on what we do, before we get into the product live demo. Does that work for you?" This helps the prospect understand what's coming, and continues the process of building agreement.

Disqualification

Of course, this is also the point in time where you can offramp a prospect that isn't qualified. That is, if the organization doesn't have the pain points that you seek to solve, or it is clear that it has no ability to pay for solutions to solve the problem, then you should seek to conclude the conversation on great terms. (Remember, though, that if it's simply your contact who doesn't have authority to expend budget, but the organization does have the pain points you solve, you can partner with him to get to the right decision-maker.)

The best way to close out the conversation is to frame it in terms of respect for the prospect's time. Something like "You know what, <name>, based on everything we just talked about, I don't think that what we're up to is going to be super helpful in your <whatever you do> efforts. We mainly help out people and organizations that <fill in the specific thing that your solution solves here>. I know you're a busy person, and don't want to waste your time on something that isn't helpful. I'm happy to send you some slides or demo videos, but I would propose that we just go ahead and conclude this call, and I can give you back thirty minutes of your time. What do you say?"

You win credibility with prospects this way, and you make it clear who you're relevant to (so they can refer their friends who do have the pain point in question). Ideally this doesn't happen too much, especially if you've done a good job of using externally available information to prequalify prospects, and if your appointment-setting process is honed to put only valid opportunities on the calendar. But in the rare case it happens, close it out.

Introducing Your Narrative

If the account is qualified, there is a set of goals that you want to achieve during the presentation before you get into the actual product demonstration. First and foremost, you need to convey the parts of your sales narrative that are better communicated with slides than with a demo—things like pain points, the failures of current solutions, how your solution works (the conceptual framing), and qualitative and quantitative proof of why it is a better way to solve the business issue. As discussed in the Sales Materials chapter, the visuality of slides allows for much richer communication of these parts of your narrative than simply speaking to them in the abstract. Communicating your product's features and how they work is typically better done in a demonstration, but for the other parts of your sales narrative, this is the exact reason you invested in building a sales deck.

While product features and their value proofs may be documented in your presentation, you generally should avoid getting into them ahead of your demo. Those slides are typically better used as offline reminders of the features you've demonstrated live. Think of them as something for your prospect and her colleagues to refer to after you've blown their socks off. The exception here is cases where, for whatever reason, a live demonstration of your software is not possible. Nowadays this scenario is pretty rare, and I would recommend figuring out a way to avoid it—even if you need to do a demo loaded with dummy data.

For your presentation, you'll want to have your "master deck," or the personalized variant of it, ready and loaded into Showpad or DocSend, or ready to project on your machine. As you progress in your presentation, especially if you're doing a good job of facilitating a rich back-and-forth, invariably topics or questions will pop up that may make you hop out of order. That's perfectly okay, and should be welcomed. You want to use all the materials you have at your disposal to achieve the goal set out above, and if that means backtracking to an earlier part of the presentation because one of your comprehension checks fails, or skipping to an appendix slide based on a question that surfaces, then you should do so. Don't think you have to slavishly progress slide by slide, on a death march through your presentation, as that will trip you up in your pursuit of a rich consultative conversation. Moreover, if it becomes abundantly clear that the goal of your presentation (comprehension of the parts of your sales narrative not covered by your demo) has already been achieved, and the prospect is ready and eager to progress to the demo, by all means, skip ahead!

You can come back to slides after the demo too. In fact, this is a fairly typical pattern. Jumping from the live demo back to a slide that talks about the benefits and ROI of the feature you just highlighted is a great way to connect the live product to the value the prospect will get out of it.

Demo

We talked about your demo script in the Sales Materials chapter, so you should be familiar with what you want to talk through in your demo. However, to reiterate, the difference between your sales presentation and your demo is that your presentation is about setting the correct mental model, and the demo is about demonstrating how the actual product delivers on the promises you've made. It's also an opportunity to do so in a way that makes maximum use of the fact that you and the prospect are synchronously looking at the same thing and can have a rich discussion (whereas slides can be consumed asynchronously at a later date).

Customization

One of the biggest differences between the sales presentation and the demo is that while the sales presentation slides will frequently be the same from prospect to prospect (with perhaps some light customization as discussed in the Sales Materials chapter), the demo is far more likely to be heavily tailored to the prospect's needs.

The best option is using actual data or materials from the prospect in your demo. There's a great old story about how Postini, a spam filter company long since purchased by Google, would have the CIO they were selling to point email traffic at a Postini server, which would immediately start filtering out spam that the CIO's existing filters were failing to catch—a great demo to be sure! At that point, the rep could say, "Pretty great, right? Shall I draw up a proposal? Or would you like your spam back?" It's a bit flippant, but it really gets the point across. The demo had proven that the solution did what was promised in the sales presentation, and did so with the prospect's actual work environment.

If your product has a partial "freemium" component, and some employees of the target organization are already using it in some regard, a good approach may be to use that particular instance, perhaps alongside one set up for a demo. "You can see what Fred, Jane, and Ian from your team are doing here. In fact, here's the reporting interface that you would get access to as a paid customer, and you can see their level of usage." Not every product is going to be easy to use with real customer data in a demo. But as you're thinking about your product and its features, you'll be well served to consider how they can best be demonstrated, not just how they work in the abstract. Remember too that you're customizing your demo not just for the account in question, but for the type of stakeholder you're talking to.

Demo-Ready Data

If you can't use your prospect's real data, you can use the next best thing—data that supports all the use cases and proofs you want to demonstrate.

You'd be amazed how many demos I've watched where the data being used made it nigh impossible to get the point across. That's not just a huge lost opportunity, it's also an ugly turnoff. You have total control of the demo instance, and you couldn't be bothered to get it into a state that easily demonstrates the value of your solution? Jeez, what other shortcuts are you taking? That doesn't instill a lot of confidence. Any time you find yourself saying things like "Well, ignore that" or "Imagine if XYZ," you probably have a data problem.

This doesn't necessarily mean that you need product investment or engineering assistance to fix the problem, but you do have to do the work to get yourself properly set up—which likely isn't all that challenging. But if, for whatever reason, you can't manually get the data in your product into a state that lets you demonstrate effectively, well, then you might need to have a conversation with engineering and product. You're going to be doing a lot of these demos, and later, if you're successful, there will be many sales reps joining you. (Not to mention that having "example data" in your product for new customers is often helpful, and makes for more compelling first user experiences.)

Think about this every time a feature ships. You likely add a slide to your sales deck breaking down a new feature, so what do you have to do to your demo to make sure that you can showcase this new feature and its implications in a high-impact fashion? If you're spending those expensive engineering resources on building something, you certainly want to make sure it's nice and sales-ready, with all the associated sales materials.

Focusing on Features that Matter

As with your sales presentation, you should think about which specific features you want to focus on to make your demo most effective. You probably only have fifteen to thirty minutes of time to do actual product demonstration, so make sure to prioritize the features that will be most compelling to your prospect. Now's the time to put to use all that excellent prospecting, planning, and discovery you did, and to remember to speak the "language" of your prospect.

If you were selling Textio, for example, and learned in discovery that the prospect was frustrated with what a mess job-description management is for hiring managers and recruiters, you would take special care to demo the templating and management features of your product. Or if you were LifeGuides, and you knew that your prospect was very much into making sure their careers Twitter feed was well stocked with compelling content, you would focus on how LifeGuides makes it extremely easy to produce dozens and dozens of lightweight employee video testimonials that are perfect for stocking an employment-focused social media feed.

Obviously there are going to be parts of your demo that you're very excited to share across prospects, and core use cases you'll include to make sure your point comes across. (We discussed this in the Demo Scripts section of the Sales Materials chapter.) But make sure you know what parts are optional and can be cut out so that you can spend more time on high-priority features.

Proof Demonstration

The demo isn't the conclusion of the sales call; it actually sits in the middle. Once you've completed discovery to arm yourself for the call, the slide presentation to set the right mental model, and the demo to show off the actual goods, it's time for the next step: "Why we know this works and why this is a great investment."

This is where I like to switch back to slides, where all of these proof points are laid out. As with the pre-demo sales presentation, the visual nature of slides makes for better communication of quantitative and qualitative material. If you talk about ROI and other proof points while the prospect is looking at features, he's not going to retain anything. Use visual exhibits.

You can refer to the previous section on "Proof Points" slides for your sales deck to refresh yourself, but the point here is that you're now talking about why everything you've presented so far is a great investment. And you're backing it up with proof. Whether that means feature-by-feature ROI studies, aggregated customer ROI information, customer-by-customer ROI examples, or qualitative proof—or a combination of all of that—you're progressing to the "this is why this is a no-brainer" part of the presentation. Don't skip this important step before attempting to close the sale.

Pricing and Asking for the Sale

This is typically the concluding part of the pitch, although you may not get to it if you haven't done all the preceding steps correctly. If you have, it is extremely important to not skip this step. For founders and first-time salespeople, presenting pricing and affirmatively asking for the sale is often where the most mistakes are made—largely because they don't do it. After going to all this trouble to find the prospect, make an appointment, and then present the value of their solution, they drop the ball short of full execution.

It's an understandable error. This is where you can feel the most exposed to rejection. It's akin to another common founder error, selling to people they know versus qualified accounts because acquaintances are less likely to reject them. But we're going to surmount this! And we're going to get good at it. Part of the trick here is convincing yourself that your solution is worth it. And if your pitch is well formed, with great proof points and a rational pricing scheme based on market comps or proven ROI, you should have zero fear. Your engineers cost money, and you need to pay them. Your solution will put money in the customer's pocket—either through reduced costs or increased revenue—so you are completely justified in taking part of that created value for yourself. Let's ask for it!

First, prospects often ask for pricing on their own. If you've followed the flow we just walked through—discovery, presentation, demo, proof—and done so with a prospect who has your pain points, validating along the way that he is qualified, you'll be amazed how frequently prospects ask for pricing information at this stage. Don't be surprised! They've been in commercial conversations like this before; that's part of what makes them qualified prospects. Particularly if a prospect is already using inferior existing solutions—paying money to solve the specific problem your solution solves—the revelation of your magical new solution to their now-validated pain points will of course lead to the logical next question: "Wow, this is all really great. What's pricing?"

If a prospect does indeed ask for pricing, you should be happy. People typically only ask if they're interested in buying, and you just captured a valuable piece of information—this prospect likely thinks your solution makes sense, provided the price is right. This is when it is helpful to have that pricing slide that you can flip to quickly. Also, this is why, when we covered appointment setting, I encouraged you to forestall discussion of pricing until you could help frame the conversation with the prospect. Telling someone "Yeah, it's ten thousand per recruiter per year" in a vacuum could result in a lot of sticker shock. However, once you've presented the problem, how you solve it, why this is better, and all the proof points associated with that—well, $10,000 might be a screaming deal.

If a prospect doesn't ask for pricing unprompted, I like to use this as an opportunity for a "trial close," rather than just driving ahead to a pricing slide. That is, I gather more information about his mindset, post-presentation—something along the lines of "Given all we've covered, is this something that you see being useful in solving your <fill in problem here> challenges?" If the answer is no, that's potentially very concerning, since they're articulating lack of interest without even knowing the price. Yikes. It will be all the more important, in that case, to dig into the prospect's objections, because this may be indicative of an issue with your prospecting, discovery, presentation, and demo process. More on handling these sorts of objections below.

If the answer is "yes", the prospect has just given you an interesting piece of information—he's excited about paying for your product, even though he hasn't heard pricing yet. This seems like a pretty good sign for you, given that he certainly knows your product will cost something. In fact, in the back of his mind, he likely indexed off of an existing solution that he's already paying for. In TalentBin's case, for example, the thought running through the prospect's head was typically "This probably costs the same as a LinkedIn Recruiter or Monster Resume Search seat. I'd pay that for this." So, in effect, the prospect has signaled not only his interest, but also, perhaps, a price floor. If the answer is "Well, that depends on what it costs," that's also fine. Just progress to discussing pricing as if the prospect had asked you directly.

Presenting Pricing

Depending on your model, the pricing you present will often be just a straw man of what you eventually put together in an honest-to-goodness proposal (more on this in a second). That is, if you sell on a per-seat basis, you would likely present the list price for a single seat to gauge reaction. Or if you sell on some other per-each basis, the same would be true. If you sell based on some other constraint, like size of an organization, it's going to be fairly obvious what pricing will be, so you'll want to jump to that. When presenting pricing, it's great to frame it in the context of existing solutions, best alternatives, or opportunity costs that you've already touched on in discovery and your presentation.

For instance, if you're Immediately, and your pricing is, say, $30 per month per sales rep, you might frame it as "It's thirty dollars per rep per month. So if you consider that your average rep is making a hundred fifty thousand, it's fifteen minutes of salary expense per rep. Of course, Immediately will save them hours and hours per week." Or if you're LifeGuides, and you know that the customer is paying for a $20,000-a-year LinkedIn Premium company profile, you might present your pricing in relation to that. Or if you're HIRABL, you might present it in the context of projected ROI based on existing experience, like "Typically we charge one dollar per monitored submission per year, so based on your organization's submission volume, that would be around ten thousand dollars. We would anticipate finding between ten to twenty missed fees over the course of a year, representing between one hundred twenty-five and two hundred fifty thousand in recovered fees for you. Not a bad deal, right?" Eventually you may do this more formally, using text and visuals, in a follow-up proposal, but doing so verbally is the first step.

When you're verbally presenting pricing, you'll want to start at the most extreme case, knowing that you'll probably end up being negotiated down. This is why presenting just a single unit of pricing (e.g., one seat, one discrete unit of use) is helpful, because when you then roll that up to the fifty seats that the prospect needs, you'll have baked in wiggle room for yourself. Don't back yourself into a corner and start negotiating against yourself at the start, like "It's ten thousand dollars per seat, but don't worry, I can get you a deal." Just state the pricing and the rationale that backs it, shut the hell up, and see what the reaction is. This is often one of the hardest things to do, sitting in silence waiting for the reaction. But you have to do it.

From there, you can take a variety of paths. If the reaction is positive—along the lines of "Well that's not bad" or "That makes sense"—you should move on to asking for the sale and closing. More on this below. If the reaction is negative—like "Wow, that's really expensive" or "There's no way we could pay that"—you'll have to get into handling that objection. And if it's in the middle—like "Well, that's a lot, but I see where you're coming from"—you'll progress along the same lines as the positive case and ask for the sale.

Asking for the Sale

When you have leading indicators of interest, it's time to proactively ask for the sale. None of this "So, what do you think?" wishy-washy stuff. Forthrightly ask for the business. Good approaches here are things like "Based on what we've discussed, this sounds like a great fit. Is this something that you would want to progress with?" or "Is there anything that is preventing us from getting you started as a customer?" As noted before, so much of business-to-business selling is simply understanding where you stand with your prospect and taking the next appropriate action. Nothing quite cuts to the chase like asking the prospect whether she wants to make a deal.

There are a variety of other slick closing techniques, but all are really just versions of asking for the sale. There's the "waffles or pancakes" approach of "Would you prefer one seat or two?". And the timing-centric, "We have a number of openings with our customer success organization for implementation calls next week. Would you like to schedule one?" and so on. You can Google around to see other approaches. But the point is, directly asking for the sale (compared to beating around the bush, or avoiding it because you're afraid of rejection) is 90% of the battle.

If the answer is yes, fantastic! You're closer to the goal. The next step would typically be to put together a proposal with a couple options for them to choose from, assuming there are different options. That is, say you're TalentBin, selling to an organization with twenty recruiters. If there was discussion as to whether the prospect might start with just one seat, or seats for all twenty, you'd want an opportunity to craft a proposal that potentially leads the prospect to a higher initial purchase. You can present along the lines of "Excellent! Would you like me to put together a proposal that covers some options that you could go with?"

If there's no reason to present a proposal with varied options—that is, it's clear there is really only one path to a purchase for the prospect—it's better to just skip to the contract. Try something like "That's fantastic. If you'd like, I can send over an order form that you can execute via digital signature, and we can get started today." Again, you would only do this if the customer is qualified, she has articulated that she wants to execute on this, and you believe she has the authority to do so. Conveniently, all of this was covered back in discovery, setting you up for this very moment. Now you can see why we do this!

If the answer is no, welcome to the most common response. But instead of meaning "No, never" or "No, no way," this is typically an "I'm not sure" masked in a no. Your job is simply to uncover the objections that are blocking you from progressing, handle them, and then loop back to "Okay, now will you buy?" More on this below.

Proposals

A proposal is a helpful way of framing a couple different options to a customer who has articulated a desire to buy.

That stated interest is crucial—you definitely don't want to be in the business of sending proposals willy-nilly to prospects who haven't asked for them. Do that, and you'll be losing out on a key signpost on the progression from prospect to customer. Proposals should be reserved only for prospects that have said they want to buy.

Why a proposal and not just a contract? Well, an order form/contract is probably the most basic proposal that you can produce, and shouldn't be disparaged at all. It has the added benefit of being executable (assuming you send it via digital signature method, like DocuSign, HelloSign, or Adobe eSign). The downside with sending a contract is that a contract is typically just for a single offering—like one seat of your solution. So if you want to show a couple options, you're stuck. Moreover, a contract or order form is more about documenting the price that someone is going to pay for a set of services. It's not a piece of marketing collateral, and to the extent that your deal isn't closed yet, you would like to use all the tooling available to get that deal slammed shut.

A lightweight proposal can help with these downsides. First, it lets you present a couple of options whereby you can direct the prospect toward an outcome that is more beneficial for you. By presenting options, you're removing cognitive overhead, so the prospect doesn't need to compose his own option. At the same time, you're making it clear that this isn't about whether he's going to buy—it's just a question of which option!

At the earliest stages, bigger purchases are better—within reason—provided they don't overwhelm your customer success resources. The marginal cost of adding another seat of software to an account is typically pretty near zero; this is the magic of software. Yes, there may be more support costs, but even those are usually added on a per-account basis. Selling three seats to a given account will not cost three times the support as one seat to the same account. So if you can figure out how to get marginal revenue out of a given opportunity, you should try to jump for it.

One strategy for maximizing a sale is to present three options in your proposal, where the middle option is your target (and the highest option is still a realistic reach). Let's say you're TalentBin, for example, selling to an organization with ten recruiters, only five of whom would get maximal use out of the solution (i.e., five are technical recruiters, and the others are generalist recruiters who might only occasionally dip into the product). You might still present pricing for three, five, and ten seats. But where the three-seat option is nearest to list price (i.e., $6,000 x 3 = $18,000), the five-seat option seems like a pretty compelling discount (i.e., maybe 5 for the price of 4.25). The ten-seat option—again, taking into account that those incremental five users are pretty unlikely to use TalentBin except cursorily—might be ten seats for the price of seven. That is, for those incremental 5 seats, you'll only charge the cost of 2.75 extra seats, recognizing that the value they provide might be lower (but still significant on the occasions the product proves useful to the casual user).

Ideally the various options land at helpful price points, just below potential psychological thresholds (e.g., $10,000, $19,500, and $24,000, as an example). You can take this approach, as well, when you know there's a certain amount of budget available. You might price your middle option for that "known good" budget, your bottom option below that (but very costly on a per-each basis), and the highest option as a "stretch goal" that is a screaming deal on a per-unit basis.

If you know that the maximum budget could potentially be in play, then you certainly want to not only present a proposal for it, but guide the prospect toward that "best deal" via pricing inducements. Many corporate purchasers are used to taking the "gold-plated" option, so having something at the top end, while also providing some air cover by making it look like a "deal," makes it more likely they can jump on it. Plus, if it's not there, they can't even consider it. So include it! Even if they don't end up going for that high end, by presenting it you make it that much more likely the prospect goes with an option above the very bottom one. Going back to our TalentBin example, if you only presented pricing for three and five seats, the five-seat option would be the "expensive" one, potentially impacting the prospect's perception of its viability.

There's definitely an art to these sorts of things, requiring an understanding of how much potential demand there is in the prospect organization, how much budget is available, and how much pain is present. You don't want to overthink it and get too complicated. And if the prospect pushes back and decides to go with a lower-tier option that wasn't presented, that's fine; send over an order form and call it a day. But there is a lot of potential upside associated with presenting options that are above and beyond just trying to sell the base-level deal and running on to the next one.

A note on cannibalization. At a later stage, you might be worried about cannibalizing potential demand via discounting what you could sell for full price. That is, if you have confidence that your solution will spread within an organization, you might be concerned that you were taking $16,500 (5 seats for the price of 2.75 x $6,000 per seat) for seats that could eventually earn you another $30,000 at full price. Early on, don't worry too much about it. Instead, strive for that incremental cash in your bank account, right now.

Another thing that proposals can be nice for is framing the projected ROI associated with those different options. This goes to the concept that a proposal is a piece of marketing collateral, helping to sell for you even when you're not engaging directly with the prospect. They can also help your champion play "show and tell" with the ultimate decision-maker, if necessary. If it's just your contact who needs to make the decision, then having this information nicely presented for her is helpful. However, if there is a CFO or some other back-check authority, having all of this bundled up in a nice tight package, ideally including your logo and the prospect's, will do wonders for the credibility afforded you, and your champion. That is, you make her look like she's done her homework and is bringing a well-reasoned proposal (ha!) to the table, reducing potential skepticism by her internal back-check counterpart.

When it comes to delivering a proposal, it doesn't have to be too fancy. To start with, you can do it manually. I'm a fan of a templated PowerPoint presentation where you can drop in the relevant options, the prospect's logo, and any sort of ROI projections. Later, you can get more involved and tie information from your CRM "Opportunity" object into a programmatically generated proposal using something like Conga Composer, Drawloop, or Octiv. Not only do these save you the time of manually putting the relevant information into a proposal, but often they will have their own e-signing functionality, or let you integrate with DocuSign or Adobe eSign. That way, when the prospect chooses which option she wants, she can just click through and sign, rather than having to tell you her selection. Anything that can remove a step of friction and back-and-forth is beneficial.

OBJECTIONS

In the grand majority of your sales interactions, it's not going to be an immediate yes, nor will it be a cut-and-dried no. Instead, it will most commonly be a "No, because of this" or "Well, what about this?" And all those equivocal responses come under the heading of "objections" that you need to handle before returning to the close.

Often first-time sales staff are afraid of objection handling, because it feels like you're starting conflict with the prospect. Why am I arguing with the person I want to sign this proposal?!

The reality is that handling objections is where some of the most important work in sales is done. If sales is about commercial persuasion, this is where the rubber hits the road. This is where you examine, one by one, the things that are blocking your prospect from proceeding, and surmount them using business-based arguments and proof.

That's not to say that this has to be contentious, but you will be best served by being direct. When a prospect surfaces an objection that runs counter to their business reality, it is your duty to address it head on. This general concept of "respectful contentiousness" has been popularized by Matthew Dixon and Brent Adamson in their book The Challenger Sale. It's all the more important in innovative technology sales, where you must change minds to popularize a new approach to a business problem—which typically requires challenging existing mindsets.

We touched on this briefly when talking about objection handling in the Appointment Setting chapter. Now, instead of surmounting objections to taking a meeting, you're surmounting objections to proceeding with the purchase. Further, you have far more information about the prospect's internal situation, thanks to all the discovery you executed, so you can handle these objections with very concrete examples that are rooted in his business realities. Moreover, you are on the far side of your presentation and demo, in which you made the case for why your solution is a solid fit for the organization, building agreement with the prospect as you went. So objections should be nothing to fear, given your position of strength.

As with the objections you were handling in Appointment Setting, objections to a sale are a good thing! You know the prospect is actively engaging with you and considering the sale, rather than going silent or just saying something abstract and content-free like "No, I don't think it's a fit." A great way to elicit specific objections when a prospect is being vague is with a line like "What specifically is blocking us from progressing right now?" That puts it to her to surface one, or many, concrete objections.

The objections that you run into will be both generic and specific to your solution. The generic ones will be similar to those we covered in Appointment Setting, around timing, budget, authority, need, and price. Then there will be those that are specific to your solution, which may be versions of those generic ones or specifically address feature and functionality concerns or competition. We'll talk about the generic ones first, then move on to the solution-specific ones.

Generic Objections

Generic Objections can generally be divided into the following categories—lack of decision-making authority, lack of need, fear of change, timing, price, budgeting challenges, and reluctance. We will discuss how to respond to and resolve each of these issues below.

Lack of Decision-Making Authority

If the objection is around authority, this is an easy one to resolve. During discovery (see how it all comes back to discovery!?), you were supposed to figure out what the organization's process is for making judgments about tooling, and who makes final decisions. Well, now you just come back to that.

The important thing to understand is whether this is the true blocker. Is the prospect sold on the solution, and honestly telling you that he doesn't have the authority to commit to purchasing? This is important because handling this objection is going to involve assisting the prospect in navigating his organization with your help—you will essentially be partnering with the prospect to sell the next decision-maker in the org. And because this can be a squirrely exercise, you want to make sure that he is fully bought in as a "champion" of your solution.

You can validate that with something like "Is the authority to make this decision the only thing that is blocking us from getting you started?" This helps you understand if there is anything else lurking, or if you can point your efforts toward this issue. If questioning elicits other objections— like price or budget or feature deficit—great, handle those first. But you don't want to get into a situation where you and your champion are sitting on a call with his boss or the CFO and something else bubbles up. Yuck.

Assuming that yes, your prospect is indeed bought in, it's now just a question of project managing the next step of the sale to engage, with the help of your prospect, the ultimate decision-maker or set of decision-makers. Ideally you would have been engaged with them from the get-go, but often the budget-holder and decision-maker are removed from the person who would understand and appreciate your solution. For example, sometimes organizations will run purchasing decisions through a finance staffer, like a controller or CFO, to make sure that there are strong ROI arguments and efficiencies deriving from the purchase. Or other times, it may be the manager of the prospect that you're engaged with, who is removed from the pain point that your solution addresses. Whoever it is, you need to elicit that information from your prospect, and then offer to run point on engaging the decision-maker to get the ball across the line.

Typically I prefer to not give the prospect the ball to run with here and, instead, like to put the onus on myself to manage that process, under the guise of being "helpful." Of course, the goal is to ensure that I have control over moving the conversation forward, and am not gated by the prospect dropping the ball. Because while your contact may be excited about your solution, advocating for it is not his day job. It's yours. Also, he likely will not be as good at it as you. So you should be the one running point on setting up incremental meetings with other decision-makers. Just treat it as another demo that will likely be foreshortened.

How to do this? Well, first, eliciting the names of the decision-makers can be dicey this late in the conversation, because the prospect may be concerned that you'll just run ahead and engage them, leaving him out of the loop—or making it look like he just dropped a rabid sales rep in their laps! Again, that's why getting this information via discovery at the beginning of the conversation is so much better. Or even before that in pre-call planning, when you figured out who the potential decision-maker could be (boss, boss's boss, etc.). The closing conversation is so far from prospects' minds at that point, they're less guarded with this information. But regardless, you can use the same gambit as before, using LinkedIn to sniff out who your contact's likely boss or likely decision-maker is and surfacing that. An easy approach here is something like "Fantastic, I am very excited to work with you to help {the_relevant_decision-maker_in_the_org} understand how helpful this will be for {whatever_the_problem_to_be_solved_is}. I know you're busy, so I would love to take point on setting an appointment so we can both present this to her. Is her calendar available to you? If so, we can get fifteen minutes scheduled right now, and keep this ball rolling!" If the relevant person's calendar isn't available, you can volunteer to start an email thread including your champion and the target decision-maker wherein that scheduling takes place. (Ideally you should just assumptively propose some times, the way you would in an appointment-setting context.)

Once a meeting is calendared, you would just approach it as a second demo, with all the associated pre-call planning, a stated goal, and customization for the type of person that you're "selling." In this case, you're selling the decision-maker on the fact that her deputy is bought into this solution; you just need to make it clear that this is a good expenditure of budget. Often you will find that the decision-maker in question is just back-checking the judgment of the deputy, and that it's a rubber stamp situation. However, this goes back to the importance of having good ROI documentation in your slides and proposal. These higher-level managers are not going to care as much about individual bells and whistles as business outcome proof.

We Don't Have a Need

Of all the generic objections you'll get, "We don't have the need" is the most concerning. As touched on above, if the prospect doesn't think your solution is a fit, there's something problematic going on. It goes back to the "persuasion formula" we talked about at the beginning of the chapter. Does the prospect really not have the need, and you just did a poor job on prospecting and discovery? Then you probably shouldn't be selling to him. Or does he actually have the need, but is not grasping the potential value? Or does he not believe that his organization would capture it? You need to figure out the issue.

On the first point—validating actual need—this is why understanding objective external signifiers of demand, and making sure to do good discovery, is key. Because if those signifiers of need are absent, well, you shouldn't be pitching that prospect anyway. But if they're present, it puts you in a much better position to get to the bottom of things.

Despite all your best intentions and efforts, sometimes through crossed wires you can get to the far side of a pitch and discover something that contradicts those previous signals of need. So your first job is to re-verify that need. For Immediately, this might be something like "I'm confused. Based on our discussion at the beginning of this call and my research on LinkedIn, your company has fifty outside sales reps. And from what we talked about earlier, your sales management struggles with getting those reps to log meetings, emails, and contact information in the CRM because they're mobile all day long. Is this not the case?"

Note that the sentence includes all of the need signifiers, so you are sure that they have an opportunity to address where the shortfall is. Is it with the number of reps? Are they not actually outside sales reps? Or are they actually quite good about logging activity in the CRM? What are you missing? Again, this is not about calling someone out as a fibber, but instead about getting clarity of information, so you should not be squeamish. If in response to this inquiry, your prospect surfaces a piece of information that makes it clear that, after all, they don't have the need for your product, well, next time you need to be better at discovery! This would have to be something specific that contradicts the prior indicators of need, though, like, "Oh, well, we do have fifty reps, but only five are actually outside sales reps." That would be a specific data point, and you should take it seriously. However, if the response is squishy, like "Well, I just don't think we need it," that's code for something else, and you need to get to the bottom of it.

It can be harder to contend with a prospect who continues to claim that he doesn't have the need after all, even though you know that he does (either from external information, things that he or his colleagues have already said, or just a general squishiness in his response to your inquiries). In that event, it's likely that he's using this generic objection as a cover for the real objection (whether budget, authority, priority, etc.). You want to get clarity on that by helping him understand that he can be straight with you. This can be delicate, because you don't want him to feel that you're calling him out, so frame it in a way that makes it seem like perhaps he was just sparing your feelings before. You can do that by adding something to the above question, like "Well, from everything I can see, it appears to me that your organization definitely has the need for this, but perhaps there is something else blocking us from progressing that we haven't discussed yet? You can be straight with me, I can take it!"

The goal here is to get down to the actual reason, so you can handle that objection on its merits. You're trying to get the prospect to surface a more specific issue, like "I'm concerned that I won't have time to use the product" or "I don't think it will be as useful as <your competitor>" or something like that. Something that is specific, and can be addressed on its own.

We're Happy with How We Do It Right Now/Fear of Change

Often when prospects articulate that they "don't see the need" or "don't think it's a fit," they're actually making this objection, in disguise. That is, the prospect validates that she does indeed have the need in question, but articulates to you that she is unwilling to make a change to her way of doing things. This is actually a much better place to be than "we don't have the need," because you have gained agreement that she does indeed have the need. Now you're just having a discussion about why she should grasp the opportunity to adopt a new way of attacking this need.

The best way to approach these objections is to take the hidden cost of continuing to do things business as usual, whether true cost or opportunity cost, and make it visible. You may recognize some of this language from the "Proof of a Better Solution" sections of the Sales Narrative or Sales Materials chapters. That's no coincidence—this is the point at which you should bring out your quantitative and qualitative proof of a better solution. Do the actual math for the prospect on what she'd be missing out on.

For instance, if we were Textio, the makers of job-posting text-optimization software, and we were selling to someone who wasn't sure if she wanted to Textio-optimize her job postings, we would compare the projected outcomes for the following twelve months using her status quo with what it would look like with our approach. In this case, we would go back to those key metrics that we know our prospect cares about—click-through rates for candidates that see postings on job boards and our career site, applicant-to-screen ratios, and such. For instance, if we knew that the prospect spent $100,000 a year on job postings on Monster and sponsored clicks on Indeed, and we have shown that we can reduce posting spend by 15–40%, we could say, "By continuing your current approach, you're wasting fifteen to forty thousand dollars a year. That's half a Recruiting Coordinator salary. Saving that from your budget would make you a hero to your CEO and your VP of Engineering." Note that you're not just making it clear to the decision-maker that this decision is something that impacts her, you're bringing in her internal stakeholders too—who would likely be evaluating this decision with a more dollars-and-cents mindset. That hint of a "stick," to go along with lots of carrots, can sometimes help focus minds.

This is a great time to flip back to the materials (like slides) you put together to crystallize your proof points. Objection handling is another reason it's important to have sales materials other than just a demo. For instance, these were some slides from TalentBin's sales deck that demonstrated the time savings associated with adopting a talent search and automation solution. In this case, we made it simple, and said, "TalentBin will save you one thousand dollars of recruiter time per week," with the model to back it up. If we ran into "fear of change" objections, we could use the discovery information we'd gathered (i.e., how many recruiters the prospect had in house) to crystallize that opportunity cost. For instance, if the company had ten recruiters, we'd make it clear that they'd be wasting $10,000 of recruiter time every week.

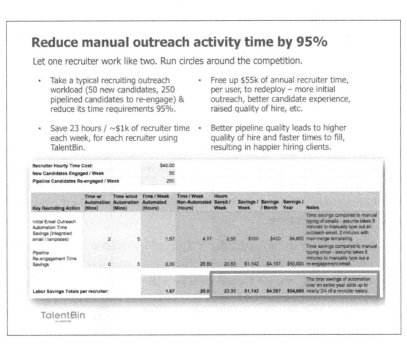

Recruiter Time Savings Analysis

Automation gets you a second full work week out of each recruiter.

Recruiter Hourly Time Cost:	$40.00
New Candidates Engaged / Week	50
Pipeline Candidates Re-engaged / Week	250

Key Recruiting Action	Time Savings Per Action (min)	Hours Saved / Week	Week	Month	Year	Notes
Candidate Discovery Time Savings	10	8.33	$333.33	$1,333.33	$16,000.00	Time savings compared to manual discovery via Google - assume takes 10 minutes per valid candidate discovered via Google.
Email Address Discovery Time Savings	5	4.17	$166.67	$666.67	$8,000.00	Time savings compared to manual discovery via Google - assume takes 5 minutes per email addresses search via Google.
Profile Data Aggregation - Qualification	5	4.17	$166.67	$666.67	$8,000.00	Time savings compared to manual discovery and review via Google - assume takes 5 minutes to do a semi-comprehensive review of a candidate's social footprint to qualify fit.
Profile Data Aggregation - Email Quality	5	4.17	$166.67	$666.67	$8,000.00	Time savings compared to manual discovery and review via Google - assume takes 5 minutes to do a semi-comprehensive review of a candidate's social footprint to elicit details for compelling outreach.
Initial Email Outreach Automation Time Savings (templates, mass mails)	5	4.17	$166.67	$666.67	$8,000.00	Time savings compared to manual typing of emails - assume takes 5 minutes to manually type out an outreach email.
Pipeline Re-engagement Time Savings	5	20.83	$833.33	$3,333.33	$40,000.00	Time savings compared to manual typing email - assume takes 5 minutes to manually type out a re-engagement email.
Labor Savings Totals per recruiter:		45.83	$1,833.33	$7,333.33	$88,000.00	

TalentBin

Beyond the pure quantitative arguments, you should use qualitative approaches as well. That is, all those arguments about how your solution is the emerging industry standard, and other types of "fear of missing out" arguments—including which of the prospect's competitors are likely using the solution. (It's kind of like a "No one got fired for buying IBM" argument—but more like "People who bought IBM early looked brilliant!") These approaches are useful in dealing with other objections as well. Frame the purchase as "inevitable" and "the next logical thing"—and subtly suggest that the prospect will be kicking himself in a year when all his colleagues and competitors have implemented these sort of solutions, and he looks like a caveman. In fact, this is an opportunity for him to look advanced, and to advance his career!

Lastly, there's the "fear of change" piece. That is, your prospect believes that she has the problem, and she believes that your solution is the right one to address it—that it's quantitatively and qualitatively better than what she has in place. But she's afraid that it won't actually end up that way for some unknown reason—a generic "boogeyman." This goes back to our "persuasion formula"—in this case, the "belief" term is where we need help. The best way to address this is with your arguments around "How we will make this easy for you," as that's often where the concern flows from. Existing proofs of success, using real customer success stories, may also help. But mainly this is a nonspecific concern—while this all sounds great, and makes sense in theory, the prospect simply isn't sure it will come to pass in practice. And the best way to handle that is to say, "Here are all the resources we have in place to ensure that you capture the value we both agree is on the table for you. We will make you successful."

Timing is Bad/We Have Higher Priorities

This is a variant of "we're happy with how we do it now," but a slightly better version. That is, the prospect agrees that his organization has the need, that the solution addresses it better than what they have in place right now, and that they will get value out of progressing with the purchase. And given that he hasn't just jumped to the king of objections—"no budget"—it would seem that he knows they can pay for it. The sticky part is that they have other things that are higher priority right now. This objection may also appear as its cousin, "timing is bad."

The reality is that your prospect always has a bunch of competing priorities, including day-to-day execution of his role, so the key to addressing this objection is to reduce the perception that implementing your solution will be a lot of work. That is, the implication here is that he only has so much time to roll out a new solution, and that that time is already spoken for. Once again, a great way to address this is with your arguments around how easy you will make it. Make it clear that all he has to do is say yes, and poof, it will be done without any more involvement from him, short of providing authority and names for users.

So something like "The timing is bad because I am in the middle of rolling out a new applicant tracking system" could be addressed by a Textio salesperson with "That's actually a great time to start using Textio, because you're already going to be changing business process around how your job postings are written and deployed. It's a great time to cement new, better habits. And the good news is, we have six customer success specialists on staff who can run daily webinars for your team on how to get the best use out of Textio, and ensure that all your hiring managers have attended and passed out of the training. This is fantastic, because as you roll out your new ATS, you'll see even better ROI from it by mixing the two solutions."

Another approach is to help characterize why working on your solution should actually be a higher priority, even assuming scarce time resources. In this course of argument, you'll now need to do some more discovery, around what other programs they are considering implementing. That is, you've just discovered a new type of "competition," which isn't pure competition—it's just something else competing for the headspace and time of your prospect. This can be dicey if the prospect has already committed to that course of action (commitment bias is a two-edged sword!). But you can certainly sniff out what those alternative programs are, and their perceived ROI, to position your solution as a higher-priority project—again, using numerical and qualitative arguments that compare the opportunity cost of not adopting your solution to the opportunity cost of not adopting that other product. This is where being a student of your market is important, because you'll have to make the other solution's ROI argument for it (in a way where your solution wins!), in a credible way. But it certainly can be done, because often prospects haven't been super rigorous in their analysis of whether to spend their scarce time and budgetary resources on this project versus that. So now you get to help them do that, with a preference for your solution!

These have been examples of how to actually change minds. But you can use sleight of hand without challenging the underlying objection—"this is not a priority right now" or "the timing is off"—and still get the deal done. That is, you can capitalize on the fact that you have the prospect's attention and buy-in right now, and that they agree that this is a project that is worthwhile. When will be the right time? In a couple weeks? In a month? In that case, let's just get this deal done now, and make sure that it gets on the prospect's dance card for when he does have time. Why would he jump at doing that now? Well, you can take a couple of approaches. You can create a pricing inducement, like "If you buy now, I can give you fourteen months of service for the cost of twelve" or "It's likely our pricing will go up in the new year." Or you could use both of those together. Or you could try "You can buy now, and I'll start the contract in a month." These various approaches can be especially helpful at the end of the year or of an organization's fiscal year, when they are making budget allocation decisions for the year ahead, even if they don't intend to take the associated actions for a couple months.

The upshot on this bucket of objections is this—if you've got the momentum of a prospect agreeing that your solution should be implemented, it's just a question of when, take appropriate actions to make that "when" now.

Price/Value

An objection around price is actually a great place to be. That is, it would appear that the prospect is convinced and wants to do this. Now you're just haggling over the price.

Pricing objections can mean a couple different things, and it's important to precisely nail down what the prospect is actually objecting to. That is, sometimes vague price objections amount to posturing for a discount. In that case, you need to just get down to pricing negotiation, rather than a deeper conversation around value provided compared to price. We'll talk about pricing negotiation in a section a bit further on, but the important thing here is to figure out which conversation you're having—one about value or one that's just about discounting. A great way to do that is to specifically ask, using language like "I'm happy to talk about the value that the product provides, and we believe that our pricing is a fair split of the value created. But could you help me understand what you think would be a fair price?" or "Are we far apart here? How far would you say?" If they come back with something that is, say, 10% below the price you quoted, this is clearly just a discounting conversation, and you don't need to make it any more complicated than that. We'll talk about how to handle that when we get to negotiation.

But if the response that comes back is something more like "Well, I couldn't pay more than {*50%_of_your_quoted_price*} for this," then you're not really talking discounts. You're talking about your prospect's understanding of the potential value your offering provides. The best way to approach that is to walk her through the way the offering will create value, piece by piece, along with the projected ROI associated with it, or the relevant market comparables. Essentially, you're going to be justifying the decisions that you made when concocting your pricing, something we touched on in the Pricing section of the Sales Narrative chapter.

In the case of something like HIRABL, the response might be "Based on your submission volume and recruiter counts, we quoted you a price of forty thousand for the year. From the hundreds of customers we've serviced, and hundreds of thousands of candidate submissions we've tracked, we know that over the ensuing twelve months, we will most likely catch twenty missed fees for your organization—not to mention the ones that we will identify from the last eighteen months of submission data. And given that you make an average fee of thirty thousand dollars, we anticipate that HIRABL will drive an incremental six hundred thousand dollars of revenue to your organization that you would otherwise miss out on. Given that, we feel that forty thousand is a very fair price, and will be nearly paid for by your first collected fee. Can you help me understand where my analysis is falling down?"

Or in the case where your pricing is based on comps, like TalentBin pricing just below LinkedIn Recruiter, it might be something like "Well, currently you pay nine thousand dollars per year for a seat of LinkedIn Recruiter for each of your technical recruiters. TalentBin, meanwhile, only costs seven thousand per year per seat. Not only does TalentBin have 3–10x the number of potential candidates for certain technical skill profiles in the geographies you recruit for, but we also provide personal email addresses for candidates—something that can double or triple response rates to recruiting outreach. Moreover, we don't cap your outreach activities. Whereas each of those LinkedIn Recruiter seats only gets one hundred fifty InMails a month, you can send as many emails as you'd like through TalentBin. And those emails are open- and click-tracked, unlike LinkedIn InMails. Lastly, TalentBin offers automation functionality, like drip-marketing campaigns, that not only raise response rates, but save your recruiters tons of time for sourcing. Given all that, can you help me understand how this isn't a fair price for the value TalentBin will offer your technical recruiters?"

In both of these cases, what you're doing is laying out the ROI argument and providing an opportunity for the prospect to object to something in the analysis. If there isn't a distinct justification for her price/value objection, then you'll quickly find yourself converging back on a different objection (likely the true objection)—maybe she only has $5,000 in budget, which is why she was saying she would only pay $5,000. Or you'll find yourself having a discounting conversation, but closer to your proposed pricing.

However, if there is a legitimate rationale for the objection, this can also be an opportunity to understand why your pricing model may actually not be set up in a way that aligns with the value that is being provided to the user. Take the HIRABL example. Perhaps the prospect would point out that her average fees are actually more like $15,000 (instead of the $30,000 you cited), and could prove that to you. Well, if that is indeed true, and your pricing targets a 15x ROI, then she might have a point, and you might consider making an exception here. Moreover, you might consider modifying your pricing model to accommodate this sort of thing if you think it's going to be a more common case.

Another legitimate rationale might be that the prospect only intends to use a portion of your solution's functionality. For instance, take TalentBin's pricing argument above. Imagine a situation where the customer already has a marketing automation solution like Marketo or Outreach.io that they intend to use for recruiting purposes, using TalentBin's profile and email addresses simply as "leads" to import into that system. All of a sudden the "bundle" that is TalentBin's search, qualification, contact information, and recruitment marketing automation becomes less valuable to them, because they've already got the automation part handled and paid for. Again, in a case like this, you might want to consider some sort of exception, and if the exception ends up being common, this could be an opportunity to segment your solution.

Lastly, you might encounter a situation where a prospect's best alternative is substantially different than most of your prospects'. That is, they may already be addressing the problem your product solves, but with a "bailing wire and duct tape" solution—still, a solution nonetheless. Take HIRABL again. The prospect might already be doing "backdoor hire" checking, but doing so in a manual fashion, using existing staff. That is, perhaps twice a year, they have some of their clerical staff take all the submissions from the last six months, sort them by the most valuable fees (perhaps cutting off those below $10,000 in value), and then manually go through LinkedIn profiles to see if those candidates ended up at places they were submitted by the recruiting agency. In this case, the marginal value that HIRABL provides isn't the same as what it provides to a prospect who isn't doing any of this at all. Rather, HIRABL's ROI argument here might be that their solution does all of this automatically, so those clerical workers who take a whole week to do this manually, at a cost of $20,000 in salary expense, could be redirected to more valuable activities—like recruiting and business development activities. Or that now they can track all their submittals, not just those above $10,000. Or that rather than doing this twice a year, monitoring happens on a continual basis, which aids in collections efforts. With all that said, it is certainly the case that HIRABL would bring less value to this prospect than to the same prospect with no backdoor hire checks in place at all. So HIRABL might consider making an exception case here.

In general, these deeper discussions around price and value (assuming they are about that, and not discounting conversations in disguise) are a great opportunity to learn what parts of your product are valuable for what customers. When you are early-stage, I suggest getting a deal done rather than drawing a concrete line in the sand. As long as the prospect meets your ideal customer profile, and will actually get value from the solution, usually it's better to have them onboard, even if it's at half of your list price. If you do engage in this sort of pricing modification (I don't want to call it "discounting," because it's really a re-imagining of your pricing model to accommodate a previously unaddressed scenario), you need to clearly document the rationale, ideally in the contract, for a couple of reasons. Firstly, when the renewal comes around, and the scenario has changed (for example, in HIRABL's case, the customer's average fee is now $25,000, not $15,000), you have it documented and can remove that concession. Secondly, because you don't want this pricing concession to be construed by a third party as "standard." That is, we wouldn't want someone paying $5,000 for a "no marketing automation" seat of TalentBin to tell his buddy who doesn't have a marketing automation solution in house that the product costs $5,000 a seat. Because that buddy is more than likely going to want to use the TalentBin recruitment marketing automation.

This does not mean that you should be selling to folks who won't get value out of your solution just because it's cheap. That is, if someone is saying he won't pay more than X because of the low amount of value the tool would provide him, and he's right (that the solution actually doesn't provide a lot of value), then you should pass on the conversation. Moreover, why are you this far along in your sales cycle and only just learning this? It sounds like something that should have been figured out during discovery and qualification. Don't sell to people who will get minimal value. They will only use up your customer success resources, churn out, and generally fail to provide you enough revenue to surmount their cost. It's also just a distraction. Avoid it.

We Don't Have The Budget For This

Not having budget is often a failure of imagination on the part of the prospect, and it's just a question of you helping them find that budget. (That is, unless it's being used as a red herring for another objection, in which case you still need to get to the real issue.). In Discovery, we talked about qualification using frameworks like BANT and ANUM (where "B" is "budget" and "M" is "money"), and how the challenge with new-technology sales is that there often isn't an already-existing budget that addresses the solution you're selling. This challenge will also show up in closing conversations as an objection to be handled.

In discovery and qualification, did you validate that the organization does actually purchase tools for solving business pains, and that the decision-maker that you are working with has done this before, or knows that it can be done? If no, well, that was a big boo-boo back then, because they really may have "no budget," in the sense that they don't have a process by which to spend money on products to help their business. Yikes. So we're not going to address that as an "objection," as that is really a disqualifier—if the organization doesn't have a notion of spending money to make money, well, we're not in the business of teaching market capitalism, per se.

If yes, then great. Now you just need to make it clear that this solution is worth spending money on in much the same way that the organization has done before. A great first step there is to sort out what the current budget is for solving the problem you address, and if it is recurring in nature or already fully committed. That is, while there may not be budget currently available and earmarked for your exact solution, there could well be budget dedicated to addressing the problem. In the case of TalentBin, for example, prospects typically spent a goodly amount of budget to solve the problem of "we need to hire engineers to build our product." Purchasing our product was a question of digging into that budget to see what was already spent, and what could be shifted. One of the ways that organizations hire software engineers is to spend money on recruiting agencies that typically charge 20%–30% of a first year's salary as their fee. Well, when an organization was budgeting for its year, they may have budgeted for one or two fees per quarter. Presto! We found our budget. Another way to do budgetary horse trading like this is to sort out if there is any existing source of budget that is coming up for renewal soon. For instance, if there were ten seats of LinkedIn Recruiter coming up for renewal, then we could propose that three seats' worth of that budget be allocated to this new, better solution and bridge the time gap with "free months."

A more complicated version of this fiscal maneuvering is when budget is "transferred" from one substantially separate bucket into another, like from payroll expense to tooling. Imagine you're selling support-ticketing software like Zendesk. The prospect's current means of addressing inbound support ticketing is a shared email inbox with very little automation, business rules, or templating support. The company's support organization is growing to accommodate a growing customer base, at a ratio of, say, one new support agent per 200 customers added. In that environment, the adoption of a mature support system like Zendesk, with all of its automation functionality, could raise that ratio to something more like one support agent per 300 customer added. That means that if the organization's plan is to add 1,000 customers in the coming year, the adoption of something like Zendesk would mean hiring three new agents in the coming year, versus five under the current staffing plan. Assuming CSRs cost $50,000 a year, fully loaded, we're talking a cost reduction of $100,000—"budget" that was already allocated for the year when the support organization signed up to support 1,000 new customers. Poof! There's our budget.

Of course, this sort of "cross-bucket" budgetary horse trading often involves more than just the budget holder you've been engaging, like the head of support, head of recruiting, or what have you. It may require looping in a finance staffer like a controller or CFO, or another CXO type. And while that's another moving part, it's actually a good thing, in that those staff are more used to looking at the "big picture."

Beyond budgetary transfers, there's also discretionary budget, and one-off budgetary justification. That is, while the individual you're interacting with—the VP of Recruiting, VP of Customer Success, VP of Engineering, etc.—may have already exhausted her allocated budget, that doesn't mean that she, or especially the CFO, doesn't have a hidden kitty of money. You just have to make sure to ask for it. And moreover, if your decision-maker hasn't considered this, you need to work with her to go together to the CFO, or other budgetary controller, to see what may be squirreled away. This is where having a solid ROI argument is key. That is, because this discretionary budget is being held aside for exactly this sort of thing, but also for other unexpected opportunities, you're essentially competing with those potential projects. So you need to bring your A game.

Typically these pools of budget are specifically earmarked for "experiments," and whoever disburses the money will be looking at your solution as exactly that. So just be aware that it'll probably be a purchase at the small end of what you do—whether a single seat, a constrained time period, or what have you—and you'll have to work to make sure it "sticks." This is the sort of budget that "land and expand" solutions are often depending on. This doesn't mean you shouldn't try to access discretionary budget if you can, it just means that you should weigh that reality compared to your other options (e.g., financing, pricing inducements, etc.).

The bigger version of this approach is a one-off budgetary justification. That is, don't go after discretionary budget that already was sitting there—create your own new bucket of discretionary budget. Doing this usually means working with your prospect to advance a one-off justification to the part of the organization that makes these decisions—again, usually finance. While this adds complexity, it can be a fantastic opportunity to grow the deal. First, your decision-maker is now going to be having a strategic discussion with the CFO, COO, or what have you to address a deeper question in their organization. It's less a case of "Are we going to buy a single seat of TalentBin" and more a question of "Should we reduce our reliance on recruiting agencies, in general?" And if the ROI justifications to embrace this change at an organizational level exist, then this is exactly what the CFO and COO are there to do—make capital-returning judgments. Moreover, given the time cost associated with meetings, and the collaborative partnering between you and the decision-maker, you have an opportunity to enlarge the deal size—the difference between $40,000 of incremental spend versus $20,000 of incremental spend may not be a meaningful one.

Outside of budgetary horse trading, discretionary spend, and off-cycle budget justification, there are a number of clever moves that can be made to paper over a "lack of budget." If it's a case of timing before the next budget cycle, then you can often "place a marker" on that budget in the future by getting the deal done now and simply starting it later, or providing "free months" to bridge the gap. This is akin to the "timing" objection above, but this is the budgetary version thereof.

If the organization is simply cash poor (or thinks it is), then you can potentially help with financing. This isn't to say that your organization is going to offer financing to your customer—but through pricing inducements, you can help them think about existing financing instruments they could potentially access. That is, if you traditionally charge $9,000 up front for a seat of your solution, for a twelve-month contract, but the customer states they don't have the budget to swing that, you can offer monthly pricing of $999 for a twelve-month contract.

Monthly payments are undesirable to you, in that they can become a collections issue, and typically you would love to have that cash in hand to cover payroll. However, offering this option can help get a deal done in a couple of ways. First, over the course of a year, that would amount to $12,000, 33% more than the organization would otherwise pay. Well, now that the opportunity cost of taking that approach becomes clear, the organization can figure out how to rustle up that $9,000 and save itself $3,000 over twelve months. A hybrid approach is to start with monthly payments (at the rate that is higher than the up-front price), but offer the customer the ability to "pre-pay" the rest of their tab at any given point of time. This can work particularly well when your solution drives a cash-centric ROI. For example, in addition to finding missed fees, HIRABL's solutions help staffing agencies sniff out new business opportunities when candidates they've previously place moved to new organizations, or hiring managers they currently work with move to new organizations. All of those things represent new revenue for a staffing agency using HIRABL. The challenge can be that that $30,000 missed fee or fee from a new client might not show up for a month or two after the organization starts using HIRABL. No problem! What would have been a $20,000 license for twenty recruiters for the year can be broken down to $2,200 a month. And then when that first $30,000 missed fee comes in, well, the client can decide to buy out the rest of that contract and save himself the 33% on whatever remains on the term! Win, win!

I Need a Trial/I Need a Reference

This is one that will show up frequently, and you need to be careful. The concept of a "trial" is not a bad one. In fact, a demo that is well tailored to the prospect, ideally including his organization's data, is pretty darn close to a trial. And the notion of a customer reference is a good one too; it is an example of a powerful piece of "proof data." But you need to use caution here for two reasons. One, the prospect may be using this as a way to avoid saying no or surfacing the actual underlying objection, and simply putting off a decision. And two, you don't want to lose control of the deal, or add unnecessary time and complication to it. When someone asks for a "trial," and you just flip them a set of credentials with no structure, you're simply asking for him to come back at the end of the week and say, "Wow, yeah, I didn't get to this. Can I have another week?" Let's make sure this doesn't happen to you, as it wastes your time, hurts deal momentum, and plants the seed in the user's head that he may not end up using the product after he buys it (he isn't using it right now, right?).

When the prospect says, "I need a trial," really what she is saying is "I'm not sure I believe this, and I need more proof points, ideally ones that I can hold in my hand/see in my browser." Her proposed solution to that is a "trial" (vague, abstract, but something she feels would help achieve this goal of "seeing it with her own eyes"). You can often address this very easily by asking what she would want to see to help address her concern. Something like "I'm happy to help you get more comfortable with the value the solution provides. What sort of further proof would you be looking for?" You will be amazed how many times this turns out to be something as simple as "Well, I'd like to see some proof of prior success." That can take the form of marketing collateral focused on qualitative and quantitative proof of a better solution, like customer success stories, ROI studies, or customer references. Conveniently, you should already have a bunch of this documentation in hand—in your deck appendix, for instance. In fact, she may have already seen it, and now just needs to be reminded. So great! Use that as your means by which to surmount this issue without adding more time and complication to the deal.

But if instead the prospect is eager to see what the tooling looks like in her own hands or the hands of her team, and won't be satisfied with collateral, that's fine as well. Firstly, when a decision-maker wants to have the team look at something, often they'll use the term "trial" when what they really want is another demo for the larger group. In which case, great! That will be a good opportunity for you to do value selling in a presentation and demo to this new group of stakeholders. Offer to do just that: "Showing this to your team sounds like a great idea! I would love to give them a guided tour, and let them get their hands dirty with my help."

If the goal is further understanding of how the UI works, or the usability of certain features, you can achieve that with a guided walk-through or "ride-along." Schedule another meeting specifically to walk through all the pieces of the product that the prospect might want to investigate, and let her control the mouse and screen so she can see how things work and satisfy her curiosity. At TalentBin our sales reps would often schedule a follow-up hour after the initial demo to do just this, and let the prospect click around and make sure that the demo she saw wasn't smoke and mirrors—and that when she controlled the mouse, the profile volume and quality was just the same. Of course, you are there the whole time, to support prospects if they get sidetracked, add commentary about the value of the various features they're using, and, most importantly, make sure the product actually gets used.

If your product is not set up for "freemium" usage, or unattended trial, just handing users the keys to the car, and assuming they're going to know how to use it as well as you or one of your customer success staff, is a terrible idea. They're not going to be experiencing the product the way they would after they've been fully trained and gone through an implementation process. Now, if your product management and engineering staff has invested in features that help users "get to value" quickly, by all means, you should leverage that (and you probably already are for the purposes of lead generation). But if that investment hasn't taken place, do not assume that your prospects will just magically "get it" if you let them have an unattended trial. Rather, if they actually end up using their trials (a big "if"), they will likely run into small issues here and there that stop them in their tracks and lead them to blame the tool. And that's hard on your deal.

While the grand majority of "trial" requests can be handled in the ways outlined above, more mature buyers with better process may seek to do a formal "pilot"—that is, a time-bounded experiment, where they go through certain key actions in the product to see examples of the promised ROI. With something like Textio, prospective buyers might want to optimize a single job posting, and set it live on Monster to see how it performs compared to their existing postings. Or with TalentBin, they might use the tool for a week to execute outreach to candidates and gauge responsiveness. In all of these cases, it's important for you to frame the pilot in a way that makes it clear how success will be defined, and for prospective buyers to be held accountable for participating in training sessions and check-in meetings and acting on defined activities, which they know will be instrumented and reportable. To the extent that you can remove the risk of non-execution on their part, you should seek to do so, because the biggest issue in trials is always non-usage.

As you can see, all of sudden it becomes clear that you only want to be doing this for the largest deals, where there is a lot of revenue opportunity. It can be worth it, but you need to be realistic about the associated time costs (you could be doing demos for new, potential slam-dunk prospects who don't need a structured pilot to prove things out). Include that time cost in calculating whether you want to offer a structured pilot.

The alternative is not an unstructured pilot, as that will simply blow up your deal. So for small customers who may not be worth the time associated with a structured trial, you can draw the line in the sand and say, "We don't do this because people don't use it and don't have success, and that's not fair to them, nor to me. I am committed to helping you get comfortable with this solution ahead of purchase, so we can do an hour-long guided session where you have control. But

I can't do an unguided trial." If this comes up enough, you can decide to prioritize product and engineering resources to make unstructured pilots and self-serve usage an easier process. Raised close rates and faster deal times may justify the investment, much the same way you can build in features that make demos better and more tailored to prospects. But just tossing the keys to a prospect is usually a losing proposition.

Solution-Specific Objections

We've looked at the major buckets of objections that show up regularly, regardless of the specifics of your solution. But that doesn't mean those are the only ones you'll run into. Undoubtedly, a number of objections that are specific to your market and your solution will pop up again and again. This is to be expected, and like the generic objections above, should be viewed as a positive—it's a signal of an engaged prospect who's actually thinking about how your solution could potentially impact her business. So you should be ready to knock those objections out of the park.

Because I don't know what those specific objections will be for your solution, I'll just talk to a generic framework for handling them, and then you can apply it as appropriate. Solution-specific objections will usually involve questions about whether this is actually a better way to solve the problem your solution addresses. So the best way to tackle those is using the same approach you did in your core narrative—with quantitative and qualitative proof—ideally documented in the form of a slide!

Say that you're HIRABL, selling software to help catch missed contingency recruiting fees. A prospect might believe everything you've discussed, but might be concerned that even if you surface these backdoor hires to them, they won't be able to collect on the fees that they're owed. So how would you address this objection? Well, you might point out your clients' aggregate collection rate to give them comfort. Or you might talk about how catching backdoor hires quickly, within a few weeks of the hire, makes collection many times more likely to happen because it's still in the "whoops, that was an accident!" phase. Or you might talk about how your customer success staff has all sorts of tools to help broach those topics with clients, so the prospect need not worry about angering them. Or you might do a combination of all of the above!

As touched on in the section on sales decks, I recommend that if you hear an objection a couple of time, you might as well build a slide to address it and put it in the appendix of your deck. This has the benefit of making you look like you're super prepared and expert in all things regarding your solution. It also acts as a handy little script so you can nail all the points you want to make when handling that objection. Beyond this, you should also just keep a running list of objections in a living document, like a Google Doc, so that you can refer to them as necessary. Moreover, when you start hiring reps to help you scale your efforts, all of those objections, and their associated responses, will already be ready for them!

If an objection gets to the point where it shows up very frequently, you can make the call to actually include it in the main part of your pitch and narrative. This can be a two-edged sword, because you're now proactively bringing up a potential concern that the prospect may not have thought of on her own. But if it's such a common objection, it's often better to just bring it up, and demolish it, proactively. Otherwise, the prospect may not think of it until later, when you're not present, and have to reason through it on her own without your help. With TalentBin, an example might have been something like "Now, I know what you're thinking. 'Do candidates get weirded out by the fact that you know everything about their activity on GitHub, Stack Overflow, Twitter, Meetup, and so on?' It turns out, they're pretty used to it, since they know that this information is readily available on the web. And moreover, they view it as a positive, because it demonstrates that you've gone the distance in actually qualifying them for this potential role, as compared to many recruiters who just spray and pray job opportunities willy-nilly. So yeah, they prefer this approach! In fact, you can see how preferable it is by the 3x email response rates recruiters get with TalentBin, versus sending generic LinkedIn InMails, based on a study our customer success team ran."

Competition Objections

Competitive objections can be a really helpful way of proactively framing the conversation around other players in your market. While bringing up competition proactively can be problematic, if the prospect brings it up, you should jump all over it. First, if you already know, based on your discovery questions, that the prospect has a competitor in place, or is considering one, you can take the initiative to address it. Or, if that didn't arise in discovery, but a question asked later in the pitch indicates that he is thinking about competition, you can run with it.

With competitive objections, it's especially important to not just address the one-off objection—which might show up in the form of a single feature-comparison question—but rather to frame the competitive conversation in the context of your existing messaging. That way, if the prospect ends up interacting with the competition again before you close the deal, you've planted seeds of how to think about the holistic comparisons between the two solutions.

Take TalentBin again. Occasionally we would get asked about "code scoring" for the recruiting profiles our talent search engine built, because one of our competitors, Gild, had long ago acquihired a small code analysis project. They ostensibly used the technology to make judgments about the quality of a given engineering candidate based on the code she had published on GitHub. When given an opening, rather than just addressing that one point, we would use it as an opportunity to frame the whole conversation about competition, specifically around how our solution was vastly superior when properly evaluated along all relevant vectors (not just this one particular one). That is, we might say something like "Well, that's a great question! We actually use a number of data signals in helping to understand what a given candidate is into, professionally, and we can talk more about that in a second. But importantly, when we think about talent search engines, it's important to think about all parts of the talent search process—that is, search and discovery, qualification information, contact information availability, and then outreach and pipeline management functionality and automation. Your question touches on data that can be used for both search and recall, and also qualification of particular candidates. On that front, TalentBin consumes candidate data from the broadest set of sources available—not just places where code is published, like GitHub, but dozens of other sites like Meetup, where folks demonstrate their interest in various software engineering technologies. We look at candidates' online activity with the widest possible lens to make sure you can see all the engineers who have a skill you're looking for. Isn't that great?"

That is, we would take the one-off question, "Do you score code?," and address the question that's under that question—"Can you help me understand how you use data to help me hire software engineers, and how does your approach compare to this other approach over here?" This strategy works for most objections. As they talk about in press training, "Answer the question you wanted them to ask."

From a materials standpoint, like with other solution-specific objections, it's good to have a slide, or potential slides, to support this conversation. To start, you could have a slide that presents the competitive framework that's pertinent to your solution, and the ways your solution wins out in those buckets. And assuming you have multiple competitors, you could have one of these "competitive rollup" slides for each. (You wouldn't want to feature multiple competitors on one slide. There's no need to present to a prospect the other solutions she might want to research...) Later, a more advanced version of this is to have "competitive mini decks" for each competitor of merit, including a handful of slides that describe how your solution and the competitor stack up in each bucket of your messaging framework. But that's pretty advanced. To start, a single slide per competitor of merit is good.

Generic Objection Flow Loop

Regardless of the type of objection, whether it's one of the more generic ones or one that is solution-specific, the pattern of handling them remains the same. That is, you should "catch" the objection; turn it to the "question under the question"; respond to the objection with quantitative and qualitative arguments that prove the case, supported by visual and textual sales materials; validate understanding of these arguments ("Does that answer your question? Does that make sense?");

and then pick up where you were before that objection. As you drive to a close, keep uncovering any further objections, with questions like "Do you have other questions or are you satisfied that this would be a fit for you?" As you can see, this is a loop, where you handle an objection and then return to your close to handle the next objection, repeating until there are no more objections left (well, or the prospect feels you've made it to the other side of the persuasion threshold, and they're willing to take the leap even with other objections outstanding).

DEMO FOLLOW-UP & FURTHER MEETINGS

Depending on the cost and complexity of your solution, your prospects probably won't be purchasing directly from you at the point of demo, or immediately thereafter. There will likely be some sort of follow-up required. In the best-case scenario, that might be sending the prospect a contract that she can e-sign immediately. Fantastic! It might be sending a proposal with pricing options as discussed in your demo. It might be the delivery of some key information to help with the decision-making process and to address objections that arose in the demo, like ROI proofs, and so on. Or it might be a further demo or meeting with another stakeholder whose agreement is required to progress to a sale. There are many permutations.

However, regardless of which variety of follow-up item is required, the approach to executing them all is largely the same. Firstly, you must directly and concretely state what the next action is. Remember our discussion above about contracting for each next step? This is where it becomes very important to guard against spending your time on useless opportunities, and to hold your prospect accountable with those "micro-contracts." None of this "Well, I'll send you some information. Let me know what you think!" Instead, you should concretely articulate the state of the deal, what you will do, and what the prospect will do in return. For instance, "Based on our agreement that this solution makes sense for your organization, and your desire to spend budget on it, after we get off this call, I am going to send you a contract for one seat using our e-sign system, and you will be able to execute that today. Is that correct?" Or "You would like to purchase three seats of our software, provided I supply you with the ROI study that we discussed in our call. I will provide that after I get off the phone, and then we will reconvene to discuss your analysis of that ROI study and whether it has resolved your concerns." And so forth.

If there is a further meeting required, calendar it. If another decision-maker needs to be involved, propose getting a meeting on the calendar with all three of you. If your prospect is going to consume some information that you have delivered or discuss the solution with his team or simply consider the information you've shared, that's fine. But set a specific follow-up appointment to discuss the outcome of those actions. By doing this, you're making it clear that you won't be chasing him around via unresponded-to emails or phone calls, and that if he's going to promise to do it, you're going to hold him accountable. Partly this is to dissuade him from faking interest. That is, if he's not actually interested, or only partially so, putting a call on the calendar where you will jointly review follow-up materials will make him think twice about asking for a proposal just so he doesn't have to say no. So if you get a "Let's touch base in a month or so," the response to that is "Fantastic, let's get that calendared right now, and set the agenda that we will be reviewing—namely, what's keeping us from progressing right now, and whether it has changed."

By setting these meetings, you are minimizing the risk that open-ended tasks will derail your opportunity. Meetings are a great way of doing this, but you can also use methods like setting a CRM task for yourself as a reminder to note whether the prospect executed on their commitment ("Did Jeff get back to me about pricing?"). If the micro-contract was articulated in an email (which I recommend, even if it was already made over the phone or in person—better to memorialize it in text), then there are helpful tools like Boomerang, Yesware, and Tout that let you bring an email thread back into your inbox at an appointed time, depending on whether or not the recipient responded. In the case of these micro-contracts, I like to set the backstop to bring the thread back into my inbox regardless of whether the prospect responded to it, because I would hate to forget about it just because he responded with a quick "Yep!"

Then, once a micro-contract for the next action is concretely agreed, execute on it as quickly as possible. This is one of the reasons why in the Appointment Setting chapter we discussed the importance of having time blocked directly after a demo to allow for immediate execution of follow-up actions. If you have to jump right into another demo, you will be less likely to immediately execute on your part of the micro-contract, which puts you at risk of forgetting about it. I have found that prospect commitments have a time decay rate. That is, the faster you deliver on the part that you owe them, the faster and more likely they are to execute on their commitment. So in addition to being clear about who owes who what, be quick in the delivery of what you promised.

While there are different permutations of follow-up based on what was discussed in the call, there is a set of actions that I feel should always be included. That is, you should always follow up a demo with a summary email, ideally in the thread that set the appointment (or perhaps in your demo reminder email) to provide continuity. By systematizing this, you'll always have a virtual venue where you can deliver on the commitments you made in your call, and provide a digital trail for your prospect to refer back to. In addition to whatever items you committed to deliver in that follow-up email, I am a big fan of including the "for sending" version of the sales presentation you used in the call, as we discussed in the Sales

Materials chapter. You may have had an amazing demo, and blown their socks off, but human memory is a fickle thing. If you send a deck, with any appendix slides that were particularly important, you're guarding yourself against lapses in recollection.

And like the "generic objection loop" that we discussed above, this post-meeting follow-up loop continues after every meeting, unless the opportunity is either closed won, or closed lost.

PRACTICE & ITERATION

There's nothing like actual "live fire" drills with actual prospects to hone your skills. That said, doing a series of practice demos, complete with objection handling, can really help get you warmed up and ready for the real deal. You might even continuously mix those in when your calendar is light. If any of your prior customer development research interviewees would be willing to do these drills with you, fantastic. But even if it's people on your team who are not revenue-facing (forcing them to ask questions like a prospect is probably good for them too!), your significant other, or otherwise, any practice is helpful.

Also, recognize that your pitch, demo, and objection responses will never be set in stone; you should be seeking to improve them as you go. Did you realize that, yes, just like Pete said, offering trials to people is a terrible idea with your current product, and you should just cut that out of your pitch? Great! Cut it out! Don't slavishly adhere to something that doesn't work. If that one slide in your deck isn't helping, or is constantly causing confusion, drop it. You should view your pitch and down-funnel protocol as a product that you are constantly iterating.

With that said, nothing drives success like raw activity. So get out there and go!

CHAPTER 8

Down Funnel Selling: Negotiation, Closing & Pipeline Management

INTRODUCTION

In the last chapter, we covered how to prepare for and execute customer-facing pitches. While you would prefer that pitches and deals proceed in a linear process from beginning to end, that's far from the reality. In this chapter, we'll cover some of the more squirrelly bits of dealing with opportunities that are in a "down-funnel" state, from negotiation, driving urgency, and closing (whether winning or losing— both important), all the way to guidance on how to deal with a pipeline of a dozen, two dozen, or maybe more of these concurrent opportunities.

NEGOTIATION

The more costly and complicated your solution is, the more likely there will be negotiation at the end of the purchasing process. This shouldn't be viewed as a negative and something to avoid, but simply another signpost on the way to a successfully acquired new customer. And this is different than the pricing objections we've discussed previously. When you get to negotiation, the prospect is convinced that there is value in your solution—it is a question of whether he's going to pay rack rate or 30% below that. Regardless, my goal isn't to make you a master negotiator; there are plenty of books on that already. It's to give you a general framework for how to think about negotiation and getting these deals across the line.

Firstly, whenever you are selling to people who have purchased enterprise software before, and especially if they do it frequently, there is going to be a baked-in expectation of negotiation and discounting. We touched on this in Pricing and Sales Materials, but don't be surprised when your prospect views your first proposal as a jumping-off point to negotiate you down. As such, you should factor this into not only your sticker pricing, but also any initial proposals you prepare. Start with inflated pricing in anticipation of being negotiated down, so that wherever you end up still provides an economically viable deal for you. If the prospect simply takes the price, fantastic, lucky you. And if she wants to negotiate, great, you've provided yourself room. And in the event you have to deal with a procurement department, you'll be really glad you built in that room; they're likely going to attempt to wrangle another discount on top of whatever you agreed to with your direct decision-maker. (Now, if you're selling to "deer" like we discussed in the Prospecting, it's unlikely that they'll have a procurement function. But something to be aware of.)

When approaching these negotiations, you want to be clear on what is valuable to you—what you want to preserve—and what may be valuable to your prospect. Then look for opportunities for trades, where you can give the prospect something he wants (which is less valuable to you) in exchange for something that you want. The big levers at your disposal will be price (per seat, per unit), amount, duration of contract (a year? two years? six months? month-by-month?), payment terms (total contract value paid up front? biannually? monthly?), and then terms like automatic renewal and opt-outs. As far as you're concerned, you would like a long contract, the entire value of which is paid up front, that automatically renews.

So what should you value the most? Cash is king for early-stage companies, and you should always prioritize getting more money in the door up front. You never know what could happen with accounts receivable. The customer could go out of business, have a new purchaser who comes in and holds payments hostage, and so on. Yuck. Get the cash in your bank account. Secondarily, you should value length of contract, in that longer terms reduce the risk that your customer will churn out. In the context of your negotiations, you'll want to maximize these variables where you can (and later, when you're training and compensating sales reps, you'll want to incentivize these variables as well) and, if you have to give things up, give them up last.

When you're negotiating with a prospect, you'll want to "retreat" one increment of a given lever at a time. There's no reason to give two or three increments when maybe they'd be happy with just one step down, and boom, they sign and your deal is executed. Moreover, when your prospect asks for something (i.e., "We'd like a pricing discount"), you can take the opportunity to give them that while simultaneously moving a different lever in the direction you favor. For instance, if a customer wants a discount per seat, you can counter by saying that you can provide better pricing if they buy more seats or extend the term of the contract. (Say the prospect wanted to start with a six-month contract. Now you can attempt to persuade him into a twelve-month contract, which totals more overall but is substantially cheaper on a per-time basis.) Importantly, often your prospect simply wants to feel like he's "getting a deal." Knocking a quick 5% off the top to get the deal done and across the line—without endangering the deal, or getting into less desirable payment terms—is a steal for you. Because now you can turn your attention to another deal, and get it across the line. That easy retreat and win frees you up for yet another win.

Basic Negotiation Tactics

Cheaper price per unit

If the prospect wants a cheaper per-seat price, propose to lower yours if they buy more of the solution, whether seats, volume ("clicks" or postings or whatever), or contract length.

Cheaper total

If the prospect wants a cheaper total (for instance, she "only has $10k of budget"), offer to remove seats or volume, and make the per-unit price more costly. Or reduce the length of the contract. "You only have ten thousand dollars to spend, but want one seat for each of your two recruiters, which would typically cost fourteen thousand? That's fine. We can do a six-month contract to get you those two seats for ten thousand. Alternatively, I just talked to our VP of Sales, and he says we can do two seats for the year for twelve thousand dollars." (To which she responds, "Wow, twelve thousand for twelve months for two is a steal, compared to six months for ten thousand. I'll ask my CFO for the extra money.")

Shorter duration

If the prospect wants to start with a shorter duration, make the per-time price for that duration at least 2–3x what it would be the full year. "I'm happy to put together a six-month proposal for you, but it's likely going to be five thousand dollars, as compared to seven thousand for the whole year." If the prospect is unhappy with this, note that onboarding is a fixed cost that is very hands-on, with lots of customer success labor. Your pricing simply reflects that the onboarding cost is only spread across six months (or three months), rather than twelve months.

Split-up payments

As with accommodating shorter durations, raise your pricing when the prospect wants to split up payments (biannually, quarterly, monthly). This puts you at accounts receivable risk, and as an early-stage startup, your cost of capital is quite high. So don't finance your customers. You want to optimize for cash up front as much as possible. If a seat of your software costs $10k for a year when paid up front, make it $12k if paid quarterly. When the prospect organization realizes they can save $2k by paying up front, and they have the capital to do so, they'll do it, save themselves money, and save you the pain in the rear of keeping track of those collections. And now you can take that $10k you got immediately and hire another salesperson to start pumping out more deals (versus getting $3k, $3k, $3k, and $3k per quarter...).

Urgency

While not exactly the same as negotiating the levers above, sometimes there's just the question of getting the prospect to execute now, rather than letting him wait to deliberate—this is related to the timing objection we covered previously. There are a couple of handy tricks there. If you're partway through the month, you can offer the rest of the month for free. Or you can indicate that your customer success team only has so many starting slots available, and that they get booked up. Or you can indicate that the pricing you're providing right now, and the associated discounting, is only valid for this month. Or that in the future, pricing may be going up, so they should lock their rate in now.

Pushing Back Against Discounts

As you are progressing through this back-and-forth, it can be helpful to have an authority backstop to refer to and push back with. You may feel like the used car salesman who needs to "check with his manager," but it can help provide a rationale for pushback. We already discussed "price/value" objection handling in the Pitching chapter; you can always use that here as well, to remind the prospect that you're offering a fair price. Lastly, it's totally fine to articulate that this pricing is the way it is because A) your company needs money to deliver the service, B) your engineers cost money and need to eat, and C) there are only so many deals you can close in a month, and each one needs to be a certain price to keep the lights on. You'd be amazed how this can humanize the discussion and help the prospect realize that your software costs money for a reason. A more direct approach is to refer to the prospect's product, and the fact that they don't give it away for free for the same reasons—though you have to be careful to keep this sort of argument lighthearted and non-accusatory!

Competitors and Pricing

In negotiation, there's this thing called the "best alternative to a negotiated agreement," often referred to as BATNA. That is, what's the best alternative the customer has to agreeing to your price and terms? If it's just the status quo, and you've done a great job documenting the cost and opportunity cost of that, you can charge for some proportion of the difference between their opportunity cost and the value your solution would provide. However, if there's a competitor in the deal who can assist the prospect with the same problem you do, and do so perhaps with cheaper pricing, well, now the prospect has a better BATNA.

The best way to deal with this sort of thing is to have a better product than the competitor, and to charge for it. That is, if there is a delta between the value your product provides and the value theirs provides, you can demonstrate that ROI and reflect it in your pricing. For instance, at TalentBin, we invested early on in adding lots of recruiting-automation functionality to the product (that is, drip marketing, self-writing email templates, and so on). None of the competition had these features, and as a result, executing certain actions—like sending fifty emails to brand-new candidates, or automatically following up with them after the fact on a cadenced basis—took far more time in those solutions than with TalentBin. We were able to document this (and had it clearly presented in slides) and show the prospect that while the competitor might be charging less, it was actually a false economy—the prospect's recruiters would be spending way more time doing things that TalentBin could do for them automatically.

If you don't have that better product, well, you probably should be pricing lower, because the value is less. And you should do your best to document why the competitor's additional features are not actually all that valuable, are overkill, and are unlikely to be used!

If the prospect says that he has pricing from a competitor that is lower than yours, and he will go with you if you match it—a not-uncommon buyer gambit—you have some options. You can make your best argument for why your product is more valuable, and choose to either stick to your guns, provide some pricing relief (that is, discount, but not match the price), or just say screw it and match the price. Regardless, you should authenticate that he actually has that pricing from the competitor, and ask politely to see the proposal or contract in which it's delineated. Don't do it in a combative way; just say that in order to justify any pricing inducements, you have to see that (or be able to show it to your boss, or whatever). Then, if you decide to provide some discounting or match, make it clear to the prospect that you will only do so if he agrees to execute the contract the day that the pricing is delivered. And if he can't commit to that, then don't deliver the pricing. Otherwise, you'll be entering into a reverse auction for your services, where the prospect is the auctioneer and you and your competitor are bidding lower and lower. And you generally want to avoid that.

CLOSE WINNING

While hearing the prospect say yes is definitely super exciting, that doesn't mean your work here is done. Don't stop to do a happy dance and risk your deal. You have to run all the way until the money's in the bank, and then run to make sure that the new customer is up and running and getting value out of your solution. We glorify the "closing" bit of selling, but it's just another step to nail, of many before and more after.

Order Forms and Contracts

Once you've agreed to a price, you need to act as quickly as possible to execute the contract. You don't want to leave any room for second thoughts to creep in—get the contract signed and the client on their way to your customer success team for implementation and training.

An important part of your toolkit will be your order form, associated contract, and e-signature software. Different from your proposal, which is more a piece of marketing collateral than anything else, your order form is simply there to memorialize the key terms that were already agreed verbally and allow for signature by the purchaser. The goal is easy, friction-free execution. This is an example of a TalentBin order form we used all the way through acquisition. At the very beginning, I would manually enter the relevant terms and then upload the document to e-signing software—initially I used HelloSign, but then moved to Adobe eSign because of its integration with Salesforce—to send to the prospect. Later we used Adobe eSign's integration with Salesforce to automate the population of terms. But the key was that we kept it simple.

This is not to say that you won't have a contract with the associated legalese. However, that doesn't need to be on your order form, and by presenting it to the prospect, you would just be reminding him that there's a bunch of legal arcana to consider. This is why I'm not a fan of Y Combinator's Sales Agreement Template in its current form, namely because it includes many pages of legalese appended to what could be a simple order form. That legalese is fantastic to protect you—or help you with things like publicity rights, and so on—but not attached to the order form, where it will just raise questions and slow down your deal process. Have it hosted somewhere else, and link to it from the order form. While there will be situations where you have a sophisticated buyer whose procurement or legal department will want to review this, most of the time the purchaser just wants to see that the basic terms are right, and then sign something memorializing that. Don't add complexity and sandbag yourself.

That said, you'll want to have an actual "master service agreement" (MSA), and using a standard one from either your corporate counsel (they likely have a template) or that Y Combinator template is a good bet. Just link to it from the order form, and in the event the prospect or his procurement or legal department wants to see it, provide it in the form of a Word document or PDF. There may be situations where you encounter "redlining"—that is, the purchaser's legal organization may want to change certain terms in your contract to ones they are comfortable with. This is always a two-edged sword. On the one hand, you don't want to delay the signature of the contract, but on the other, you don't want to agree to something that will be problematic for you down the road. One way to handle this is to indicate that your contract is the one that is going to be used, and that otherwise, it's a no-go. If you feel that you have the power to make that claim, try it out. If there's pushback, you can always cave. Otherwise, you can get help from your corporate counsel to review the redlines. This can be tricky, because if you have corporate counsel that costs $300 an hour, pretty soon a big chunk of that contract's value can be consumed in legal fees. So be mindful if you encounter this. It's another reason why selling to "deer"—mid-market companies without legal departments and procurement departments looking for something to do—can be nice. They don't have the resources to redline your contract. They just want to get things done, like you!

Always, always, always use an e-signing solution—it will reduce the friction associated with "Hey, can you print this out, sign it, scan it, and send it back?" Instead, with the right templating, you can fire an order form over to the prospect while she's on the phone, or even while you're sitting together in a conference room, and have her e-sign it. Less risk of dropped balls or stalls. Further, it'll make it easy for you to store those contracts; they should be saved in your CRM, tied to the opportunity for the prospect in question.

Getting Paid

Once you have an executed contract, that's not the end of things. You'd be amazed how many times I've seen startups with outstanding contracts for many tens of thousands of dollars, simply because no one was collecting on them. First, make it easy for the prospect to pay you. At the earliest stages, using something like FreshBooks, with an e-payment option like PayPal turned on, can be very helpful. While paying a 3% fee on a $10,000 contract can feel aggressive, if you consider the cost of an employee to manage collecting a dozen of those contracts a month, the distraction of having to do it yourself, or the risk of not collecting that money (remember, when you're early-stage, cash is king!), credit card collection suddenly becomes pretty appealing. On the other hand, especially given that you should target being paid up front for annual contracts, recurring solutions like Recurly, Stripe, or even something more advanced like Zuora are less interesting. Maybe later, but for now, you want to get paid ASAP and avoid all those accounts-receivable headaches.

Customer Success Prep

We'll cover implementation and customer success basics in more depth in the next chapter, but as you are tying up loose ends before moving on to that part of the customer life cycle, there's a set of things to pay attention to.

First, you actually have to consider customer success as a seamless transition from "closing" to "succeeding." That means that you should be facilitating a kickoff call or training or whatever the first step of your customer success process is. Whether that's calendaring a new meeting for you to train the user(s) in question, or introducing them via email to the person who is responsible for that, make sure it is executed. Relatedly, there is information that's easily captured at closing that will make your customer success process much easier. This may change from company to company, but a good example might be the name, title, and contact information of the decision-maker, executive sponsors, and users of your product. Especially if they are different people. Eventually in your customer success process you'll be reporting on success to executive or decision-maker stakeholders; make sure you have their information captured now.

CLOSE LOSTING

While we would love to win every deal that comes through our pipelines, it's just not going to happen. In fact, if you're winning all your deals, you could even make the argument that A) you don't have enough deals in your pipeline (Are you doing just one demo a week, and bird-dogging that one like crazy?), or B) you're not talking to enough customers who are lightly qualified (that is, you're cherry picking only the best ones, but not taking enough shots on goal). If you're fully utilized (ten demos a week or more), and you're winning all of them, okay, something you're doing is magic, and I'd like to talk to you. But with a new solution—or even worse, a solution in a newly forming market—win rates in the 10% or 20% range will be more typical. If you hit 30%, you're doing pretty great.

And this isn't something to be ashamed of. Think about all the reasons why a deal might not happen—it turns out that there really isn't budget available right now (but maybe in four months!), priorities shift away from the problem that your solution addresses (don't worry—they'll likely shift back!), or the person you're selling to leaves the company. There are myriad reasons why this time may not be the right time for that deal. So closing out an opportunity as "closed lost" is totally okay, and certainly better than spending your emailing and calling time on a deal that's never actually going to come to fruition. Remember, your time is your most valuable asset in enterprise selling. So being dishonest with yourself about the likelihood of a deal closing, and letting it take up time and space in your pipeline, is actually far worse than closing something out.

When to Close Lost Something

When should you close something out? Well, the easiest is when you've tried to handle the prospect's various objections, and she still gives you a direct answer to a direct question that she's not going to move forward right now. This is almost the best-case scenario (aside from a win!), because you have a clear understanding of where you stand, and the opportunity to ask specific questions about why she didn't want to progress. Was it competition? Was she not convinced of value or that she actually had the need? If that's the case, then it's probably low likelihood that you'll be able to get her later. The more likely scenarios, though, will be the prospect not having the budget to purchase, or the prospect largely going dark—which is usually indicative of some sort of issue with priorities changing, an unstated lack of budget, or an unwillingness to go to bat to purchase the solution. This case is actually not bad, because presumably the prospect still has the need for your solution. It's not a "no," but a "not now."

How can you know when it's time to close something out, even if the prospect isn't telling you directly? First, you can make sure that you're not in this situation of indeterminacy by making sure that you always have the next meeting on the calendar. That way, you'll have a call in which it's much easier to suss these things out. Of course, if you have a call scheduled and the prospect misses it, or somehow makes it hard to schedule a next meeting, your spidey senses should pick this up as the beginning of a deal going sideways. If you aren't seeing specific movement forward, and instead you're seeing a series of broken "micro-contracts" on the part of the prospect, the deal is probably on its way down. In these situations, it's actually better to just be direct and give the prospect an offramp. Remember, as we discussed in the Sales Mindset Changes chapter, you want to have a mindset of plenty, not scarcity. You don't want to grasp after this opportunity when there are thousands of potential accounts to be addressing. Spend good time with good opps. Recognize when the prospect may be trying to let you down easy by not saying no, even as his actions say no, again and again.

Address these situations head-on. It might be as simple as an email that says something along the lines of "We've missed a couple follow-up appointments. While I think that our solution would be extremely valuable to your organization, as we agreed that <some citation of ROI that is specific to them>, I don't want to occupy your time if it's unlikely we'll be able to help you out. But I'd really like to know so I can prioritize my time effectively, and also not bother you unnecessarily. Are you still interested in working toward becoming a customer? Is now a bad time? Or does it turn out that this is something that doesn't make sense for <their company name> after all? I can take the truth, but I would like to have clarity!" Or something like that. Always be respectful, and don't burn bridges, because you'll just be resurrecting this opportunity again in three months. And who knows, maybe your contact moves to another company in the short term, and was so pumped up on your solution that it's the first thing he wants to purchase in his new role! That is, provided you weren't a jerk when you closed the book on that opportunity.

Closed Lost Metadata

When you choose to close out a deal and not work it anymore, make sure that you document the reason in your CRM. This will position you to pick up the opp later if it's potentially resurrectable (you'll create a new opportunity on the same account). It will also help you better understand what is driving lost opportunities, which can help inform your product roadmap. If you lost the deal to competition, make sure to have a picklist of options in the CRM so you can see who you're losing to. If the reason was pricing or value perception, have a text field in your CRM that lets you capture closed lost notes, and make sure that you, and your eventual reps, take the time to record information there. You will likely be resurrecting these opps in two or three months, by which time you will have forgotten all the current context, unless you note it now. Think of it as jotting down a treasure map for your future self, so when you pick up the opp, you'll be that much closer to winning it the next time around.

Coming Back Around

One thing that early-stage companies have a problem with is "one and done" prospect engagement. That is, they get the appointment set, they do a discovery call and validate pain and lack of good existing solutions, they do the demo and follow-ups to build excitement and consensus, and then something goes sideways and the deal is shelved. As discussed above, it happens, probably way more than 50% of the time. So this is to be expected, and you definitely shouldn't leave opportunities sitting open in your pipeline, taking up resources.

But what's shocking is how often founders and other sellers don't circle back around after a certain amount of time. That is, if the timing was off, but everything else was primo, when will the timing be right? Ask! Note it down, and reengage at that time, with a new opportunity. Or if it's not clear when the right time will be, reengage in sixty days regardless. "Hey there, Jim! We spoke a few months ago about how TalentBin can help you guys accelerate your technical recruiting, but it just wasn't the right time. We've shipped a ton of great new features, making the solution even better, and from what I can see on your jobs page, you are still hiring lots of engineers. Want to hop on the phone and catch up on what's new in your world, and the new hotness we've made?"

To the point about "inevitability" touched on in Sales Mindset Changes in Chapter 1, until the prospect stops having the need you solve (e.g., no longer hiring, goes out of business), or implements a competitive solution (thereby soaking up the demand you sought to fill), they should be considered a target. And given that you've taken the time to sniff out a variety of things in your discovery and demo process that your competition doesn't know until they do the same work, you should harvest that investment! Make sure that you are "looping back around" on those opportunities that you have closed lost. Don't leave them open in your pipeline, limping along with no particular next action. Rather, close lost them, and at the appointed time, as reported in your CRM, make a concerted attempt to pop that prospect back to the top of the funnel, in a new opportunity. You'll be amazed what a fresh pass through the funnel—with renewed urgency, and an opportunity for the prospect to see what new features you've shipped (and by implication, what awaits them after they purchase)—will do for close rates.

PIPELINE MANAGEMENT

Now that we've talked about what a trip through the funnel looks like for any given opportunity, how do you manage a few dozen of them at once? Depending on the length of your deal cycle, and your average contract value, you can imagine working between a dozen, fifty, even up to a hundred deals concurrently, each spanning 30, 45, 60, or maybe even 180 days from beginning to end. This goes back to one of the most jarring things about selling for the first time—trying to manage that many concurrent threads, and herd those cats toward a finish line, is a shockingly large adjustment from non-sales work.

And while a holistic rundown of how best to manage a pipeline could be a chapter unto itself, these are some general guidelines.

Staging

One of the most important things in enterprise sales is having control of the deal and knowing, truthfully, the "state of the opp." The first step here is obtaining the information by asking good, direct questions, whether at the top of the funnel in qualification, or further down the funnel as you're pushing an opportunity toward completion. But the second step is ensuring that you've recorded that information in a way that lets you easily report and act on it. One of the most important parts of pipeline management is "deal stages"—that is, making sure each opportunity is tagged with the specific "step" it's currently in. That will signify to you how far a deal is from the finish line and, relatedly, how likely it is to get across it.

As your go-to-market evolves, you'll start figuring out the specific steps that are required in your sales process. For example, your product may require a "security review" that comes after getting all the sign-offs necessary from the relevant stakeholders. So that would be a stage. Or you might need to do stakeholder interviews with others who are impacted by your solution, even if they are not responsible for the decision. That would be a stage too. The important thing is that your stages have crisp definitions, and always mean the same thing to you and to anyone else who is using them (i.e., your eventual sales reps). Be careful if your CRM, like Salesforce, comes with a generic set of stages (e.g., "needs analysis", etc.) and associated "close percentages" (which, at your stage of selling, are pretty silly). Those aren't super helpful, and could distract you from defining your own solution-specific stages.

At TalentBin, through our acquisition, we had some pretty basic steps, because our sale was pretty basic; a single recruiter could buy us if she had budget, and it didn't really require a lot of other stakeholder coordination. Our stages were something like "Demo Scheduled" (we created an opportunity once a Sales Development Rep scheduled a demo with an account that had requisite qualification criteria), "Qualified," "Seeking Approval," "Sent Proposal," "Negotiation," "Verbal Agreement," "Contract Sent," and then "Closed Won," "Closed Lost," and "Closed-Unqualified."

Each stage was associated with specific criteria. For instance, "Seeking Approval" was used when pain was validated, and the stakeholder that we were engaged with was interested in proceeding, but there was another stakeholder whose permission or involvement was needed and was being sought. "Sent Proposal" meant that the prospect had specifically requested a proposal to consider pricing options, and that the next step was an up or down decision (or negotiation).

"Negotiation" meant that we were negotiating price, but that all other hurdles had been passed. The relevant stakeholders had bought in, and it was just a question of agreeing on a price and terms.

"Verbal Agreement" meant that the prospect had agreed on a pricing option, and that we needed to send a contract. Things should not have been in this stage for long. But it was useful when an agreement showed up in the rep's email, and he didn't have the fifteen minutes to send off a contract just then because it was the weekend and he was away from his laptop, he was about to hop into a demo, and so on.

"Contract Sent" is pretty damn clear, but it meant that those opportunities should be watched like a hawk. The prospect had agreed to a price, we'd sent them a contract to sign, and now it was a matter of crossing our fingers and toes that they signed it.

And of course "Closed Won" meant that the contract had been signed and that prospect was now a customer for the term of the contract. "Closed Lost" meant that we'd decided the sale was not going to happen on that pass through the funnel.

"Closed-Unqualified" was a special case, for opportunities where we should never have done a demo to begin with, because it turned out that the account didn't have the need for our solution. We would pay close attention to these to figure out what we'd done wrong to end up doing a demo for an account that could never buy—which of course is a terrible waste of sales time, and cause of prospect irritation!

"Qualified" was for opportunities where the demo had been done, and there was some indeterminate next step that wasn't better captured by any of the other stages ("Seeking Approval," "Sent Proposal," etc.), like when the prospect needed to "think about it" or "talk with my team." This stage usually was a catchment basin of cats and dogs that needed better next steps, and I should have done a better job with specific modeling criteria here.

Across the board, these probably could have been better, but they were a good start. As noted, your go-to-market may have more involved, or maybe less involved, stages, and you'll tune them over time. But the important thing is to have stages, and to make sure your opps are tagged as best they can be. Not only because this allows you to quickly scan them, and remind yourself which needs what action, but because it's crucial for your reporting. CRMs have helpful features like "time in current stage," so in your pipeline report you can see, for instance, opps that have been in "Contract Sent" for nine days. WTH? Better see what's going on there, because there's no reason a contract should be hung up that long!

While stages are important, one of the best ways to make sure that a pipeline doesn't go sideways is to follow the approach documented previously regarding "explicit next steps." At each stage, there should be an explicit next step, it should be captured in your CRM ("Reconnect with Brian on his team's feedback" or "Do group demo for Susan's reports"), and, most importantly, there should be a calendared time for that action to happen. Pipelines get out of control when there's no explicit next step, and when there are specific next steps but no clear time and date for when to complete them.

Cadencing

Successful selling is managing a rolling set of opportunities, each at a different stage and out of sequence with the others, with some dropping out of the funnel as won and others as lost, all while adding more to the top. It's a lot of moving parts. So making sure you have a recurring cadence by which to loop across your pipeline and avoid dropped balls is key. This is why in more mature sales organizations you have recurring weekly meetings like a "pipeline review" or "forecast call" (the bane of many reps' existences) as a forcing function to make sure that deals are not going sideways, and that reps are on top of them.

When it's just you, this is a two-edged sword. On the one hand, you want to make sure that you are on top of the deals that you're working—you've spent so much time and energy getting them on the calendar, demoing them, and so on, squandering that investment would be terrible. On the other hand, you don't want to create unnecessary overhead for yourself. This is why calendaring next actions can be so helpful. If you have meetings set to discuss the outcome of a prospect's consideration of your materials, or to do a demo with her broader team, the good news is, they're right there on your calendar. Kind of hard to screw that up. "Past you" compels "future you" to have good pipeline follow-up by putting it on the calendar.

But for when you can't do this, making sure that you have a set amount of time calendared for pipeline review is good. At TalentBin, I used to set two hours for the whole team in the later afternoon every Wednesday. Later, as you become more familiar with your go-to-market, you'll start getting a sense of your natural "carrying load"—that is, the number of opportunities you can support before you start dropping balls (which is not good, and typically signaled by a fall in close rates). At that point, you can start constraining the number of new opportunities you add to the top of your funnel. Maybe you decide that you'll only do three net-new demos a day, bumping up to four if there's something particularly exciting, to leave three or four other hours in the day for down-funnel follow-up meetings. Or maybe you'll have a floating hour a day for pipeline execution, which you can move within the day or to the next day (adding it to the hour you had blocked for pipeline follow-up that day). But the point is, you need to block the time to do the work, or it won't get done. And if it doesn't get done, you'll be wasting perfectly good opportunities.

Pipeline Prioritization and Cleaning

While allocating proper time for pipeline execution is a minimum requirement, there are definitely things you can do to make this time more effective. Generally speaking, it's always better to work "close to the money." That is, when you're reviewing your pipeline, start at the bottom, where you have contracts, verbal agreements (why haven't you sent the contract yet!?!), or proposals out. Those have more invested in them and are further along and thus more likely to close; focus your time there first and foremost to make sure they're in the state they need to be. Do you need to dash off a check-in email? Something else? Even among these opportunities, prioritize by the magnitude of the sale, crossed with the ease of closing. Sending emails and following up with a $10k deal may take the same amount of time as doing the same for a $30k deal. So make sure that you're happy with the state of the $30k deal first, because it's three times as valuable!

Once all those deals are in a clean state, start moving up your funnel. Are there any opportunities that don't have a calendared next action? That aren't "backstopped" with some sort of meeting? Fix those. Again, prioritize by value, focusing on whatever action will drive them to the next stage in the pipeline.

When it comes to cleaning your pipeline, it's okay to be ruthless. Are there opps that are clearly stuck and need to be cleaned out? Can you send them a final breakup email (as discussed above), and see if they come back with a "No! No! We're still good!" or otherwise kick them out? If you are honest about only having forty to fifty hours a week for selling, the opp that's sitting mid-funnel—with no future meeting on it, and a couple unanswered emails—is just taking up space for a juicy new deal waiting to enter your funnel. Don't think of it from the standpoint of "But, but, but, I don't want to lose it!" but instead "That little bugger is taking up room for a much more deserving opp. Out you go!"

There are a number of ways you can be more efficient in prioritizing and managing your pipeline. Reporting that ranks the opportunities by stage, and then projected revenue within those stages, can be good. You can also set up reporting that helps with error checking, like down-funnel opps (those in stages "Seeking Approval," "Proposal Sent," and below) that haven't seen activity in seven days (e.g., an inbound or outbound email, or a call over a certain amount of time). You should also catch opportunities that have been stuck in a certain stage for more than, say, two weeks (these time intervals may change depending on the nature of your go-to-market) or opps that don't have a future meeting calendared ("uncovered opps," as I like to call them). But these are all more advanced concepts. At bottom, if you have set time to review your pipe, and clean it in a prioritized, rigorous fashion, you'll already be miles ahead of purely reactive salespeople.

Calendar Management and Role Specialization

Up until this point, we've been largely assuming that all of this work would be done by you, as an individual seller. We've occasionally referred to the notion of Sales Development Reps who can help set appointments on your calendar, or a customer success function that takes a closed deal from you and runs with implementation. Even before you have a proper team, though, you can and should be segmenting the work you're doing into different "roles" and allocating your time accordingly.

As you've seen from all the various actions described above and, moreover, all the activities described in Prospecting and then Appointment Setting, this is a lot of stuff to do, and you only have those forty to sixty hours in a week. How can you get leverage? Well, the first way is to make sure that you focus on good accounts with great qualification criteria, and to always ask them good qualification questions so you never let crap into your pipe.

Calendar Management

But even if you're being vigilant about only spending good time on good targets, and later good opportunities, how can you best allocate that time? Well, when starting out, before role specialization, a great way to make yourself more impactful is to split your calendar time into blocks and spend each one focused on a particular role. That is, allocate time in two-hour chunks to do prospecting—to find the fifty or one hundred or two hundred points of contact that you want to engage with—and another block of two hours to execute your initial outreach to those folks. Then block another two hours over here to follow up with those prospects. If you're successful, you'll likely have demo calls, follow-up meetings, and closing calls peppered throughout the week. In addition to making sure that you have sufficient prep and follow-up time blocked immediately before and after those meetings, make sure you have enough time set aside for top-of-funnel activity. And, of course, don't forget to leave time for your pipeline cleaning and to follow up on opportunities that are already in flight.

As you organize your calendar, be mindful of what times are good for what activities. First thing in the morning is probably good for prospecting and initial outreach (or at least staging emails to send later for maximal open and response rates), as your prospects are just getting settled into their days. Whereas planning calls and demos for mid-day and early afternoon is typically a good bet, in that prospects allocate that part of the day to meetings. Lastly, the end of the day can be good for summary and wrap-up items, email follow-ups, sending deliverables that weren't sent immediately after a call, and such. Be thoughtful about intra-week time management too. Mondays and Fridays seem to have high cancel rates for demos; people agree to a Monday call a few weeks out, then realize they're slammed and cancel on you Sunday or Monday morning. Or they cut out early on Friday. Consider doubling up on prospecting and pipeline management on Monday and Friday instead. This is why field reps often push all their admin work out to Friday, when they're back in the home office, so they can use the rest of the week for customer-facing engagement. This, of course, is naughty from a CRM excellence standpoint, but potentially good from a time management stand-point—assuming every single hour the rest of the week was used for customer-facing activity.

Role Specialization

That said, if you're feeding your own pipeline with your own prospecting and appointment setting (in addition to doing all your own demos and down-funnel activity), that could absorb something like half of your time. So now instead of doing two or three demos a day, fifteen a week, and sixty a month, maybe you're doing just one or two demos a day. That means that instead of winning, say, $60k of ARR a month—20% of sixty opps at an average contract value of $5k—you're at just $30k a month—20% of thirty opps. Wow, that really changes your economics. You're not paying for as many engineers with that revenue anymore.

Conveniently, there's a solution to this. As popularized in the groundbreaking sales book Predictable Revenue by Aaron Ross and Marylou Tyler, by abstracting the role of prospecting and appointment setting from the role of demoing, deal running, negotiation, and closing, there are fantastic efficiencies to be gained. Namely, by hiring a bright new college grad to take over setting appointments against that list of fantastic accounts and points of contact as your Sales Development Rep, you can now spend more time focused on new demos and pipeline management. And this raises your revenue efficiency. Now instead of spending 50% of your time prospecting and 50% demoing and doing down-funnel work, you can spend 100% of your time demoing and down funnel. The $40k–$60k a year you'll spend on a junior sales staffer to pop demos onto your calendar at a clip of 5–10 a week will pay for itself—if each of those demos has a 25% chance of closing, at $5k apiece, you're looking at $1,250 of potential revenue from each one. So an SDR putting ten demos on the calendar a week (which might be appropriate for a smaller ACV solution, while three to five might be more appropriate for a higher-ACV, slower-velocity solution) is creating $50k of pipeline a week, of which you would expect $12.5k to close. Meanwhile he'll only cost you something like $1k a week. Your math may differ, but the point remains compelling.

In this fashion, using the metrics above, a $50k Sales Development Rep plus a $120k total cost Account Executive can drive something like $650k in revenue a year, while costing $170k—a 26% cost of sales. Or better, if it's a ratio of one SDR to two AEs, you're looking at $1.3M a year off of $290k in salary expense, or 22% cost of sales. This might be compared to a full-cycle rep that costs $100k driving $325k a year, a 30% cost of sales.

These examples start to reflect the language of scaling sales organizations (more on this later). I'm rehearsing it for you, though, so you can understand the power of making a "pitch & close" rep more effective by adding a wingman. In addition to making yourself more efficient now, you're also starting to build a bench of talent to become AEs in the future. This upwelling strategy—hiring SDRs who pump opportunities onto the calendar of AEs, and who then become AEs themselves, while pulling their friends and colleagues into the org as new SDRs— can become an extremely powerful virtuous cycle.

For the purposes of early specialization, I always recommend that founders or single sellers get an SDR wingman as soon as possible. Once you can reliably set appointments for yourself, you've proved that it can be done. Get someone else doing the labor, using the materials you've built for yourself and your list of targets. Moreover, you can have her both doing the outbound and being much more immediately responsive to inbound lead response than you were able to be. Obviously this adds the complexity of now having to manage someone else's performance, but this is probably a good thing. You'll need to get your hands dirty with sales management sooner or later.

Managing the complexity of down-funnel opportunities is hard enough on its own. Add in the fact that you're managing a few dozen of them, and it can feel completely overwhelming. Behind the mindset change to raw directness that sales begets, this multi-threaded project management is one of the hardest skill profiles to master. Even seasoned reps drop balls left, right, and center. However, if you're able to be intentional and mindful about your down-funnel cadence following the advice above, you'll be extremely well positioned to make the most of the opportunities that you've gotten this far, and to get a good chunk of them over the finish line.

Once you've done that, you'll have a whole new challenge to contend with— customer success! Thanks to the nature of SaaS, you can't just sell a deal, send the prospect their login credentials, and touch base with them in a year to renew the contract. Instead, you're going to be responsible for setting them up for success, and then monitoring the achievement of that success over the length of the contract. More on this in the next chapter.

CHAPTER 9

Customer Success Basics: Implementation, Ongoing Success & Renewals

INTRODUCTION

You've just closed a new deal. You're pumped up, having gotten a customer across the line and booked the revenue, with the check in the mail. You're ready to repeat your success and get another contract signed. In fact, you're starting to forget about the customer you just sold and turn all your attention to the next prospect.

Don't give into that temptation! In a SaaS world, the reality is that the moment you close a new customer, it's a countdown to when they will be renewing, or not renewing, their contract. And if you don't ensure their success with your solution, they won't be renewing. But that's not the worst of it. Even before renewal comes up, they certainly won't be buying more seats or units of your solution. And while they're not buying more, they certainly won't be telling their friends and colleagues nice things about your solution. They won't be providing you with delightful marketing-ready testimonial quotes and videos. Worse, if a new leader comes into the organization and does a tool review to see what is being used (and what isn't), she could easily decide to break your contract—and not pay the remaining installments. Yikes!

WHY CUSTOMER SUCCESS MATTERS

While losing out on a renewal is a big problem for your business, unsuccessful customers present all sorts of other problems ahead of that. And you don't necessarily have a year to fix them. While we talked in prior chapters about the benefits of longer contracts—they give you more time to get a customer to success—that doesn't mean you can get away with skimping on customer success and then save the contract in a last-minute scramble. There's actually only a short window in which you have a customer's attention and faith and can work them to invest their time and attention in adopting your solution. It's far easier to get a customer up and running as an extension of the sale process, with all the associated excitement, novelty, and executive buy-in, than to resurrect something that has fallen by the wayside and been deemed a failed purchase.

Now contrast this to a happy customer getting value from your solution. In their first couple weeks using the product, following a successful implementation, they already have some massive wins. And those wins are exactly in line with promises that were made during the sales process, demonstrating that they're well on their way to achieving the expected ROI. So they decide that more team members should have licenses and ask to double the size of the contract. All the while, because they're so proud of themselves for being smart purchasers of a new solution, they're happy to take customer reference calls. In fact, they've already recorded a nifty little webcam video raving about your solution, which you've embedded into your sales deck. When the decision-maker who purchased your solution gives his talk at the fancy new-technology conference, he cites you as being core to his company's success. And when one of their users leaves for a new role halfway through the year, her first call is to you guys to get a license for her new company.

That's the virtuous cycle you want to be a part of.

Do customer success wrong, and bad things happen. Do it right, and great things happen. How great and how bad? Well, check out this chart detailing the monthly recurring revenue for three versions of the same hypothetical businesses. The 0% line shows what recurring revenue would be assuming that all customers stay customers forever. After fifty-eight months, the company is at $4 million in MRR. Then look at the yellow line. With 2.5% monthly churn (that is, at the end of every month, 2.5% of total revenue is lost due to customers who cancel), after the same fifty-eight months, MRR is at something like $2.8 million. With 5% monthly churn, it's below $2 million. That is, you would have less than half the revenue that you won at some point in time, and paid marketing and sales expense to acquire.

Now take a look at the green line. This is what you get when, every month, 2.5% of your existing revenue upsells via expansion. That is, users and groups that are having success tell other users and other groups, and they buy more widgets, seats, or what have you. After that same fifty-eight months, you're over $7 million in MRR. Pretty impressive.

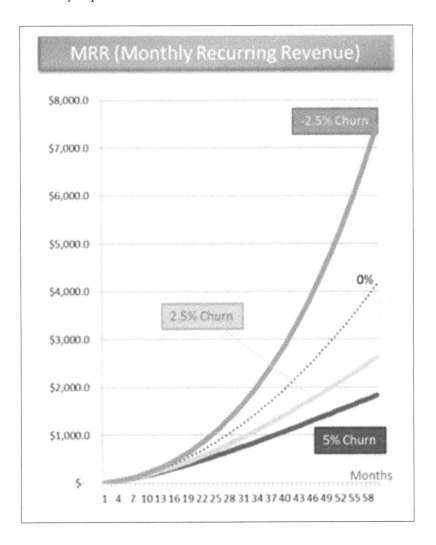

While this demonstrates the importance of customer success as you scale, it's even more important when you're just starting out. Getting those first few customers to take a leap of faith on your solution is hard. Make sure that they get the promised value out of it, and it'll be that much easier to get the next few customers. And those prospects will have to take less of a leap of faith, since your existing customers have already told them about you over a beer!

Yes, your product can have features that naturally make it viral within an organization, or make it sticky by getting users to put in lots of data. All of that can help with churn reduction and upsell. But none of that happens without first getting customers up and running and successful, quickly. So let's get you set up to do so.

So what is good customer success?

Above all else, customer success is about fulfilling the promises that were made during the sales process. The customer handed you money in exchange for a promise of value, and now you're going to deliver that value.

What does that value look like? Conveniently, it's documented in your Sales Narrative. Those KPIs that you said you were going to raise or lower for the customer? That's customer success. So if we were TalentBin, this would be all about driving more engineering talent into the top of the customer's hiring funnel. And if we were Textio, it would be about optimizing job postings such that more applicants would apply per post and posts would attract more diverse applicants. Customer success is about delivering on your ROI promises, and doing so for each of the involved stakeholders. Was there a certain set of value propositions for the manager, but others for the individual? Well, you're going to want to check both of those boxes, and make both of those "customers" successful.

You methodically, and in a stepwise fashion, engage with prospects and drive them down the sales pipeline toward being a customer. Now, the same approach will ensure that you deliver the success you promised those customers, and find yourself on the happier versions of those revenue graphs above. Methodical, in that it will be rigorous the same way your discovery, presentation, demo, and pipeline management was. And stepwise, in that it's not a question of getting a customer implemented, handing them the keys, and forgetting about them. Rather, after implementation, customer success turns to cadenced check-ins, instrumentation of success markers, and documentation of ROI achieved, all aimed at supporting an airtight case for renewal at the end of the contract.

MECHANISMS FOR CUSTOMER SUCCESS

When it comes to customer success, there are a broad array of tools to get the job done. That said, don't think that you need to employ all of the approaches we'll touch on. They are presented in order of most integral to more optional. All will deliver value, but depending on your bandwidth, you may need to pick and choose until you have dedicated customer success staffing. Regardless, they're all good to have in the back of your head.

Implementation

The broad bucket of "implementation" is the set of steps that you take after a customer has signed to get them quickly up and running, and can include technical implementation steps, user training, and more. Depending on the complexity of your solution, this could be as simple as a thirty-minute call and guided tour, or as complicated as a multi-month, full-blown professional services engagement. In either case, though, implementation is the first step on the road to customer success, without which you're putting yourself at a substantial disadvantage. Invest in it accordingly.

The goal of implementation is to execute all the preconditions needed for your customer to have success with your solution. So the first step is to understand what those first steps are. This ranges from the completely mundane, like securing credentials for a user, to the more involved, like integrating with existing systems, migrating data over from legacy systems that your solution is complementing or supplanting, and so on. It also includes user training for all archetypes of users—individual contributors, managers, and beyond.

So for a company like Textio, makers of job posting optimization software, implementation would start with securing credentials for all the recruiters who would be using the solution. Next, they'd hold training sessions with those users to understand how best to use the system, and with their management to help them understand that the system is being properly used and creating the promised value for the organization. And it would keep going all the way to securing proper integration with the customer's existing applicant tracking system to ensure that Textio could start learning from the organization's prior job postings (and the applicants and eventual hires that came from them).

Once you understand how many of these steps need to be taken, and have a sense of how much time that should take, you'll start to see how involved this might be. This is important, because it will indicate whether your implementation process can be as simple as a "one and done" call and screen share with the primary user of your product (or even a self-guided onboarding tour, for extremely inexpensive, uncomplicated solutions), or if it will require a series of meetings with various stakeholders, project managed to completion.

There isn't a single correct answer. It's simply a question of making sure that you are doing all the things needed to get your customers to success, and not stopping short. So if that means it will be a multi-person project that spans several weeks, that's fine. Just set that expectation during the sales process and, importantly, make sure that your pricing can support this level of engagement in the long run. If implementation takes 120 minutes all-in per customer, and a customer success rep who costs $50k a year can do fifteen a week, that's $70 of implementation labor cost right there. If your product costs $20 a month, that math doesn't work. Either your product will have to cost more or you'll have to think about how you can use cheaper, non-labor-intensive resources (e.g., in-product tools, documentation, etc.) to reduce that implementation cost. For our purposes, we're going to assume we're dealing with a fairly costly product, around $1k+ per user per year.

For reasons touched on above, early in your go-to-market, it's fine to over-invest your personal time resources to ensure that your first customers get to success. But in the back of your head, you should be thinking about the salaries you will eventually need to pay your dedicated customer success staff, which will have to come out of licensing revenue. Make sure that what you charge can support that customer success burden. Moreover, if implementation is particularly beefy for your solution, consider charging a one-time implementation fee to account for that. (A good rule of thumb is to triple the labor costs associated with the implementation process—so if it takes a week of employee hours, costing you $1k, you might charge $3k.) With most SaaS products, though, by virtue of their "flip the switch" nature, implementation doesn't require that kind of heavyweight implementation. But your mileage may vary.

Implementation Calls—One and Done

If your solution is straightforward enough that you can thoroughly cover implementation in a 60-minute meeting, or less, then that's a tried-and-true approach. It's a nice block of time in which you can hold the customer's attention and walk through a checklist of things to take care of, concepts to explain, and actions to take.

Early on in your go-to-market, on-site implementation can be a good approach. I suggested selling locally to start so you could go on-site to present and demo without getting in a plane; now you can do the same with implementation, ensuring rich communication and getting your customer bought in. Face-to-face time is so important early in your company's life (and it never hurts to bring cookies and your latest logo schwag to set a friendly tone). Eventually, though, holding these meetings by phone and screen share will be the more scalable way to do this.

Pre-Call Planning and Pre-Work

Your implementation meetings should be run from your sales presentations. That is, there should be pre-call planning, where you review your CRM for information from whoever sold the deal (early on, likely you) about who the user(s) will be, who the decision-maker and other stakeholders are (if they are different from the users), and what the business rationale for the purchase was.

Beyond simple pre-call planning, if there are specific pre-work actions that need to be handled to make your "face-to-face" time more efficient—like securing user credentials, loading the client's logo into the UI of their instance of your product, or what have you—do that too. And make sure you're familiarizing yourself with the parts of their business that your solution helps, and the specific user or stakeholder you'll be working with, using available resources like LinkedIn, their career site, or whatever else.

At TalentBin, our planning included reviewing the customer's careers page to see what sort of technical roles we would be setting up searches and "folders" for during the implementation call. We would also check out the LinkedIn profile of the user we'd be implementing to see if they were a technical recruiter, a generalist recruiter, or maybe concerningly, an engineering leader or HR generalist (which would require that we delve into recruiting actions and best practices, not just new software tools). Just as with a sales pitch, you want this information in your back pocket so you aren't blindsided and are best set up for success.

Rediscovery

Just as you start your sales presentations with discovery, you should typically start your implementation calls (and kickoff calls, for more involved implementation projects) with "rediscovery." That is, state what you believe the customer's business goals are and how the solution is going to be used to achieve them. At TalentBin, this might have been something like "It's my understanding that you're going to be hiring a dozen software engineers over the coming year, mixed between Ruby developers, and some front-end specialists. And to help with that, you bought this TalentBin seat. Is that right?" You want an affirmative statement of what your "agenda" is for the coming twelve months (or whatever the term of the contract is), so you know that you're on the same page, and can start working together, toward these goals.

And if there is some sort of slippage between what the customer's goals or beliefs are, and what you thought their goals had been, fantastic—now you know that and can course correct, rather than charging through an implementation call that drives toward the wrong goals. Or if, for whatever reason, they purchased the solution to solve problems that it doesn't solve (yikes! How the hell did this deal get sold?), you can quickly act to correct there too. Whatever goals you agree to during this rediscovery, make sure that you are documenting them in your CRM. Or, at very least, make sure that you memorialize them in a follow-up email to the user and stakeholders after the call, so it's there to refer to if there is confusion down the road.

Agenda Items

As you think about the agenda for your implementation calls, begin prioritizing the points you'll cover, from those that are crucial to success to other important items, with optional topics last. Things that absolutely must be covered might include ensuring that the user can actually access and log in to your solution (I know, you'd be shocked), that they have the relevant software downloaded onto their computer, that your solution is obviously bookmarked in their browser or shortcutted on their desktop or "dock" (you want to make it very easy for them to get back to your solution), or that any relevant data feeds are set up.

For instance, if your solution requires a user to OAUTH into their email or another system, it's critical to walk your new customer through that process first and foremost. If you train them on everything else but that action can't be completed, what was the point? If setting these data feeds or authentications can end up being fiddly or time consuming, it may make sense to have an initial "setup call" before the longer, more formal "training call." That way, you can put all those setup items to bed, and deal with any tripwires that come up, and you'll still have the full time allocated to the implementation call to tackle training and higher-value work.

Having covered "setup items," you should next focus on the core actions that are taken in your solution. A brief refresher (perhaps with a couple slides) may be appropriate here to set the context of the training. If you end up selling to larger organizations where the user hasn't seen the solution before (ideally less the case when you're selling to "deer"-sized, mid-market, not-too-small, not-too-large, accounts to start, but not uncommon), you'll also need to sell the users on why they should be excited about the solution. (Use the same rationales discussed in the Pitching chapter—it's going to make their jobs easier, make them smarter and better at their work, and potentially get them a better job in the future!)

During implementation, to whatever extent possible, have the user execute actions and, ideally, do actual, productive work. Often implementation staff will just flip on their screen share and do a "show and tell." This is inadvisable, in that your user will not be engaged, and will quickly whip out their iPhone to see the latest on Instagram. If you can, use a screen-share solution that allows the users to share their screens. If it allows you to use some sort of pointer or cursor to show them where to click, even better—do that. You want them to be mousing and typing and doing things, with your coaching. Things like join.me or Zoom.us, or heavier-weight solutions like GoToMeeting or WebEx, can be good here.

For example, a typical TalentBin implementation call included setting up a job requisition project folder, setting up and saving a search, demonstrating how to view and dismiss profiles, reaching out to viable candidates, and dropping those candidates into a drip-recruiting marketing campaign. At the end of the call, the user had ideally executed outreach, put a handful of candidates in drip campaigns, and maybe even gotten a response from a candidate, or at the very least an email open notification. Talk about a great outcome from an implementation call—a user who is fully set up, has executed and familiarized herself with the business motions necessary for success, and has actually done some "work" that can provide the promised ROI! That's the ideal.

If you're wondering what these steps might be for your solution, think back to your demo script. You set it up to rehearse the most important, valuable elements of your solution for your prospect, and to do so in a logical, progressive fashion. Your implementation process likely should align with that. It's kind of like a demo, but one where the user is doing the driving.

Group Calls vs. One-on-Ones

When it comes to implementation calls, you'll often be tempted to do "group calls." That is, if there are going to be a dozen users of your software, you might think, "Well, I can do this once, get them all with one call, and move on to the next. Efficient!" This can be really dangerous, especially early on in your go-to-market.

Group implementation calls suffer from the same issue that group sales demos suffer from—lack of accountability. Everyone thinks that someone else is responsible for paying attention, so no one does. Even if you've instructed everyone to follow along with your screen share and do the work on their side, you can't tell if they're actually doing it. Not to mention that you now have, say, five folks who can potentially trip up and need to ask a question, slowing down everyone else. The result is typically an uncontrolled call that fails to achieve your objectives. Worse yet, now you have five half-trained, half-implemented users who are responsible for that account's success with your solution. Remember that churn thing we were talking about? You now have five churn time bombs. Again, your ability to conduct one-on-one implementation may be constrained by what you can charge for your product. But if each of those users represents $1k of revenue (multiplied by many years of renewals), then you shouldn't be skimping. Especially at the beginning.

Oddly, you may run into managers who want you to do a group training, thinking that it's somehow more efficient for their team. You should feel empowered to push back against this—if it's an hour per user separately, or an hour with them all on a call together, it's still an hour of each user's time. It's actually your time that's being expended to a greater degree. Just explain why the way you do it drives success. Help them understand that more value is provided through separate calls, and that they'll look like heroes for allowing it. And remember, if you acquiesce, you're setting up more churn time bombs for yourself to deal with later.

Homework, Follow-Up Calls, and Monitoring

When you conclude your implementation, you want to be sure that a "summer break" mindset doesn't set in for your users. That is, don't let them feel like students sprinting out of class on the last day of the school year, looking forward to a couple months before they have to think about school again!

A great way to avoid this sort of thing is to set a back-check meeting for a couple weeks out. Then, assign some specific homework to be executed in the interim, which the users know you will review by monitoring their usage. One of the beauties of SaaS software is that you have insight into the actions that users are taking or not taking. Make it clear that you will keep an eye on that information to make sure that users are having success, to jump in if there appear to be problems, and to report to deal sponsors (like their boss!) that the promised ROI is being achieved. We'll touch on monitoring more later, but even just talking about it from the outset can help create a usage tailwind.

Ideally this monitored homework assignment should require very distinct, measurable actions—for instance, doing X specific action Y times by the end of the first week. Be clear that users who do this homework have X% more success than folks who don't, which is why it's assigned.

Take, for example, Teamable, makers of clever referral recruiting software that helps recruiters mine their internal networks for potential fits for open roles. Say they spent their implementation call demonstrating how a recruiter should process referral candidates for a single internal staff member. The homework goal might be to reach out to ten referral candidates of ten internal staff in the first week, for a total of a hundred potential candidates, and to get ten interested responses. Eminently achievable, and a mild scale-up of what was done in the implementation call, all focused on driving demonstrable ROI as quickly as possible.

As with down-funnel sales work, don't end the implementation call until that next meeting is actually on the calendar and you've sent the meeting invite for it. When it comes to scheduling a follow-up meeting, it can be just as time consuming to chase down a customer as a prospect. Avoid being in that situation!

Materials and Support Contacts

Before concluding the meeting, verify that the user knows how to get in touch with you if he has an issue. More on this in a bit, but making sure that there is an easy way to get in contact with "Support" (which might be you right now), both in the product and via email, is key. If you are able to record your onboarding call and provide it after the fact, this can be a helpful reference for the user (and a "tale of the tape" to go back to, if there are any issues in the future). You can share the script or checklist that was used too. If the customer is trying to remember that one really neat thing that you showed them, well, with those materials, they can easily access it.

Missed Meetings and Re-Implementations

If meetings are missed, you should push hard to reschedule them, to ensure that implementation is happening the way that will enable success. Make sure that you have tracking in place to know which users and accounts have had their implementations, which need to, and which need to be reschedule. Again, you don't want to plant churn time bombs to be discovered at a later juncture.

That said, a video-recorded "canonical" implementation call can be a helpful piece of collateral for someone who needs a refresher (again, better if you record their actual call for them to refer to), or for someone who would like to see what a call looks like.

Occasionally you may find that users need to be "re-implemented" in some regard, because they've either gotten out of the habit of using your solution or need a refresher. Or the original user of your product may leave the org, meaning that you need to onboard her replacement. In addition to preserving that customer's implementation recording, having weekly "group implementations" for this purpose can be helpful. That is, if it costs $70 in labor to execute an implementation, and a user needs one or more refreshers per year, now add this up across dozens of customers, that could add up if done individually on an ad-hoc basis. For users who've already had an initial implementation, a standing group call can be a great way of accommodating the five, ten, or more users, across customers, that might need some help in a given week. Early on, though, you probably want to overinvest in going the extra mile to make sure that people are successful. So if someone needs to be re-implemented, by all means, get it on the calendar and do it, whether it's an individual user or, even more importantly, a decision-maker or manager who is responsible for the people using the system.

Implementation Projects/Multistage Implementations

If your solution is more complex, and requires the involvement of different parties, you may not be able to take a one-and-done approach. This is fine, and shouldn't be avoided. Just be sure that your pricing supports more involved training. Multistage implementations can actually be a good thing—the more effort it takes to get something up and running, the less likely someone is to rip it out down the road. So getting good at these implementation processes can be a substantial competitive advantage for you.

When approaching a more complex implementation, think of it as akin to a multistage sales process, not unlike the one you probably went through to get the initial contract executed. Meetings should be calendared, and you should use the same "micro-contract" approach to ensure that you have commitment for the next step at each stage of the process.

Project Kickoffs Calls and Discovery

When your implementation involves multiple steps, it's often good to have a kick-off call with all of the relevant stakeholders and participants, where you can review timelines and what is needed from each participant, and get collective commitment in front of all of the other stakeholders.

It's important that this sort of call involves the sponsor or sponsors of the project, and any internal vendors whose help will be required to get everything up and running. Make sure that those folks are identified and commit to attend the call. During the meeting, as with "one-and-done" implementation calls, make sure to restate the customer's goal for the solution and walk stakeholders through what they need to do to get there, along with the ideal timeline.

Having visuals for this meeting can be really helpful. This could be a slide that demonstrates the major steps, and timeline, for implementation (which you might have already created for your sales presentation). Or it could be a live, shared Google Sheet, with line items for each deliverable or action, their customer-side "owner," a targeted date associated with it, and the relevant status of that item (i.e., "To Be Done," "Scheduled," "In Progress," "Completed," "Hung," or what have you).

This is a good example of something pretty basic from the folks at Teamable:

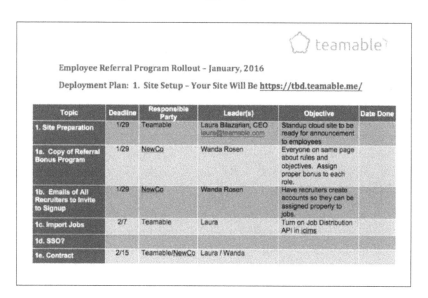

One favorite approach is having a templated Google spreadsheet from which you can create a copy for each customer. Ahead of your kickoff, identify, with the help of your deal sponsor, the various customer-side stakeholders for each item (e.g., "This is the CMO. She owns this, this, and this. This is the VP of IT. He owns this, this, and this."). This is an example that I threw together, patterned after some spreadsheets I've seen.

A "live status" spreadsheet like that can later serve as a wonderful "source of truth" as you progress through the various steps. Introducing it at the start sets the expectation that you'll be marching down that project plan, and that everyone will have access to it to see what's being accomplished (or not, if things go sideways). There are fancier professional services project-tracking tools that provide this functionality, but to start, a simple shared Google spreadsheet is probably good enough.

Progressions and Status Reporting

Once you have all those stakeholders identified, it's time to execute the various steps you've listed. As they are completed to satisfaction, mark them as completed in your implementation project plan.

Status reporting can end up being a substantial amount of overhead, which is why it can be so valuable to streamline things with a shared spreadsheet and a dedicated "implementation thread" via email. As important items are checked off, you can update the spreadsheet, and then link to it in an email notification to the group thread. This gives stakeholders a reassuring sense of forward momentum that their project is progressing and further establishes your credibility. It also creates a way that customers can get status updates whenever they would like, even between weekly status emails.

Advanced Progress Tracking

Your granular project tracking will likely be executed in a project spreadsheet to start, but as you acquire more customers, and as you have multiple implementations in progress, you'll want to think about moving this to your CRM. The problem with keeping status information in different spreadsheets is that it's difficult to query across multiple documents to see the aggregate implementation status of your customers. The right way of dealing with this is to track this information in your CRM.

This could be as simple as a post-sales status field on the relevant opportunity in your CRM correlated with different meaningful implementation stages. Or if you want to get fancier, it could be distinct activity items that need to be retired, each associated with the closed opportunity. However you approach it, the important thing is the ability to say to your CRM (or substitute system) something like "Show me all the opportunities that are closed won, but in various states of completion." For example "Show me all the opportunities that have close dates in the last fourteen days, but which haven't yet had their initial kickoff call." That way, you can see if any accounts are in some sort of red-flag situation.

Implementation Item Execution Proactivity

As noted in the "one and done" section above, to the extent that you can do the work for the customer, do it. And to the extent that you can make things as simple as possible when you can't do the work yourself, do that too. A great example of this is Outreach.io's implementation process. They sell a sales email and calling automation solution, so it's critical that they connect their software to the customer's Salesforce instance. In fact, this is so important that they build in a specific call with an approved Salesforce admin on the customer side to get that set up. It's a fifteen-minute call if all goes according to plan (and sometimes it doesn't), but it's so important to the rest of implementation that they make sure to get that executed first and foremost. And they do so by using screen-sharing software so the implementation specialist can take control of the customer's mouse if the customer okays that, just to make it as easy as possible. You should consider how proactivity like this could be used in your implementation process to make sure that the things that need to get done, get done.

Snags and People Wanting to Diverge

Be mindful of snags in your implementation process. Firstly, as noted with one-and-done implementation calls, if something falls off the calendar, always get it back on. This becomes all the more important with a multi-step implementation, as there are more opportunities for those failures to occur.

If a further meeting falls off the calendar, reschedule it. If, for whatever reason, there are multiple failures, then be clear about the implications of this to the customer-side party who is precipitating the issue. Something along the lines of "The reason we need to have this call is because I need fifteen minutes with you to XYZ. That is important because it's required for the next step of our implementation, which <overarching stakeholder name> was hoping to get completed by <date>. What can I do to help get this completed so we can attain that goal?"

If for whatever reason you keep being stonewalled by an ancillary stakeholder, be careful about running back to your sponsor to tattle. Implementation projects are like multi-stakeholder sales, but after the sale has already taken place. You don't want to be seen as going around tweaking noses, even if you have the imprimatur of the CMO, CIO, or whatever. Your goal should simply be to act as the agent of your deal sponsor, doing your best to advance the goals of the project and diligently documenting those efforts in the form of well-written emails, meeting invites, and status update emails, along with a tracking spreadsheet. You never know when that person you're working with to execute an implementation action, post-sale, can end up at another organization and have something nasty to say about your solution while it's being considered for purchase....

Completion

When you've completed all the relevant steps of implementation, and the solution is "operational," memorialize that to your various deal sponsors so they know that it's time to start expecting to see the return on their investment. That is, if it takes two months to get things up and running, you don't want your deal sponsors thinking, "Why haven't we seen a return yet?" and holding it against you. This is another benefit of good status reporting during the implementation project—your deal sponsors are seeing the work that you're doing, and the value that you're providing in driving the desired change in their organization.

Charging for Implementation

If your implementation process is drawn out, and requires a substantial amount of labor on the part of someone in your organization, consider charging for it as a professional service. This can be helpful if your customers' implementations vary significantly in complexity, and therefore demand varying resources from your team that haven't been built into the pure licensing costs of your solution.

A good example of this would be a solution that hooks into others enterprise systems, but could potentially be used without those hookups. If a customer doesn't require any implementation hookups beyond their standard onboarding and training, then standard licensing would cover them. But if a different customer needs integration with three or four other systems, which represents 20+ hours of meetings, calls, and so on from a systems engineer on your team, well, you might consider charging for that.

Inducements for Users/Stakeholders

While you would hope that everyone involved in implementation would be excited about embracing new technology that will help them do their jobs better or, at a very minimum, follow through on something that their superior has instructed them to do, you can't always rely on that. You have to consider your solution's different value propositions to different stakeholders (individual users, line management, leadership), just as you did during the pitching process. That is, "What's in it for me?" continues even during this stage.

One great way of helping with that is to provide inducements to individual users to heartily embrace implementation. That is, in addition to helping them understand how this is going to make their job easier and why it's going to be make the organization more successful, consider positioning how this will make them more in-demand professionals, now and in the future. A more advanced version of this could be actual "certification" in your solution. That is, when the individual goes through all the steps of implementation, executes on the various pieces of homework, and attains some version of success with the solution, you can "award" them with certification.

At TalentBin, we offered TalentBin Certification, awarded to those who passed a lightweight test after implementation (that really just acted as an open-book quiz to compel paying attention to the topics we covered, or at least going back to the materials later) and completed a certain set of actions (i.e., putting 50 candidates into drip campaigns). Certification included a digital PDF certificate and entry into a registry that could be checked by employers. Of course, this aligned with the interests of our customer success team—if users were familiar with how to achieve success, and incentivized to take the actions that would drive ROI for their companies, that was a big win for everyone involved!

Inducement can also be as simple as sending hearty helpings of company schwag to users who have gone through implementation. T-shirts, Post-it notes, high-quality pens, you name it. If you're selling software that costs hundreds to thousands of dollars per user per year, then $5 worth of nice pens and Post-its is certainly worth it, and a nice reminder to users that their customer success manager loves them and is invested in their success. Plus, it can't hurt to have a reminder of your solution papered all over their desks. It is absolutely amazing how much buggy software and occasional hiccups can be papered over by sunny, delightful customer success. Constantly remind the user that you're in their corner.

This is one of the reasons why customer success staff are often compensated not on renewal metrics, but instead on success precursor metrics (i.e. the proportion of the users they are responsible for who have logged in or attained some measurable outcome in the last 30 days). Alternately, you might compensate customer success managers based on their assigned users' net promotion scoring or customer satisfaction survey scoring. The point is, guiding and rooting for your customers' success—whether that means making them better professionals, helping them prove their value to their bosses, getting them raises, or positioning them for better jobs—is a great way to make sure that they are excited about your solution.

Inbound Response & Support Tickets

Once you've completed implementation, it's time to drive your users to a return on their investment as quickly as possible. Let's talk about the tooling you'll need to achieve that.

The first bucket of tools allows users to easily contact you when they hit snags and need help. We'll talk later about proactively identifying users who are having issues and engaging them before they even reach out. But the first step is having a means by which users can get in touch with you when they have issues.

You'll recognize a lot of the same tenets from the Inbound Marketing chapter here, in that support is rather similar—it just happens to be for existing customers rather than prospects.

Inbound Support Request Capture

The key here is to ensure low friction to get in touch. If you make it hard to ask a question or provide feedback, your user will simply close your solution and go back to the way that he used to do things. You want to make sure that when folks have an issue, they can complain and complain easily, because hearing that feedback is a requirement to fixing the root issue!

At the most basic level, this can be a big "Help" or "Support" link. Ideally it should live prominently on the side of the browser window or app screen, and allow users to quickly jot down their issue and fire a message off to a monitored inbox with a click. This could be something as simple as a "mailto:" link that points to <support@yourdomain.com>, where that email address has been set up as a listserv that people responsible for support (maybe you!) at your organization monitor. A more advanced version might be a Google Form that asks for structured information—keep in mind, though, that this can add friction for the user who needs help. Really, the most important thing is simply to know that someone is unhappy so you can jump all over it and help them get to success.

There are a variety of shared-inbox solutions that make managing a dedicated support email address easy like Front, Help Scout, and others. More involved support solutions like Zendesk, Desk.com, Freshdesk, and Salesforce ServiceCloud can also let you easily present a <support@domain.com> email address that then gets "captured" by the support software, and ticketed in a way that lets you understand which issues need to be addressed, which are in progress, and which have been solved.

General Support Tenets

While they might sound obvious to some, I'm going to take a second here to note some general tenets of support communication. Though customer success should always be viewed as helping the customer to achieve the value they were promised during the sales process, inbound support is a bit of a two-step process. That is, unlike implementation, where the user is typically excited to be trying out her new toy, in the case of inbound support the new toy probably let the user down and broke in some regard. Now she's pissed, and wants to both get her toy back and express some frustration.

So while your longer-term job is to get the user back on track and successful, the first step is usually to diffuse frustration, and to do so in a way that makes the user feel heard and empathized with. It's often very tempting to "blame the user" when you realize that the cause of the issue can be something very basic ("Is it turned on?"). Resist this temptation and instead focus on making sure that you can "save" this relationship, by taking all the blame for the issue and validating the source of frustration. Moreover, they're probably right. If it wasn't turned on, why wasn't that clear? That's your fault, as a product development organization, for not putting the power switch on the front, where users can see it's switched off.

Your goal is to soothe the angry customer, progress to fixing her problem, and persist until the issue's been resolved—or she tells you that it's no longer an issue.

Rapid Response

The next most important key to inbound support is quick response. Eventually you may get into "Live Chat" (more on this in a second), but to start, even asynchronous support email requires extremely quick response time. If you're at a very early stage, you may even consider a direct phone call back so you can quickly solve the problem in a rich, synchronous conversation. This may not be scalable later, but early on, the quicker you can solve problems for your users, the more excited they will be about your solution—and the less time they'll spend stewing, frustrated with how your solution let them down. Furthermore, your support will have an air of honest-to-goodness TLC that will reflect highly on your solution. Again, you'd be amazing how much awesome support can paper over issues with a solution, especially when it's early and things may be rough around the edges.

Even if you can't solve the issue for the user instantly, at the very least you should aim to quickly acknowledge that the ticket has been received and communicate some time frame within which they should expect follow-up. Most of these more involved ticketing systems include automatic email acknowledgment functionality, which is helpful, but I like to let the customer know the moment that a human starts working on the ticket too.

Response Tracking

As with sales opportunities, you'll want to keep track of the state of a support request, so you can know which ones need you to act, which are "in progress," and which ones are "done." Basic support software will help you do this, but make sure that you're practicing good hygiene when you respond to requests, marking them as "in progress" and only closing out tickets when it's become clear that you've solved the problem. And not just "Okay, I didn't hear back from you, so I'm going to close this." Make sure you have an affirmative statement that you fixed their issue, or that they no longer need your help. Otherwise you're going to have a hot mess of confused email threads, customers waiting for help, or unnecessary follow-up with folks whose problem you've already solved. Like an inbound marketing and sales pipeline, you want to work the ones that came in most recently and haven't been acted on first; once those have been addressed, fall back to the other open tickets.

Canned Responses and Macros

Once you get a goodly number of users on your solution, you'll start seeing patterns in your support queries—namely, multiple users running into the same issues. This is good. Not only can you construct "frequently asked question" responses that will make you more efficient, you can usually also identify opportunities to fix this user frustration in the product, so it won't become a support ticket. (A good way to think about it is if a user takes the time to complain about something, there's probably 10x more who ran into the same issue and didn't complain!)

Support software includes what are known as "macros," which allow you to use "canned responses" (the support version of an email template), along with automatically updating certain statuses and tagging with your tickets. As soon as you start seeing patterns in your support requests, you should start creating canned responses. At first they can just be text based, providing the information that is requested. But as you get more involved, consider providing links to more robust support articles you create using the "support site" functionality of most of these support software providers.

For example, if you're were NextWave Hire, makers of recruitment branding software, and you constantly saw people asking how they could load their NextWave Hire employee testimonials into social marketing software like HootSuite, you might consider spending thirty minutes to stand up a support "article" on how to do that, step by step, with screenshots. This way, you know you're providing a richer educational experience, and each time you get that question, you can quickly fire off a macro linked to that article, getting the user exactly what they need and on their way. Moreover, when you later add a front end and search to your support site, users may be able to self-serve these solutions without involvement by a support agent—helping them get their solution faster, and freeing up support agents for stickier issues that need their involvement.

Ticket Tagging/Product Feedback

Above and beyond helping your users get the value they were promised when they purchased your solution, rigorous support can be extremely valuable in guiding your engineering and product efforts. That is, the information contained in support request often points toward the highest-impact moves you could be making next—whether bug fixes that reduce common issues or new features that address the unmet desires users are surfacing. However, in order for this information to make it to your product development organization, first it has to be cataloged and tagged appropriately. Typically, this means adding tags to tickets that describe the features that they stemmed from.

So if you were Textio, makers of job posting optimization software, and you saw users having issues trying to save job descriptions from the editor interface and complaining to support that they were losing their work, you might tag those tickets with the part of the product ("editor") and the desired functionality ("saving") in question. Don't go overboard, but keep in mind the ultimate goal of this exercise—to be able to take this information at, say, the end of the month and see what features are causing the most support tickets—the better to guide decisions about product development.

Other Inbound Support Tools

While email-based, "ticketed" support is the expected industry standard across SaaS, there are a number of other methods of providing responsive support, and a number of other venues where you may end up engaging with your users.

Live Chat

Live chat is becoming more and more popular, both for desktop-based customer success and, more and more, for mobile-based solutions. The value of live chat for support again echoes the value of live chat for lead capture—immediacy. Being able to quickly solve a user's issue at the moment of their frustration keeps them from disengaging with your solution—and on their merry way to achieving the value you promised them. Not only can your agent resolve the issue quickly, which is a benefit to the customer, the rapid back-and-forth of chat provides the customer a sense that "something is being done to help me."

Moreover, chat makes it much easier for you to elicit further information from the customer about their issue. If a customer's initial email to support is half-formed or missing information (which they often are), then asking for clarification is an exercise in email-tag. With chat, on the other hand, the rapid back-and-forth allows your support agent to pull the relevant information out of the customer.

And while it might seem that live chat would be more costly, typically a support agent can hold a handful of these conversations at once. So ultimately it may not require more personnel time than email-based support tickets. That said, it does require someone to be "on call," at least during certain times, which can be challenging if your support team is only you, or a single customer success person who's handling implementation calls, follow-up calls, and inbound support requests. (More on this later when we talk about support specialization.) Some chart support software, like Intercom or Zendesk Chat, gives you the best of both worlds, behaving like chat software when you or your customer success staff are "online" and available, and behaving like more traditional asynchronous email when they're not. So if you have to be on an implementation call, and a customer files a support request, it is received like an inbound email request; other times, when you're "on duty" for support, you'll receive a chat.

Social Support

Twitter is another place you might find yourself providing customer support. Well, issue diagnosis and resolution rarely takes place on Twitter, but it's another channel where your customers may end up venting their frustrations about something wrong with your solution.

Firstly, if you're seeing this kind of frustration on Twitter, consider that you may not be making it as easy as you should for customers to vent directly to you. This is where the fallacy of trying to make support "hard" (that is, requiring users to fill out lots of fields in a complicated support request form) may bite you in the ass. Your customer may just decide to open a new browser tab and dash off 140 characters of pissed-off diatribe that will unfortunately be consumed by all of his followers!

That said, even if you make things as easy as possible, you'll likely still end up with folks talking about you on Twitter—whether it's existing customers or people considering your solution. Most support software now includes some version of "social listening" to bubble up potential issues and create tickets out of them. Early on, this may be unnecessary; you may have too few customers to worry about them taking to social. However, if your accounts happen to have lots of users of your solution (for instance, a customer has 100+ employees using the software), pretty quickly you could end up with a few thousand folks with the potential to create social media headaches.

Supporting consumer products on Twitter is far beyond the scope of this discussion, and typically much harder than doing so for enterprise users. With enterprise users, the best approach is to simply treat social comments as an initial "inbound" support request—do your best to acknowledge them, let them (and others who follow them) know that you're on the case, and describe what action you're going to take, or need them to take. Thankfully, at an earlier stage, you likely won't have too many users, so it should be pretty darn easy for you to take their names and geography (typically included in their profiles), look them up in your database, and then engage them directly via your typical support process. Ideally your first outreach should include a proactive suggestion of what the solution might be, based on the tweets. And of course tell them in a public reply that you emailed them with a proposed solution, or with a follow-up question. If you can't figure out who a user is because he or she has an atypical alias that doesn't align with the name of a user in your database, reply that you tried to find them and couldn't. Then give them the URL for a support article that best solves their issue (if you have one), and tell them to email your *<support@yourdomain.com>* address so you can fix their issue.

Of course, social can also be a great place to encounter people raving about your product, or asking questions about it before they actually enter the sales process. Taking the opportunity to give those folks a high five or to direct them to a sales rep (or, even better, direct a sales rep to them) can be a cherry on top of a social support mechanism.

Phone

Phone support can be costly, in that you have to have someone who is "standing by" to answer calls (much like you need to do with chat). That said, early on, we're not really interested in being as cost efficient as we can; we want to sniff out early indicators of issues so we can systematize their solution. So at the outset, having a phone number for folks to call—and you'll be surprised how many would prefer to chat and file email support requests than talk to a human—can be a great way to give early customers the white glove treatment. Take the opportunity to learn fantastic information about their challenges with your product, and their hopes and dreams for what it could be for them. Later on you can make the choice to remove that option as you seek to manage the economics of your support mechanisms.

Proactive Customer Monitoring

While low-friction inbound support and rapid response is fantastic, there's a step beyond—proactive, preventative customer support. One of the beautiful things about modern software, particularly SaaS solutions, is that the customer actually uses it on your servers, or at very least, in a way that allows you to instrument their usage. This is in stark contrast to how things worked back in the day, with on-premises enterprise software that was installed on customers' servers and racked in their data centers. Then, you might have had no idea whether the software was being used, and value was being provided to customers.

Now, SaaS delivery means you see what sort of usage customers and users are engaging in. And that's crucial to your business. Because users are subscribed (and didn't "purchase" a perpetual license of the software), they can just stop subscribing if they aren't using the tooling (and deriving the promised value). The logical implication of that turns out to be—pay attention to whether customers are using the tooling the way they're supposed to! This notion of "customer success monitoring" has really taken off only in the last few years, and the associated tooling is still being developed. However, there are fairly basic ways that you can accomplish this now.

Inspection

It's fairly common to architect your application such that a customer success manager can log in "as" the user to see what's going on. This is helpful when troubleshooting, but can also be great for customer success. as you can dip into customers' accounts to check for the telltale signs of proper usage. You would be looking for those "value precursors" and "value outcomes" discussed above—the actions and outcomes that lead to the value you've promised.

Custom Reporting

The more advanced version of inspection is reporting that you can get from your engineering team (or, if you're handy with SQL, maybe you can do it yourself). The downside here is that it can be expensive to have your engineering team stand up reporting for you. But if you have enough customers, it can be worth the investment.

There are a couple different types of reporting. One is comprehensive reporting for some trailing time interval that shows the key value precursor and outcomes for each user and each customer. That way, you can easily scan across and identify potential problems to address (and, on the flip side, users having great success for use in marketing materials and customer references).

Then there are more prescriptive reports that alert you to just the specific users who need help by showing which users and customers fell below designated usage levels. This can be as basic as surfacing users who haven't logged in for some period of time. Or you can look for more specific indications that a user is struggling. On TalentBin, for example, running searches that yield zero results, or unusably large numbers, suggests a problem; we could have designed reporting to alert us to that usage issue, which was likely to block success. The important thing is to instrument leading indicators of non-success so you can jump on them before that bad or nonexistent usage becomes ingrained.

Dedicated Tooling

You may also be able to hack existing tooling to provide you this information. If your product and engineering team uses something like Mixpanel or similar, you can sometimes use that software to set up this kind of customized reporting. Or, if you want to get really fancy—and likely you would do this only after you have a customer success rep or two—you can use purpose-built customer success instrumentation software like Gainsight or Catalyst, which not only pulls user activity into the system, but allows you to act on it with communication templates, playbooks, and the like. You can almost think of things like this as the CS person's "pipeline," which they're constantly combing to see where they can move a customer down the road to success, the same way a sales rep would with prospects in the CRM.

Acting on Data

Of course, having this data is all well and good, but if you don't do anything with it, it's not super helpful. First, that means consuming it. You have to prioritize time, on a recurring basis, to review this information. Identify people who are having great success (and give them kudos, and log them as potential customer references) and those who are not doing well. Once you've done that, you need to act on it.

Doing so is a little more delicate than responding to inbound requests. In this case, you're calling out that the customer appears to have an issue with their usage that makes them "aberrant." So this takes some finessing, and is best approached from the standpoint of "I want to help you have success," "I want to help you be the best you can be," "I want to learn what's keeping you from being able to achieve success, and fix it," and so on. Remember the "pitching" we talked about in implementation, and the importance of those user-facing value props? This is where you trot them out again. Later you can get into the heavy artillery and involve their management or original decision-makers (if that's a different person).

Shockingly enough, a lot of the time, it can just be a case of the user or customer having competing demands on their time, and being not great at prioritizing use. Often you can take on the role of manager here to ensure that they're blocking sufficient time, and can even use calendar reminders to help with this.

Other times there are actual issues that need to be resolved. Engaging users and prompting them in an open-ended fashion about what the issue is can be a fantastic way to see where there are weaknesses in the product, or where there are out-and-out bugs. Sometimes it's a simple fix. Perhaps the user was just confused about a feature, and once you show him how to resolve it, he's off to the races again.

Another fairly common situation is that the user to whom a license was assigned leaves the company, and their manager doesn't have a rigorous transition plan in place. That's also easily resolved; you'll want to engage with the relevant decision-maker to secure a new user, and run them through the relevant onboarding programming. The same is true if you have a decision-maker who leaves the organization. This is why you'll want to instrument usage even at the managerial level.

If someone's usage disappears from your reporting dashboards, perhaps they've disappeared from the org—which is important to resolve for this particular implementation. But if that customer was excited about the product and having success, then perhaps that decision-maker is in the market for your solution again at the new company she landed at! Another reason even managers are important users to proactively instrument.

Of course, there are occasionally problem users. That is, folks who, even after you've resolved all their supposed issues, continue to not do the things required for success. Often these are folks who either have another competitive tool or process that they prefer or weren't involved in the process of procuring your solution, and aren't bought in on it. To the extent you can, make your case about how this will help them do all the great things they want to do, now, and in the future at other jobs. Help them understand the opportunity cost of not using the solution—whether that's missed hires, lost revenue, or whatever your product's value proposition is. If that fails, involve the deal sponsor to see if you can secure a different user. Of course, do so in a respectful way, but make sure to detail all the efforts you've undertaken. If it's a situation where the entire organization has licenses, like a CRM, and there isn't a question of swapping in another user, just make a note in your CRM about the problem user (almost like "Closed Lost" notes for prospect opportunities) and move on. If it's a situation where only a subset of staff at the organization have licenses, and your licenses are "scarce," then seek to get another user in that seat.

It's important to remember that you can't spend all your time on every user, and at a certain point, you have to cut your losses. In fact, typically you want to spend your time on the "C+/B-" users—you may never be able to save the users who are at F and D levels. The B+ and A users are on their merry way and don't need much attention. So spend your time getting those C+/B- users up to B+ levels. This is especially true when you as a founder are doing the customer success, but it continues to be true even when you have a handful of customer success staff.

Many of these issues are really easy to resolve, but the important thing is being able to identify that something is amiss, and jump into it, before things get worse. And to do that, you need to have proactive monitoring!

Success Outcome Capture

In addition to monitoring usage to get ahead of any problems, a successful customer success function needs to understand and quantify users' success—and then make sure to tell them about it! In business speak, this evidence of success is often known as "outcomes."

In the sales process, you promised certain kinds of business value to your customer. Instrumenting the achievement of that value is important for a variety of reasons. When customers can see that they are achieving the desired business value, they're more likely to stay customers. Moreover, by documenting and capturing success outcomes, you'll be able to use that information in go-to-market materials, like sales decks, customer success stories, and so forth—more on that later in the chapter. There are a couple of ways to go about this.

In Product

If you can design your product in a way that captures outcome value, all the better. For instance, in TalentBin, there was a concept of "stages" associated with candidate profiles, and one of those stages was "hired." If people were buying TalentBin to help them hire hard-to-find engineering talent, chronicling when that happened was one of the most direct ways of proving its value.

Sometimes successful outcomes may be harder to capture, so you can look to instrument the precursors to that outcome value as well. If you were Textio, for example, you could capture the number of job postings that had been improved, and what the level of improvement was, by comparing the Textio score of the job requisitions before and after optimization. Of course, the best of all worlds for Textio would be capturing that precursor behavior and also capturing the improvements of job-view-to-apply, phone-screen-to-apply, and phone-screen-to-hire ratios that even more concretely prove the value of the product.

Survey/Conversation

Sometimes instrumenting value directly in the product is challenging. Moreover, while quantitative indicators of value achievement are great, they leave out more qualitative measures. For both of these reasons, eliciting value attainment feedback directly from users can be really helpful. There are a variety of ways that you can go about this, and some may be more doable than others depending on the scale of your customer base. The simplest approach is just being mindful to ask your users what they've accomplished when you interact with them or during scheduled catch-up calls. For instance, we discussed the notion of a 30-day check-in call. Part of that call could be focused specifically on documenting value that the user has achieved (or not achieved, in which case, you now know what you need to fix).

More involved versions of "asking your customers" are net promotion scoring survey software like AskNicely, Delighted, and so on. Surveys can be implemented to automatically send at certain times (i.e., 45 days after initial kickoff), or can even be embedded directly in the UI. You can customize them to not only capture standard net promotion data like "On a scale of 1 to 10, how likely are you to recommend this product to a friend?" but also explicitly ask value capture questions like "Does this make you more efficient?" or "How many hires have you made?" and so on.

However you capture this information, it's important that you do it in a way that is reportable after the fact. Your CRM can be a great way to do this. If you can get proactive about capturing these success signifiers as "Activities" with time stamps on them, suddenly you can report on them to answer questions like "How quickly do customers get to ROI payback?" or "What proportion of our customers get to what level of success in the first month? Second month? Third month?"

Quarterly Business Reviews

There are all kinds of benefits to instrumenting and capturing success signifiers. But you can't forget to reflect this customer success information back to the customers themselves. That might sound a little weird—if they're having success, you'd think they'd know, right? No! Customers are super busy, use dozens of tools, and have all kinds of competing vendors whispering in their ears that their software would provide a better, faster, smarter solution than yours. You need to do a good job of documenting and reflecting back the success your customers are having, so it's super clear that they're getting that all-important ROI.

If you're proactive about sharing this ROI information, great things happen. You'll be top of mind with users and decision-makers, who will understand why this was a great investment of their time and budget. And if there are other potential users of your solution in the organization, it'll be that much easier for you to sell more seats. These decision-makers and users also interact with friends and colleagues that share their business challenges. Making sure your ROI proof is readily available will arm them to be great promoters to others. And it helps cement their existing commitment bias (that is, aren't they smart for choosing you?), which is very helpful if competitors and alternative solutions show up in their inboxes. Why would you open an email about a competing solution when you know that you're getting great value from the one you're using?

If don't do a good job reminding customers of their successes, the opposite can happen. You'll miss out on upsell opportunities, as no one is clear on why your solution is a great investment. You'll miss out on word of mouth because your decision-makers and users aren't armed to advance those arguments for you. And you'll leave yourself wide open for competitors to come in, making a case that their solutions can provide more value. Not good.

The best way to achieve scenario A, and to effectively share success data with your customers, is to implement quarterly business reviews. Oddly named—probably better to call them something like "success reviews"—these are formal quarterly checkpoints between a vendor and a client to document progress against joint business goals. That is, this is the means by which a vendor can present formally the value that has been delivered to the client so the customer can say, "Wow. This is great. I'm so glad that I'm doing business with you. I'm totally going to renew when the time comes around. In the meantime, I'm going to think about how I can maybe reallocate some budget from the other solutions I'm using, since clearly yours is working so well. Oh, while I'm at it, I'll tell all my peers at different organizations about this next time we have cocktails." At least that's the best-case scenario!

Participants

Quarterly business reviews should generally include the same participants who were involved in the selling process, with a particular focus on the decision-maker who spent his budget on your solution. A decision-maker who is a seasoned software purchaser will typically expect this sort of thing—and, in part, expects you to do his homework for him vis-à-vis the ROI that has been generated to date. I know that sounds a little weird. You clearly have an incentive to demonstrate substantial ROI, so why would customers leave that up to you to prove? Well, again, your customers are busy people dealing with the day to day of their jobs, so if you can do this for them, they'll love you for it. Plus, they'd love for you to make them look smart for choosing your solution.

Involving users may make sense, however if there are too many to be practical, better to focus on the primary decision-maker. So too if there are problems in adoption or usage in parts of the user base that need to be addressed candidly with the decision-maker—you don't want users "in the room" for that discussion.

Tooling and Approach

As with many of these things, a nice slide deck template that outlines the information you want to transmit is a great start. This is an example of a QBR deck for a solution provider that helps telesales organizations do a better job handling their inbound calls.

Your template should include a place to list the shared goals that drove the purchase of the solution—an opportunity to do "rediscovery" and ensure that the same business pains continue to be priorities. Start with something like this: "When you first purchased TalentBin, it was because you had five open headcount for Ruby on Rails engineers, and were looking at this tool as a means to help with that. Is that still the primary technical hiring challenge you're facing?" This rediscovery should be paired with the KPIs for the key business process that you were looking to improve, both before and after the solution was implemented.

If things are going great, and you can demonstrate that substantial value is being captured, then you should feel empowered to note opportunities for more ROI with more adoption. That is, say only five recruiters are using your fancy software, and you can show that they've saved fifty hours per recruiter per month over the previous quarter, aligning to $30,000 in saved salary expense. Well, if you know there are twenty other recruiters in the account, they're clearly wasting $120,000 in salary expense across the rest of the recruiting team for each quarter those others aren't users. What are we waiting for?!

This is a slide that focuses on how much key performance indicators have improved as a result of implementing a solution.

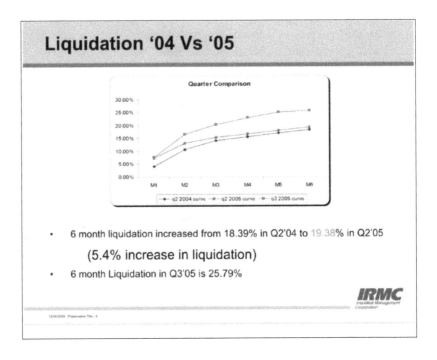

If there are issues, you should know this ahead of time from your success instrumentation, and address them in the presentation. Are seven of the account's users adopting well, and gaining ROI, but three aren't? Present this, along with the opportunity cost of non-adoption, and come with a proposal of how you'd like to address this issue to ensure maximum ROI for the decision-maker. Again, you're being proactive and doing a bit of her job for her, which will be welcome. Also, if there are issues, attempts at upsell and cross sell in a QBR will probably be looked at as pretty lame. So don't do that until you're delivering on your promise for the existing folks.

Ultimately, the goal of the QBR is to assess the state of the relationships and "sell" the next steps that are most beneficial to you and the client. If that means retraining for problematic users, then you should be selling that. If everything is great, you should be "selling" participation in customer success marketing collateral, like videos, slides, and case studies, and such, wherein the success metrics that you just reviewed and everyone gave each other high fives over can be documented in an easily shareable format to get in front of potential customers, and in so doing, make your client look like the brilliant thought leader she is for being so forward thinking!

These recommendations should be the conclusion of the QBR, along with discussion and buy-in by the decision-maker that these are the right next steps, and a proposed action plan to achieve them.

Depending on the size of the customer and the amount of revenue that you're looking to preserve, this QBR could be done on-site or digitally. If you're going to do it on-site, you can often add in some user-facing activities, like retraining, a live Q&A session, or even just a customer appreciation thing like pizza, cookies, schwag, and so on. If the QBR is delivered over a digital presentation, you should ideally record it so it's available for reference after the fact.

Lastly, if your solution isn't revenue intensive enough to justify the staff time to execute a QBR of the type described above, this doesn't mean you shouldn't be explicitly sharing success information on a cadenced basis. Your goal remains the same—getting a customer excited about the value they're getting out of your solution. So if your product is particularly low cost, consider how you might develop an "automated QBR" that delivers all the same metrics and proof that you would cover in a face-to-face, or digital, presentation, but does so via email and potentially in the product.

Outcomes and Next Actions

Coming out of the QBR, guess what—you need to implement those next actions. So whatever the plan of action, you should summarize it in a follow-up email to the relevant participants. Then the responsible party should start cranking on that, as the clock is ticking on execution of that ahead of the next QBR.

Reporting on QBRs

Just as you report on your deal pipeline, you want some sort of method to report on QBR execution. Early on, this could be a Google Sheet that simply lists each QBR in its own row, which you populate when you first onboard the customer. Eventually, of course, this should live in your CRM—a standard way to approach this is to have an event of type "QBR" with a completion state field that you can set to "To Be Scheduled," "Scheduled," or "Completed." And when an opportunity is closed won, set that QBR field to automatically populate at quarterly intervals such that you can easily run a report to see the "To be Scheduled" QBRs in the next sixty days that you need to schedule and prepare materials for.

SUPPORT SITES & ASYNCHRONOUS SUPPORT MATERIALS

While most of the things we've discussed have been one-off actions that are either proactive or reactive in nature, asynchronous support materials are also a powerful way to drive more and better success with your customers. Much like we look for places where we can templatize and collateralize our sales message—with email templates, slides, videos, PDFs, and so forth—we can do the same in customer success. And the benefits are the same—you can make sure that the information that you're providing is correct, since you wrote it once and double- and triple-checked it.

But even more importantly, customers usually just want to solve their problem and get on their merry way. If they can do that by reading a success note or watching a quick video, that can often be more satisfying than having to file a support request, or engage in a chat conversation with an agent. Not to mention that by letting customers answer their own questions, when appropriate, your success staff can spend their time on implementations, QBRs, and thornier support issues.

The traditional way to do this is via a support site. Most support software like Zendesk, Desk, Freshdesk, and so forth have lightweight content management systems that allow you to create a dedicated page for a given topic (usually in the form of a how-to answer) with text, embedded images and screenshots, and even videos, that lives on a hyperlink. Moreover, they typically let you embed links to these pages in support response macros/canned responses to let support staff quickly respond to inbound requests with the relevant answers.

Most support software also provides functionality that allows users to search across the support articles, or suggests support articles that match the initial input a user puts into a form. Lastly, they provide analytics on these documents to show how frequently users are reading them, which helps you understand the benefits they're providing, and also where there might be confusion about the product.

As you build your support site, you can definitely start basic and work your way up. Support materials have a tendency to accrete over time, and that's a good thing. To start, one valuable item to house on your support site is a fully recorded kickoff call—Camtasia and ScreenFlow are great tools for this—to which customers can refer if they get confused later. Even better is a kickoff call that is broken into its constituent parts, like "This section is how we set up our account" and "This section is where we learn how to use basic search" and "This section is where we learn how to use advanced search" and so on.

Like with your sales deck slides, you can think of this sort of materials as "object oriented" instead of monolithic. Take that same work you did to record the entire implementation video and slice it up into individual snippets that address key parts of using the product. Each of these can later be used to create a specific support article that is focused on that topic.

Another great thing to house in a support site are new product announcements. Frequently the marketing and sales org will make video, screenshot, and text materials to explain new features when they're launched. These can easily be repurposed in a pinch as support materials (though typically your marketing demo videos will be more focus on benefits and value than "how to" use the features). But until you have the time to make support-specific versions that are more detailed in nature, by all means, use what you have! Either way, a dedicated support article that documents the goals of a new feature and how to use it can be a great resource to email to your existing users, and for merchandising in the product if you have a means by which to do so.

Beyond core workflows and new features, it can be hard to know when to spin up a support article. On the one hand, they can be really helpful in reducing time spent answering support queries. On the other hand, they can be time consuming to produce, so you don't want to go off the deep end creating one for every edge case. The rule of thumb I like to use is similar to the one I mentioned in the Sales Materials chapter for creating appendix slides for your sales deck. If a question comes up more than once, it's probably worth the time to spin up a support note addressing it and a macro to answer the question.

It might seem like a pain to take an hour out of your day, but if you're using good support software, you'll create all sorts of great benefits. First, you'll make it possible for users to self-serve support on yet another topic. Beyond that, for the queries that still make it into your support queue, support software will often recommend the right article and macro to use—you'll be setting future you up for success, because your past hard work will be resurfaced to you magically. And you'll be well set up for when you start hiring support personnel to help out too. Lastly, you'll have that nice note available to shoot over to the customer rather than having to re-type it again and again.

One note on notes (heh). While many of the benefits of support notes flow from time efficiency, you don't want to lose the opportunity to make a customer feel loved. So when responding to inquiries with a support note, first make it clear that you have a hunch that this support note will answer their question. (I like to bake this caveat into the macro text so I'm less likely to forget it.) Moreover, make sure to articulate that you're simply sending the note in the interest of perhaps expediting the solution for them and that if they would prefer to get on the phone to address things in more detail, that of course you'd be happy to do that.

What do you don't want—especially early on—is a situation where a fantastic, high-satisfaction interaction with a customer is spoiled by them thinking that you're just trying to get rid of them. There will be many customers who are ecstatic to get that well-documented support note, and use it to solve their problem. They likely have a busy schedule, and the notion of trying to calendar something with you seems not so exciting to them. However there will be a class of customer (the same one who might use your inbound phone line!) who really wants to talk to a human. If it looks like you're stiff-arming them with a macro and support note, with no offer to talk live, they're not going to be happy campers.

New Release Communications/Ongoing Training

It sounds obvious, but one of the biggest missed opportunities in early-stage customer success is insufficient investment in the documentation, announcement, and adoption of new features. In early-stage software, the reality is that you're likely iterating your product pretty substantially as you go, adding new features and extending existing ones. The funny thing is that while new features get incorporated fairly regularly into prospect-facing materials—like demos, slide decks, and so on—folks forget about the customers who have already bought a version of the product that didn't yet have these magical enhancements.

That's a problem. If your customers are not being kept up to date on your advancements, but are being wooed with the latest and greatest versions of your competitors products, you're missing out. And if your evolved features are addressing pain points that were surfaced via support channels, well, all your customers likely have those pain points. If you aren't communicating that they've been solved, they're likely still being frustrated by them. Further, while customers primarily buy your solution, as is, to solve an immediate problem, there's a part of them that is "buying the company." That is, they're also buying into the belief that you will continue to get better at solving this problem for them, with better and better technology. If you are indeed iterating your product and shipping new features, you need to show it to your customers and get credit for that momentum. You want them to say to themselves, "You know, it was a really great idea that I bet on these guys. They're always coming out with great new things for us." Lastly, appropriate communication of new features and functionality is a fantastic way to reengage disengaged customers who are at risk of churning.

Materials

What materials should you use for this? Well, as noted above, creating a support site note as part of your release process will help ensure that you at least have the key information readily available—what the goal of the feature is, why it is helpful, and how to use it. This is a pretty good example of a TalentBin new feature support note:

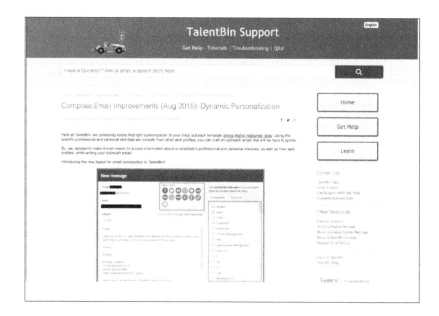

Recording a lightweight demo video to show this off in a visual fashion is also good. This is an animated gif that demonstrates the "automatic personalization" referred to in that support note:

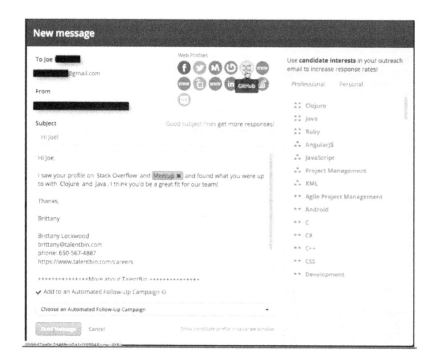

Of course, having this information available is great, but merchandising it solely on the support site isn't nearly as good as bringing it to your user—in the product, in their inbox, and on your various other properties. Use your support note and associated screenshots and videos in customer-facing emails, or even "webinars," about the new features. (If you record those webinars, you now have yet another great support asset.) You can also merchandise announcements in your product using "new feature announcement banners" that can be dismissed. Some support solutions like Intercom include banners or fly-ins as part of their customer communication features.

Finally, once you've taken the time to create new-feature notes and announcements, get as much mileage as you can out of them. Even after the initial announcement period, this sort of material can be used for email campaigns to introduce users to features over the first few months of their onboarding.

Recipients

You might think that you should only be sharing this information with your users. On the contrary, you want to share new features with anyone in your accounts who has a stake in the successful deployment of your solution. So while non-user decision-makers likely won't need a demo, you definitely want to have them on the distribution list for these email announcements. You want them to be glad that they made the decision to buy your solution. And if you are doing a good job staying top of mind—with a drumbeat of ongoing releases and customer success support—that can be a great source of upsell opportunities.

Be mindful of adding those users and their email addresses to your CRM in such a way that you can easily execute these communications. Extra credit if you have various stakeholders modeled in a way that allows you to execute different reporting for different communications. For instance, do you want to execute a webinar on ROI calculation for your solution, which would be appropriate for decision-makers but not for end users? Well, having a "type" field in your CRM that can be set to "User" or "Manager" can help you with that.

Implementation and Monitoring

Communication of a new feature isn't where responsibility ends, though. As noted above, customers have to actually adopt those new features to get value from your ongoing product improvement. So what does this mean? Well, often you'll have new features that require substantial implementation effort.

Take TalentBin's "automated follow-up campaigns" feature. At one point, TalentBin shipped the ability for recruiters to automatically send follow-up emails to candidates that they discovered in the TalentBin database—"drip marketing" functionality that substantially raises response rates from candidates. To make it easier for recruiters to adopt this feature, we actually provided a bunch of "canned" campaign email templates on various topics that would be relevant to candidates. Still, a number of these templates needed customization to be specific to the customer before they could be truly usable. Which is why, when we released the new feature, the TalentBin customer success team went through their assigned accounts and engaged the relevant stakeholders to get on a "new implementation call." That way, we could walk them through the new feature, and get those templates customized so they would be ready for use. It was worth the time investment, because customers using campaigns would get much more value out of the solution than those just sending "one and done" emails. Of course, as soon as the feature went live, it became part of our onboarding training—but we had to loop back to hundreds of existing customers to make sure that they could access the new functionality in an impactful fashion too.

Renewals

It bears repeating—the goal of customer success is to ensure that customers get the value they were promised when purchasing, so they will continue to be customers. In a SaaS world, if they don't get value, they won't renew. Everything we've covered has been in support of that goal. So by the time a year has passed (the typical length of a SaaS contract), it should be just an absolute no-brainer for the customer to renew. After all, you've done such a good job helping them capture tons of business value from your solution, in a way that was fully documented. So first things first, to ensure renewals, make sure that folks get to value.

But even if you've done all those things right, you still need to capitalize on it by executing a good renewal process. These are some ways to do that.

Automatic Renewals

First, in your order form and master service agreement, you should have an automatic renewal clause. Customers may seek to negotiate it out, but most will never consider it, and this way, your solution just default renews. When the time to renew comes around, you just run the credit card on file using something like Recurly, Zuora, or Aria Systems. With automatic renewals, it can also be nice to provide a courtesy email note a month or so out. This doesn't mean that you can skimp on getting customers to success, but it can help in some edge-case scenarios where implementations have taken far longer than they should, stakeholders have left a company (resulting in a new "sales" cycle simply to get adoption of what has already been paid for), and so on. Further, automatic renewal at existing pricing can be a boon to a customer if you raise your pricing as you add new functionality and the product gets more robust.

Renewal Calls

If you don't have automatic renewals, then you'll have to have whoever is in charge of your renewals process—either you as a founder when you're small, or a Customer Success Manager or Account Manager when you're bigger—execute a renewal call. This is very similar to the quarterly business reviews that we discussed earlier in this chapter, where the goal is to summarize success to date as compared to promised goals, and to discuss customer business goals for the period ahead. But in this case, the goal is to summarize the customer's success across the entire term, and to discuss of organizational goals for the year ahead—a sort of "jumbo QBR."

Timing

Renewal calls should be close enough to renewal that you can immediately send a renewal contract to be signed, but far enough out that if there seems to be a snag, there's enough time to help remediate and get to a renewal. If your final QBR is three months from the end of the contract, then a renewal call six weeks from the end of the term can be a good compromise. Calendar that renewal call as soon as the final QBR is executed.

If you're doing a good job in your QBRs, by that second-to-last QBR, you should have a sense if the account is going to renew; if it looks like there are issues, start a plan to fix that as soon as possible. However, if for whatever reason you get to your renewal call only to find out that there are showstoppers, there's always the option of adding some more time to the end of the contract to resolve those issues. This is to say, you can often extend a contract a month or two without requiring payment in order to resolve those issues.

Materials and Prep

As with QBRs, come to the renewal call prepared with all the success metrics that the account has accrued over the contract term; you'll want to have all the proof necessary to show that they have gotten value for their investment. All the success metrics that your CS staff has been counting up and logging in the CRM? Those should be brought to the fore for the call, in what amounts to a "grand finale" QBR deck.

Closing and Upselling

As with pitching itself, it's important during the renewals process to actually ask for the business, again. Even if you have an auto-renew clause in your agreement, you want to validate that the customer is indeed bought into a renewal. In that scenario, that might sound something like "Fantastic. Well, I'm glad that we got to review all of this and that we're helping you <business goal your solution solves>. Your contract will be renewing on <date> and we're looking forward to working together in the year ahead."

Part of the renewal call discussion should be focused on the business goals of the customer organization for the year ahead, and that's where potential opportunities for upsell can be unearthed. Are they planning on hiring thirty more salespeople, each of whom could potentially be a user of your product? Now is the time to discuss whether it would make sense for them to buy those additional seats now so they can get a volume discount, rather than adding them one at a time over the year.

LEARNING FROM YOUR CUSTOMER SUCCESS TEAM

While all of the above activities are key to getting customers to success, and eventually renewing their contracts, an effective customer success function can and should play a larger role in your organization. That is, because it's uniquely positioned to have meaningful, ongoing interactions with your customers, customer success can often pass on a wealth of information to sales and marketing, product development, and other key functions.

Product Development

An outcome of all of your customer success activities—rigorous onboarding, inbound support request capture, and proactive monitoring—will be a wealth of information on what customers like about the product, and what they don't. Customer success uses this information to resolve issues and enable success, but it's also important to feed this intelligence back to the product development organization. If certain features are hard to use, and create a large amount of inbound support requests, product and engineering can prioritize refactoring those features. That will in turn not only reduce the support resources needed to paper over that issue, but will ideally enable more success, creating happier customers who are less likely to churn (and more likely to generate positive word of mouth).

Sales

Your customer success team will also be the first people to know that a user or decision-maker is departing from one organization to join another. This is a prime opportunity to follow them to the next company as well, as typically the settling-in period in a new role is accompanied by setting up new tooling. Handing this information off to sales to execute on in a timely fashion is paramount.

Customer success can also be extremely helpful in surfacing customers willing to do customer reference calls with prospects. Connecting prospects with customers who are rabid fans due to their success is a great way to get deals across the line, and your customer success staff can help you achieve that.

Marketing & PR

As your company matures, your pitch should too. That is, you no longer have to speak about hypothetical success—now you can point to real-world examples of how your solution is changing how your users do business. Customer success plays a key role in finding valuable usage data and product evangelists and passing that information back into your marketing and media outreach.

Success Proof

Earlier in the chapter, we talked about the importance of capturing successful outcomes in your CRM so you can report that information back to the client. Equally important, though, is having the ability to report those outcomes across all users, or particular subsets of accounts. As customers reach their goals, customer success can harvest this information and provide it to marketing for use in "proof of success" collateral like slides, videos, and so on, as discussed in the Sales Materials chapter.

Events/Customer Advisory

Customer success will be best positioned to identify cheerleaders and advocates who can be helpful in the context of conferences, speaking opportunities, and customer feedback on new product.

If customer success is going to help all these other parts of the organization, the first step is to make them aware that these are activities that they should be engaging in. The second, more advanced, step, especially as you start establishing a specialized customer success function, is to provide compensation inducements to them. For instance, offer a $50 bonus for each upsell or new opportunity (again, contingent on the size of your typical deals) identified by customer success that ends up getting sold.

CUSTOMER SUCCESS CALENDAR MANAGEMENT & SPECIALIZATION

As discussed in the previous chapter, as you start to have more responsibilities that occupy your time—but before you bring on staff to hand those off to—you'll have to be mindful of splitting your calendar to achieve them.

Previously, you had to find time for prospecting, initial pitches, and down-funnel follow-up meetings; now, you're adding implementation meetings, monitoring success KPIs, QBRs, and renewals! It's a lot, so it's vital that you be vigilant about blocking segments of time on your calendar, or those activities won't get done.

The first step is to make sure that meetings for customer success activities— implementation calls, kickoffs, check-ins, and QBRs—get on the calendar as soon as deals are closed, so your future time is "burdened" appropriately. The second step is to start tracking these activities in your CRM. The same way you may have a "Demo" event activity or "Follow Up" meeting activity, you should track "Implementation Meetings" and "QBRs" such that, with a simple report, you can see, for example, all accounts that have a Closed Won opportunity but have not yet had an implementation meeting.

After you have onboarded a dozen or so customers (depending on the size of your deals), you should start to think about how you could hire someone to take this responsibility off of your plate. Importantly, because of your experience onboarding, getting to success, and doing QBRs for that initial set of customers, you should have the beginnings of a customer success "playbook." Codify it in documentation and process (again, to be tracked in the CRM), such that you can hire that first CS specialist, get him to success, and then start the process of stamping out more of him.

When you get to the point where you are adding a substantial number of customer success staff, you'll want to be clear about who is responsible for what to get the most out of your investment.

Responsibility Specialization and Compensation

The compensation of customer success staff is heavily influenced by the responsibilities they bear. Firstly, as an aside, as of the mid-late 2010s, the compensation models of customer success staff have not yet seemed to wake up to the realities of the importance of customer success in a "renewals world." That is to say, if you refer to the revenue growth chart in the introduction of this chapter, and look at the scenarios with differing churn numbers, you can see the deep importance of customer success. That should be reflected in the level of talent you are willing to pay for, and the compensation requirements that flow from that. Historically organizations have viewed support and customer success as a cost center to be minimized, rather than considering the opportunity cost of under investment in the function: higher churn rates, lower lifetime customer value, and reduced opportunities for upsell and positive word of mouth.

That said, one of the most important determinants of how you compensate your customer success staff is their commercial responsibility, or its absence. That is, will your customer success staff be responsible for renewals? Or will an "account management" staff or even the primary account executive staff be responsible for these? Generally, focusing account executives on new business is the right approach; focusing efforts and not splitting attention is typically the best way to assure that things are done right. AEs that are "responsible" for renewals often follow the same pattern, showing back up to an opportunity 60 days from renewal—270+ days from the last time they exchanged emails with the client. Approaching a client with the attitude of "OK, so catch me up!" is not a recipe for a functional success and renewal motion. The best organizations specialize this responsibility.

Who, then, should be responsible for renewals? There are typically two approaches. Customer Success staff can be responsible for renewals; you might even base part of their compensation, in a variable fashion, on renewals and upsells. The other approach is one wherein responsibilities are split, and Customer Success is responsible purely for "success" activities, like implementations, ongoing support, quarterly business reviews, and so on, but another "commercial account manager" is responsible for seeking out upsell opportunities and ultimately renewing the business. This latter approach offers the benefit of specialization and eliminates the concern (oft stated but dubious, in my opinion) that success staff can't "close."

My take on this is that early on, when there are fewer customers, that level of specialization creates unnecessary overhead. That is, creating specialization between Account Executives who are hunting new business and Success and Account Management staff who are "farming" existing business certainly makes sense—the behaviors and operational tempo of a new-business hunter are very, very different than those of an existing-business farmer. But at the very early stage, specialization between Customer Success staff and Account Management staff creates more complexity and overhead than benefit. Having a class of customer success person that's responsible for the implementation, ongoing support, quarterly business reviewing, and eventual renewing of customers seems to be the best balance. You get both specialization and the "close to the metal" benefit of a rep who's deeply familiar with the 100, 200, 300 accounts that he is responsible for.

Later Specialization

Later, as your customer base grows into the hundreds or thousands, more substantial specialization of success and support roles may make sense. For example, you might split out inbound response support versus implementation versus ongoing "success" versus account management and renewals. The benefit of this is that you can get efficiencies of specialization and scale. You can provide a better level of service to folks who are chatting on your support chat widget or sending in tickets if people are staffed purely to deal with those; otherwise, they'll be left waiting until a customer success manager gets off an implementation call and can turn her attention to tickets. Or you can have more senior, more skilled, and thus more expensive customer success staff focused purely on implementation, quarterly business reviews, and project management of success activities, while more junior (and less expensive) staff focus on first-line ticket response—not dissimilar from the specialization of SDRs and AEs in a pre-sales environment.

Regardless of how deep you get into customer success in your company's earliest days, the most important thing is to think about it at all. The biggest error founders and other first-time revenue leaders make, aside from the inability to sell at all, is insufficiently investing in the success of customers once they have been sold.

If at very minimum you have a success mindset, and choose from the approaches above, you will already be far ahead of the game.

Taking What You've Proven Can Be Done
& Getting Others to Do It Too

CHAPTER 10

Early Sales Management & Scaling Concepts

INTRODUCTION

What the hell is "scaling?" People use the term all the time, but I find that about 80% of the time someone talking about "scaling" is usually a great sign that they have no idea what they're talking about!

In B2B sales organizations, "scaling" is when you take something that has been proven to work at the unit level—one sales rep, one sales "pod" (i.e., an SDR, two AEs, and a CS rep)—and you start adding more of them, by which to parallelize your go to market. This is an important thing to realize—the way that most B2B organizations scale their revenue acquisition is not through magically selling more deals through your existing reps, but rather by adding more reps. At a certain point, your sales reps only have so many hours in the week, and executing discovery calls, demos, follow up meetings, email, and closing calls with prospects takes time. So the way you "scale" revenue is by adding more people to do these actions.

And now that you've proven that you can reliably sell your solution yourself, your job now becomes proving that you can take that ability—that "sales and success motion" that you've developed across dozens and dozens of demos, closed deals, and onboarding and successful customers—and instill it in other sales and success professionals that you hire. You are moving from creating the "way to sell this" and now starting to build the organization that implements that approach in a repeated, scalable way. This is the beginning of scaling, which, in turn, requires management.

SCALING ANTI-PATTERNS & KNOWING WHEN TO HIT THE GAS

There are a couple anti-patterns related to "scaling" that I'd like to discuss before we talk about sales management basics, namely "premature scaling" and "lagged scaling." Both are problematic in different ways.

Premature Scaling

Premature scaling involves adding sales staff (or adding many more sales staff) before you have proven that the sales motion actually works. This approach typically results in an inefficient or aborted go to market effort that destroys cash and enterprise value, and often leads to layoffs of those sales staff, and maybe others, and an injured fundraising position. This can happen a few different ways. The most common way is for a founder to try to avoid having to figure out the sales and success motion himself, and instead try to "sprinkle some sales on it" by hiring a sales leader or a bunch of sales reps to "figure it out." Usually what happens in this scenario is a sales leader who follows the playbooks that he's previously seen to work at organizations where the sales motion has already been cemented, typically by throwing bodies at the problem. The result will frequently be very inefficient reps and often customer success problems, leading to low customer satisfaction, churn, and eventually the laying off of that sales staff. I would give some examples of companies where this has happened, but you likely won't recognize them because typically it kills the company—they're not around anymore so you won't recognize the names.

For instance, imagine a scenario where a founder thinks that he's "got it", even though he hasn't sold the requisite few dozen deals on his own to prove that the product solves the problem that it seeks to solve, that the customer does indeed get value out of it, and that the customer is willing to pay for that value, and do so on an ongoing basis. Instead, in this scenario the founder hires a "VP of Sales" at $250k total compensation, with a six month draw (the leader gets his whole target salary, $125k, for at least six months while the team ramps up) and that sales leader in turns hires three SDRs at $80k each, and three AEs, each of who target a $150k total compensation, each of whom are on a three month draw. In this scenario the founder just added around $70k of month burn. Now, this can be totally fine, at scale, if each of those AE and SDR combos that costs ~$20k a month can deliver something like $80k+ of bookings (ideally paid up front) per month.

But that's the sort of sales efficiency you would typically see only after the sales and success motion has been honed by a founder who engaged in founder-led selling for dozens and dozens of opportunities, resulting in a couple dozen deals, and then proved that this could be repeated with some reps that the founder herself hired. Rather, in this case, what you would typically end up seeing is a bunch of AEs who don't cover their own costs—because they can't close enough business to cover their own salaries, and that of their SDR partners and their share of the sales leader's salary they need to cover. And then things get even worse from there. Because the AEs are being relied on to define the Ideal Customer Profile, and simultaneously are expected to close business, they'll start selling to anything with a pulse, regardless of whether or not that prospect will actually get value out of the solution.

And sometimes those reps will have success—which of course is good in the short term, because that AE will at least defray some of his own cost, but in the long term is terrible, as that "bad customer" becomes a drain on customer success resources. Moreover, when that customer comes up for renewal, and churns out, it will hurt your metrics, and your ability to raise further capital, because it's clear that customers aren't getting value out of your solution. It's no good. Some good recent examples of "premature scaling" can be seen in the cautionary tale of Zenefits, who sold epic amounts of deals without fully considering the costs associated with servicing the customers they brought onboard—creating a situation where as reps sold more and more deals, they had more and more negative unit-economic customers on the books bleeding the company dry of resources. Eventually this lead to massive layoffs of these inefficient reps who loaded the company with "upside down" customers.

The payments company Square had a similar situation when trying to take their Square Stand product to market into higher end retail outlets beyond basic coffee shops in 2014. Instead of de-risking their go to market and validating that this new product fit the new market they were going after at a smaller scale to start, Square hired 20 fairly senior AEs—all with substantial salaries—raising the burn of that business unit dramatically under the assumption that they would be selling into higher end segments. They eventually realized that the product did not have the functionality required for those customers, which showed up in unsatisfactory win rates as compared to lower end, "coffee shop" deals that had previously been their bread and butter, and started to react to that, but unfortunately their hiring profile for AEs was far more senior than necessitated by the high velocity, transactional sale that Square Stand "coffee shop" opportunities required.

Ultimately most of the team left or was let go after having wasted large amount of time and salary expense. The good news was Square has senior leadership whose reputation made it easy for them to raise lots of capital, and they had an existing Square Reader and Register business at the low end to help sustain them, but it put a huge cash divot into that business unit while they were figuring it out—the kind of cash divot that would destroy a smaller company with less capital firepower behind it.

Lagged Scaling

The other anti-pattern you commonly see in "scaling" is simply not doing it. This is different than organizations that think that they "don't need to do sales"—we already addressed that in the first section of the the book. Rather, this is the situation where a founder or early salesperson has gotten good at selling the solution, and can reliably and repeatedly turn new meetings into closed deals at a consistent win rate. But rather than recognizing that they need to move on from just "turning the crank" on more deals, they get stuck doing just that, either motivated by running up the customer count, or because they're unaware of the need to move on, or afraid of the next set of challenges that need to be addressed.

Whatever the root cause, this failure mode, while less common than "premature scaling," and also less existentially threatening, is problematic in its own way. That is, unlike premature scaling which threatens to burn cash reserves and shorten your runway, lagged scaling is more about eating opportunity cost.

Once you have proven that a founder can reliably sell the solution, the next step in scaling the organization is "packaging" that ability so it can be scaled out across multiple sales reps—which is the key to scaling a B2B sales organization's revenue acquisition. The more time that is wasted before moving from "doing" to "packaging" and then proving that this derisked sales motion can be replicated by others, the more time is lost as your runway shortens (you likely have far more engineering salary expense than revenue at this point—so the quicker you can ramp up your revenue acquisition, the faster you can get to cashflow even) and the more time is lost to competitors attacking the market. Moreover, if you consider that your goal in building your org is to build enterprise value as quickly as possible, and the means by which organizations are valued for either acquisition or public flotation is multiples of revenue, then time lost acting as a sales rep when you could be acting like a sales manager, and adding multiple units of revenue production (sales reps!) keeps you from building enterprise value in your org.

When is the Right Time to Scale?

So if this is indeed a "goldilocks" situation where we don't want to scale too soon, and don't want to wait too long, then how do you know when you're ready to go? First, it's less of a binary "now you're not ready, poof, now you are" situation, but instead it's typically better to treat this like making your way into a hot jacuzzi, a bit at a time, validating that things are working as you go, but always making constant progress.

How do you know the time is right for you to take that first step of bringing on another sales rep, or two, to prove that someone other than you can sell the solution? Usually the answer can be found in the math of your sales metrics. A "good" b2b sales win rate is typically anywhere between 15% and 30%. That is, of all "demos" or first meetings you do, eventually 15-30% turn into closed won deals (while the others either closed lost or fizzle out into nothingness). If you find yourself in this range reliably, then it's probably time to bring on other reps and prove that you can get them to close at a similar pace. If your win rate is substantially above that—well maybe consider raising your pricing, but certainly get a move on on abstracting and scaling your sales function! If your win rate is below that, then it probably makes more sense for you to figure out why only, say, 10% of your initial engagements are turning into customers before you turn to scale up customer engagements. Whether it's the result of your messaging, product feature deficit, or pricing, sort that out first before scaling up.

The motivation behind these efficiency metrics is that to have an efficient sales organization, the total cost of your AE and SDR and sales engineer costs (if you have a very technical sale and have sales engineers) should not add up to more than 20 or 25% of the amount of revenue they close, a rule of thumb. So if your sales motion seems to require a single sales reps who set his own appointments, does demos, and closes deals, and he costs $100k a year, you'll want to see him booking around $500k of revenue a year—because after you pay him out of that kitty, you want there to be plenty of other money leftover to pay for engineering, customer success, and so on.

This is what is known as "cost of sales" and you want it to be 20-30% (at the highest.) As a result, that rep needs to be able to close deals reliably, based on a good win rate, or else that $100k rep might only be able to bring in $300k of bookings, resulting in a really inefficient sales motion and difficulty scaling up. That is, imagine that a rep can do five new prospect demos a week, and 10 other "follow up" meetings in a week. That's 20 new potential deals a month (5/week times 4 weeks in a month), and if he can win four of those deals (20%), and each deal is worth $10k each, that's $480k in a year—not a bad clip. But now imagine that the win rate is 10%—even still doing 5 new demos a week, with 10 follow up meetings, and the same average contract value of $10k, that rep will only be able to do $240k in revenue per year. If he costs you $100k all in with base salary and commission, that's a 40% cost of sales—only $140k is left over for marketing expense, customer success costs, and then paying for engineering salaries, and so forth. No good.

This is why having a "good" win rate, coupled with a good average contract value and a reliable and consistent deal cycle is a good leading indicator of being ready to scale up to that first step. Otherwise you'll be hitting the accelerator on a car that leaks most of the gas out of the engine.

ABSTRACTION & SPECIALIZATION OF SALES ROLES

We talked about the basics of role specialization in Chapter 8 when discussing how hiring an SDR rep early on can be a force multiplier when you're running through your first few dozens sales cycles. Whereas that goal was to help you free up your time to do more selling meetings (demos and follow up meetings) and do customer success activities, now the business of specialization is about preparing your sales team for scale up—we are proving that AEs other than you can successfully sell the solution, and that CS staff, again, other than you, can successfully implement, monitor, and drive success of customers. Because doing so prepares you for hiring and managing many of these successfully, which allows you to ramp your organization's revenue.

Role Specialization

Importantly, even as you abstract the selling behavior into other staff, you'll also be working on specialization of those staff as well. This will likely happen in a stepwise fashion, as discussed in the maturity model to follow, but ultimately specialization of sales and success staff is a very powerful "modern" way of selling.

The benefits of specialization are an extension of what you found when you hired an SDR to help set appointments for your calendar. Not only does specialization lead to individuals being better at the thing they are specializing in due to doing more of it (i.e., AEs doing demos and closing calls constantly versus Account Managers doing QBRs versus SDRs cold calling and emailing), but you also remove the cost of context switching between different "roles" that would otherwise be present within a single person. And of course this has all been enabled by the trusty CRM, which acts as a repository of "truth" with respect to the state of a prospect, from lead to opportunity to customer to renewal.

Ultimately, assuming you have the revenue model that can support it, specialized roles, with SDRs setting appointments, AEs pitching and running deals, and CSM/AMs "farming" accounts, is the gold standard of a B2B revenue acquisition apparatus in the 21st century. That said, there can be situations where specialization is not merited. For example, if the majority of your deals are "one call closes", transactional, with low average sales prices, then it might just make sense for you to have junior reps who act like "closing SDRs". Generally speaking, specialization makes sense when efficiency gains offset enlarged coordination / complication overhead—which for higher sales price, longer sales cycle situations is typically always the case, with some exceptions.

Specialization and Sales Maturity Stages

Of course I don't recommend jumping straight to the end state of a fully specialized sales organization just as you start to scale up. Rather, we need to approach the scale out of your sales and success organization in a similar "validating hypotheses" fashion that we did when proving your sales motion—by getting more complex, step by step, and figuring out what's broken along the way, and then fixing it before you take the next step. And importantly, this is your number one job at this stage of the organization.

What are the steps? And what should you be focusing on at each stage, and what are the exit criteria for moving on to the next? We detail them below.

Founder Doing It All

This is what we've largely been addressing up to this point in the book. A business founder engaging in lead gen, outbound appointment setting, pitching, demo, and closing, and then customer success for an early set of customers. The goal of this stage is to prove that you can reliably convince customers that your solution is valuable, get them to use it in a way that demonstrates that your product moves the relevant business metrics for the customer in a way that they desire, and prove these customers will pay for the right to have those business metrics positively impacted like this.

The exit criteria for this stage is a handful of early customers paying money in exchange for the value your product provides, and, after being implemented and using the solution, continues to both use the solution (acceptable levels of engagement) and believes the solution provides the value being paid for—such that if another prospect asked them about the solution, they would say it's worth the money, and when it comes time for renewal, they will do so.

The main anti-pattern for this stage (as is largely the topic of this whole book!), is hiring a "sales guy" to figure it out. Throwing the product "over the wall" to someone who was not involved in customer development to execute this. "Sprinkle some sales on it." Other anti-patterns here can be not charging for the solution, thus not proving the actual value exchange. And another common one is selling the solution, but not investing sufficiently to prove that the customer attains the promised value (that is, you got money, but they did not get value, and they'll eventually churn.)

Founder Plus SDR / Founder Plus CSM

This is the first step of abstraction we referred to quickly in the Closing & Pipeline Management Chapter. Because the process of prospecting qualified Accounts and Contacts, and then engaging them with outbound email and calling behavior with the goal of setting an appointments is more basic and "packageable" than pitching and demo'ing, assisting a founder-seller with an SDR can be one of the first ways of putting specialization into your sales org. It's a tried and true way of getting leverage for a founder seller, and leaves you with more time to focus on nailing repeatable selling and success activities by filling your calendar with new pitch meetings, relieves you of prospecting work, and leaves you more time for doing customer success.

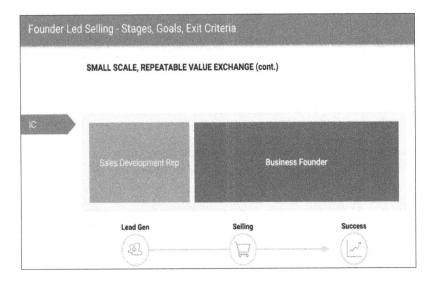

That said, another way of providing specialization can be by adding a Customer Success management resource to assist the founder seller in supporting these early customers that you're onboarding. This approach can make sense when lead generation and appointment setting isn't a time suck for the founder seller. If, for instance, the founder seller is very well networked, and getting access to new prospects to engage is relatively easy, then the more important place to get leverage can be in packaging up the to-date validated customer success model, and handing that to a CS rep or CS lead to run with and evolve, so the founder selling can focus her time on scaling up customer acquisition faster. In both cases, the notion is to abstract off part of the founding seller's workload into another specialized resource.

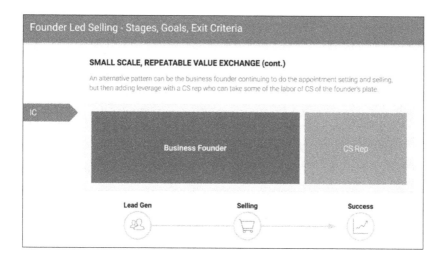

Founder Led Selling - Stages, Goals, Exit Criteria

SMALL SCALE, REPEATABLE VALUE EXCHANGE (cont.)

An alternative pattern can be the business founder continuing to do the appointment setting and selling, but then adding leverage with a CS rep who can take some of the labor of CS of the founder's plate.

IC

Business Founder

CS Rep

Lead Gen   Selling   Success

The exit criteria for this stage would be a few dozen customers acquired, onboarded, and getting to success, along with a clear, repeatable, documented sales motion, ready to be tested on one or more new, non-founder sellers, all while maintaining healthy sales KPIs like win rate, attainment (in a monthly or quarterly period) and son on.

The anti-pattern here would be trying to get someone else to do this for you. Hiring a "sales guy" or even worse, a VP Sales to prove out that this is repeatable a handful of times. Another is acquiring a bunch of customers, only a fraction of which get to success. Spraying and praying.

Founder Plus SDR and Two AEs

This is the stage where we start seeing the beginnings of true leverage setting the stage for scale. The goal of this stage is to prove that someone other than the founding seller can sell the solution. The key activities here are the hiring, training, and management to success of one or more sellers (typically two, to start), aside from the founding seller. There can be continued selling activity by the founder, but more and more time should be focused on proving that these additional sellers can sell the product, in a repeatable fashion. Training, management, coaching, inspection, correction, and tooling are more and more the focus.

The exit criteria for this stage would be those sales reps engaging prospects, presenting, and closing ideal customer profile customers, who are then getting to success and value, at least as efficiently as you were, previously.

The anti-patterns in this case are twofold. This is a "goldilocks" scenario. You want to do it "just right." The first anti-pattern is too much "leverage" by hiring too many, too fast. Hiring too many raises burn rates without proof of success and too many reps makes it difficult for the manager-founder to get each to critical mass. Instead, you try to "boil the ocean" and get none of them to success. The second anti-pattern is non-leverage. Instead of focusing on proving AE1 and AE2 can get to success, founder spends too much time still "playing" instead of "coaching." Doing so robs the future of the company by slowing the process of "packaging" and "distribution" of the sales motion into something that can be dropped into 5, 10, n reps in the future.

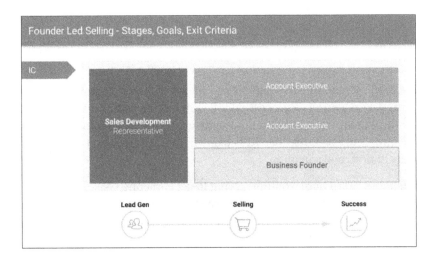

Initial "Sales Pod"

This is the next step in specialization and scale out, where the founding seller now steps entirely out of the day to day work of selling. The goal of this stage is to prove the successful performance of a "complete unit" of revenue production, including lead gen, selling and closing, and onboarding. The founding seller is now focusing her time fully on sales orchestration refinement and management, sales process definition and implementation, along with tooling creation and adoption. Depending on whether previously there was not specialized customer success or sales development staff, now is the time to introduce that specialized role and work to cement the interaction and rules of engagement between the various functions to ensure they are tight and without gaps.

The exit criteria for this stage is the unit producing revenue at a predictable rate, all members are hitting their goal KPIs (meetings product by the SDRs, deals closed for AEs, onboarding customers with high NPS scores for CS), with smooth handoffs & proper backchecks to prevent dropped balls. The unit of revenue production and retention performs with solid unit economics—where the unit more than pays for its own salary costs, and throws off cash to the business. You are confident you can now clone this.

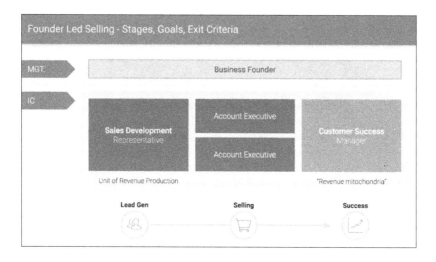

"Sales Pod" Abstraction & Initial Scale

This is the point at which you can really start to see the power of "scale out" via replicability, whereby cloning that initial sales pod, you are able to double or triple through throughput of your team.

While the activities to focus on here are largely the same as before, there will be more managerial complexity, as you will be adding more staff, and thus there will be more of a focus on metrics and analytics. This might be the stage at which you add a professional sales manager—though there can be value in proving the successful hiring and onboarding on another cohort or two of addition reps in order to fully develop those management motions before handing them off to someone else.

The exit criteria for this stage is for the complete unit to be producing revenue at a predictable rate, with all members hitting their goal KPIs, and successfully returning lots and lots of contribution margin back to the business. You are now confident that you could hand a unit like this to a professional sales manager, and she would be able to manage it, and start cloning these units out, herself.

The anti-pattern here isn't entirely clear. Potentially handing the beginnings of this unit off to a manager before fully baking it yourself. Or by racing through this stage to the next one before proving that this stage was successfully achieved. Or by not tending to the additional complexity or ensuring that there is sufficient lead generation to power the incremental AEs.

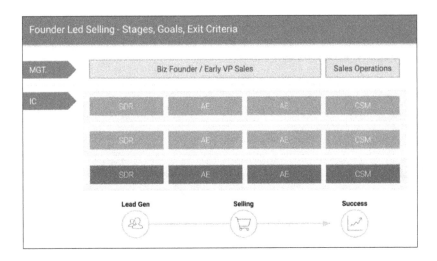

Full Scaled Sales Team of Teams

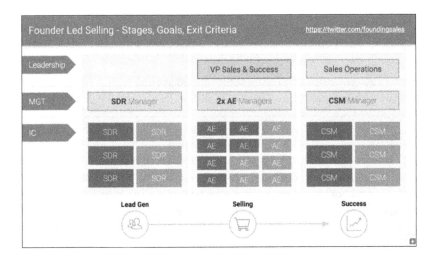

See Chapter 8's Role Specialization section.

Conveniently, you should know it works, because you have already been doing it yourself.

Sales Operations

A note on "sales operations" as part of scaleout, above. Sales operations (and also "sales enablement", "sales effectiveness", and "sales strategy") are efforts that are focused on making the entire "machine" that is the sales organization more fluid and effective, using metrics analysis, process refinement, and technology adoption to facilitate that goal. You might think that this is something that is the responsibility of sales leadership and management, in general, and of course you'd be right. But sales operations is a pure refinement of this—where their job is purely focused on those efforts, whereas those efforts are just one thing of many that sales management and leadership are responsible for.

Typically introducing sales operations will make sense when you have enough reps that a single sales ops headcount salary, blended across all the reps will be worth the time savings and revenue lift that stems from the addition of that headcount. It can vary, but this could be as early as 10 reps. For example, if an $80k sales operations person can help each of your five sales pods composed of one AE and one SDR each deliver $50k more in bookings per year through better process, automation, and technology adoption, then $80k of salary for $250k in incremental bookings seems like a sweet deal to me! Now imagine that leverage with 10 sellers. Sales ops is a powerful tool.

Even before you decide that your sales org is ready for that investment, that doesn't mean that this isn't anyone's responsibility. Rather, it falls on the shoulders of you as the leader, other leaders and managers, and even to the reps themselves. I like to refer to this concept as the "product management of the sales org", where we are constantly looking to enhance the go to market through the removal of existing friction and problems ("bugs"), and by adding functionality to the sales org ("features").

EARLY SALES MANAGEMENT

Sales management is the practice of enabling, coaching, inspecting, correcting, celebrating, and generally, managing, groups of salespeople in the pursuit of taking your product to market. Understanding what drives the success of a B2B go to market is instructive in how to think about your role as an early sales manager.

Ultimately what drives sales and customer success performance is a high quantity of high quality customer facing selling activity. We can improve the output of this formula through raising either the quantity of sales activity, the quality or both. We can raise the quantity of this activity through better focus and effort through better management of staff in their execution of these activities—like helping staff focus on customer facing activities rather than internal facing communications or other non-work distractions. We can further raise the quantity of activity, through the specialization or automation of tasks that are automatable— like by doing mass prospecting and filling the CRM with Accounts and Contacts for reps to target rather than them splitting their attention to do so themselves. And of course we can also raise the raw quantity of this customer facing activity by simply adding more sales people doing this selling activity—this of course being the crux of "scale out" in a modern B2B sales org. Adding more cylinders to an engine adds horsepower and makes it go faster.

The quality of customer facing activity also matters—the discovery, presentation, pitching, demoing, and deal running. This can be raised through better training and messaging—by ensuring that reps understand the pain points that the product solves, the conditions in which those pain points exist in a prospect's business, and being able to effectively discuss these points. Quality of customer facing activity can also be improved also through better process—by preventing reps from losing track of their opportunities, being diligent in their follow up, and generally running a good sales process across their opportunities. You can think of this as ensuring that these "cylinders" in the engine are burning cleanly and not leaking, and so forth.

Sales management is adding those cylinders, getting them properly hooked up to the fuel system, the exhaust system, and ensuring that they're pulling their own weight in an effective fashion, and continuing to do so on an ongoing basis.

THE ROLE OF THE SALES MANAGER

Much the same way we discussed Sales Mindset Change at the beginning of this book when characterizing how the mindset and behaviors of acting like a salesperson are substantially different from that of other professionals, it's important to pro-actively point out here that moving from the role of "founder seller" (or even just "seller") to sales manager also requires a substantial mindset change.

And most of the changes in actions and mindset flow from one high order change—you are no longer supposed to be "doing" the sales, but instead are now focusing on helping others do the selling. As noted above in the discussion of "scaling," the way that B2B sales organizations get leverage is through more reps—your job is now to achieve that scale through the successful hiring, onboarding, training, monitoring, and coaching of reps. So any time you find yourself doing actual individual sales work—doing a demo, sending a prospect facing email, etc., you should ask yourself if you should be, and consider instead a manager activity you should be doing instead.

As an example of why this matters, let's say you're a really good founder seller. Because I mean, you read the first parts of this book and totally took it to heart and implemented it, right? So now you're a total killer. And you close 30% of the first demos you take, and do so at a $50k average deal size. And your poor reps, they're good, but not as good as you. They only close deals at a 20% rate, and their deal sizes are only $30k. So you should be running deals right? You're so much better, right? Nope. Wrong conclusion. That incremental $80k you book per month, $30k over your other reps' $50k per month is nothing compared to adding four more reps, each of whom becomes a machine pumping out $50k a month. Moreover, it's unlikely that you're inherently magic (sorry), and that only you can close $80k of business per month. If you can, they probably can, and thus you should be figuring out how to make it such that they have the same win rate and average deal size as you. Again, the goal is to hire, onboard, and get to ongoing success incremental reps. That is the way you will win as a sales manager.

I see this anti-pattern all the time in more "mature" organizations—especially when "seasoned" sales management is brought in from larger sales organizations like an Oracle or IBM or SAP or what have you, where there are specialized recruiting, onboarding, and sales operations functions in the organization that take care of many of the true tasks of "management". When these "managers" transition to startup sales management, rather than realizing that the key lever they have to hitting their numbers is in adding more successful reps and instrumenting their success, they instead spend their time doing actual selling activity alongside reps rather than tending to the "pipeline above the pipeline"—the hiring pipeline. Don't make the same mistake—and when your org gets to that larger scale, don't let your sales managers make that mistake.

Manager Activities

What should you be doing with your time instead of selling activities? If there's a compressed rule of thumb, it's that you should be doing sales management activities with leverage. Building systems, playbooks, processes, and materials. Engaging in hiring and onboarding activities, and then later systems and tooling for hiring and onboarding. Monitoring, inspecting, and coaching reps, and later building processes for doing just that. I generally yell at managers who are not doing high leverage things. When considering what to spend time on always think "does this action have recurring impact? Does it make more than one person more successful?"

And once you are clear on that set of activities you ought to be engaged in, you need to make space on your calendar to do them. As a manager you can frequently be tempted to "jump on calls" for the sake of being the big man (or lady) in the room—but doing that three times a day means you'll be robbing yourself of all the time you should be spending on, say, phone screens with new sales candidates, or mock pitches with new reps, or reviewing team metrics to identify potential soft spots in your team. Make room for the activities of management or they won't get done—and then you're not getting leverage, and you risk having a bunch of inefficient, expensive reps bleeding your org instead of contributing recurring revenue.

With all that said, these are the set of management activities that you ought to be filling your days with.

Hiring & Onboarding

If the way to get to scale in a B2B organization is the hiring, onboarding, and ramping to success of a large number of reps, then the first step in that process, clearly, is hiring and onboarding. Ensuring success in the "pipeline above the pipeline," or, your hiring pipeline, is the first step on the way to scaling up. More on this in the Sales Hiring chapter to follow, but approaching hiring with the same sort of rigor, process orientation, and execution as your selling activities is key.

And while hiring is the first step to success, hiring without rigorous and excellent onboarding and ramp to success is self-defeating. Discussed in greater depth in the Sales Onboarding chapter to follow, intense, detailed, and rigorous sales rep onboarding is paramount. The old school approach of hiring a class of five or ten AEs, with the expectation that 50% will wash out is a vestige of a time before high quality, instrumented hiring and onboarding, and massively wasteful. Successful sales managers focus on filtering the wrong people out in the hiring process, getting the right people onboard and trained up through tons of hands-on repetition, and off to success—so the manager can then turn to repeating that process with a new cohort of reps.

Process Construction, Adherence Monitoring, & Tooling Adoption

Once reps are hired and onboarded, they need an operational framework within which to perform. It's your job to construct that, as prototyped in your own founder selling work, and now formalize that into a stepwise process whereby the inputs of selling are made available to SDRs, AEs, and so forth, they are able to act on them, and the outputs are then passed to other parts of the organization for next action, like customer success, all the way to eventual renewal. This typically means investment in documentation of that process—written out in a bulleted process flow, or perhaps graphical flow chart—generally know in the jargon as Rules of Engagement. This is where you start to really understand the difference between being an individual seller and a manager of sellers. No longer can you keep in your head what the qualification criteria are for an ideal customer profile prospect. You have to write it down, make it available in a Google Document, and make sure all of the SDRs and AEs have seen it, know they are responsible for acting based on those criteria, and have a means by which to come back to it and refresh themselves if they forget.

This is particularly important when you have a multi-step, specialized sales motion that involves SDRs, AEs, and maybe even CSMs or AMs, where there are points of customer handoff, and where responsibilities are split amongst different actors.

With this process formalized and well documented, then the work turns to monitoring the execution of the process parallelized across the reps that you have, verifying adherence, and looking for soft spots where either reps need to do a better job of adherence, or the sales process itself needs refinement. Also involved in this is tooling selection and administration, in that tooling (like better CRM administration, reporting and analytics, and various sales automation solutions) is typically a force multiplier. This function is what's typically thought of as the bread and butter of "sales management"—but in an early stage environment, it's only one part of the job, and is contingent on the above described prerequisites being in place.

Metrics Harness Construction & Monitoring

Gone into in far more detail below, the construction and monitoring of a sales performance metrics harness is the sibling of sales process excellence. Understanding the quantity and quality of sales activities that need to be done by your reps, who is meeting that bar, and who isn't, and why, is a requirement of the modern sales manager. A good metrics harness will help you with all of the above and below sales management activities by providing an early warning system for if things are not going according to plan, either for an individual in his ramp period, a rep who's been selling for a year, or, more importantly, across a whole team or team of teams, which can be indicative of a shift in the market. A strong metrics harness will allow you see all of this and act accordingly to correct. (Making this way easier and way better than the status quo is why we started our performance analytics company Atrium.)

Inspection, Coaching, and Correction

Beyond getting out of the business of doing pure sales work, the second biggest shift in mindset required in sales management is getting used to telling reps what to do and correcting them when they are off. As a first time manager, this can be truly mind warping, but it's of paramount importance. If you've hired and onboarded a set of reps, but aren't ready to proactively instruct, coach, and correct them when they go astray, you're setting yourself and your org up for eating substantial opportunity cost. You can have the most rigorous, efficient sales process specification in the world, but if reps diverge from it, and you don't correct them, it doesn't matter. You can have the most precise, nuanced metrics harness, but if you aren't willing to take a concerning metric (say weakness in the ratio between first meetings and follow up meetings for an AE, or even just the raw number of customer meetings an AE is having), and dig into its root cause with a rep, and correct the causal behavior, what's the point? Inspection of sales activity, identification of improvement areas, coupled with the correction of underlying issues is vital.

I understand that it may feel weird to tell someone "No, you said that wrong." Or "the way to present this slide is by saying, X, Y, Z", but it's something you're going to have to get good at. Otherwise you'll be at the mercy of the reps you've hired and their ability to magically self-coach and correct. Which, don't get me wrong, if you've hired and onboarded well, may be a pretty solid ability. By why would you stop there? Your ability to inspect activity and then communicate correction like this is key to your success as an information router in your sales org. You are the one responsible for routing the correct behavior in the pertinent context to a struggling rep, or discovering an emergent best practice innovated by a rep, centralizing it into your sales org's collective knowledge, and then, importantly, pushing it back out to the rest of the reps—and ensuring that they adopt.

If you aren't comfortable with digging into a rep's activity as necessitated by something you saw in the metrics or heard on the sales floor, you'll end up with reps not adhering to process, not presenting messaging in the best way possible, ultimately injuring their win rates and bookings. And if you aren't comfortable, once you've identified the root cause, communicating the shortfall, and then working with the rep to resolve it, and validate that the "fix" has stuck, not only will your sales efforts suffer, but you'll also end up fostering an environment of "moral hazard" in your sales org. If reps know that they can get away with not adhering to process, unsurprisingly, you'll see less process adherence. Moreover, if they know that you know process non-adherence is happening, and you still aren't doing anything about it, well, now you have a situation where you can end up with full blown rudderless sales org. That is, what other things will you not correct? Seller activity levels? What about quota requirements? What else? This is why this behavior change is so key as a manager. There are plenty of resources on how to best navigate those conversations, but you must, with directness. This article and book—Radical Candor—by my friend, Kim Malone Scott, is one of my favorites. And this document on making performance conversations easy from Atrium is a good one too.

As a note, the above is why it is so important that you, as a founder seller, initially sell a statistically significant number of deals yourself. By doing so, not only are you discovering and building the selling motion that other reps will adopt, but you are building your confidence in that sales motion. You are fully empowered to correct divergences from this process because you know it works. You did it. And that puts you in a strong place from which to inspect, coach and correct. Imagine the alternative. Having not sold a number of these deals yourself, you may have a hunch about why something isn't working—but do you really have much proof as to why one approach over another is the right one? And even if you're right, are you in a strong spot to make that argument? "Come on man, you have never sold a day in your life, it's clearly the product isn't any good." And so forth. wA terrible spot to be.

Same with an excellent metrics harness (more on this below). If you are without a solid instrumentation harness monitoring your team, and the individuals within it, you'll be hampered in not only your ability to catch issues early, but even if you are able to catch issues early, your ability to coach them will be impinged. For example, imagine a scenario where a rep is having bookings attainment issues. You have a theory it's because he's not winning as many of the opportunities he is assigned as his peers. But unfortunately, because you don't have win rate instrumented, you may have a hard time making that argument. Moreover, he might just say "it's actually because I'm not getting enough new opportunities" (get ready for the age old "we need more leads" rep complaint—you'll hear it a lot). Without having a good metrics harness in place that instruments all parts of the sales motion, you'll be hampered in your ability to diagnose and then act to correct, because without data, there can be room for disputations—and guess what...sales reps are good at objection handling and persuasion!

Materials & Documentation

Another key sales management activity you should prioritize spending time on is documentation and material creation and maintenance. Sexy, right? Nope, not at all. But extremely important. As you grow, building materials for asynchronous consumption by onboarding reps, and reps who are already ramped, is a key way to get leverage in your org. No, it's not sufficient to write an email to your reps once with the proper way to handle an objection. Or dumping it into a Slack channel, never to be found again. Lol. Rather, these are opportunities for building documentation and tooling that houses this information in a way that is consumable by reps, on their own, or even if they struggle to find it themselves, you can quickly route them to the information, rather than having to recreate and re-articulate the information. Yes, we are quite literally taking advantage of that age old technology, "the written word." Well, and video recordings, and online shared documents, and so forth. But the core tenet is the same—you should be looking for opportunities to document processes, messaging, materials, and so forth.

You might be thinking "man, that really sounds like a lot of administrative, secretarial work," and you'd be totally right! But this is your job now! Unfortunately, the reality is that your reps won't proactively decide to create a centralized document with common objections, and their answers. And they won't proactively decide to centralize a repository of call recordings from the best demos your team has done. And they won't create new slides to reflect newly shipped features. So you have to. Because if you don't, they won't have access to that "right" answer, and instead will make something up. Or they'll do their best, and present a partially right answer, which is better than nothing. But it's nowhere near as good as it could have been if they had that information collated for them. And they certainly won't take the time to update those materials on an ongoing basis.

Every time you do this, and every time they leverage those centralized email templates, objection responses, new slides for new features, updated and fresh sales deck, they will be selling better because of your efforts. And this is a key point of managerial leverage. You making sure that all your reps are equipped with the latest sales deck, with all the most refined messaging and product screenshots, published into Docsend, Showpad, HighSpot or whatever tool you use for sales materials management will be multiplied across all 5, 10, 20, etc. of your reps. But if you don't do that, instead, all 5, 10, 20, etc. of them will be dying a death of a thousand cuts day in and out as they don't have access to those materials. So do it!

Performance Management, Professional Development & Off-Boarding

The last major bucket of activities to spend your time on as a budding sales manager is people and performance management. That is, the professional development of staff, and, in the event that the development doesn't meet requirements, the managing out of reps who aren't performing at required levels.

With respect to professional development, this should be focused on identifying growth opportunities for individual staff, and soft spots that need correction, and then working to resolve them. Typically this is implemented via staff one-on-ones (more on this in operational cadences below), and quarterly / bi-annual / annual performance reviews. But the key to successful performance reviews is to ensure that frequent, regularly cadenced, documented, performance management conversations are happening. In the short term, these sort of performance conversations would revolve around tactics to improve desired sales outputs—for AEs, more and bigger deals, for SDRs, more and better opportunity creation, and so forth. This would be the venue where issues that were discovered in metrics review can be discussed, potential solutions can be prescribed, and progress against these prescriptions can be checked in on until the issue is resolved. For example, if you had noticed that an SDR was having problems with his appointment hold rate, this would be the place to investigate what the root cause of that problem might be, and prescribe a potential solution—perhaps sending meeting reminders to prospect attendees the morning before they are supposed to have a meeting—and then setting a reminder to yourself and the rep to see if this prescription is being implemented, and that it's having the desired impact—raised meeting attendance rates—two weeks in the future from that.

Over longer timespans, staff professional development should focus on helping reps grow and achieve the next step in their career. That is, while addressing performance shortfalls and improvement areas in the short term is important, you also want to keep an eye on helping them get to the next natural step in their career because if you don't, someone else will, and you'll be left with reps churning out of your organization. Which, if our goal is to hire, onboarding, and then successfully maintain productive reps, leaking them out the back door is not an effective way of achieving this goal. The first step to doing this is identifying what that desired path is for a given rep. Does she want to progress from SDR to AE? Or is she more interested in moving from SDR to SDR management? Same with your AEs. Are they interesting in moving into more complex deal cycles? Or moving into sales management? Identifying that desire is the first step, which is followed by putting in place actions to help them achieve that goal over a set timeline. Does a rep want to try her hand at some managerial activities? Assigning her responsibility for a particular managerial task from your plate—like perhaps being the "owner of all objection handling information" can be a good way to give her the beginnings of that experience. Many orgs implement these at "10% projects", where, assuming a rep is hitting his numbers from an output standpoint (bookings, meetings created, etc.) he can have a project that he can spend up to 4 hours a week (blocked, on the rep's public calendar, and identifiable) that helps the organization, and specifically helps him advance against those professional development goals. Another example here might be a rep who desires to move into more substantial enterprise selling cycles to ride along with a more senior rep on one of her enterprise deals, to watch how that is done, in the flesh.

It's not separate from professional development, but within this bucket is the notion of monitoring employee engagement and morale. That is, one of the things you as a manager will need to be aware of with your staff is their engagement and general morale. While positive or negative morale can frequently be seen in performance metrics—generally people who are happy are higher performing, and engaged, and people who are performing will often be happier, and vice versa—it's not 100% guaranteed. You can have reps who are performing well from a pure output standpoint, while having impacted morale, and while a good metrics harness can sometimes catch this in degraded performance over time, sometimes this can result in a rep that unexpectedly gives notice, even before negative performance indicators start showing up. This is, of course, no fun because we want to retain great reps, and we certainly don't want to flush an entire pipeline worth of deals. So being on top of staff morale, again through the mechanism of one-on-ones, and other performance conversation checkpoints is key.

If you look back across the preceding few pages and look at the types of activities you need to engage in as a manager, you can quickly see that is a whole different ball game compared to when you were doing individual selling activity yourself! Importantly, though, this is the way that your organization will start on its way to scale—by you getting out of the business of selling, yourself, and instead getting into the business of taking what you've learned, and validated is a repeatable, predictable selling motion, and spreading it across a growing number of reps. No longer a player, but a coach, and no longer a doer, but a teacher. Moreover, when you eventually move from being an early sales manager yourself to either managing other managers, or getting out of the business of directly managing the sales org altogether, knowing the above activities cold will help you monitor whether they are happening sufficiently within your managerial base—because sometimes even "seasoned" managers will skip out on any number of these activities, which of course is bad for your organization.

The Modern Metrical Sales Manager

We touched on the importance of a rigorous metrics harness above, but it is so important in modern sales management, I believe it merits its own section.

In old school sales management, the process of hiring, onboarding, and getting reps to success typically relied on spending lots of time riding along with reps either on their sales calls, whether in the office via phone or web presentation, or out in the field. And by doing this, managers were able to identify potential issues with a rep's sales motion before it turned into attainment issues by visually or audibly inspecting selling activity. In modern sales organizations, however, thanks to better instrumentation, with the rise of modern CRMs, the model has flipped to where sales managers use metrics to continuously monitor the quantity and quality of reps' selling activities, and based on this information, identify potential soft spots in their reps' performance, before then zooming in on that specific part. This is in contrast to simply "being along for the ride" and hoping to catch a potential problem with a rep in that particular call that the manager sat in on or follow up email that she was CC'd on.

This is not to say that managers in modern sales organizations do not ride along for calls or don't get CC'd on occasional correspondence, but rather a metrics-driven approach allows managers to focus in their time on places where it can be most effectively deployed to address rep improvement areas, rather than being inundated and overwhelmed with tons of rep activity—even if it doesn't need inspection.

How can you as an early sales manager achieve the above? It's a process that builds on top of prior steps.

Goal Setting

First, we have to be explicit in what our goal is. In sales, conveniently, this can be pretty straightforward, in that we're trying to drive revenue. That said, depending on an organization's stage or priorities, pure revenue acquisition might take a backseat to acquiring more customer logos. And for different roles, that goal might be a bit different. For SDR teams, that goal likely is the creation of qualified appointments for the AE team to execute on. But importantly, first, you have to define that goal clearly so all are on the same page, and have a metric around that goal. For example, $80k of new business bookings closed per month, per rep. Or 10 new qualified meetings per SDR per week.

Sales Methods Definition & Benchmark Setting

The next step is to clearly document and define the methods by which you achieve this goal. Conveniently, this was the aim of all the founding selling that you did yourself before you decided that you were ready to add more salespeople. That is, you should likely already have a very clear idea of the kind of selling activities, and stages, required to get a deal done based on having done a good number of them yourself. And not only should have an idea of what those actions are, but also the quantity and quality of them that are required to get a deal done, and, thus, in turn, five deals done, ten deals done, twenty deals done. That is, the number of meetings, the type of meetings required (initial discovery meeting, demo, proposal, security review, etc.). The amount of customer facing calling, the amount of customer facing email. The total number unique accounts engaged with in a time period. The number of opportunities being worked. You should not only have these component parts listed out, but also have their relative quantities noted. That is, how many meetings should be done, per AE, per week? How many of them should be first meetings with a prospect? How many should be follow up meetings? How many opportunities should a rep be interacting with per week? How many new Opps should an SDR be creating per month? How many emails per week? How many accounts should they be engaging with per month? These baselines are important, because it will allow us to validate that our reps are engaging, again, in the necessary quantity and quality of selling activity, once we actually start measuring it. This is a good example of a framework for explicitly documenting the levels of activity and mix for your sales motion.

Recording & Capturing Selling Activity

Once you have the above clearly set, the next step is ensure that these activities are properly instrumented so we can definitely say that we are indeed engaging in the right quantity and quality of selling activity as prescribed in our selling motion, such that we will get to our goal, or if we're not, we know it before it turns into a problem. Of course this starts with the recording of deals closed, and revenue booked, but that's only the very basics of things. For instance, if we know that customer facing meetings are an important part of selling motion for account executives (and generally, they are), we need a means by which to record those. So too with different types of meetings, and other part of the sales motion (email, calling, presentations, proposals, and so forth). The most common means by which this is done is with a CRM for ease of reporting on, but to start, this can be as basic as a whiteboard with people's names on them, and daily, weekly, monthly tallies for various tracked items. But the important thing is to start recording these actions, because we're going to need to report on them. Even better if you can record this in an automated fashion—like having email activity automatically logged in the CRM, or using software like Zoom and Chorus to record digital presentations that are delivered.

Metrics Consumption

Once you have this "metrics harness" in place, the next most important step is to ensure that you're actually monitoring it. Having this information instrumented and ready to compare to intended baselines, but then not actually doing that, is a big problem, in that as a sales organization, you'll be flying blind with very little conception of if you are actually advancing against your stated goals. Moreover, it can be one of those things that can slip by the wayside in the crush of reps asking you questions, one-on-ones, team meetings, and more. This is why specifically cadencing the consumption of these metrics is vital. The best way to ensure that this gets done is to bake metrical review into the day to day, week to week, month to month operational cadences of your sales org. That is, set a recurring calendar event for yourself to do just that at different intervals. And not only should you, as the manager, be cadencing the consumption of these metrics, but you should be ensuring that your team and reports are doing so as well. Create a "metrics section" in your team meeting wherein you review team metrics and call out divergences from intended baselines. Review individual slices of these metrics in one on ones with reps. In your monthly postmortem, reviewing the prior month's performance, have a section that focuses on these metrics on both an aggregate, but also a pre-rep level.

Anomaly Detection

All of the above culminates in our ability to sniff out potential issues in our sales org before it turns into underperformance of the team and individuals in the form of insufficient bookings. How do you do this? Well, as you're consuming these metrics in your operational cadence as noted above, you should be looking for potentially concerning divergences. Those can be divergences from a stated goal, i.e., "Our sales reps should be having at least 15 customer facing meetings per week, and Joey has had 8 customer facing meetings per week for the last two weeks."—or it could be a divergence from what the rest of the team is doing. If all of your sales reps win 25% of the new Opportunities that they engage with, and one of your reps starts winning 20%, and then the next month, 15% while the others maintain at 25%, that would be concerning. Anomalies can be divergences to the positive as well. If a rep suddenly is engaging 100% more accounts than he has historically, or that his colleagues are in the same time period, that could potentially be a good thing—where he has innovated some sort of process to make himself more efficient—or it could be an indicator that he is doing that activity instead of other activities that might be more important, which could be a bad thing. Either way, it's something that you as a manager will want to investigate and discuss with the rep to make sure that everything is cool.

Root Causing Issues

Frequently when an issue shows up in rep and team metrics, that metric itself won't be the ultimate root cause. For example, if a sales rep's revenue attainment in a quarter doesn't get to the goal that you've set, that itself is not the root cause. There's something underneath that metric that likely points to the issue in question—which in the future you probably would want to monitor ahead of time to see leading indicators of the issue, rather than the unfortunate outcome that shows up months later. This is where diagnosing the root cause of a sales issue that you discovered through metrics is important. How do you do this? It's helpful to think of metrics as being composed of the metrics that flow into them and those metrics being composed of those that flow into them, forming a sort of "tree". That is, while bookings is an important metrics, if a rep is having a bookings issue, there are a number of things that go into bookings. Did he close fewer deals than usual? Or did he close the same number of deals as usual, and they just happened to have smaller deal sizes, each? If this was the case, was this because he was engaging a different class of prospect who were smaller, and thus had less potential demand for the solution he was selling than the prospects he had previously been engaging? Or had he still been engaging with the same segment of customers, and for some reason selling less of your product into them? Or is he instead selling the same amount of product (as measured maybe by number of seats of software), but putting more discounting into the deals than usual?

Or, running it back, if instead he did indeed have the same average deal size as usual but just ended up closing fewer deals than in a usual month or quarter, was that because he won fewer of the opportunities that he engaged in that time period than usual, impacting his win rate? Or did his win rate maintain as usual, and he just had fewer opportunities to engage? Or did he have the same number of opportunities to engage as usual, but somehow did a poorer job than previously at running these opportunities, perhaps as indicated by his frequency of interacting with his opportunities or his total level of customer facing meeting, email, and calling activity?

By starting with the "loose thread" and starting to pull to see where it leads you, as a sales manager you'll get closer and closer to the root cause of the issue, and then fixing that issue at the root. And by doing so, you can solve that issue before it turns into a bad outcome by being repeated, eventually compounding into poor output performance for that rep, or even worse, across the entire team and company.

This process can be repeated any time you see a potential anomaly in a key performance indicator, even if that indicator is further up the funnel from attainment. For example, is a rep down on the number of customer facing meetings he's supposed to be having per week? That could be concerning, but perhaps he has ramped up his prospecting activity to fix that customer meetings weakness, which prospecting activity would then show up in a commensurate rise in his customer facing email and calling activity. Has he done so? If not, why not? Or was the decline in customer facing meetings because he was overwhelmed with a bunch of internal training meetings, so this was momentary blip. Either way, you want to know.

Sales Motion Inspection

Of course, while a good metrics harness can help you flag potential leading indicators of issues and in many cases be enough to diagnose exactly what the issue is, it won't always be enough to allow you to come to an out and out conclusion. In those scenarios it will require specific inspection, and getting your hands dirty with the rep. While seeing a dearth of rep activity metrics, like customer facing meetings or email, is typically solved—"Hey, I need you to focus and get these numbers higher" issues of selling quality typically will require you to dig into the actual content of those activities by inspecting the actual calls, meetings, and emails.

To go back to our example above about a degradation of win rate, once we were confident that it wasn't an issue of prospect selection, it would likely make sense for the manager to dig into how the rep is running his deals, either by listening to recorded calls (again, this is where software like Chorus, Gong, and others can be helpful), or by making sure to ride along on a number of this rep's new deals. As noted at the beginning of this section, this is how a manager can use metrics to spotlight an issue that needs deeper engagement to diagnose—versus spending all of his time riding along on calls and meetings with all his reps—even the ones that don't have problematic win rates, which is a more old school sales management approach. And which, while nice and hands on, requires far higher ratios of managers to reps than otherwise, since managers spend a lot of wasted cycles paying attention to things that don't need their attention—this is how being metrically excellent can make your org more efficient. If you're only paying a $200k sales manager per every 8 rep instead of every 5, you're paying 40% less management overhead which makes your cost of sales, and your organization's Saas valuations that much better.

Or another example might be an SDR whose meeting creation metrics are lagging as compared to his prior performance and compared to that of his peers. By looking at his metrics, we might see that his calling, emailing, and unique accounts engaged metrics are steady as compared to his own previous performance and that of his peers, but that for some reason the response rates on his outbound emails seem to have degraded while others' have stayed steady. This would be the point at which the manager would dig into what those emails looked like—digging into the CRM to see what the subject lines, email content, so forth looked like to see if there was a specifically identifiable issue that popped up to be coached.

Coaching & Spreading Success

Once our inspection reveals what we think is the issue, we need to fix it. This means specific coaching of what we have identified as the problematic behavior. If our inspection of degraded win rates leads us to riding along on some calls, which then lead to identifying that a rep was having specific issues handling certain objections, well, that's now our job to fix with him. This can be done a couple of ways, but normally what it involves is the specific identification of the shortfall of the selling activity—in this case, handling an objection—demonstrating the correct way to do execute that selling activity, and then engaging in mock repetitions of that activity until the rep gets it right. If this sounds hands on, you're right. But it's a far better approach than letting the problematic behavior persist. If you or the rep have trepidation about this sort of hands on management, perhaps thinking it sounds like "micromanagement", get over it. Think of the kind of diagnosis, coaching, and practice repetitions that occur in professional sports. At-bats, snaps, shots, etc. are recorded and diagnosed when the stats point to particular issues, at which point the "right" way of executing that shot, snap, play, etc. are practiced until it is nailed. Can you imagine a scenario where a professional baseball player or football player has an identified performance issue, and the coach was afraid to help him resolve it because it felt like "micromanagement"? The concept sounds absurd. Sales management is no different. Dig in and be hands on.

If some of this sounds reminiscent of the sort of work that should be done with reps during new rep onboarding, you're exactly right. In fact, many potential problems in selling behavior can be prevented by rigorous and thorough onboarding, which we discuss in the sales onboarding chapter. But even the best onboarding can't prevent all issues, and even solid reps have improvement areas that can make them better, raising their win rates, contract values, and attainment, and humans being how they are, issues will crop up from time to time even for behaviors that previously were just fine.

And in cases where our inspection of something like a particularly high win rate, aberrantly high contract values, or ramped customer meeting counts, leads us to identifying what appears to be a new best practice and additional "feature" to be added to our sales motion, it is similarly the responsibility of sales management to capture that new best practice, and seek to spread it around to the rest of the sales staff. Is this "micromanagement"? No, it's management. And it's going to make the rest of your reps more successful, you a better manager, and everyone's stock worth more money more quickly.

Stage-Specific Management Rigor

While above I map out the framework by which to have rigorous, metrics-driven, performance-centric management, as usual, there's a maturity ramp to how far down the rabbit hole you need to go based on how developed your organization is, and especially how large it is. There are rarely demerits for being too rigorous too soon, and you can often get away with being looser in a smaller organization—but there are huge downsides to being a more scaled sales organization with the management capacity of a infant. That's how you kill a company.

Early On

Early on in your sales organization, like when you have your first couple reps, this process of training and expectation setting, monitoring, inspection, and coaching can be more organically done. That is to say, early on, as it's paramount to get your first couple sales reps to success, and prove that this solution can indeed be sold by people other than the founder, it's fine to over-invest time in monitoring and inspection. That is, sitting in on calls, being Cc'd on prospect communication, and so forth so you can have a far more granular understanding of how deals are progressing, and how reps are, or are not, taking the right actions to progress them. While the instrumentation overhead here will be substantial (if you're sitting in on two reps' worth of calls a day, you won't have hardly any time to yourself for metrics review, hiring and onboarding work, not to mention all the other things you probably need to be doing), to start, it's worth it to make sure those reps get to success, and so you can see quickly if they're going sideways. However, what you're doing now, in addition to making sure that these reps get to success, is learning the common places where reps have issues with your sales motion, so you can iterate your onboarding and training to proactively address those issues ahead of them showing up in later cohorts of reps.

At Scale

At larger scale, like a half dozen reps or more, it will be much harder for you to do this sort of "instrumentation via osmosis", and rather it will be incumbent on you to have a solid metrics harness in place so you can see early warning indicators of potential problems, and then be able to "zoom in" on potential hot spots. Getting good on this early on will be a benefit for your organization, but also when you get to the point where you are hiring sales management, and are able to give them this metrics harness, and methodology for monitoring that will help them be better at ensuring good yields on hiring classes (few hires that flame out), quick ramps to success, quicker identification and managing out of bad hires, and in general will lead to a more effective sales org. That is to say, the same way that earlier on, you were focused on creating the model for selling your solution, so that you could eventually get out of that business, and teach it to others, now we are engaged in creating the model of managing those reps, as required for your specific business.

Sales Performance Instrumentation

So if instrumentation is so vital for modern sales management, what are the right metrics? As with so many things in early stage organizations, you can start basic, and get more advanced. But the important thing is to start.

Quantity, Quality, Mix

One thing to internalize is that successful sales behavior comes from a high quantity of high quality customer facing selling activity. As such, that is what we need to instrument. It's not enough to simply measure outputs.

Frequently you will get old school sales managers saying things like "I don't care about inputs, I just care about the outputs." That's the hallmark of a sales manager who is too afraid of management and metrics to do either. Look for him to probably be unemployed soon. Don't fall into this trap.

Quantity metrics are frequently counts of things. Number of customer facing meetings, number of first meetings, number of new opportunities created, number of emails sent, number of calls made, number of presentations made, number of proposals sent, number of opportunity forward progressions, number of contacts engaged for the first time, number of accounts engaged, number of opportunities currently in the pipeline, amount of pipeline value, number of deals won, number of deals lost, amount of revenue booked, and so on. But quantity metrics without quality metrics are severely impeded in their efficacy.

That said, you can get pretty far based purely on quantity metrics, so if you can only choose one, start with quantity metrics, but aim to add quality metrics as soon as possible.

What are good quality metrics? Of note, quality metrics are typically ratios and averages and are helpful in understanding how an AE or team of AEs are doing with the activity they're engaging in. For AEs, some examples of quality metrics would be win rate—the number of opportunities that are won as compared to the number of opportunities that are opened or first meetings that are taken. Other examples would be average deal size, average deal age, average age of opportunities in the pipeline, pipeline conversion rate, number of contacts engaged per account, number of meetings per opportunity, average time between interactions with an opportunity, average age of an opportunity in a stage, ratio of first meetings to follow up meetings, and so forth.

These metrics, or their relative level of focus, will change when it comes to different roles. For example, with Sales Development reps, who are primarily focused on setting appointments and creating pipeline for AEs (assuming your sales motion can support a two-stage sales process), the metrics will tend to be more activity focused. The "quantity and quality" model applies here as well, but will be applied to behavior that engages a broader set of accounts less deeply, versus AEs who will be working a smaller number of opportunities, but more deeply over a longer time interval. Some good quantity metrics for tracking SDRs are, well, meetings created of course, but then amount of pipeline created (the summation of the projected revenue of all the opportunities that this SDR created), emails sent, calls made, connected calls, talk time, number of accounts engaged, number of contacts engaged, and so forth. For SDR organizations where reps take care of the discovery part of the opportunity, this would also include number of meetings held. With respect to quality metrics from SDRs, these could be response rate on emails, connect rate on phone calls, contacts engaged per account, number of activities per contact, activities per account, conversion rate of accounts engaged to meetings created, all the way to quality metrics on the outputted pipeline created, like win rate on opportunities created, average deal size on those created opportunities, and so on.

An especially nice thing about quality metrics is that in addition to be able to compare between reps, and track historical changes, you can also use them for reporting on deals that have indicators of less-than-stellar quality of execution. That is to say, while tracking "untouched opportunities" over time is valuable for assessing how on top of their pipeline a given AE is compared to his colleagues, the list of opportunities that right now, this instant, have gone 30 days without an activity can be a very helpful "to do" list of what a rep should be spending his time on—namely, close those out, work them, or explain why it's ok for them to not have that activity! Or with respect to SDRs, an example might be the list of accounts they are engaging that have fewer contacts engaged than a specified goal, say, three contacts per account—assuming you're doing a serious enterprise sale that touches many stakeholders.

As you can see, these metrics can go from pretty basic—like number of customer meetings—to pretty advanced—the average time between interactions on an opportunity. At TalentBin we got pretty far along. By the time the company was acquired, for AEs we were tracking, with respect to quantity metrics, bookings (duh), demo meetings, proposals sent, and email activity. With respect to quality metrics on a per rep basis, we tracked win rate, average deal size, average deal cycle, and untouched opportunities. With SDRs, for quantity we did demo creation, email and calling quantity, unique accounts engaged, and for quality, we did calling connect rates, win rate on opportunities created. Clearly we could have done more, but I would give that metrics harness a solid "B / B+" especially for an organization without a formal sales ops function, and with <10 sales reps. Nowadays the metrics harness I use on myself and my reps is far, far more advanced, especially with the help of Atrium, but again, it's ok to start basic with an eye towards getting more advanced later. But at minimum you have to start or you're flying blind.

Reading Metrics

What does a great metrics harness like this get you? Importantly, it gives you a fingerprint of the behavioral information for each of your sales reps. And once you have this behavioral fingerprint, you can use it for all manner of effective management needs. First, you can use it to understand, demonstrably, the behaviors your best reps engage in. That is, you know who your best reps are based on their bookings outputs. But when you are able to see what all of these other metrics look for those top performers, you can see that it's not really that they're magical sorcerers, but rather the specific behaviors and ratios that are different for them as compared to your other reps, which allows you to dig into what allows those top performers to achieve those metrics. Spoiler alert—very frequently it will just be that your best reps do more work. But it may also be that their selling behavior is better in certain regards. Their higher win rate may be due to them involving more stakeholders in the deal earlier on—which would show up in their higher metrics of contacts engaged per account, for example.

Further, with this behavioral signature of success, you are better able to see changes of rep performance over time. A key example of this is in new hiring. If you are onboarding a new class of five sales reps, having a metrics harness like this in place allows you to see the degree to which the new hires are starting to engage in the quantity and quality of behaviors that are demonstrated by the the existing top performing reps. If those new hires are ramping into band with your existing ramped and top performing reps, this is a good thing! Alternatively, if one or more are not, now you know, and you can move to address that issue quickly—and specifically with respect to whatever the metric points to as an issue (e.g., do they not have enough customer facing meetings? Or is their opportunity creation quantity that's problematic? Or are they not getting to second and third meetings?). And if whatever the issue is is not solvable—that is, even with coaching directed at improving the selling behavior that is showing up in the problematic metric, the behavior doesn't improve, well, now you've realized this far ahead of time, and can move to remove the rep from his seat, rather than allowing him to burn salary expense and opportunity cost (in the form of the prospects he's working, poorly, that another rep could be working successfully), and replace him with someone who will be successful.

Not only can these sort of "changes in metrics" be helpful during onboarding, they can be helpful in sniffing out potential issues with rep motivation that can pop up from time to time, and unchecked, and can turn into unwanted attrition. That is, if a rep's metrics start negatively diverging from his existing behavioral signature, that can be an indicator of potential issues. Having a great metrics harness in place can help you see that before it turns into major problems.

Managerial Operational Cadence

While knowing what you, as a manager, should be doing, and knowing what your reps should be doing, is the first step to success, making sure that those activities actually take place is how to take that to scale. If you know that you should be taking time to consume the metrics of your team and look for potential issues, but then your entire workday and week is eaten up by sitting in on calls with your reps—well, you're never going to get around to those important tasks.

This is why "operational cadences" or "operational rhythms" are so helpful for managing teams, and yourself. That is, rather than treating your workdays, weeks, and months as never ending, monolithic expanses, it's far more effective to chop them up into manageable time blocks with checkpoints marked down at specific intervals, and recurring times where specific activities happen.

The most common means by which to do this is with "meetings," including stand-ups, team meetings, pipeline reviews, individual one-on-ones, monthly retrospectives, and quarterly business reviews. Meetings of course get a bad rap most of the time because they are typically terribly undefined and executed, and end up just wasting time. However, done correctly, they will ensure that the things that need to get done, as a manager, and for your reps, will have a designated time and place for them to be done—and as such will actually be executed, allowing you to capture the value from doing them.

On Meetings

You might say "Wait a minute?! Meetings are those things that waste time and are for big companies!"

On the contrary, meetings are for richly communicating information, and receiving it. For ensuring that the things the organization is supposed to be doing is being done, that people within the organization understand what the larger goal is, their place in it, what they should be doing to proceed towards that, and to raise issues if they see divergence there.

If you don't do them, the core needs will still be there, and they'll just get served other ways. If you don't have private venues for surfacing issues, like one-on-ones, they will happen in back-channel conversations in ways that erode morale. If you don't have a means to communicate, and reiterate, top priorities, then people will work on whatever is in front of them, or things they like, versus things that organization needs. If people don't know when information will be shared with them, they will assume you're hiding it from them. Fix all of this with a thoughtful meeting cadence, wherein certain meetings have a certain purpose (and stated anti-purposes), and proactively handle these information distribution and feedback solicitation needs.

And no, a company-wide Slack channel does not count.

How to Implement Operational Cadence Meetings

Meetings should have a stated purpose, a stated set of attendees, a format (which supports the purpose), a specified length, and a cadence to them.

The best way to do this is to use Calendar invites, setting the recurring time frame to what the recurring period is specified to be, inviting the relevant attendees (those who are required—avoid "optional" as much as possible. If they're optional, they're likely not needed, and should be doing other things), and putting the specific format and recurring agenda in the meeting description.

Like this:

Or this:

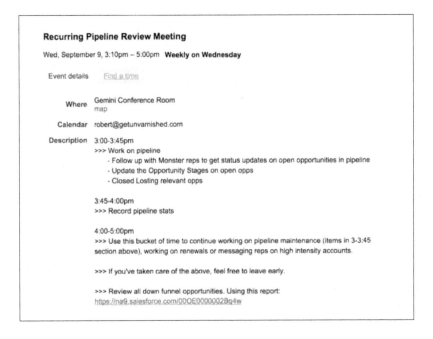

Breadth of attendance is where you can be most efficient with meetings. Are most of the attendees sitting around not receiving information or contributing information in the meeting? They're probably not required, think about splitting that meeting into a bunch of individual ones.

Cadencing serves the purpose of letting staff know that if something does not get covered this time, it can be put on the agenda for next time. It also ensures that staff knows that what was discussed and agreed in this meeting will indeed by checked on next meeting—so promises can't be empty. Cadence also needs to be appropriate to the attendee base, depth of the meeting, and purpose. There is no need for weekly all-hands. You're likely handling things in that meeting that should handled in others. One-on-ones done monthly is probably too infrequent—you run the risk of staff irritation boiling over if they do not have a release valve.

Time frame should be constrained to what is needed, as well. No sprawl. If have more content than can be handled in the meeting, prioritize the content, and then save the unhandled stuff for the next one. Either have a tracking document to record what was covered, and action items, or actively put the next content in the next meeting's Description field. If there is special content that is required, can it be handled in an email? If none of that will work (it better be an emergency), put another meeting on the calendar to address that specific topic.

Timing of meetings is important to pay attention to. Scheduling team meetings during lunch (one of the benefits of bringing lunch into the office) makes it such that you don't stomp on productive time during the rest of the day. Otherwise, meetings at the "edges" of the day—either at the very beginning, to compel a sprinter's start, or at the end of the day, when people are burned from their day of work and can use a break.

Content and Format needs to be explicitly set. If there is lack of clarity as to what this meeting is for and what content is to be covered, you will get creep, which will dilute the purpose of the meeting, and keep you from achieving the goal of the meeting. The owner needs to be the goal keeper of keeping the meeting on track, and not diverging from its purpose.

Examples of Sales-centric Operational Cadence Meetings

Sales has a faster, more frequent tempo than the rest of your organization, typically, along with a set of actions that requires more instrumentation and accountability than, say, engineering, so the meetings cadence will reflect that.

Sales Stand ups

Owner: Sales lead.

Purpose: To provide a checkpoint to the day, promote shared learning, and promote transparent accountability. Quick and up tempo to help maintain in-day tempo.

Anti-purpose: Not for exhaustive rehashing all work done, questioning strategy, etc.

Attendees: Sales team "pods". If you have a 3 AEs and 3 SDRs, this can be done together. If you have 8 AEs and 8 SDRs, each pod has their own standup.

Format: <30 seconds per person on key metrics that were achieved in the prior interval—Demos set or done, Calls made, emails sent. Show up to the meeting with the numbers, and put them on a shared whiteboard dashboard as a means of shared transparency. Share any key items "of note" (would be exciting wins, could be big flubs to share with others to avoid.) If someone is out of the office (working), they need to dial in for it. If they are occupied at the time (try not to be) with a demo, traveling, working from home or such, numbers and comments should be emailed to team ahead of time. Field sales team members can report out via a set-format email to a dedicated list-serve or slack channel.

Cadence and Timing: Depends. For a small team including SDRs, could be twice a day. Noon just before lunch and 5:00pm. For a larger team, could be once a day at noon.

Length: <10 minutes. If you get to a size of organization where <30 seconds per person will add up to greater than 10 minutes, split the group as noted above.

Sales Team meeting

Owner: Sales leader.

Purpose: To review prior week's metrics, out-performance or shortfalls, promote team shared accountability and transparency, and provide information and solicit feedback as regards product to date and product future, and customer success.

Anti-purpose: Not a roundtable, ideation session. Not a group bitch session.

Attendees: Entire sales team (and potentially CS team if it is embedded in your sales team). Product leadership representative, customer success representative.

Format: Have key team metrics that team is focusing on achieving more/less of, and start meeting by reporting on them. Demos held prior week, month to date, revenue month-to-date, etc. Have segment of meeting (5-10 minutes) focused on product leadership sharing what shipped last week, what is shipping this week, and soliciting product feedback. Have segment of meeting (5 minutes) for Customer Success to share information, make requests, and solicit feedback. Product and CS participation can be front-loaded so those representatives can peel off after their role is concluded. Team should go around and share a personal win and a personal learning from the prior week. Review any particular information that needs to be underscored in a group environment (which may have been emailed, previously). Are there particular new programs that are shipping? New materials for reps to be aware of? Changes to CS protocol? (Again, many of these could have been previously emailed, but may need reiteration to ensure "they stick.") Solicit questions and feedback on the go-to-market, and issues that might impact the whole group (not personal issues.) Solicit feature requests on sales operations, marketing materials, etc. (as long as touch whole team.) If first meeting after end of month, or end of quarter, use it as a retrospective. The meeting owner should have 15 minutes calendared ahead of this meeting to ensure that the content is in order for the meeting, and to review the metrics that will be discussed as a team, himself, ahead of time.

Cadence and Timing: Weekly. Mondays, lunch. Bring lunch in.

Length: 60 minutes.

Pipeline meeting

Owner: Sales leader.

Purpose: To provide a venue for shared accountability and focused work on pipeline maintenance.

Anti-purpose: Not a ideation, bitchfest meeting.

Attendees: Full sales team of AEs (not SDRs). As AE team gets larger, split into pods at ~five AEs per.

Format: Each seller reviews last week's closed deals, and which deals will likely come in this week. Time is spent on concerted down-funnel work around pipeline maintenance (ensuring that relevant Opps are in correct stage, Closed Losing dead opps, and general pipeline.) Because this is unpleasant work that reps avoid, compel it in a group environment. And bring in pizza to make it suck less. Close meeting with reporting of activity in the meeting (Opps closed, Opps updated, contacts touched). People shouldn't miss this meeting. Or schedule demos over it. It's here to be a place to make sure work that may not otherwise get done actually gets done.

Cadence and Timing: Weekly. Wednesday end of day. Get pizza.

Length: 60-120 minutes.

One on ones

Owner: Sales lead (whoever is the sales rep's manager.)

Purpose: The purpose of this is solely for direct manager to proactively extract issues as viewed by the rep, and share information in a private setting.

Anti-purpose: This is not a status meeting. This is not a pipeline review. Those are handled other places. Focus purely on rep issues and needs and career development discussion.

Attendees: Direct manager and sales rep.

Format: Have a recurring set of items to go through, every time. I like the format "What do you need from me?" (As in, what needs to be better?) "What do I need from you?" (As in, how are you performing, and what changes do I need?"), and "What do you need to know?". In the "What do I need from you" case, it's appropriate for sales staff to review past-week, or month-to-date, quarter-to-date metrics, to ensure that things are tracking appropriately. If there are performance issues, this is where that needs to be addressed, and remediation plans made. As regards information sharing, this is "What information do I need to share with you with commentary that may not be suitable for a public setting"). By always following a format, it will be a forcing function to surface this information, and ensure you don't have blowups and surprises. Focus deeply on extracting issues. If you have observed things in the wild that you feel are underlying issues, bring them up. In sales orgs, issues typically show up in metrics, and should be discussed here.

Cadence and Timing: Every two weeks. Ideally have all meetings on the same day (if team is larger, have them on consecutive days). If there is a topic that needs to be addressed privately with team members in parallel, one on one, having them all on the same day, or quickly together, will allow you the megaphone to do this. Do NOT skip these. If you have to skip, do NOT skip. Move the meeting to later that day. Or the next day. DO NOT SKIP THESE. It will bite you in the ass.

Length: 30-60 minutes, depending.

Monthly Retrospective

Owner: Sales lead (whoever is the sales rep's manager.)

Purpose: Akin to the weekly sales team meeting, but with a specific aim to look back over the prior month, and ahead for this month. This meeting specifically allows the manager and staff to take stock of the prior month's performance, evaluate if the team hit desired levels, or, if not, to figure out why, quickly, before the underperformance becomes chronic.

Anti-purpose: As with sales team meeting, not a roundtable or ideation session.

Attendees: Entire sales (and potentially CS) team, and potentially product leadership and customer success representative.

Format: Start with a restating of previously agreed to standard metrics that the team had previously agreed to as goals, and then review team's metrics harness to see if goal metrics were actually attained. This is not just lagging indicators like booking, but rather all quantity and quality leading indicators, as well. Do so on a team level, but also on an individual level, specifically citing metrical outperformance, and eliciting sharing from out-performers on what drove that performance. Like a big weekly team meeting. Share what's coming up. Diagnose issues. Share successes that need to be shared around. Accountability.

Cadence and Timing: Once a month, at the beginning of the month—but with enough time standoff from the end of the month for the sales leader to do sufficient analysis on what outcomes were and what he or she wants to focus on in the meeting. I like to take over the existing sales team meeting with this meeting. Ideally over lunch.

Length: 60 minutes.

End of Time Period Celebration

Owner: Sales leader

Purpose: After a successful month close, I like to do something like a team lunch or dinner as a means by which to drive team camaraderie, etc. It doesn't have to be huge, and if you want, you can make it contingent on team hitting certain goals, but generally I like to have some sort of team-wide recognition of the completion of the just-ended sprint.

Attendees: Full sales team when you're small. Split into pods once full team gets bigger than a dozen folks.

Format: Dinner or lunch.

Cadence and Timing: Monthly, after close of prior month, during the first week when folks are taking a small breath, and before you get too far into the next time period.

Example of an Operational Cadence Calendar

This is an example of a calendar month-based operational cadence for a <10 person sales team composed of SDRs, AEs, and CS.

	Monday	Tuesday	Wednesday	Thursday	Friday
Week 1	Mid-day Standup Sales Team Meeting: Prior month retrospective, this month forward looking.	Mid-day Standup Close of Month celebration lunch / dinner.	Mid-day Standup AE Team Pipeline Review.	Mid-day Standup One-on-ones with all team members.	Mid-day Standup
Week 2	Mid-day Standup Team Meeting: Progress to date in the month.	Mid-day Standup	Mid-day Standup AE Team Pipeline Review.	Mid-day Standup	Mid-day Standup
Week 3	Mid-day Standup Sales Team Meeting: Approaching end of the month. Last chance for adjustments.	Mid-day Standup	Mid-day Standup AE Team Pipeline Review.	Mid-day Standup One-on-ones with all team members.	
Week 4	Mid-day Standup Sales Team Meeting: Last opportunity for getting deals / opp creation across the line.		Mid-day Standup AE Team Pipeline Review.		

On a quarterly cadence, you would add a Quarterly Business Review that is a more robust version of the monthly retrospective team meeting, but with similar content focused on clear eyed evaluation of what has been executed to date, and what you expect to be the case going forward, and where adjustments need to be made.

Executive Meeting: Non-Owner Executive to Owner Executive

Owner: CEO (who is not sales lead)

Purpose: Track progress against stated sales goals, as measured via agreed key metrics.

Anti-purpose: Not a one-on-one as relates to performance or extracting issues.

Attendees: CEO and Sales Lead (if they are separate people)

Format: Review key agreed metrics that track success of sales organization, their improvement, degradation. Discuss, and identify constraints that are blocking forward progress. Agree and prioritize proposed solutions to constraints, and document next steps for execution and timeline in Google Doc, for review at next meeting. At next meeting, review agreed outcomes from prior meeting, and success or divergence.

Cadence and Timing: Every two weeks. End of day. (To avoid mid-day work disruption and occupying manager time while team is executing.)

Length: 30-60 minutes.

Annual planning

As you have more data, can have a real bottoms up plan.

Adding Managerial Layers

As discussed above, the goal of sales management is to make individual sales staff, SDRs, AEs, and so on, more successful by having someone (or a group of someones) that are purely dedicated to that success. But as we also detailed above the activities that managers should be engaging in in order to make their staff more successful are many! It turns out that management is a lot of work! And given that there are only eight hours in a workday, at a certain point, your ability to manage your staff will cap out, and you'll start dropping balls and being unable to fully execute all the management tasks you should be. And this will be the point at which you should probably add some managerial help under you.

When to add management help? The time to add management help is the point at which your ability to do the work you need to do, outside of managing sales, becomes no longer possible. Partially this is related to when you decide that you want to professionalize your sales leadership function (that is "bring in a VP of Sales."). But if you consider all of the tasks listed above—one on ones, standups, team meetings, cross-functional org meetings, pipeline reviews, and so forth—the time really starts to add up, even before you get to things like metrics consumption, coaching and training, riding along on calls, and so forth.

In part your ability to manage successfully before adding more managerial help is related to your ability to "manage by metric." The better your metrics harness, the less time you'll spend uselessly inspecting work that doesn't need inspection, and instead, you'll be able to spot precisely the issues that need your attention and work, and spend time on those, only, saving your time, and forestalling your need to add more managerial help. But that still only goes so far. So too the rigor with which you keep 1:1 notes, and improvement areas that you're working with a rep on. The more rigorous you are, and the less you rely on remembering these topics, the more folks you'll be able to manage concurrently before you need additional help. Another thing to keep in mind is the diversity of roles that you're managing. Managing fewer types of roles means more shared managerial tools and materials—so the more diverse the group of staff you're managing—for instance, AEs, SDRs, and CSMs, the more challenging as compared to a similarly sized group of, say, just SDRs.

All that said, conventional wisdom typically notes that a manager starts having issues keeping full understanding of her reports' performance in her head anywhere between 6 and 9 reports, so you should probably use that as a rule of thumb yourself. At what maturity stage does this show up? Somewhere between having an initial "sales pod" and having a group of sales pods is probably the right time to add some help.

What does that look like? Early on, your management structure could be you as the early sales manager managing a couple SDRs, AEs, and CSMs, together. As you add more pods—say the example that we noted here, you could add an SDR team lead to manage the day to day metrical performance of the SDR team, leaving you to directly manage the AEs and CSMs.

Team leads can be a helpful short-term force multiplier, where you take an outperforming individual who has a professional development interest in management, and give them partial responsibility for managing a pod of a certain function. This frequently shows up in SDR and CS, and the slice of management that the team lead takes on is typically metrics monitoring and report out, being a "first line of defense" when there is a question about product, rule of engagement, etc, intercepting those questions, and handling them, and any number of other managerial activities discussed above, saving your time for other managerial activities for other teams, and higher leverage managerial activities like hiring, onboarding, and performance management topics. Relatedly, the management activities that are typically not given to a team lead are people management topics—like one-on-ones, performance management, professional development, hiring, and onboarding.

That said, team leads can only get you so far, and at a certain point, all of the 1:1s, team meetings, professional development work, and so on will add up to beyond the point of your ability to do it all in a 40-60 hour work week, at which point, you'll know the time will be right for adding a managerial layer that can shoulder those responsibilities for you. Be wary of waiting too long to do this, in that like the failure mode of "lagged scaling" discussed above, while it might feel like you're being efficient, because you've gotten so good at sales management, the likely reality is that your AEs, SDRs, and CS team is probably underperforming by 10, 20, 30% as compared to if they had dedicated high quality management versus you, spread across 10 of them. Moreover, if your organization is having this level of success, probably the highest point of leverage for your time would be more hiring and onboarding versus all of the other managerial activities detailed above. So get some managers to handle all that, and you focus on hiring and onboarding, or, even better, building the machine that does that function without your involvement!

Professional Development & Promotion Paths

Depending on how long you plan on managing sales staff before you "bring in pros" to take over management, you'll likely have to consider the professional development needs of your staff (and once you have professionalized sales management you'll want to make sure they are paying attention to that as well). That is, while SDRs and AEs hitting quota and making their targeted compensation, or beyond, is our primary goal, your staff will want to understand how their role will help them develop towards bigger and better things. Being mindful of this will be key in 1:1s ("What do you need from me?"), and in keeping your staff growing, happy, and retained in your org (that is, not looking for a new job.).

Further, professional development in a sales org is something that can be an extremely powerful driver of value creation for your organization. If SaaS startups are valued on multiples of their revenue (say, 5-10x revenue), and each additional AE, once ramped, adds, say, $40k in annual recurring revenue per month, each additional AE you add who successfully adds $40k in ARR per month is adding $400k in value to the organization, per month. This reiterates why successful sales hiring and onboarding is so important. But now imagine that you have a team of SDRs who are primed to become AEs—each SDR that you are able to successfully promote from SDR to AE, who then gets to success in ramping into that $40k in bookings per month range, you have now added another piston adding $400k in enterprise value, per month.

Similarly, while professional development for AEs typically revolves around moving into larger and more complex deal situations, this too can be extremely beneficial to your sales org. A mid-market AE, depending on market, can do between $30 and $60k in bookings a month at $10-20k deals at a time, netting to $400-700k in bookings a year. Whereas an enterprise rep working with much larger deal sizes, north of $50k can do $1-2m in bookings a year. Again, if an organization is judged on its recurring revenue, developing a mid-market rep to an enterprise AE can add millions of dollars in value to your organization. So don't skimp on the professional development plans!

What do those professional development plans typically look like? Well, it depends on the role. For SDRs, AEs, and CSMs, you can have the traditional "individual contributor progression" path—which for SDRs is moving from SDR to senior SDR, then junior account executive, and beyond. The activities that you would want to layer into their professional development work would be specifically those need to progress to—like practicing discovery calls, open ended questions, presentation and demonstration, and objection handling—all the things that you would expect to cover in an AE onboarding. And these can be done on a recurring basis—a couple hours scheduled weekly specifically for these tasks—with managers, or can involve "riding along" with AEs on discovery calls and demos (or, even better, listening to recording of these outside of callings hours.) For AEs and CSMs in the individual contributor development path, this would typically involve working with larger and more complicated deals and clients. In this case, this can involve helping more senior AEs with their accounts, or being specifically assigned individual larger opportunities that a senior AE or management helps out with.

There's also the managerial development path to consider. Which path a given rep is more interested in is something you need to specifically discuss with them, and then help them progress towards. In this latter case, the best kind of professional development exercises usually revolves around implementing programs that make others on the team more successful, or helping with specific management tasks that you might otherwise have to deal with yourself. This could be tooling or process projects, or even being responsible for analyzing and improving a specific part of your organization's sales motion—whether prospecting, outbound engagement, inbound response, pipeline management, and so on.

Building a Strong Organizational Culture

Early on in a sales organization, and in early stage organizations more generally, culture can often be a bit of an afterthought. This is unfortunate, because a strong culture can be a source of competitive advantage through supporting and cementing an organization's ability to execute, how attractive it is as an employer, and via retaining talent once hired.

Because it's often an amorphous thing, we'll define culture here as the set of implicit behaviors and mores an organization considers appropriate, rewarding and celebrating them, and, conversely the behaviors that your organization considers "not ok" and censures. And this reward, celebration, and censure can be both explicit and implicit. Or as Netflix once put it in their famous "culture deck", company values (and thus culture), are shown by who gets rewarded, promoted, or let go. Beyond that, I like to think of organizational culture as what the operational "spackle" that fills in the gaps between management processes. That is, while your values and culture inform how you manage, there will always be gaps in even the best run management harness, and this is where culture acts as an operating directive in absence of explicit instructions, and helps people "do the right thing." And given that there can be lots of ambiguity in an early stage startup sales org, even if you've taken to heart the various recommendations of this chapter, a robust culture ends up being more important that you expect.

Conversely, without a strong culture that aligns with the needs of your organization, you can end up with all kinds of bad things happening. Many people are familiar with the issues that organizations like Zenefits ran into when a culture of skirting regulations, taking shortcuts, and clever "hacks", and partying collided with a market steeped in rigor and regulations, dealing with extremely sensitive topics—customers' employees' healthcare coverage. As demonstrated there, the results can range from company-killing fraud to rampant attrition to hideous Glassdoor reviews that make it impossible to hire.

Specification

The first step to fostering an intentional sales org culture is having a sense of what your culture should entail. Well, what kind of organization do you want to run? What kind of organization do you want to grow into? What markets do you sell into? Are you selling into conservative markets like healthcare, HR, or government? Or more informal markets like developer tools? Who do you want to be able to recruit? A more junior or more senior staff base? What is the existing culture that has accreted into place over time from founders and early employees?

Documentation

Once you know what you want your culture to be, you need to document it for distribution and reference. It doesn't need to be as involved as that Netflix deck, and it won't be set in stone, either. It can evolve, of course, but at minimum, bulleting out the things that your organization values and that which is doesn't in a shared Google Doc, is needed for broadcasting, and repeating these values, again and again. That way whenever you want to give a shoutout to someone who has done something great in line with your culture, you can point directly to the document, and the specific line item when doing so, thereby reinforcing its importance.

Articulation

Once you have your culture specified and document, the next step is to proactively share and articulate it. This should start all the way back in the beginning of an employee's experience with an an organization—at the hiring and interviewing stage. Being up front about your org's culture early in the hiring process can help you screen out folks for whom it's not a fit, and will be an attraction for those who are fired up about it. Onboarding. Team meetings. All hands.

Proactively articulate it (in hiring, in onboarding), but have to demonstrate from the top. Reiterate it. Spot bonuses. Shoutouts. Screenshots sent out. Kudos channel. Opposite as well.

CHAPTER 11

High-Impact Sales Hiring

INTRODUCTION

Now that you know that your initial go-to-market strategy is working, based on the metrics we covered in prior sections, it's time to scale by adding more people.

For good and for bad, the way that traditional SaaS sales organizations scale is by incrementally adding humans to execute the sales work—calls, emails, demos, negotiation, closing—that leads to revenue.

On the one hand, this can be challenging, because humans are complicated; it's difficult to make judgments about an unfamiliar person when hiring and, later on, when managing. On the other hand, if you get the right folks in-house—professionals who are hungry, intelligent, self-directed, and results oriented—it can be magical, and not just for individual execution of calls, demos, and so forth. There's a "rich get richer" flywheel mechanism to sales hiring—high-quality folks produce high-quality work, leading to high-quality business outcomes, leading to a more engaging, rewarding work environment, leading to more high-quality employees and recruits. And the cycle reverberates throughout the company. Let's make sure this scenario applies to you.

STARTING TO SCALE & THE CRITICALITY OF QUALITY SALES HIRING

It's hard to overstate the importance of high-quality hiring in early-stage sales organizations that have hit the point of scaling. When you're taking a new solution to market, your biggest cost is opportunity cost. In a greenfield market, it's generally a land grab. Every week you don't have that next market development rep calling against qualified accounts is a week your competitors have an advantage. And every week you don't have that new account executive doing demos and closing business is a week that your competitors are doing their darnedest to lock those customers in for good. Not to mention, if your startup is not yet profitable, it's a race against time before you run out of money; you need to quickly demonstrate sufficiently attractive metrics to raise funding.

Conversely, bad sales hiring can be the death knell of an early-stage sales organization. The cost of a bad market development rep isn't the three months of salary before you fire him. It's the dozens of demos that a good hire, sitting in his seat, could have been setting, 20%-30% of which would have turned into deals. And the cost of a bad account executive isn't her salary for two quarters while she's supposedly "ramping," but rather the fact that customers she should have been closing have now been signed by your competitor. Now their customer success org is getting those customers set up, locked in, and succeeding, so you're never going to get a shot at them again.

Sales hiring is, quite simply, mission critical, and it's something you're going to have to get good at. I have zero doubt whatsoever that the ability to attract, hire, and onboard successful, high-quality sales staff can be a monster competitive advantage that startups have against ossified incumbents, riddled with legacy sales staff with bad habits, poor technology usage, and massive layers of managerial overhead. So this isn't just a task to get done. It's an opportunity to pull further ahead. Again, SaaS sales organizations scale by adding more high-quality humans, so a core competency is going to be getting those folks on board in a repeatable, sustainable fashion. It's not really something you can have someone else figure out for you. You need to get your arms around it.

In this chapter, we'll cover what you need to know to start growing your sales org, from hiring by specialty and specifying your hiring profile to identifying hiring sources for that profile, through screening and interviewing, all the way to closing candidates and understanding the basics of compensation plans.

SCALING BY SPECIALIZATION

As I've noted previously, a hallmark of a modern sales organization is specialization, which ultimately fosters greater expertise and efficiency in executing each step of the sales process.

As you start to hire, then, you should be thinking about what part of your sales process you're hiring to support. Generally speaking—given that a founder or product manager starts out doing both the "market development" activities of calling accounts and setting appointments with decision makers, alongside "account executive" activities like sales presentation, demo, negotiation, and closing—the first thing you'll need is market development help to load your calendar with appointments. Then, once your lead-generation function is sufficiently ramped that your individual calendar is overloaded (that is, when you don't have enough time for sufficient down-funnel follow-up and closing conversations), it's time to add more account executives. Later, when you have enough customers approaching renewals, it's time to add account management functionality.

Depending on the role(s) that you're hiring for, your approach may change at the margins, typically with more involved hiring processes for more senior roles. But the kernel will be largely the same.

We'll start with the most general components, then move to the specifics of hiring for certain key roles.

Determining Your Hiring Profile

To start, you should converge on your hiring profile. A "hiring profile," not to be confused with a "job description," is the set of characteristics that define your ideal hire, including both raw and professional characteristics. I started, grew, and refined the TalentBin sales organization and later extended that to a 1,000+ person sales organization at Monster, all while working with other early- and mid-stage sales organizations to help build or refine their sales orgs. Along the way, I've come to deeply believe that your sales staffing should be of the same quality as your engineering staffing. And thus your hiring methodology should reflect this.

This flies in the face of decades of sales hiring theory, which has in large part treated a sales dude as a sales dude as a sales dude—fungible, coin-operated, cannon-fodder infantry to march into the field. We'll talk about this more in the onboarding chapter, as well, but the approach of hiring large numbers of sales staff that seem to meet a moderate bar, then firing them if they don't work out, is especially pernicious in an early-stage organization selling a high-innovation product. It may work for organizations that are trying to value-engineer—hiring the lowest common denominator at a thirtieth percentile market cost in order to keep their cost of sales low. But it's no good for twenty-first-century software sales. The opportunity cost you're eating using this approach is terrible.

Raw Characteristics

What I look for in potential sales staff, and what I have coached others to hire for, is high intellectual acumen, a high "figure shit out quotient" (practical, resourceful street smarts), and a high "grinder quotient."

Smart solutions require smart sales staff. Having the brains to quickly understand things is a prerequisite for understanding the dynamics of the market—the business models and economics of prospects, the existing solution ecosystem, the competitive landscape, and so on. It's also representative of a potential hire's ability to internalize new features and their customer-facing benefits as your engineering team ships them. If you are in the business of bringing a new, innovative solution to market, one that changes and improves constantly, the importance of staff that can quickly ingest, comprehend, retain, and express the value of that solution cannot be overstated.

The alternative is sales staff who don't and can't understand the business processes and economics of their clients; without that foundation, they can't position the positive impact of your solution, will not be facile with the market landscape, and will have difficulty expressing the value of new engineering efforts. You can probably see why I compared sales and engineering hiring above—because you can have the smartest, hardest-shipping engineering and product organization in the world, but if the folks who take that to market can't do those efforts justice, you're screwed.

And while intellectual acumen in your sales staff is required, it's not sufficient by itself. That intellectual horsepower needs to be leveraged by practicality and resourcefulness. For starters, analysis paralysis—that hair-twirling noodling you get from intelligence absent practicality—is anathema to the high-activity execution that is required for enterprise sales success. Spending five minutes thinking about the perfect way to respond to that email is not helpful when there are thirty more you need to send by the end of the day. Moreover, nothing in sales takes an elegant, deterministic route from point A to point B. Every deal has twists and turns, so an ability to "figure it out" and do whatever it takes to get the ball across the goal line is paramount. The tooling will never be perfect. The decision makers will never fall into line the way you want. It is the role of the sales professional to figure out how to succeed in spite of that. So look for people who can just figure it out.

Lastly, in enterprise sales, activity is king. And a lot of that activity isn't particularly fun. Making eighty phone calls a day isn't pleasant. Getting shot down on the phone isn't either. Doing five demos back to back is actually physically taxing effort. Sitting down and ripping through dozens of emails as you clear a pipeline is boring. And all of these activities are certainly less fun than checking out what's happening on Facebook, Twitter, or Instagram, or chatting with colleagues or mindlessly responding to colleague-facing email. But those unpleasant tasks are all important for sales success. The staff who will be able to thrive in this sort of environment have what I like to refer to as "high grinder quotient," or the ability to work through large amounts of not terribly pleasant work because they know that it's important for their success.

You want to select for sales staff that can comprehend the space in which they operate and where your solution fits in, constantly update that mental model as both the space and your solution evolve, and resourcefully execute at a high tempo. I've boiled it down for myself to a sort of cheat sheet of the leading indicators of these characteristics.

Smarts

The best way to get smart sales staff is through referral by people whose judgment you trust. That's why proactive referral recruiting can be so helpful (and we'll get to that in a few pages). You understand the judgment of the referrer, and they have inside information on the person they're referring. But you don't always have that insight.

Failing that, college can be a helpful indicator. Top and second-tier colleges, like first- and second-tier private schools, UC schools, other top state schools (e.g., University of Washington, University of Oregon, etc.) allow you to "draft" off of someone else's authentication. In order to be admitted to these schools, graduates had not only solid acumen scores (SATs, ACTs) but also a pattern of academic achievement to meet GPA requirements. Both are good leading indicators.

By no means is alma mater a sufficient indicator for an automatic "hire," nor is the absence of a top school an automatic disqualifier. This should be considered as just one term in a scoring algorithm. Beyond just school, look for a historical pattern of achievement academically, professionally, and with respect to extracurriculars. All of these will be good leading indicators.

Resourcefulness

Look for patterns of having "figured things out" in the past too. What does that look like? It could be a history of starting businesses, clever "hacks" or creative shortcuts of some sort or another, or meaningful hobbies with a progression of excellence. Sports participation is often a great indicator of resourcefulness as well. Candidates paying their way through college is another great example, as are decisions to move great distances to do something new.

Competitiveness

Competition is an intrinsic part of sales, and there is no better way to look for a competitive streak than prior sports activity. This is especially true of multi-sport athletes who have engaged in competitive athletics from an early age, through high school or, better yet, college. High end musical or academic competition is also a good indicator.

Coachability

Sales reps will not be perfect when they start selling your product. And there is little worse than reps who think they know what they're doing, actually don't, and won't take coaching to improve, preferring to throw leads in the Dumpster. Usually the only solution is letting them go and eating the associated opportunity cost. But this scenario can usually be avoided, and learning curves can be compressed, by hiring sales reps who have experience taking coaching. Competitive athletics, or anything that involves taking coaching in pursuit of the correct way of doing things, are a great leading indicator here.

Likeability, Charisma, and Leadership

While being a persuasive and smart sales person is required in early stage, there is nothing like pure likability, charisma, and leadership ability to give reps a tailwind. Look for leadership positions within teams, clubs, and service organizations, and prior experience winning elections as leading indicators of likability and charisma.

Detail Orientation

The stereotype of the charismatic, slick sales rep exists for a reason. Sales is about people and persuasion. However, more and more (especially in inside sales), it's also about methodical execution of multistage processes, precision follow-up, juggling hundred-opp pipelines, and CRM excellence. So hiring a "big picture" person who can pitch like greased lightning, but fails to follow through on down-funnel opportunities, amounts to setting tens of thousands of dollars on fire. And that's not going to work.

How do you sniff this out ahead of time? Throughout the screening and interview process, look for errors in details, like typos and grammatical errors in the written screen and resume. I like to ask in the written screen how candidates organize their lives: Do they use a calendar or to-do list to make sure things don't fall by the wayside? What does their Gmail inbox look like? Do they archive emails for which there is no "next action" after they read them? What do they think about messiness and how clean do they keep their desk/room/house? If you think their desk is a disaster, just wait to see what their pipeline will look like....

Persistence

Sales inevitably includes some unpleasant slogs. Look for staff who are used to that sort of thing—to enduring unpleasant, necessary precursors in order to achieve desirable outcomes. Certain types of sports demonstrate this in spades: crew, swimming, cycling, long-distance running, track. Seeing something on a resume like achieving the Eagle Scout rank suggests persistence too, as does a self-started business (provided the candidate stuck with it).

Positivity

Related to persistence is positivity. Even an amazing win rate of 35% means you lose 65% of your deals. And most of an SDR's outreach will result in people saying "not now." So remaining positive in the face of these micro-failures is key. Moreover, in early-stage startups, there are all manner of setbacks, whether related to fund-raising, competition, or larger market currents. Lastly, not all prospects are peaches; being able to grin and eat it in the face of a prospect with an axe to grind will be required. This trait is more observable in the context of interpersonal interaction, so throughout your screening and interviewing process, pay attention to the tenor of candidates' references to failures or difficult experiences.

Teamwork

While individual contributorship and individual responsibility are paramount in sales, in modern organizations with SDR to AE to AM handoffs, teamwork is also important. Sales reps need to rapidly learn go-to-market best practices and share them with their management and colleagues, while feeding market feedback back to the product organization. Prior team sports experience, of course, is the best way to find this, but team environments can show up in other activities as well—like founding a business or participation in service organizations.

There are doubtless many other characteristics to look for—and presence of these traits doesn't take the place of proper screening and interviewing. But if you look for candidates who embody these characteristics, you'll have a great head start on a strong interviewing funnel.

Professional Characteristics

When hiring for market development staff, those raw characteristics are probably sufficient. You're likely hiring folks who are straight out of college, and who won't have a lot of professional characteristics of note. But as you start to hire more senior staff, you may want to consider prior experience.

Personally, I'm of two minds about this. On the one hand, I'm a huge fan of creating an "upwelling" effect by bringing on market development staff who are fresh out of college, training them over a six- to twelve-month period as they become familiar with the market and solutions, and then moving them into closing roles. It ensures that they are inculcated in your culture and system—Gregg Popovich-style—and that they don't bring any bad habits or preconceived notions to bear.

On the flip side, sometimes you need to scale, or hire those first account executives, and you don't have time to wait for your bench to grow. In those situations, you can use prior organizational membership as a great heuristic for the characteristics you need on your team.

I'm going to start with the warnings, because I feel that I've seen (and made) way too many mistakes of faulty analogy when looking for professional experience that matches what I need.

Industry Focus

For instance, thinking about "industry" wrong can be a problem. Just because someone sold "human resources" software, doesn't mean they can sell all HR/recruiting software. When I'm hiring for TalentBin, for example—which sells software into the recruiting part of organizations, and is a fairly transactional sale (perhaps purchased on a budgetary cycle, but just as often, purchased off cycle)—it would be a mistake to look for sales staff that have experience selling, say, performance management systems like SuccessFactors, Halogen, etc., just because they also "sell into HR." The sales cycle, tempo, and even value propositions (one is about human capital acquisition and proactivity, the other is about compliance) are substantially different.

Instead, when it comes to industry focus, look for those who have sold to the same decision makers that your org sells to, at a similar price point and budgetary tempo. For instance, if you're selling recruiting software, then people who have previously sold recruiting agency services could make sense. Both sell to the recruiting organization (not "HR," which is responsible for time cards and payroll), and both sell something that can be purchased outside of a budgetary or RFP cycle. So be mindful that "industry" is a more nuanced thing than "SaaS" or "analytics" or "HR."

Role Execution Focus

Another thing to be wary of is the notion that "sales is sales is sales." This is not the case. Your organization will likely be focused, to start, on new customer acquisition, the most difficult of the sales exercises. In mature organizations, there is typically more abstraction between roles—account executives do new business acquisition, and account managers focus on renewals and upsells and cross-sells. So if you're giving someone credit for "sales experience," you need to make sure it's the sales experience you want.

This is also true when considering staff out of organizations where this abstraction does not exist. These are typically legacy sales organizations, like Oracle, or younger, more loosely architected sales organizations like ClearSlide, where reps are responsible for lead generation, appointment setting, demoing and negotiation, and closing, followed by onboarding and later upsell and cross-sell—every stage of the sales cycle. Because the focus of these reps is so heavily split, they may have only a fraction of the necessary experience compared to someone who has been focused exclusively on new business acquisition. Be sure to consider this.

Sales Cycle Tempo Mismatch

Ignoring sales cycle tempo can be problematic too. If your solution is one that requires a long sales cycle, herding many decision makers and influencers to an eventual conclusion, then hiring folks who are used to "one call closes" or, at most, fifteen-day sales cycles can be a problem. They won't have the "cat herding" experience, and will have muscle memory of high-volume, rapid-fire engagement to work against.

It's the same on the inverse. If your solution has a more transactional, "quick hit" sales cycle, with a lower average contract value, hire for the activity required for that—lots of interaction with disparate clients, high volumes of demos on a weekly basis, and management of a pipeline of many smaller deals. Someone who has years of experience shepherding more complicated, slower-moving deals— where a pipeline has a much smaller set of larger opportunities, requiring less disparate activity—will have a lot of baked-in muscle memory to unwind to have success in your solution's deal cycle.

This isn't to say that either of these tempos is better than the other. It's just that they need to be in alignment with the tempo of your solution's sales cycle—something that you should have a pretty good handle on, since you've been doing it yourself. So be mindful of this.

Industry Bellwethers

Similarly, be wary of pulling staff out of the "standard" industry bellwethers—the monoliths of your space that you're looking to steal share from. The challenge with these sales reps is that they've been selling behind established brands, working with established marketing organizations that drive lead generation, and handling existing contracts that are on renewal "cruise control." All of these benefits will be nonexistent in your organization. So if the old saying is "No one ever got fired for buying IBM," then the corollary is "An IBM sales rep probably won't crush it selling a no-name, startup solution."

So if you're a new payroll industry entrant, former ADP people may not be a great idea. Or if you're a new recruiting solution, be wary of senior sales executives out of a CareerBuilder, Monster, or even LinkedIn—anyone who has become "baked into the budget" and will expect clients to take their meetings and the renewal to show up on time, with a bow on it.

Moreover, the older the sales organization, and the longer the rep in question has been there, the more likely it is they have adopted ineffective legacy behaviors from that organization. For instance, most older sales organizations have poor sales technology adoption practices. They have legacy CRM systems that are hard to use, and thus reps and managers grow complicit in avoiding them. Sadly, this leads to a culture of CRM disuse, which in turns leads to a culture of low transparency and low accountability, which leads to low execution, and excuse making.

In lieu of technical adoption, there will likely be less efficient process workarounds to paper over the gap, like time-consuming weekly meetings and line-level managers who spend their time on sales calls alongside their staff. Unfortunately, this consumes time that leaders should instead use on higher-value activities—consuming information from sales leadership, product marketing, and product management and distributing it to their team, or monitoring CRM metrics to spot issues as they show up in the data. Poor technical adoption also tends to foster bad email behavior, like CC'ing management on every action, because there is no trust in the CRM. That quickly leads to overflowing email inboxes that crowd out actually valuable information, like new product releases, marketing collateral, and so on. All of these expectations and behaviors can be very hard to unwind, so be aware of that when considering staff out of organizations that meet these criteria.

But there is a caveat when it comes to more junior staff. Many of these industry bellwethers have the infrastructure to support solid sales training programs and to instrument good sales behaviors, like high calling and emailing activity. So looking there for junior sales staff, like market development reps, who are ready to move on to a closing role could make sense. And laggy promotion timelines in these larger orgs can end up leaving staff who are ready for the next step languishing six months or longer beyond when they became capable for that step. Just be cautious that the potential hire hits your other requirements, as many of these larger organizations have a lower bar for other important criteria.

Now that we've covered some areas where you'd be wise to use extra caution, there are a couple of places that are often great sources of the professional characteristics startup leaders are after.

Mid-stage startups

One place to look is the set of organizations in your space that have hit escape velocity, and whose sales staff may be looking to jump onto the next rocket ship. They just finished selling a new, paradigm-shifting solution into an existing market, and thus would be more likely to have success doing so again. So if you're one of the newest set of applicant tracking systems going after the recruiting market, like Greenhouse or Lever, this could be sales staff out of Jobvite, iCIMS, and so on. It probably isn't sales staff who are still at Taleo or Kenexa, or selling applicant tracking solutions for Oracle, SuccessFactors/SAP, etc.

Customers

Another place to consider for potential sales staff is the customer base that you sell into. For instance, if you sell IT infrastructure, the in-house IT administrators who implement and administer your solutions are deeply intimate with the problem space—they live it. Or if you sell recruiting software, recruiters who experience the exact business pains you're looking to solve can be great fits.

Again, though, familiarity with the space is not sufficient by itself. For instance, an IT administrator who is introverted, and unable to conduct high-activity outreach and engagement, is never going to work out. But paired with the other characteristics you're looking for, this kind of subject-matter expertise can be gold. For instance, former recruiters are great salespeople for recruiting solutions because they not only know the pain points, but they are used to a recruiting workflow that revolves around high-activity outreach, persuasion, and pipeline management—just like sales.

Achievement Characteristics

Once you have identified candidates with the professional characteristics you're looking for, one benefit of looking at staff with prior experience is that you can ask them for artifacts of the sort of achievement you're after: quota attainment, activity metrics, and such. One thing to note, though, is that salespeople are used to selling, and spinning anecdotes and data to support their goals—and they will sell you on hiring them. So while their resume or LinkedIn profile may speak to quarters of outside achievement with regards to quota, I've seen enough "embellished" titles and stats from existing and prior staff to know that those self-reported metrics should be viewed with a gimlet eye.

Instead, ask for actual proof. Screenshots of activity graphs and leaderboards, directly from a candidate's organization's CRM, are hard to spoof. A truly clever approach I've heard of but not used is asking for a screenshot of CRM revenue leaderboards and the candidate's place in them. This, of course, not only shows you the candidate's ranking, but also the other top performers in that org, in case you want to recruit them next. Asking for W2s is also a popular approach, but my issue with this is that it's a top-line outcome; it doesn't show me the key metrics, like calls, demos, win rates, etc. I'd rather have the underlying data. But generally speaking, something is better than nothing, and something that comes from a third-party source is certainly better than something that is essentially marketing collateral, i.e. the candidate's resume and LinkedIn profile.

Relationships or "Hiring a Rolodex"

"What about relationships?" you might ask. Isn't there value to sales staff coming out of organizations where they have worked with hundreds of clients, and have their direct-dial phone numbers and email addresses? The notion of hiring a sales professional for his or her Rolodex is a dying one. It may even be dead already. This concept is a vestige of the time when there were no easily accessible alternatives for identifying and engaging with relevant budget holders. This is no longer the case. The sources vary by vertical, but with LinkedIn, Jigsaw/Data.com, and Hoovers/D&B, identifying decision makers requires only rudimentary searching by your lead-generation function.

While relationships with existing clients can be helpful, this value proposition should by no means excuse the absence of other requirements. There is no reason for you to hire someone who fails your other criteria in order to access their Rolodex. A twenty-three-year-old market development rep armed with five hundred accounts to call can get you the same thing (while building your bench), so you can give that account executive seat to someone who meets the requirements that are going to drive success. There may be exceptions for industries where the decision makers can't be found via other means, but this is generally going to be less and less the case over time, as the world moves toward more information transparency for prospecting.

Articulating and Documenting Your Hiring Profile

When you're getting started, it can be helpful to consider how other success-ful SaaS sales organizations approach their hiring profiles. Consider these examples:

TalentBin

At TalentBin we targeted new grads out of high-quality universities—Stanford, Cal, other UC schools, etc.—with a history of achievement in both taking initiative and building things. We also looked for indicators of success in team endeavors and athletic excellence (particularly in those unpleasant "grinder" sports). Alternatively, we targeted existing market development staff from LinkedIn—an industry bellwether in the recruiting market—with the promise that those market development reps (SDRs) would have a faster path toward becoming account executives at a fast-growing organization like TalentBin, compared to a slower-moving, larger organization like LinkedIn. We also hired former technical recruiters who had high subject-matter expertise, but also the high-activity execution characteristics needed to sell software. We specifically did not pull account executives out of LinkedIn, or legacy sales organizations like Monster or CareerBuilder; these more senior staff were typically inured to selling existing solutions that the market is well aware of (job postings, resume search, and LinkedIn Recruiter) and thus were less suited to presenting a new, innovative product that substantially departed from legacy solutions. They were also typically more focused on maintaining and renewing existing contracts than acquiring new customers, and relying on an established brand for making contact with customers than being a tip of the spear and penetrating and proliferating within accounts.

Meraki

A highly successful hardware sales company, Meraki adopted the strategy of pulling high-impact sales staff out of IT value-added reseller (VAR) shops. In those small IT consulting shops, which are largely undifferentiated from each other, sales professionals need to hustle hard in order to beat others out for business. Moreover, because they are dealing with organizations that typically are without IT leadership (CIO, VP of IT), reps are serving in a very consultative role. IT resellers constantly see new technologies come across their shelves, so the ability to understand customer pain, and then identify new technologies to solve those problems, was paramount for these folks. Lastly, there is a high level of inside-sales execution on the part of these VARs, in order to keep their efficiencies high and cost of sales low in a low-margin business. All of these characteristics aligned with Meraki's needs, and drove sales excellence in the organization.

Yelp/Groupon

Yelp and Groupon would be examples in the other direction. Because of low average contract values, a massive market of hundreds of thousands of small to mid-size accounts, and a relatively uncomplicated value proposition, their sales teams are architected for extremely high activity in support of a fairly transactional sales cycle. This mean lots of junior go-getters—fresh out of college and willing to make hundreds of calls a day—looping across thousands of accounts. And while having intimacy with the local merchant's business pains is helpful, because of the fairly straightforward sales being proposed reps aren't required to have a high level of selling expertise or technical acumen (unlike a Meraki, LinkedIn, TalentBin, etc.). Thus the hiring profile is one of scale and cost reduction; junior staff straight out of college are less costly than more senior staff.

When you look at the talent pools that both Yelp and Groupon have tapped into, it's recent grads out of second-tier regional colleges with lots of graduate volume, particularly in humanities, communications, and business majors. In the case of Yelp, for their Tempe call center, that's Arizona State University, or for their San Francisco sales center, it's San Francisco State, San Jose State, UCSB, etc. In the case of Groupon, much of their talent comes from Indiana University, De Paul, Ohio State, and other schools surrounding the Chicagoland area. Both companies found high volumes of charismatic, articulate, non-technical staff to mop up thousands and thousands of $1k contracts here and there.

As you work on your hiring profile, spend some time considering examples in your space. Once you've converged on what you're looking for, document it in a manner that can be easily shared with potential candidates. At the most basic, this could be part of a "job post," or a post to your application tracking system's career site. But you must have this profile, and role characteristics, documented in a way that can be easily shared and consumed, regardless of whether or not you have it up on a job board.

This can be as basic as a Google Doc that has its sharing setting set to "anyone with the link can view it," like this: https://docs.google.com/document/d/13eaM-vpMgDTZf_omRpbCYFdcIMQQ1ZrdT_tvDupVfG0w/edit

SOURCES OF HIRE OR HOW TO FIND YOUR PROFILE

Now that we've discussed the profile that you'd like to see on your sales team, we can talk about where to go to find it—or how to get it to come find you.

It's important to realize that not all sources of hire will require the same approach or be appropriate at every stage of your growth. Some sources make more sense earlier on, but become less relevant as you grow. And some sources make it easy to home in on higher quality from the get go, while others will require more screening. These are the various sources to consider early on.

Staffing Agencies

When you're hiring your very first "real" sales staffer, agencies can be a great source of hire. Staffing agencies are set up to provide you with ready-to-go, qualified candidates who are seeking new roles, and for this, they typically take a fee of 20%–30% of that candidate's first-year salary. While 25% of a $60k base salary for an account executive is substantially more costly that a job board posting or even a staff referral fee, there are a variety of benefits to this approach.

Firstly, you should target a sales-specific staffing agency, like TheLions in San Francisco, Betts Recruiting, or Rainmakers. Staffing agencies, like talent agencies, have first crack at all the best talent, because they have crafty recruiters in-house who are both proactively seeking it out and also filtering and vetting that talent. And because salespeople have short average tenures at organizations, they typically stay in close touch with recruiters who have placed them before—meaning that those recruiters have a "hot list" of great candidates they can engage. So not only do these recruiting agencies have ready-to-go candidates, those candidates are typically pre-vetted and screened "known good" hires.

Now, this isn't always the case. Remember that these recruiters work with all manner of sales staff, from candidates who sell $1k advertising packages to small businesses at Yelp to enterprise reps who sell $1m deals to Fortune 500 clients. So it's very important that you proactively characterize the profile that you're seeking (which we conveniently defined above) to the recruiters that you're working with. And continue to emphasize that profile as you get resumes. If you see candidates that do not fit your profile, it's very important to drop the boom on those recruiters quickly and correct that. If you don't, you could end up in big trouble. Because these recruiters are paid based on placement, they have a big incentive to work quickly to get a "butt in a seat," and to place a candidate that they have in-hand.

This is good, because they work with urgency; it can also be bad, because they want to place that candidate quickly, before he takes another role or decides he doesn't want to move roles after all. So if you are seeing candidates that don't match the profile that you're looking for, and you don't push back, these staffing agency recruiters will smell a pushover. As a result, they'll not only shove other, less qualified candidates toward you, but now they'll actively push their lower-quality candidates your way too, reserving higher-quality candidates for clients they know are pickier. So be stern in maintaining your filter.

Relatedly, make sure you screen well. We'll talk about screening—written screens and phone screens—below. Don't skimp on that with candidates coming out of staffing agencies.

Warnings aside, there are great benefits of working with staffing agencies to fill your earliest roles. As noted, they are quick, and can help reduce your sourcing workload so you can focus on other things. Eventually, referral recruiting will likely be your highest-volume and highest-quality source of hire. But when you're first starting out, you don't have an existing staff of folks to refer candidates. Nor do you have a network, personally, to draw from. Candidates provided via staffing agency can help you with exactly that—so when you're looking at these candidates early on, you should consider that "network value" in your thinking. For instance, if the candidate is coming out of a SaaS sales organization that's currently peaking, he can help be your future funnel of talent out of that organization into yours, and give you inside knowledge as to who was good and who was not. Staffing agencies can also be helpful with respect to compensation details. On the one hand, they have an incentive to enlarge any compensation offer to a candidate they place, since they are looking at a 25% piece of whatever incremental money is paid. On the other hand, they have extremely accurate state-of-the-market compensation information for the candidates they are placing, knowing both candidates' current salaries and the offers made to those they've placed.

There are a number of other things to be mindful of when working with staffing agencies. One is to not skimp when it comes to negotiating fees. While it may be tempting to try to get that agency down to 20% or 17.5% of first-year compensation for their fee, what you're actually doing is setting up an incentive for them to only show you candidates that they don't think they can place with other clients paying full freight. And given the opportunity cost of an unfilled, or poorly filled, sales position, this sort of "savings" can end up being extremely costly. However, what you can sometimes negotiate is a biannual or quarterly payment plan on your hires, which will help lessen the impact on your cash flow.

Another trick is to not work with too many agencies concurrently. Again, these recruiters are motivated, so if you have three or four agencies sending you resumes, you'll quickly be overwhelmed. I find that one or two is usually enough. It can be helpful to let them both know that you're working with another agency, as well. It adds some additional motivation.

I learned a trick for constraining resume overload from the CEO of Pure Storage: one in, one out. That is, tell the agency recruiters that you're working with that you will only take one resume at a time, and that they cannot send you another one before you have given the thumbs up or down. This creates a helpful incentive wherein the recruiter has to be mindful of sending you the best fits for the job, and the highest-quality staff first, lest you get turned off by bad resumes and don't respond. This cuts down on the incentive to test you with a lower-quality candidate to see if you might take them off their hands. If you have a good working relationship with your agency account manager, have done a rigorous intake meeting, and have a well-specified and documented candidate profile, a lot of these tricks will be less necessary. But proper incentive alignment can make sure that things don't go sideways.

Later in your scaling process, when you have a base of staff from which to draw referrals, and potentially in-house recruiting staff to do proactive sourcing, you will likely not need agency help as much. But at the very beginning, it can be extremely helpful, and worth the cost.

Referral Recruiting

When you're making your first hires, referral recruiting can be challenging; you don't have any staff to refer candidates to you, and you yourself likely do not have a network of sales professionals to pull from. However, once you have established those precursors, referral recruiting is simply the lowest-cost, highest-quality source of hire that you can leverage.

First things first—make sure that your staff has access to recruiting marketing materials, like the job postings in question. It doesn't have to be sexy, but it needs to be available as a hyperlink that can be emailed/texted/tweeted/shared on Facebook. Here's an example, and here's another one. Additionally, you'll want your staff to be intimate with the hiring profile that you're looking for. Just as you communicated that clearly to staffing agency recruiters, you now need to communicate it to your own staff—who should be fairly familiar with the type of person you hire—as your agent in sniffing out talent.

Second, you'll want to have a referral-recruiting bonus in place. Depending on the seniority of the role, you can do something between $2500 and $5000. The goal of a referral-recruiting bonus isn't to keep referral recruiting top of mind for your staff; you generally won't be able to get your folks to constantly think about recruiting, because they have their jobs to do. That will have to be your job. However, the referral bonus is there so that when someone does fall into the lap of one of your team members, they'll work hard to get that candidate across the line.

Lastly, and requiring the most amount of labor, is the recurring activity of both reminding your staff about your hiring needs and engaging in proactive referral-recruiting activity. The best way to keep recruiting top of mind for your staff is to bake it into recurring team meetings. When you're in team or all-hands meetings, note the open roles that the organization is trying to fill, and the successes you've had to date. When it comes to proactive referral recruiting, though, it's going to take some more elbow grease. I wrote an article in the First Round Review about proactive referral recruiting; the long and short of it is that sitting down with your staff—walking through their LinkedIn and Facebook connections, flagging those who fit your hiring profile—is a great way to create a lead list of potential candidates and fill your hiring funnel.

When you have successes via referral recruiting, spread them around. Make sure that everyone knows that this approach works, that the best hires come from this source, and that you too can get a nice referral bonus check for helping out!

Even though your quality of candidate will likely be the highest coming from referrals, in that your staff will implement a good filter, it's still important to maintain the level of screening discussed below. And at the same time, you'll want to provide a feedback loop to the staff who refer people. If a candidate ends up not being a fit, it's important to express why, so that your staff can get better at referring good fits. Feedback also ensures that your staff knows that you are executing on their referrals—even if it didn't end up in a hire, this time.

Job Boards

Job boards get a lot of crap. The primary ding against them is that because the candidates on job boards are looking, they must not be any good; if they were, they'd be promoted and happy in their existing organizations. There is some truth to this; there will be candidates that come through postings who are lower quality or less apt to fit your profile. But that doesn't meant that all candidates that come through postings will be a poor fit. It just means your "signal to noise" ratio may be noisier than it is with referral recruiting or direct sourcing. However, sales professionals are active networkers, career-minded and "riser" oriented. They are typically on the lookout for good options, so even the best staff can have an eye open for their next opportunities. Couple this with the fact that the candidates on job boards are active candidates—they are actively seeking new roles—and job boards can be a high-velocity source of candidate flow for your sales hiring.

The one thing that you will have to be particularly mindful of is screening. There is no filter on candidates who apply from your job board posting, so you'll have to have a screening mindset from the very beginning to ensure that you don't chew up unnecessary time running poorly qualified candidates through a time-consuming interview process. Even as you write your job ad—using the hiring profile you've documented—you should be clear about what your "requireds" and "nice-to-haves" are. You can even make it clear what your screening and functional interviewing (mock pitches, etc.) process is, both to excite those who are eager to tackle a challenge (the folks you're looking for), and to proactively turn away those who are turned off by that sort of legwork.

Depending on what the candidate flow looks like from a job board, you may have to tune your postings. For instance, if you aren't getting enough candidates, you may need to dial back the commentary on screening rigor; if you are getting a large number of unqualified candidates, you may have to dial it up to dissuade those folks from applying and crufting up your candidate flow. Generally speaking, if you're getting a dozen or so good-quality resumes per week from a posting, that's a good rate of candidate flow.

Direct Sourcing

Direct sourcing is the process by which you use candidate databases—like resume databases, professional social networks like LinkedIn, or talent search engines like TalentBin—to search out and proactively qualify potential candidates, and then reach out to those that look like they could match your profile.

On the one hand, direct sourcing is great because you can find exactly those candidates that have the characteristics that you're looking for, and not waste time on potentially unqualified inbound applications that don't match your profile. On the other hand, it takes a substantial amount of work, and the potential candidates that you're sourcing may not be looking for a role (known in recruiting parlance as "passive candidates"). Not only do you have to search out relevant candidates in the talent pools you're sourcing from (say, LinkedIn), you have to build a lead list and reach out to those potential candidates. Sound like sales? Good catch. It is.

As such, be mindful of the labor requirements for this sort of exercise. At the earliest stages of your hiring ramp, when you don't have a recruiter on hand to assist you, you may be better off sticking to staffing agencies, referral recruiting, and job postings. Read more on stage-appropriate recruiter usage in this article I wrote in the First Round Review.

However, if you do decide that you want to allocate a few dozen hours to a passive candidate- sourcing campaign, these are some things to think about. Unlike software engineering, design, or product professionals, who don't spend much time proactively on LinkedIn, salespeople are on LinkedIn constantly. They use LinkedIn for prospecting and learning about their prospects; they spend almost as much time there as they do in their CRM and email. For that reason, they tend to have extremely up-to-date, and well-embellished, LinkedIn profiles, often with direct contact information.

This is a boon to you, as a direct sourcer, because you can use the criteria we established above—company membership, role execution focus/title, and so on—as search criteria, so that only those who match those criteria are returned in search results. Effectively, you can screen via search query. You will likely have to pay for one of LinkedIn's premium products, but you won't need the top of the line, LinkedIn Recruiter. And if you tune your search queries correctly, you'll cut your searches down substantially so that you get under any results limits that a cheaper version of LinkedIn imposes.

For example, don't just search for "Sales, San Francisco Bay Area." Instead use a combination of specific titles and companies of interest, for something like this: "market development" *or* "sales development" *or* "business development rep" *or* "business development representative" *and* "LinkedIn" *or* "Simply Hired" *or* "Indeed" *or* "Box" *or* "Salesforce." And don't forget your industry's acronyms; these reps are just as likely to turn up by searching "SDR" *or* "SDR" *or* "BDR."

Contacting these candidates shouldn't be hard. While LinkedIn provides InMail access for a fee—and sales professionals will see their inbound LinkedIn messages because they're strong LinkedIn users—InMails are generally a contact vector of last resort. Email and phone is preferable. Again, because salespeople know that prospects are often looking at their profiles, they will merchandise their work email and phone; because salespeople are typically open to new opportunities (everything's for sale for a price, right?), they'll often post their personal email and cell phone too. Make use of that in your outreach. It will make you more efficient and raise your contact rates.

While you are able to hone your searches and qualification criteria more minutely in this fashion, these folks are often not actively looking for a role and may have less motivation to jump through screening hoops. This does not mean that you should not screen them. Instead, this may required a "sell, screen, sell" approach. That is, you will have to start the conversation in a selling mode, getting the candidate excited about the role and the opportunity, until they say, "Yes, I would like to go through an interview process." At that point, you should run them through the same screening and interview process you'd use with any candidate. There are a lot of really bad salespeople at industry bellwethers who would jump at the opportunity to work at an exciting startup, but who turn out to be absolutely terrible, and just haven't yet been flushed out of their organization. I can't tell you how many LinkedIn AEs failed our basic written screen at TalentBin—typos, grammatical errors, the works. Do you want that person to be your first line of offense with clients? Don't be the place to which they "jump before being pushed."

SCREENING, INTERVIEWING, & CLOSING

While sourcing for the top of your hiring funnel can stock your pipeline with high-er-probability candidates, your screening, interviewing, and closing process is what will maximize your conversion of these potential hires.

I find that a lot of organizations don't know what they're looking to achieve in the screening and interviewing part of the hiring funnel. I boil it down to this: the screening and interviewing process exists to authenticate that would-be candidates have the characteristics required for success in your sales org. "Authentication" is the key. While experience at a prestigious organization, a degree from a compelling school, or a shiny-looking resume may be potential leading indicators of success at your organization, the goal of the screening and interviewing process is to "prove it," and once proved, to close the candidate on working at your organization. All the steps in your screening and interviewing process should support that goal.

Screening

Hiring, while of extreme importance, can be a large time suck of inefficiency if you aren't mindful. This is why I am a big proponent of the use of asynchronous screening approaches earlier in the hiring process—it puts the time cost onto the candidate, while at the same time creating rich "interviewing artifacts" that are better reflections of a candidate's abilities than a resume or personal statement that has been polished to perfection. This can be all the more important when working with staffing agencies whose incentives are to shove a "butt in your seat." Having a strong screening mechanism in place that doesn't consume all of your time, and gives you a high-signal outcome on which to base judgment, is all the more important when working with recruiting agencies.

"Artifact-Based" Pre-Screens

For that reason, I'm a particular fan of implementing screens involving the production of some lightweight work artifact as the first step in my hiring process. One of my favorites is a written screen. It's not an essay test, but rather a series of a dozen or so open-ended questions that the individual can respond to. I generally give instructions to spend no more than an hour on it, and I keep the questions in the template lighthearted (but pithy enough to allow for the demonstration of crit-ical-thinking acumen). Some of my go-to questions include:

Tell me about something you've built that you're proud of.

What do you think about Google Glass?

What sort of team sports did you play in high school/college? What was your favorite?

Scale of 1-10, how messy is your room? Be honest.

Tell me what you like about sales/recruiting, in your own words.

Document for me a deal (either sales or recruiting) that went terribly. Be totally honest.

What am I looking for in the written screen? Well, modern salespeople spend most of their time communicating value and persuading people to do things in written, spoken, and visual formats—so the ability to clearly communicate is extremely important. An inability to do that with cursory subjects will reveal an inability to do so with your solution. If you can't explain—with a beginning, middle, and end—something you've built that you're proud of, your favorite bar and why, or how a deal went sideways, you're going to struggle to do so with our product. While high activity is important for sales, executing those activities with attention to detail is required. Those who can't demonstrate thoroughness and attention to detail in a task where it is specifically called for will fail to do so in day-to-day work activities.

This is similar to how recruiters look for typos and grammatical errors in resumes—except that those are the most highly polished pieces of hiring collateral that candidates present. It's much better to use a tool that is specifically designed to catch a lack of attention to detail or thoroughness, in a time-constrained approach. For instance, if the candidate can't be bothered to tell the difference between "there," "their," and "they're" in what has been identified as a test, what will her emails to prospects look like? And what will her pipeline cleanliness look like?

Another artifact-based screen that I like is a mini homework assignment involving account research and voice mail pitching. At the end of the written screen, I tell candidates to leave me a 30-second voice mail, pitching TalentBin as if I were the head of recruiting at Airbnb. Firstly, I like the fact that it's a composite homework assignment. It requires going to TalentBin's website and consuming its value propositions, which tests initiative, comprehension, and retention. It also requires qualifying Airbnb as an account, and allows for varying levels of execution on the part of the candidate.

A cursory level of execution would be abstractly pitching TalentBin. A better level of execution would be doing account research on Airbnb and their hiring requirements in order to tailor the pitch in question. And I don't provide my cell phone number—but it's in the signature of every email I send. And easily available from some cursory Google searching. Email responses asking for my cell phone number receive a raised eyebrow.

I've seen other approaches too, like providing some written GMAT questions to be executed ahead of an interview. These could have benefits too by providing more rigor, but I'm partial to a "guerrilla" screening test. Its less-than-rigorous outward appearance invites the candidate to act in a way that comes naturally to them, which is I want to surface. If their natural way of being in the world is to be rigorous, with high attention to detail and execution, I want to see that. If that's not their natural way of being in the world, then I definitely want to see that too.

Note that these approaches are quite different from "video interviewing," where standard interview questions are presented to someone so they can verbally respond to them while being recorded by the webcam of their computer. I'm actually not a fan of this approach, because it's just a time-shifted, place-shifted version of traditional interviews (or phone screens); those are typically more narrative-based, and less about authentication of the ability to do the work required for a role. And ability is a much more important thing to authenticate earlier in the hiring process.

Like video interviews, though, written screens are asynchronous in nature. I don't have to be on the phone at the same time as the candidate, and can consume them later, when I have available time for it. Written screens also allow me to take an off-ramp as soon as it's clear that the candidate won't make the cut. If the first couple questions make it clear to me that this is someone who doesn't have the requisite written communication skills or attention to detail to succeed in our sales organization, I can stop and tell the candidate that, while I appreciated their effort, it's not going to make sense to proceed at this time.

Contrast this to the traditional approach of setting up a fifteen- to thirty-minute phone screen that requires synchronizing calendars and synchronous communication (which is valuable, but for more nuanced judgments). And, let's be honest, it's more difficult to extricate oneself from a phone screen that has gone sideways after five or ten minutes; it's just human nature to play it out. Written screens help avoid this time suck.

Be forewarned that senior staff will likely be more attuned to a traditional hiring workflow—typically an initial phone screen and, if they pass that, a series of on-site interviews. While you may be tempted to skip written screens of more senior staff based on their "pedigree," don't you dare do it. As I've noted, senior experience at a legacy organization can actually be an indicator of all kinds of bad behaviors. If a would-be senior rep is insulted by being subjected to the same screening approach as others, how do you think he's going to be when it comes to coaching by you, or others? Or new process adoption? Or a transparent sales org? He should be excited that the organization has a rigorous process for identifying great staff and stocks its sales team with high-quality folks that are a joy to work with. And he should welcome the opportunity to show off how great he is.

Lastly, your approach to written screens doesn't have to be complicated. Our organization (both Sales and Customer Success) uses a templated Google Doc that gets forked ("Make a copy of") and shared with the candidate in question. We give them editorial rights and instruct them to execute it at their convenience and email us when they're done.

The time savings and insights that are surfaced through the use of written screens in sales hiring can't be overstated.

Phone Screen

While written screens can be great for efficiently qualifying/disqualifying sales candidates, phone screening can be used to authenticate more nuanced parts of the profile that you're looking for.

While it's not the same level of clarity that you'll get in a mock pitch—more on that later—or in-person interview, a thirty-minute phone screen can be helpful for understanding if this person really has the characteristics that were highlighted in their profile (resume, LinkedIn profile, etc.) and demonstrated in their written screen. For instance, I like to use this opportunity to authenticate the "intellectual acumen" part of the profile that I look for. Specifically, with respect to sales staff, I like to talk about funnel optimization and leverage by asking the candidate to take me through a lead-generation and sales funnel that they're familiar with. This could be in their existing role, or it could be as simple as a business they worked at in high school, like an ice cream store, lemonade stand, or even a personal-training business (one of my key sales hires was previously a personal trainer!). In the context of this conversation, I ask several key questions:

What were the inputs to the sales funnel in question?

What were the characteristics of the prospects, and how could we find more of them, scalably?

What were the competitive characteristics of the market?

What would lead to higher conversion of the sales funnel?

And so on and so forth. I try to do this in a rapid fashion to see how the candidate does in a "keeping up" environment, how well they do at explaining their answers, and if they are able to apply a problem-solving, scalability-focused mindset to their example.

Once we converge on the constraints in the situation in question, then we get into how to solve that problem. (This speaks to their "figure shit out" quotient.)

How would the candidate solve the issue of insufficient customers for the ice cream store, or whatever sales funnel they discussed in their example?

Could that funnel be made more efficient, for instance by serving more of those scoops of ice cream in a given time interval?

How could the candidate ensure that customers were happy with the value being provided?

How do we know that they like the ice cream and will tell others about it?

How can we do a better job of allowing sales reps to do more demos in a given period?

As I like to say, "If you were the king/queen of the world, how would you solve this?" And that's an important question, particularly in startup sales hiring. If the candidate is coming out of an organization with a fixed set of processes, they may have a bit of tunnel vision. This is their opportunity to break out of that, and show me that they can break out of it. Because figuring shit out is going to be required in an early-stage sales go-to-market.

I try to execute all of this in less than twenty minutes. (You'll note that the phone screen I'm describing is longer than the "traditional" phone screen. That's because I've already confirmed that these candidates are "worth" more time with my written screen, so I can invest more of my time at this stage to extract better information for my hiring decision.) If it's a successful exercise, I like to devote the last ten minutes to questions they have about the organization—this would be the beginning of "selling" the job. That is, the candidate made it through the initial hiring funnel and profile/resume screening, through written screening, and now through a verbal screen. It's looking like this thing could have legs, so let's start engaging with that and getting them excited about the organization, since we're already on the phone!

You can even throw behavioral components into this, as well. For instance, I occasionally like to purposefully "miss" inbound phone screen calls (I always have candidates call me to test punctuality), so I can see what candidates' voice mail sounds like, how long they wait to call me back, and if they email me immediately. All of this speaks to proactivity and persistence, which are behavioral characteristics that we value highly.

It's important to note that—unlike the written screen, which leaves an artifact—phone screens don't naturally leave you with something to review later. It's critical to either record the screen (for instance, using a presentation software like Zoom or call recording software like Chorus) or take good notes afterward. If you're going to spend twenty to thirty minutes on the phone, the least you can do is jot down five minutes' worth of bulleted notes structured as "green flags" (things you were encouraged by), "yellow flags" (things you weren't excited about), and "red flags" (things you thought were actually concerning). This way you'll have data to come back to when engaging with candidates further down the process, or when comparing different candidates and making a choice between them.

Mock Presentation Screening

As you can tell, this part of the process is focused on finding opportunities to authenticate a candidate's ability to succeed in our sales organization. When it comes to market development staff, these screens are typically sufficient to progress candidates to in-person interviews.

But when it comes to staff who are moving from customer-facing presenting and closing roles in other organizations to closing roles in your organization, an incremental "presentation screen" is definitely called for.

While some sales leaders half-ass this with approaches like "sell me this pen" in an in-person interview, I find that sort of approach silly. I'm dealing with sales professionals, so I'm going to have them sell me their existing solution. I can learn about whatever solutions they're currently selling, their competitors, and so forth with fifteen to thirty minutes of web research, so acting as a mock-prospect is fine; I either ask the candidate to tell me what prospect I am, or I concoct a profile of a prospect I am going to inhabit (like Airbnb in the voice mail example above). I instruct candidates to treat me as a prospect that has agreed to a demo and run the process from soup to nuts the way they would with a prospect; this means sending me a calendar invite, (complete with whatever online screen-sharing or presentation software they want to use), executing a full-blown thirty- to sixty-minute presentation and demo, and following up with a proposal.

Because this is essentially a mock funnel pass, it's incumbent on you to pay attention to all parts of the sales and presentation process, looking for both excellence and soft spots.

Is the calendar invite clear, and does it include all pertinent coordinates for the online meeting?

Do candidates send you an email ahead of time confirming the meeting? Do they send a reminder?

How do they conduct the call?

What pre-call preparation did they do to ensure that they know pertinent details about my mock business (which they likely assigned me)?

Do they start with discovery questions?

Do they then proceed to the problem and solution statements in a way that is tailored to what we discuss in the discovery questions?

Are they consultative in their approach?

Do they engage in presentation comprehension check-ins, making sure I'm paying attention?

Are the facile with ROI and business-driver calculations pertinent to my business?

Do they build agreement through the presentation?

How do they react when I feign confusion on an important topic?

How do they handle my objections?

How do they react to aggressive, verging on combative, questions?

How do they handle my questions about the competition?

And, importantly, do they ask for the sale?

Aside from judging how well they execute the pitch from discovery through next steps, this is also a prime opportunity to judge "coachability" in a rep. That is, if you stop them partway through the pitch, provide them some pointers, and then request to start that section again, you can get a sense of how they take feedback and incorporate it, or don't. As discussed above, coachability is a key trait in sales staff, and the mock pitch is a great place to authenticate it's presence or absence.

I've done this dozens of times, with folks from Groupon, LinkedIn, Indeed, website hosting businesses, and payroll software businesses. And while I haven't been the perfect prospect every time, that's almost a feature of the process. Candidates should know what the key characteristics of a prospect would be and guide me as necessary, which is a good thing to do with a sale, regardless.

Based on the outcomes of this process—after comparing all my green and red flags against the hiring profile I am looking at—candidates will either progress to on-site interviews or end the process there.

Interviewing

Once you've progressed through all of your screens, you're ready for in-person, team-wide interviews. Have you noticed that we've been through a ton of screens—resume/profile, written, phone, and mock pitch—before progressing to in-person interviews? That's on purpose. First, your sales reps will likely be doing most of their work via phone and other telepresence (WebEx/screenshare, email, PowerPoint); if a candidate can't get the point across in those formats in a screening process, moving into face-to-face interactions won't solve the problem. Secondly, face-to-face team interviews are extremely time-intensive—not just for you, but for your team. A four- or five-person team doing multiple interviews across an on-site day will double or triple all the time you've spent on screening the candidate up to this point. Instead, guard your team's time against wild goose chases by doing the heavy lifting yourself via a screening process. Keep your reps setting appointments and doing demos instead of interviewing candidates you should have kicked out of your funnel way ahead of time. A candidate shouldn't be coming on site unless you're already pretty damn sure that they're a hire. Otherwise, you're pissing away your team's time.

That said, there is definitely value to the on-site interviewing process. First, there is the chance that you may have missed something that kicks a candidate out. Not likely, but possible. Secondly, and more important, is the opportunity to get your team's perspective and build consensus among the team about the validity of the hire. If you are running an organization that is highly mission-driven, passionate, and bought-in, they're going to want to feel a candidate out themselves. Of course, you should remind your team of the rigorous screening process that candidate has already passed, and that you feel that they meet the bar of the team. But folks will still want to road test the potential hire.

Team Interviews

You should have specific goals for every staff member assisting in the interview process. For instance, in our rep hiring process at TalentBin, we have one of our reps who's particularly expert in recruiting interview on recruiting understanding and acumen. We have our sales ops lead interview on tooling adoption and technology understanding. And we have one of our most socially attuned reps interview on "team culture fit." At this point, the only reason a candidate is spending any time with the team is that I believe they're probably a hire, so I spend my time running the interview process. In my allocated interview segment, I ratchet up the "selling" part of hiring, answering questions and articulating very directly the organization's and the sale team's culture—what's okay and what's not okay.

It isn't enough for each part of your hiring team to "know" what they're interviewing for, though. They should have a set of questions and interactions scripted so that they are applying them to each candidate in the same way. Either sit with them to set up these tools or set them up yourself; even a simple Google Doc that can be "copied" for each new candidate is fine. Moreover, interviewers should have a unified method for recording the outcomes of their interviews. Again, I like the "green flag," "yellow flag," "red flag" approach, followed by a "summation" (strong hire, hire, unsure, pass, strong pass), with rationale bulleted under each category. When scheduling interviews, I make sure to allocate time specifically for sufficient note-taking after the interview is concluded. Again, if you're going to take thirty or forty-five minutes to interview someone, take five minutes to record the outcome of that effort.

At this point, I'm typically looking for red flags. If someone sniffs out an issue that somehow didn't arise previously, it's good to dig into it. However, barring that, and assuming that the interview team gives the green light, we like to do one last pass with the rest of the sales team in a group "cultural interview" by having the team take the candidate in question out for a beer or two.

Social "Beer" Interview

A "beer" interview (could be a "coffee" interview, if you prefer, but let's be honest—this is sales) serves a few purposes. First, it allows the broader team—outside just the interview team—to interact with the candidate, looking for cultural fit and potential red flags. But it does so in a way that is far more time-efficient than giving each person a thirty-minute session. It also allows the staff to share their experience with the candidate, further establishing the norms of the sales organization in the eyes of the candidate (who, if they don't like it, can self-select out). And it allows the candidate to ask more candid questions in the context of a social atmosphere. This usually helps cement a feeling of transparency, so the candidate can believe what I, and others in the organization, have been telling her. Lastly—and these are partially closing tactics—I get to leverage our high-quality staff, who are great to be around, as a fringe benefit of being in our organization, and start building a sense of camaraderie. That can help in the offering process if there are compensation sticking points or it's a competitive offer situation.

As with all parts of the interview process, outcomes should be documented. In this case, I require all participants (and who doesn't want a beer or two on the boss's dime, and the chance to meet the new potential teammate?) to give me their feedback in the standard green/yellow/red flag and summary format. Again, I'm mainly looking for red flags from the staff here.

Based on the outcomes of the event, we'll either offboard the candidate or move toward offering them a role.

Deciding Between Multiple Candidates

Ideally you should be running a parallel process with multiple candidates to fill the roles that you have open, and biasing toward filling your pipeline to ensure full classes of staff to onboard.

As a result, especially if you do a good job of filtration at the top of the funnel, you may end up with more candidates making it through the bottom of the hiring funnel than headcount allotted. So how do you choose? Well, the good news with sales in an early-stage environment is that it's all largely greenfield. On balance, it's far worse to have accounts going uncalled than extra salespeople who may initially consume salary, but then quickly become value-positive. That is, if you've done a good job of filtration (and later do a good job of onboarding) and you have sufficient customer lead generation, even your "silver medalists" in the hiring process should be revenue-positive in short order.

So if you have extra folks who make it through the funnel, and they meet your bar, hire them. More rainmakers are a good thing. They might even buy you some shiny new engineers.

Reference Checking

Once you've decided that you want to move forward and have compensation largely agreed (this could come before that step, too, but often candidates want to know what their offered compensation is before they will entertain an offer), you'll want to do some reference checking. There are two types of reference checks— provided reference, and "back channel references." Both can be helpful, but need to be approached differently. In the first case, the candidate is going to provide the references, so you know they're going to be good! The challenge here can be pulling signal out of those references. All references are going to be loathe to provide anything in writing, but you can usually get folks to hop on the phone for a chat. My favorite approach there is typically asking something along the lines of "On a scale of 1-10, how highly would you recommend the candidate?" At this point, they're going to drop an 8, 9, or 10 on you. (If lower, wow, you need to find out why.). I let them chat a little bit about all the great things the candidate did, etc., and then go for the good information by asking: "What would need to do to become a 10?" This is where can you often get improvement areas surfaced that otherwise would never be talked about. This isn't saying that these will be "kick-out" questions, but it's good information to have.

The second type of reference is a back channel reference. That is, finding a reference that is jointly known by you, or someone on your team, and the candidate, who can provide back channel information that either validates or potentially discounts what you've learned in the interviewing process. The best way to do this is to look for shared LinkedIn and Facebook connections between you and the candidate, or people on your team and the candidate, and then look for folks who are closer to you and your team than to the candidate. That is, they aren't in his back pocket, per se. This can sometimes be a crapshoot, and there may not be any, but if you can find one or more, it can help provide more signal to validate your existing decision. These type of references can be extremely helpful, as they may surface potential knockouts that the candidate-provided references have been pre-vetted to hide.

Other approaches where you have more than a few references can involve trying to divine patterns through multiple conversations. That is, if you ask "what are the top three characteristics" of the candidate to four people, you'll start seeing patterns emerge. And if none of those characteristics include those that the candidate has positioned to you as being key reason to hire him, that's a potential flag. Further, if the candidate has cited any particularly large projects or wins, and those don't show up without prompting, that might be a yellow flag.

Again, the goal here isn't malevolent or to "gotcha" the candidate, but simply to validate our decision to move forward, and make sure we have all available information to support that.

Post-Interview

The purpose of screens and interviews is to authenticate that a candidate has the characteristics and skills to do the job, and will fit within the culture of your organization.

Once you've done that, step on the gas, fast. The sort of high-quality staff you're recruiting will not be on the market for long, and much like a sales deal, there is a tempo and momentum to hiring. If you let that excitement start to cool off, it will make things much harder for you. You will lose that candidate to another opportunity, and none of the work that you did to authenticate them will be recoverable. Dillydallying sets the hard work you've done on fire. And it will create questions in the mind of your team—if you can't close a candidate, should they still be working here? So stop agonizing, Hamlet, and get this show on the road.

If you're not sure, on the other hand, then pass. "If there's doubt, there is no doubt" is a helpful way to think about it. Move on to the rest of your pipeline, where you can find someone that you're truly excited about. This is why recruiting, like sales, tends to be a volume game; if it's a bad deal, close it and move on.

The hire doesn't represent just the hire and their salary expense. You will be investing substantial time and energy onboarding him. He will be looked at by his colleagues as a reflection of what is deemed valid in your sales culture. You will be filling his pipeline with valid opps and giving him bluebird deals. If you're not sure that the candidate in front of you is worth that investment, then pull the ripcord. Trust your process and know that you will find those who are worth the investment.

Compensation

When making an offer, compensation will be a key part of your discussion. Firstly, you need to know what you're paying. You can't make this crucial decision based on whatever a candidate asks for or has earned previously.

The better way to think about this is that there is a market for the sort of labor that you need, with an associated market rate. At the same time, there's a certain value that you're going to be able to get out of your hires—this will go to quota and commissions. That is, if the mechanics of your market and solution tell you that your average deal size is $10k, and that a sales rep can close five of them a month, netting you $50k in bookings (at a 20%–25% cost of sales), you can't be paying that staffer more than $10k a month in base and commission. So talking to sales staff who are targeting a $100k base and $200k on-target earnings (netting to $16k a month) is simply a non-starter.

This can be hard early on, when you're not sure of the natural rate of sales for a typical rep. That's why I like to look at analogous roles at analogous companies—for TalentBin, that was looking at LinkedIn's SDR and AE teams—for guidance. It's generally pretty easy to surface compensation specifics at these benchmark organizations, either by asking agency recruiters or by using tools like Glassdoor or PayScale.

Variable Compensation

When it comes to variable compensation, or commission, nearly all sales roles follow the concept of variable compensation derived from bookings, appointments set, or some other key performance indicator. Typically you'll see a 50% base/50% commission split for new-business acquisition account executives, with more of a 60/40 or 70/30 for market development (appointment setting) or account management ("farming" existing accounts).

Related to this is the concept of quota, and how much revenue your sales staff will need to earn, or appointments they'll need to set, in order to attain that variable compensation. Quotas are funny things. On the one hand, nothing focuses the mind on taking care of business like knowing that you will be paid for these activities over here, and not for those over there. The notion that sending one more email or making one more call can lead to an extra $500 in your bank account does a remarkably good job of motivating those incremental calls and emails.

On the other hand, quotas are somewhat vestigial, leftover from a time when sales activity was not sufficiently instrumentable (via CRM, and sales instrumentation) to help sales management see if sales staff were doing the requisite activities, and doing them well. In pre-CRM sales organizations (or present-day sales orgs with abysmal CRM execution), it was hard to see how many calls, emails, appointments, and so forth were being done by a rep. So the backstop was a macroeconomic "carrot/stick" combo in the form of a quota. If the rep didn't do the work needed to generate sales, their missed quotas would demonstrate that, eventually (over a series of quarters) leading to dismissal.

If you run your organization like a modern sales org, that particular function of the quota has largely gone away; instead, you have activity charts and graphs, win ratios, and so forth, which are far better tools for instrumenting and verifying activity. Moreover, this sort of activity instrumentation presents that under-achievement information much faster than the three quarters of quota under-attainment historically needed to realize that a rep wasn't doing his job and should be fired. With all that said, incentivizing and focusing incremental activity is still an important part of variable compensation, so it is worth implementing quotas.

Setting quotas works better when you have a sense of what the natural rate of sales will be, but looking at existing market examples will be helpful. And if you have been selling yourself, and have a sense of what is achievable, you'll be able to set goals that are attainable. That last part is key—unrealistic goals will lead to unhappy sales staff who will be looking for new jobs, leaving you without an engine for your revenue growth. In fact, if your would-be hires are smart (and they better be, if you've been following along!), they're going to want to know what proportion of their would-be colleagues are hitting their numbers. It's all well and good to tell a potential hire a narrative of how she's going to make $200k a year if she hits certain goals. But if she digs in and no one is attaining those goals, you're going to lose that hire (and likely your existing staff). It's a bit of a balancing act, which may require retooling as you go. But let's look at how the numbers play out for two key sales roles.

SDRs

Compensation for appointment-setting roles depends on what you're selling. High-end, high-ticket software that is more complicated and hard to set appointments for will be compensated at a higher rate. But a LinkedIn/TalentBin/Box.net/Salesforce SDR in the San Francisco Bay Area will be making a $45k–$55k base with on-target earnings (OTE) of $65k–$75k. For something higher-ticket like Workday, it may be something more like $50k, with a $75k OTE. The $15k–$20k of variability is based on the number of appointments that are set and subsequently held. Your mileage may vary based on region.

Some people determine variable compensation by counting verified qualified opportunities; that is, if the account executive has the meeting and says that the account isn't qualified, it doesn't count. I don't like this approach because sometimes the aspects of the account that made it unqualified aren't discoverable from external information (like employee counts, job openings, etc.), or even on an initial discovery call, and you shouldn't be punishing SDRs for something outside their control. But it works for some organizations.

The number of appointments that are required to attain the total on-target earnings will vary, again, by how hard it is to set those appointments. If you're setting appointments with CIOs of Fortune 500 companies for $1m average-deal-size opportunities, then one or two a week is probably a good number! For something higher volume and more transactional, it could be ten to fifteen a week. You're going to have to experiment. The important thing is that you want your goals to be attainable with the correct amount of quality work. If an SDR makes one hundred calls a day and sends one hundred emails, and they are quality and not BS, whatever number of appointments that turns into should be a good target (and you'll note that quota is the carrot and stick that backstops your activity tracking). You also don't want to cap attainment here. If you're paying $50 per appointment set and held (this would target eight appointments set and held per week for $20k variable compensation), do not cap the upside. If someone can set sixteen appointments for you per week, by all means. Go for it! If you set your quota too low, by allowing this upside will allow them to "reveal" what maybe the true goal should be, so you can later adjust it. Also, don't require the attainment of the goal in order to achieve an all-or-nothing payout. If you don't have a lot of data supporting that someone can attain five meetings set and held a week, and that person hits four, and doesn't get their payout, that's going to be a demoralized rep. All or nothing variable compensation attainment is something that far, far more mature organizations can dabble in, like payouts only occurring when a rep attains 85% of attainment in a quartet, though usually this is an account management capacity, versus lead gen or new business acquisition—like what AEs do.

AEs

AE compensation can be a little more complicated. But generally speaking, for account staff who are acquiring new business ("hunting" as compared to the "farming" of account managers who are focused on maintaining, renewing, and proliferating existing business), you'll be seeing a 50/50 split between base and variable.

As with SDRs, this will typically vary based on the average deal size you're talking about. Higher deal sizes will mean more expensive AEs. Again, to benchmark off a San Francisco SaaS AE—out of LinkedIn, for example—you'd be looking at something like $50k–$60k base, with an OTE of $100k–$120k. Again, for a higher-ticket item like Workday, that could be a $100k base, with a $200k OTE. Usually you should be able to benchmark against other organizations selling similarly priced software as yours. (And if you're pulling people out of a related company, their approach to compensation will certainly influence yours.)

Quota and commission can also be challenging with AEs. Once you know what a "natural rate of execution" is, and thus what a reasonable goal is, it can be straightforward to set quota. Usually you don't want your entire cost of sales to be more than 20% of your revenue. So if you're shooting for a $100k OTE, with $50k variable, that AE will have to bring in $500k of bookings a year to keep that cost of sales under 20%. That would mean that a commission rate of 10% would be fine in this situation, and you'd expect $42k of bookings a month, or else the rep would be let go. However, it's important that those numbers are clearly attainable, and job candidates will want to know that they're attainable. Conveniently, since you'll be such a CRM-excellent sales founder, you'll know what your win rates are and how many opps a typical rep gets a month from SDRs, and you can show that either you or others on your team are hitting their goal, making their commissions, and paying their bills.

When setting this number, you want it to be attainable to start, so look at how much you were able to sell in a given interval of time, what your win rate was on new demos, and such, and then figure out what you think that someone whose full time job is just doing demos and closing deals should be able to do. Understand that this is a work in progress, and you can characterize this to reps what the math-based rationale is behind the numbers, and note that if they go above goal, they get paid on that. Like SDRs busting through their appointment goal, AEs who have a $40k number, but are doing $60k a month is a great problem to have. It pumps them up, gets them excited to recruit others (who will be excited about an environment where they can make great money), and later on, you can choose to raise the goal to be inline with this "natural" rate of selling, once you have more data from more staff. If you can, you'll want to pay commissions on cash in the door, not bookings that then get collected over time. If your reps can sell a $10k deal for a year, and have that cash paid up front, that's great for your cash position. So if you make it clear that you pay commission when the cash comes in the door, that will create an extra bit of focus for those AEs to sell those types of deals, and not let customers negotiate for quarterly payments.

There's another approach popularized by Jason Lemkin, founder of EchoSign, who likes to hedge against potential low performers and bad hires by pushing the risk onto the rep. That is, he suggests allowing reps to make very strong upside when they execute well, provided they have covered their own costs (more on that here: https://www.saastr.com/a-framework-and-some-ideas-for-your-first-sales-comp-plan/). The broad strokes look like this—offer a competitive base, say $4k per month, or whatever the best alternative is at a comparable company. The only wrinkle here is that reps don't start making commission until they cover their own cost. That is, they have to bring in $5k (or whatever 125% of base is, to cover benefits) before there is any commission. Then, once they cover that, pay 2x the commission. That is, instead of paying 10% of a deal, push the entire 20% cost of sales to the rep. And there's one accelerator—pay 25% for cash up front. This creates a large incentive for reps to do up-front deals, because cash is king when you're a startup—it's money you don't need to take from a VC. Importantly, though, you only pay that commission upon receipt of cash, not signing of the contract. You don't want to be cutting a $10k check to a rep for a $50k deal that is paid quarterly. He gets his 20% of each paid installment. And if the account becomes a bad debt, that's on him.

Since a lot of this is a work in progress at this stage, you want to keep things flexible. And typically you want to be understanding and generous with your reps. Early on, you may have to get pulled into closing calls to be the big fricking deal. Just because you're helping out doesn't mean the rep should get paid less on the deal. Or if a company goes out of business and doesn't pay the second part of their biannual billed contract, just pay the commission. As long as you have money to support it, don't put acts of god onto the reps' shoulders.

However you structure your compensation, it's important to have a unified plan that is based on market comps and the economics of your business, not gut feel. Typically I prefer to discuss compensation with staff after concluding the interview process that authenticates them as someone we would actually want to hire. If it shows up earlier than that via candidate proactivity, I like to articulate that we pay competitive market compensation for the well-defined roles we hire for, but that we'll dig into specifics after it's clear that it's a fit on both sides, from both a competency and cultural-fit standpoint.

Equity

Part of the attraction of working at early-stage companies is the opportunity for equity upside in the event of an exit. This is typically a meaningful portion of the compensation of engineering and other non-sales staff. With sales, it can be more mixed. Generally speaking, sales is compensated with cash commensurate to the amount of revenue that is acquired. That said, there is value to instilling an "ownership" mindset in your staff.

Again, you can use market comps for this, but equity for sales staff will generally be substantially lower than for engineering or product staff. Depending on the stage of the organization, a few basis points of ownership, vested over four years, is fair. For management, charged with building an organization, this can be more generous. But the goal of sales is that the compensation you pull from your role is tied to the revenue-attainment value you bring to the organization. Eat what you kill.

Offering and Closing Candidates

In terms of offering and closing candidates, I find a two-step process helpful, a verbal offer via phone followed by a formal offer letter once I know the hire is interested in progressing. With the verbal piece, when you've concluded whether this is someone you want to bring onboard, email to let the candidate know you'd like to get on the phone to discuss outcomes. When you're on the phone, let him know the result, whether you've chosen to proceed or not.

If you're electing not to proceed, just say that the team conversed and concluded that it "wasn't a fit." Unfortunately in this litigious world, you don't want to get deeper than that, for fear that it might come back to bite you. So even if the candidate tries to dig in for more information, politely let him know that you appreciated his time, but that the conclusion when weighing input from all stakeholders was that it wasn't going to be a fit.

If you are proceeding, the approach I recommend is to let the candidate know that people were positive on him and that you'd like to proceed with an offer, if he's going to accept it. This would be the point at which you would discuss compensation, and I like to proactively state what we pay, and the rationale associated with it. Some like to see if they can get a deal and ask candidates what they are looking for first, but I find that this starts a conversation that isn't principles-based and grounded in the economics of the business. Also, if you are scaling many market development reps or account executive roles, consistency in compensation will prevent the cultural discord that can come from having varying compensation for folks executing the same role. Besides, your variable compensation helps ensure that everyone is compensated fairly for outcomes.

If you've done a good job on the interview process up to this point, and your team left the candidate fired up to work with a bunch of great folks, he will hop right on it. In that case, you can proceed to discussing start dates, and then send over an offer letter. Other times, the candidate may want to mull over the offer before agreeing, or may come back with a counteroffer. That's fine as well, but I generally prefer to get verbal agreement before sending over an offer letter for digital signature. I would prefer that the offer letter not be used as leverage against a current employer to drive a counteroffer, or a competing offer from another suitor organization. I simply say, "I only want to send over an offer letter if you're going to sign it, so will you accept this offer when I present it?"

When it comes to negotiation, I generally prefer not to do it. If the compensation being offered is principles-based, and backed by strong market comp and business economics rationale, then I prefer to state why an offer is fair. There is a large supply of qualified sales professionals in the market, and the potential issues that substantial compensation variation introduces aren't worth making an exception. With that said, if there is back and forth, you can make sure to sell other parts of the role as well—personal development, the opportunity for career progression, and if needed, you can put a role and salary review on the books six months out from start. All of these are levers that can help you close a candidate, even as you want to hold the line with sales compensation plans that are consistent and principled.

After Closing

Once you've got a signed offer in hand, move as quickly as possible to generate and maintain momentum. Try not to leave too much time between when the offer is signed and the start date. After so much time investment, you don't want second thoughts to creep in. Furthermore, try to target starting classes of staff together. More on this in the Sales Onboarding chapter, but having three, four, five SDRs or AEs starting together offers all kinds of benefits.

Use whatever time you have, though, to set your inbound hires up for a successful start—that means doing the less fun things (lining up materials for onboarding and assigning trackable pre-work) and the more fun things, like including inbound hires in team happy hours. They're not really "on the team" until they're at their desks and doing their jobs, the same way a deal isn't done till the contract is signed and the cash is in your bank account. Treat inbound hires with the same level of urgency.

Sales hiring is the engine of your organization's revenue success. Treat it seriously and methodically, aiming for high-quality staff who are well matched to the needs of your go-to-market strategy, and you will be well on your way. Treat it haphazardly, and you are sabotaging any chances you have at success.

CHAPTER 12

High-Impact Sales Onboarding & Training

INTRODUCTION

The lessons below wouldn't have been possible without Manny Ortega, Brad Snider, and Robert Perez who were instrumental in the evolution of TalentBin's onboarding methodology.

Now that you have gone and invested all this time and energy in hiring sales staff, the next step is to get the most out of your investment. You want to get new hires up to speed—selling and closing business—in the shortest amount of time possible.

WHY ONBOARDING MATTERS

In early-stage B2B sales, once you've hit product/market fit, your biggest cost is the opportunity cost from missed, or even just delayed, sales. This is especially true in greenfield markets, where the competitive landscape is only just forming and it's a true land grab. The salesperson you haven't hired yet, and haven't gotten productive yet, isn't generating the $50k, $100k, $200k a month in sales they could be. Consider the future value of those customers as they recur, proliferate, and refer other customers, and that lost revenue looks even more troubling.

Moreover, if you are losing 30%–50% of each sales hiring class to flameouts, in part due to faulty onboarding, you are eating this terrible opportunity cost again and again—not to mention the pure cost of the time, treasure, and energy put into recruiting those flamed-out reps.

This is why the lack of rigor around sales onboarding in so many organizations astounds me. You've ideally done an excellent job (and presumably spent a lot of time) screening and interviewing your new hires. Why would you then half-ass their liftoff? Why spend the time and money to get a great race car, but not tune it up, fill it with premium, and top off the tires? Why risk a failure to launch?

Yes, there is a temptation to get new hires facing customers as quickly as possible. See previous comment about opportunity cost of lost and delayed sales. This is a false economy. You will simply be burning good leads and injuring new reps' confidence and, ultimately, their chance for success. Mitch and Murray paid good money for those "Glengarry leads", and they would be wasted on your poorly onboarded staff.

If you are hiring experienced staff, there is also a temptation to rely on their ostensible expertise and let them "do their thing." But you are making false assumptions, and it will bite you. You have no idea what bad habits their past organizations have instilled in them, or what gaps there are in their knowledge of the market.

Resist the temptation to shortcut onboarding. In an evangelical, consultative sale—the kind your staff is most likely engaged in—business and product expertise is vital. Equally important are high-impact presentation and demonstration skills, persuasive objection handling, and the basic blocking and tackling of CRM, calendar, and email excellence. Relying on your staff to simply know this is a losing proposition.

Instead, design the right sales boot camp for your team—a week to two weeks of rigorous onboarding—and implement it with your newly hired classes. Every time. Depending on the complexity of your offerings, you might find that you need even longer. This boot camp should include pre-onboarding homework and acclimation to your company culture; lessons in business and market subject matter and product; tooling and process training; drilling and repetitions; and eventually ramp and monitoring.

Hire right. Enable right. Position your human capital for success. You will not be sorry.

ONBOARDING 101

So what should your boot camp look like? I prefer a "university"-style onboarding for new hires, with a singular focus on imparting the knowledge required for high-impact selling conversations. You should be hiring smart; now the goal is to fill those brains with the necessary information, and then run them through enough repetitions that muscle memory takes hold and your hires' confidence grows.

Remember, like a university, you want to be conducting this training with cohorts and classes. The traditional thinking in sales management is that you'll lose 30%–50% of each class within six months of hiring them. That statistic is frightening; I believe that with proper screening and onboarding, you can have a much higher yield. However, even if you're amazing at hiring, it's a similar amount of work to onboard four salespeople as it is to onboard one. They're all sitting there, listening to the same instructor (you), so why not force multiply? You can even give them team names and use training cohorts as a chance to foster a sense of shared identity. TalentBin classes included "Gryffindor" and "The Three Amigos," underscoring a notion of shared identity. Onboarding a class creates a sense of both competition and camaraderie that pays off—one person may miss something, but his teammate didn't, and they can help each other out. And when it comes time for sales drills, you have natural sparring partners. Hire in classes and run your onboarding as classes too.

As for your curriculum, obviously as your go-to-market strategy evolves—and you learn as you go—you'll fine-tune it. When you start out, it could simply be a really big Google Doc that you fork with each new class, highlighting sections in green as you cover them. That may eventually turn into a series of Google Docs, each linked to a Google Spreadsheet checklist to track the execution of each class. We started this way, and after a couple iterations our sales ops lead, Manny Ortega, codified a pretty curriculum in Google Docs. From there, you can go all the way up to onboarding software that tracks (in a much fancier way than a spreadsheet) the execution of each step, like Parklet or Kin. The important thing is to have a holistic set of topics to cover, and to work your way—exhaustively—through them each time, adding and removing as you go.

These are the general buckets that I have included in each iteration of my onboarding curriculum.

Pre-work

You can actually start onboarding before your hiring class's first day on the job. Whether you're hiring new grads who are "taking a break" before starting their first job as a market development rep (I'm partial to this) or pulling new sales reps into the organization from a similar role at a different company, new hires will often have a certain amount of excitement and momentum headed towards your organization. Capitalize on that by assigning a not-insignificant amount of work ahead of time, to better prepare them to hit the ground running when they arrive.

Pre-work has the added benefit of ensuring that new hires are tracking correctly and won't fall victim to cold feet, or counteroffers from their existing employers. They're not truly hired till their butts are in seats on your sales floor, so engaging them even before they arrive helps.

What manner of pre-work should you assign? It depends on what materials you have available, but a mixture of readings, presentations, and recordings is good. For instance, because we record our demos at TalentBin, we have a library of "awesome calls" and "terrible calls," organized by customer type (enterprise vs. mid-market vs. SMB, and staffing agencies of varying sizes); I ask new hires to watch a set of those ahead of time. You might include any recorded feature demo videos or webinars; if you have a support portal with video content, that could work too. Just provide new hires a set of hyperlinks to work through (and don't rely on the abstract "go review these materials").

If there are particular readings that are appropriate, assign those. For instance, there are some "technical recruiting for nontechnical recruiters" books on the market, which TalentBin has used to put together a course reader of sorts. You could also just assemble an assortment of hyperlinks from relevant blog posts. If there are any whole books that your organization is partial to, assign those. I'm a big fan of The Goal, to get sales staff into a goal-oriented, deductive-reasoning mindset, and Getting Things Done, to stimulate an office-efficiency mindset, and The Score Takes Care of Itself as an introduction to the importance of sales precursor behaviors being connected to outcomes. Just be sure that everything you assign is high quality and relevant; mere busywork sets the wrong tone and feels like a chore. Also be mindful of the total amount of pre-work you assign, relative to how much time your hires have before their first day. Ten hours of work over two weeks is probably a fine amount.

Lastly, they should know that their execution will be monitored and audited. (Just like CRM! Welcome to sales!) You need to say, "Here's this. It's not optional. It's important. There will be a test." Deliver the materials in a manner that allows you to openly track progress, and which they know you have the ability to track. This can be as easy as sharing them in a Google Doc and instructing new hires to highlight the sections as they complete them.

Don't forget, there is pre-work for you too. When your new staffer shows up on day one, their first impression is what will start them on the right, or wrong, foot. Make sure that all of their technical infrastructure (laptop, monitor, mouse, etc.) is in place, and at least cursorily set up. Provide any other materials they're expected to make use of in their day to day. (I'm a fan of lab notebooks—graph paper, clearly—high-quality pens, Post-it notes, pen cup, etc.) And if you have it (and you should), put out some quality schwag, like a company T-shirt, sweatshirt, travel coffee mug, water bottle, etc. A new staffer's desk should look like the organization was waiting for them with bated breath, and executed preparations accordingly. It should say, "We're glad you're here. This is how we do things. You will too."

Standard Administrative Work

Of course, there will be all manner of standard forms that you need to take care of, like W-2s, payroll setup, direct deposit, any stock 83(b) forms, and so forth. I recommend setting aside time for side-by-side execution with each new hire to get this out of the way. Unfamiliar forms can be confusing, which is unpleasant for new hires and risks casting a pall over the rest of your onboarding. Crank out the paperwork so you can move on to the important stuff.

Cultural Onboarding

Acclimating your new hires to your company's values isn't just a single conversation; it's the way you demonstrate how your organization executes, what is celebrated, and what is censured. This is the case during onboarding, but also day to day. However, I find it important to have a proactive, explicit, candid discussion of what is valued within your sales organization, and what is not okay.

For instance, in the TalentBin sales organization, we lived by three key tenets:

1. You don't have to be an engineer to operate with an engineering mindset.

2. We are the product managers of our sales organization.

3. Intellectual honesty is paramount.

We explain them to new hires as follows:

Because the sales team grew out of the engineering and product organization and was built by a non-sales person, and because for much of TalentBin's early existence, we were leanly capitalized and had to make do with fewer humans, heavily leveraged with technology—we like to say that we have an "engineering mindset." That is, our approach is to identify constraints, propose solutions, test them, and then either reject or embrace the outcome. Rinse, repeat.

Similarly, because there are only so many things we can work on at one time, we have to prioritize resolving identified issues based on their impact on revenue. We refer to "features" of the sales organization, whether process, tooling, or materials, and hold ourselves responsible for "product managing" the sales organization in this conceptual frame.

Lastly, TalentBin itself was the child of initial failed product hypotheses and subsequent pivots toward success. The organization is highly aware of both the perils of sticking your head in the sand and the benefits of eyes-wide-open self-assessment, regardless of the outcome. We value intellectual honesty in the sales organization, just as you might in an engineering organization.

Your organization may share these tenets, or you may have your own. But the important thing is to proactively state them as a baseline during your onboarding process.

Better, of course, to start articulating these tenets in your hiring process. For starters, once you've identified your organization's values, you can look and screen for candidates that exhibit them. By articulating how you roll from the get-go, you can also excite potential hires for whom those tenets are compelling and allow bad fits to disqualify themselves.

Finally, a great way to contextualize the important pieces of your culture is to frame them in your organizational history. As in, "this is where we started, this is where we've gone, this is where we are, and this is where we're going." A robust review of the organization's path (both your company's and the sales team's specifically) is important in and of itself for cultural onboarding, but can also be a useful way to underscore key themes.

Business and Market Subject-Matter Onboarding

It's likely that your organization will be selling an innovative solution that, while it fits into an existing market, is a substantial departure from existing products.

Because your sales staff will be engaged in presenting this new, less proven solution in a evangelical and consultative fashion, they will need to be expert in the market, business drivers, and technical realities of your solution. They need to be able to sell authoritatively, interacting with customers as equals, not just vendors.

All of the above speaks to the importance of a rigorous general subject-matter onboarding process.

When you start out, it should be sufficient to simply cover this training with basic materials (slides, and so on). As you scale, though, you may find it valuable to construct a testing harness that ensures reps are retaining material or, if they're not, requires them to re-review the materials before they "test out." Early on, this is likely not necessary. But if you're trying to onboard 500 sales reps, distributed across geographies, it's kinda required.

You may have additions, but the subject-matter buckets we focus on at TalentBin are Market Understanding, Business Driver Understanding, and Technical Understanding.

Market Understanding

There's very little chance that your solution operates in a vacuum, so it's important for your staff to understand the market. What is the field in which your solution operates? How has it evolved over time? What are the big epochs of technology that have impacted the market? What is the current state of the market, and who are the major solution vendors that operate in your space—especially those that are tangential to your solution?

For instance, if you work in the human capital management market, you would want to cover job boards, recruiting workflow software, and even downstream solutions like HCM cloud suites that include onboarding, learning and development, and performance management stories.

Or if you work in the sales automation/customer relationship management space, it would be important to cover marketing automation and campaign management solutions in front of your solution, other CRM players (past and present), and various add-ons, along with downstream finance and enterprise resource planning solutions.

You don't want a customer who asks how your solution interfaces with a tangential workflow solution ("How do these candidates get into our applicant tracking system?") to be met with silence across the phone line.

Our training includes a full hour session on the history and state of the art of the talent acquisition space as impacted by the Internet, including job boards, applicant tracking systems, large recruiting agencies, professional social networks, and the large HCM and recruiting workflow players that all work together.

Business Driver Understanding

Relatedly, you also want to ensure that your staff understands the key business drivers that your solution is addressing. How does your client's business work, what are the key cost and revenue levers, and how do solutions covered in the market review impact them? How does this calculus change for different segments or verticals that you address? What are the common metrics by which these business drivers are measured? And where does your solution fit into this puzzle (more on this later in the detailed product training)?

For instance, if you are selling to the recruiting market, then it's important to know all the things that will be important to your client: number of inbound candidates, quality of candidate, response rate of candidates, cost per hire, time to hire, quality of hire, and hiring funnel drop-off (from engagement to phone screen to interview to offer). For staffing agencies, which are focused on earning fees from client placements, metrics around new candidates discovered, outreach per day, submittals per week, and eventually placements will be the key metrics. If your solution can increase amount of outreach in a given amount of time, increase response rates of candidates, increase submittals, reduce cost of hire, or reduce time to hire, and do so by substantially more than its cost, you're in business.

If you're in the sales and marketing automation space, the key metrics might be number of qualified leads per week, cost per lead, calls per day, presentations per rep per week, close rates, bookings per rep per month, and so on.

Whatever space you're in, the first step to being able to have a consultative conversation with a potential client is to understand the base economics of their business.

The way that we achieved this at TalentBin was by having one of our sales team, Brad Snider—a former technical recruiter—give a rundown on all things recruiting in a live hour-long class. We called it "The Brad Class." It was always awesome because Brad knew his stuff cold and was a great storyteller (which makes for a great sales rep too!). The class covered in-house recruiting, agency recruiting, recruitment process outsourcing (RPO) recruiting, and the key parts of the recruiting cycle, plus business drivers for each. Later we recorded it, and have had hundreds of sales reps and customer success staff watch (and be tested) on it.

However you want to approach training, just make sure that you're preparing your staff with a base-level understanding of the business drivers they're working with. Their understanding won't be perfect, but it will provide groundwork for them to build on as they have more sales conversations.

Technical Understanding

As a founder or senior executive on your team, you likely have extensive technical understanding of your space. But this will certainly not be the case with all of the reps that you hire. (Ideally you're hiring for this acumen, though.) Just as you need to ensure that your team understands the market and your clients' business drivers, you need to familiarize them with the key technological drivers in your space too.

For instance, TalentBin is a great technical recruiting solution. However, not every sales rep we hire (and not every recruiter we sell to) will have the technical underpinnings, to start, to understand that Java and JavaScript are not the same thing. If you work in, say, storage, nontechnical staff might not immediately understand the differences between spinning hard drives and flash, storage area networks (SANs) and network attached storage (NAS).

The important thing is not to cover each and every technical component out there, but to focus on the most important terms and innovations. Again, your goal is to provide a base layer of information for reps to build on—the understanding to engage in consultative and authoritative conversations with prospects from the get-go.

The way we handle this at TalentBin relates specifically to technical recruiting. Ensuring that our staff knows the difference between a front-end technology and a back-end technology, SQL and NoSQL, or scripting and compiled languages makes them much better sales staff. I want my team to have compelling conversations with their technical recruiting prospects—oftentimes, they are more authoritative and grounded than the folks they are selling to.

Product and Presentation Onboarding

There's a reason we've made it this far into the chapter before we even started talking about the specifics of your product and how to present it. Your solution exists in the context of a larger market, and it's critical for reps to understand that before you delve into your particular solution. One builds on the other, and if you start in on your solution before your staff understands the problem space, they'll be seriously hampered in presenting it in a persuasive, high-impact fashion.

But once that foundation is in place, take the time to give new staff a thorough education in your product, and how it should be presented to the market.

Initial Product Walk-Through

Rather than diving right into training on the pure sales presentation and customer-facing demo, I like to start by giving staff a less formal product walkthrough. Specifically, we look at all the key elements of the product, correlating them to use cases for our users, all while speaking to the business drivers each feature addresses.

To achieve the above, you can use an abridged version of your customer-facing demo (the structure for which I address in much more detail in the "Building Your Materials" chapter).

As with other topics, this product walk-through can simply be presented to new staff, or, in a more scaled onboarding environment, it can be tested on too, with quizzing software.

Sales Presentation and Segments

Once you've walked through the product, you're ready to move on to a more formal sales presentation training. Because of the pre-work that you've assigned, which ideally included recordings of your sales presentation and demo, your reps should already be familiar with your approach. The goal of this class is both to do a one-on-one (or one-on-group, if you have a class of four reps, say) presentation and to contextualize the different "chapters" of your presentation.

Your presentation *should* have chapters, with individual slides supporting the general thrust of each one. Go through these chapters with your new hires, contextualizing the intention of each, and explain how your slides support those goals. This will be important later in your onboarding process, when you start drills and repetitions. (For more detail on sales presentation construction, refer to "Build Your Materials" chapter section on that.)

Customer-Facing Demo and Demo Segments

Having completed this more formal sales presentation breakdown, I like to train reps on the various segments of an actual sales demo. This is different than the initial walk-through; it's a mock demonstration—live, to the class—in the style you would use with a customer.

Like your sales presentation, your demo ought to have sections—dedicated to presenting the various parts of the product that resolve the business pains you're attacking—and those sections should flow logically. Take this opportunity to contextualize each section for the class. As in "the point of this section is to demonstrate features A, B, and C, which are designed to help the user do X, Y, and Z, which solves business pain M, N, and O." Do this for each section while the team follows along, asks questions, and takes notes.

Often new sales reps who haven't made a strong connection between the features they are presenting and the business pains they aim to solve will end up presenting features in a "and now we have this, and now we have this, and over here we have this" fashion, without connecting them to use cases. This makes for a wholly uncompelling demo that relies on the prospect to make that association—which they may, but there's no reason to risk that. The goal of this class is to set the groundwork for presentation and demo drilling, and to give new reps a framework for presenting features and functionality in the most compelling fashion possible.

Objection Handling

One thing that I don't spend much time on during onboarding is objection handling. That is, you will hear a myriad of potential objections from your prospects, so trying to go through them all is a losing proposition. Instead, try to fold in common objections or prospect confusion throughout the rest of the sections of onboarding—presentation, demo, and so on. Keeping an exhaustive list of common objections for reference is certainly helpful, and letting reps know where it lives and how to use it is helpful too. But you need not tackle each one at this juncture.

Competition

Depending on the amount of competition in your market, dedicating a section of onboarding to reviewing the competitive landscape can be useful. I suggest tackling this after the market landscape, business driver, technology, and product sections, because there will then be a conceptual framework in place for reps to understand key differences between competitors. Ideally you already have competitive product marketing materials in place, so utilize them for this class.

TOOLS & PROCESS ONBOARDING

While cultural, market, business driver, and product expertise onboarding lays the foundation for sales rep success, it's important to not underestimate the importance of training in the nuts and bolts of tools and process.

The modern sales rep ought to be a software-enabled, highly levered professional. An average day will include office basics like email and calendaring and sales standards like Salesforce.com, all the way to more advanced software like email open and click tracking and presentation software like Showpad. If you simply assume your staff understands how to use the tools you provide, and use them well, you run the risk of setting them up to underperform.

Provisioning & Configuration

An often-overlooked part of onboarding is simply the provisioning of the proper tools for success. You might be chuckling to yourself, wondering how that could possibly be overlooked, but you'd be surprised how often it happens.

Before your new hires show up, make sure that you have purchased all the equipment your existing staff is expected to use in their day to day—even better if you already have a Google Spreadsheet listing all the pieces of hardware and software that will need to be set up (ideally with a hyperlink to the item on Amazon, for easy ordering in the future).

For us at TalentBin, this amounts to a desk (sitting or standing), chair (yes, seriously, this basic—I've seen new hires show up to find that there's no chair ready for them) or standing foot pad and task stool, laptop, external monitor, laptop stand, keyboard, mouse (with navigation buttons for rapid browsing), mouse pad, desk phone, and headset, all the way down to lab notebook (graph paper preferred), pen cup, and high-quality pens.

This level of specificity may seem odd, but it all comes down to equipping for expectations. TalentBin sales staff are expected to use their lab notebooks to record discovery question results and other notes from every call for later transfer to Salesforce.com—so providing lab notebooks and high-quality, pleasurable rolling ball pens is the first step. If they don't do it, there's no excuse; the very existence of the equipment reinforces the expectation. Same with standing pads, headsets, and so forth. If you have an expectation for high performance, equip for it and train for it. The salary expense of quality sales staff far outstrips the capital cost of a quality headset, pens, and monitors—and the opportunity cost of lost $10,000 deals certainly far outstrips any of these other expenses.

Pre-provision your staff's software too, so you can get down to actual value-adding onboarding activities faster. We will get into configuration in a second; I recommend holding off on that and tackling it in a group setting. But for things that can be stood up ahead of time, do it. It demonstrates to your staff a mindset of preparedness. At TalentBin, this meant that every new sales rep was ready to go with a Google Apps identity, a Salesforce account, an Act-On sales account for Salesforce, Yesware for email open and click tracking from Gmail, ClearSlide and InsideSales.com's Click to Call for account executives, InsideSales.com's PowerDialer for market development reps, and RingCentral phone accounts. Typically, you can quickly provision these software offerings from a single administrator dashboard. Also, make sure to add new staffers to all relevant recurring meetings—like your sales team meeting, standups, all hands, one-on-ones, and pipeline meetings.

Lastly, and I mentioned this in Cultural Onboarding, is schwag—shirts, hoodies, water bottles, coffee mugs, pint glasses, pens, Post-its. (And for morale and customer-relations reasons, not marketing reasons, I recommend investing in schwag.) Make sure that these items are present and accounted for on your new hires' desks on their start dates.

Not only does pre-provisioning make your onboarding more efficient, it sets the tone from the moment your hires show up—you mean business and have a culture of preparation and execution, from hardware to software to T-shirts.

While pre-provisioning equipment and accounts is efficient, I recommend stopping short of meaningful configuration, largely because it's often more efficient to have four or five people in a conference concurrently setting up, say, their email signatures than for you to do it individually. The act of configuration can also be an important first step in training your staff to get the most out of the tools you provide.

As with your hardware and software provisioning checklist, it's crucial to codify your configuration steps in a Google Spreadsheet. Simply block off an hour or two, and with your newly onboarding cohort, walk down the list, configuring as relevant and speaking briefly about usage. For instance, at TalentBin, these "configuration parties" include:

Google Chrome setup (and proper bookmarking)

Gmail setup: creating email signatures and turning on keyboard shortcuts, "undo send," "send and archive," auto-advance, and other enablers of inbox zero

Adding browser and Gmail plug-ins, like Rapportive, Yesware (along with BCC to CRM setup) and some of our custom developed plug-ins for lead generation

Voice mail setup for phone

Jing for screenshotting and screen-casting

Setting up corporate email on iPhone or Android

A demo environment in the product they'll be selling

You'll customize your own list as you go. The point is simply that you shouldn't leave it up to the reps to do it by themselves. It either won't be done, or will be done poorly.

Training: Basic Tools

After configuration is complete, it's time for pure tool training. If you have given your staff a tool to use, and expect them to use it, you need to train on it (and the cost of that training should be baked into any purchase decisions). Assuming they know how to use it is a recipe for disaster. But it's also important to recognize that you're never going to cover everything, and mastering these tools is a process. You're just laying the groundwork, and setting your reps up for better adoption.

And when I say you should cover all the tools your staff is expected to use, I mean all—from the most basic to the more advanced.

Browser

When you're hiring staff that may be fresh out of college, office basics—ones that may be standard for someone who's been in the industry for five years—will actually be quite foreign. Similarly, if you're hiring more senior staff, you never know what sort of bad habits they may have, or what their prior employers failed to train on.

At TalentBin, the basics we cover start with the browser. (Yes. This basic.) Our team standardizes on Google Chrome because of its speed and broad plug-in support. We train on the "Getting Things Done" mindset: closing tabs that are no longer needed (to clear cruft from one's workspace); creating a new window for a new "task" that may spawn new tabs (to avoid the case of dozens of confusing tabs, and a confused sales rep); closing windows when a task is complete; and mastering a variety of keyboard shortcuts. In a nutshell, we include anything that will make our reps more efficient and save them from distracting off-ramps from execution.

Email for Sales

Basics training extends to Gmail and calendaring as well. Email is extremely powerful, and extremely dangerous when misused. In sales, it's a great way to create multiple touchpoints with clients in a scaled way, to deliver impactful collateral, and to juggle many concurrent conversations in a way that is documented and CRM-able. It can also be a massive time suck, and without discipline, your reps' inboxes will become a disaster of erroneous, unimportant emails ("Would you like at attend DreamForce!?!?!?! Click here!") mixed in with extremely high-value client communications ("Can you send me a contract for 10 seats?").

The "Getting Things Done" notion applies to email too. The idea that, if there's not a next action on an email, you should archive it and get it out of your inbox is a new concept for most reps. Teach it (and later, audit it—when I come up to a rep and they have an already-read, not important email still in their inbox, they hear about it), and connect that lesson to the additional functionality in Gmail that you should have turned on in your configuration party. (This works with Outlook as well. Remove all email push notifications that lead to treating email as instant message, and train reps to close their email and work out of their CRM and calendar—their actual to-do lists.)

Train on well-written emails. Show reps how to write clear, topical subject lines (no, not "Quick Question" or "Hi"); how to use CC appropriately and reply-all to ensure thread continuity; and how to compose messages that have sufficient white space for readability, use bold, bullets, and headings to identify key sections of an email, and ensure that individuals being responded to are properly called out. Show how to write for searchability (that is, so you can easily recall a message from your Gmail archive). Show how to proofread, and set expectations around rigor and grammatical excellence in client-facing communication. (Ideally you screened for this in hiring, but it's good to reiterate.) Make it clear that these factors will be audited in the CRM as all email communications to clients are captured.

Train on a templating mindset. Common, repeated, sales communications take up a disproportionate portion of a rep's time, so templating can be a massive time saver, and reduce errors (grammatical, otherwise). Helping reps embrace this (by both example and explicit statement) will make this top of mind. After onboarding, continue to demonstrate this by providing templates for new product releases, but also by encouraging reps to create their own. Create a culture of template sharing—most reps will have the same needs, and a tool created by Rep A will likely apply to Reps B, C, and D. Just make sure templates aren't stored in email, but in a common repository for recall and access.

Lastly, train on keystroke shortcuts. Gmail's keystrokes are amazing. You turned them on in your configuration party, now train reps on how to use them: *J* or *K* to navigate up and down their inbox respectively, *X* to rapidly select unimportant emails, and *E* to archive them are extremely helpful for maintaining a clean inbox. *C* to compose a new email, *Command + Enter* to send it, *Enter* to open a message, *R* to reply to it, and *G + I* to get to your inbox will help reps be quick and efficient with their communications and drive more outreach and response in a given time period. Print out the Gmail shortcut cheat sheet and provide it to all your reps. All of this will not only keep them from being lost in Inbox Hell (and losing contracts in there), but make them email ninjas.

Calendaring for Sales

With sales, all you have is your time. Training on calendar excellence should not be overlooked. This comes down to two things—using your calendar to manage others (prospects) and using your calendar to manage yourself.

Many first-time staff will be unfamiliar with the notion of sending meeting invites, and that the sending, confirmation, and declining of those invites is an important part of enterprise sales. So show them how this is done, and what to include in a compelling calendar invite: venue information in the "Where," a clear and actionable title, and agenda items in the body (what is to be covered?), along with a repetition of venue specifics (Zoom link, join.me, phone bridge, etc.). Setting expectations here will lead your staff to better meetings and fewer cancellations.

Relatedly, teaching calendar hygiene is important to ensuring that your staff manages their time well. That includes the removal of items that are not relevant to free up time slots for meetings (especially important if you have market development reps setting appointments on account executive calendars); proper prep and follow-up blocks for meetings (going from meeting to meeting to meeting is a great way of ensuring you don't record or execute your follow-up actions); and even blocking stretches of pure follow-up time for mid-pipeline management and inbox maintenance. Teach the idea of "painting the calendar," whereby you book, block by block, the entirety of your day so you can make sure you're spending time on the correct things. That will keep your reps spending their time on the most important things they can, rather than bouncing through their days in a less directed fashion (or, worst of all, as directed by their email inboxes).

Training: Sales-Specific Tools

Once you've covered the basics, move to the sales-specific tool chain. This is where you may end up with more variation in what you need to cover. However, there are some important common denominators.

CRM

The basis of any high-performance sales organization will be excellent use of CRM, as it is the central hub for activity, efficiency, and reporting. Every time I help out a sales organization that's on the rocks, invariably so many of their issues come back to CRM fragility. We use Salesforce, so I'll largely tailor this conversation around that (but you can easily swap it for your own preferred CRM).

From the start, make it clear that "If it's not in Salesforce, it doesn't count." If you are basing reporting, activity tracking, and so forth out of Salesforce, it needs to be clear that if a demo happens outside of Salesforce it doesn't count. Or get paid. If emailing happens that isn't BCC'd into Salesforce, it doesn't count. Set this expectation now, and audit and demonstrate it consistently.

Data Model

For many reps, the data model of CRM is confusing. Accounts, contacts, opportunities, leads, activities. If they're new to sales, this will be foreign. Even if they're coming out of a prior sales role, there's so much muddiness around these things that you can't rely on existing understanding. So make sure to go through the basic concepts (on the whiteboard) of accounts, how contacts are children of accounts, that an opportunity is a "unit of potential commerce" with an account, and how activities are used to record information about interactions between sales reps and customers, but also as to-dos for future activities. Show how to create the various objects, and the important fields associated with them—like projected revenue and stage for opportunities, size of total opportunity ("size of prize") in an account, contact information and title in contact, and so forth. Cover how to properly disposition items, like marking demo events as "held" and recording pertinent notes, retiring tasks, and noting closed won and closed lost opportunities.

Key Reports and Task Views

If you have specific reports or dashboards that are key to your reps' execution, make sure to go through them and ensure that they are sufficiently bookmarked. An example would be Salesforce's console viewer, which allows for easy task viewing and execution (for to-dos that need action). Examples of key reports could be specific pipeline reports set up so reps can view what opportunities they have open in what stage, or error-checking reports that help reps see open opportunities without sufficient activity, or demos or tasks in unexecuted states.

Sales-Enabled Email

There are a variety of sales-specific email tools on the market, some of which were covered in prior sections more completely. At TalentBin, we use the Act-On marketing automation suite, and each of our reps has Act-On email integrated directly into Salesforce for templating, open and click tracking, and mass mailing. We also use Yesware for BCC'ing to Salesforce, open and click tracking, and templating integrated directly into Gmail. And we use iHance for "catching" and pushing to Salesforce inbound emails from prospects.

Whatever the tool chain you have set up, the important concepts to cover with sales-enabled email are BCC'ing to Salesforce for record keeping, templating and mass mailing for efficiency, and open and click tracking for deal insights.

Demonstrate how BCC'ing into your CRM works for ease of recording deal progress, and how email activity is recorded and reported to track rep activity levels. Demonstrate how templates work—why they are there, which ones are available for your team, and how to create new ones, or request that new ones are made. Show how mass mailing works out of Salesforce views, and the pertinent use cases (for instance, sending a targeted "check out this new feature" email to mid-funnel opportunities). Demonstrate open and click tracking, and what it's good for—for MDRs, that's seeing how their cold outreach is being received and for account executives, it's understanding whether follow-up collateral is being engaged with and shared around the prospect organization.

Presentation Software

If your organization has invested in sales-specific, or even generic, presentation software, like Zoom, WebEx, join.me, and so forth, make sure you cover common cases. (And if you haven't invested in presentation software, you should rethink that decision.) At TalentBin, we used ClearSlide, so we covered how to send ClearSlide meeting room credentials via calendar invite or email, how to use the standard slide decks or clone and modify decks, how to execute live screenshares, how to record pitches for later audit or to send to contacts that missed the presentation, and how to execute post-presentation follow-up, like sending instrumented deck hyperlinks to prospects and proper dispositioning of demo notes.

Power Dialing Software

If your organization has power dialing software set up for top-of-funnel activity by market development reps, or mid-funnel follow-up by account executives or account managers, cover the common use cases there as well. At TalentBin, we use InsideSales.com's PowerDialer to enable our MDRs to quickly cycle through lists of prospects, making calls, leaving pre-recorded voice mails, sending follow-up emails (PowerDialer integrates with Act-On's emailing), and quickly dispositioning tasks. And our account executives use InsideSales.com's "Click to Call" to quickly reach contacts directly from Salesforce and easily disposition tasks and notes directly from that console.

You may have other key sales-specific tools that I haven't covered, and you're also not going to be able to handle every single case during training. (Even if you do, your reps won't retain it; they'll need to learn through doing.) The important thing is to ensure that your reps understand the goal of each piece of equipment, where it fits in their process, and its key workflows.

Sales Cycle and Cadence

While training on tools is important, it's equally important that new reps understand how and when to use those tools in the sales cycle. Make sure that you fully cover the specifics of your sales organization's process and cadence.

Different products have different enterprise sales cycles, based on how the typical customer purchases, the size of the average contract value, budgetary cycles, and more. Walk new reps through the sales tempo for your product: How long does it typically take to close a deal? Is it a bottoms-up or a tops-down sales approach? Or a combination? Who is responsible for what part of the sales cycle? Does market development set appointments, and with whom? Or are account executives responsible for the full cycle? Does a sale typically require multiple presentations, or is it more of a "one call close" sort of cycle? Does it involve trials or pilots? At what point should a rep know that the deal is not going to happen and close the opportunity to make room for more productive uses of time?

Also cover the cadence of your sales organization. Having a solid weekly, monthly, and quarterly cadence is the cornerstone of a grounded, focused team. Whatever your team's rhythm—meetings, standups, team meetings, pipeline meetings, all-hands, even happy hours—review it, and the goals associated with each get-together.

At TalentBin, our cadence includes once-weekly hour-long sales team meetings on Mondays to review the previous week's stats and revenue progress, and to share product and customer success progress, team wins (things they're stoked on), and learnings (mistakes from the week before to help others avoid); twice-daily standups (just before lunch, and at close of business) to check in on activity, wins and learnings; once-weekly hour-long pipeline meeting to review deals, drive accountability, and get team feedback; a once-monthly company all-hands; and a weekly happy hour at close of business on Friday. And the cycle begins anew after the weekend.

DRILLING, REPETITIONS, & SHADOWING

One of the things that I have seen sales organizations really drop the ball on when it comes to onboarding and training is the repetition and practice of key actions. The irony of this, of course, is that sales teams are usually full of former athletes and often analogize themselves to sports teams. But somehow they forget that practice is as important—often more important—than the actual games. Presenting information from slides, even with testing, is not sufficient. No way. Drilling and repetitions, paired "sparring," and shadowing are all critical to ensure your reps develop muscle memory before they go live.

Group Drilling & Repetitions

The biggest thing your reps are going to need to drill is their demo and presentation. They can (and will) learn on the job, but there's no reason to burn through actual, valid opportunities as they do so.

During your presentation and demo onboarding, you went through each "chapter" of the presentation and demo, step by step. Now, have each rep do the same thing. I prefer to do this in the class setting, with each person presenting each chapter of the presentation or demo, and then stopping to get feedback from the instructor (you) and the rest of the team. It's a slow process—that's why you only do it once—but it really drills the heck out of the material.

Sparring

When you're done with the group drilling and repetitions, split the class up into groups of two for what I refer to as "sparring." Time-intensive, per-section drilling is good as a baseline, but after that, it's going to take a series of mock presentations to really nail the material. I have each pair trade off as presenter and prospect. And while you might think that the individual playing the prospect is really just there as a static foil, it's actually a very important part of the training; they are being forced to think and react like a prospect—to inhabit the mind of their eventual counterpart in the sales cycle—which will in turn make them a better consultative sales professional. This can be done both with presentations and negotiation calls (account executives) and with pure cold-calling for lead generation (market development reps). And, of course, run your sparring in full "game situation" mode, using whatever tools reps would use in their day to day—that is, not sitting in a room looking at each other, but using the phone, presentation software, etc. that they will use when facing prospects.

Pair Programming/Ride-Alongs

Generally speaking, I'm not a fan of the notion of "riding along" on calls to learn. This can be done outside of selling hours (or even ahead of onboarding) with recorded calls (as assigned in the pre-work). However, there is something to be said for following along as full cycle workflow is executed. One of the things we do for onboarding is what we call "pair programming," where a new hire is paired for a day with a seasoned individual in their role, and follows key workflows in a "production" environment. For market development reps, this would be sitting at the desk with other market development reps as they go shopping for prospects to call, review and execute their tasks for the day, or rip down a calling list, firing off follow-up emails or setting an actual demo. For account executives, a ride-along could be sitting in on an initial or follow-up call, or participating in pipeline management and maintenance.

Bluebirding, Ramp, and Monitoring

All the training and drilling in the world is great, but when new reps come into contact with live opportunities, it is by no means the time to let up on your onboarding focus.

There are three things I recommend to ensure that all the investment you have made to date pays off as the rep goes live: bluebirding, proactive call review, and KPI tracking.

Bluebirding, Throwaways, and Teaming

When account executives are just getting started, assign them "bluebird" opportunities—that is, opportunities that have a high likelihood of closing. Usually these will be ones that come inbound (through lead-capture forms, which naturally have the highest purchasing intent) and have strong qualification characteristics.

But putting these bluebirds on the rep's plate isn't sufficient. Generally, I like to team with reps on early calls, or have another senior rep team with them—not to run the call, but simply to offer backup in the event that they runs into something that they doesn't think they can handle. Often, the pure availability of backup, coupled with the strong prep to date, makes it unnecessary.

But be sure not to jump into a call if the rep just isn't hitting messaging at an A+ level; you're there only in the event that the wheels come off, not to correct slight wobbles. I also find it very helpful for reps to have a printed script of the sales presentation and demo on their desks as they execute calls, even if it's just the major buckets—not so they can follow along in minute detail, but so they can make sure they don't miss any key parts. And if they get knocked sideways, they can quickly look down, see where they should be, and regain their footing.

The converse of this strategy is throwaways. There are all manner of leads that will come inbound that are unqualified. In TalentBin's case, these are organizations that don't have sufficient technical hiring requirements, or don't have recruiters in house to do proactive, passive-candidate recruiting. Generally speaking, assigning these unqualified opportunities to a sales rep would be a waste of time, as compared to the other, valid opportunities on which they could be working. However, in an onboarding use case, these can be helpful practice demos; the rep knows that it's not a qualified lead, and isn't under a ton of pressure for fear of losing a potential sale.

This can cut both ways, though, in that it's important that the rep treat it as a real call—that is, go through discovery and qualification questions, and "discover" that the opportunity is not qualified. In these cases, I recommend that reps offer to do an abbreviated presentation for the prospect, in the event that their situation changes down the road (for instance, they move to an organization more focused on technical recruiting). As you can see, these presentations are an expensive form of practice, as they not only consume rep time that could be spent on valid opportunities, but also occupy the time of a customer that is unlikely to close (that is, it's not 100% respectful of the client's time). That said, a few of these can be helpful in getting the rep set up for success.

Proactive and Ambient Call Review

After these initial bluebirds and throwaways, though, teaming is an extremely expensive form of training and audit, and one that I believe sales managers use far more than they should. It robs sales leaders of time they could spend actually managing—consuming product and program materials, distributing information to teams, building and managing leveraged processes, and auditing and enforcing existing processes. It's often a form of managerial laziness that masquerades as productivity. However, there are strategies for achieving the goal of call review without the time cost of sitting in on new hire sales calls.

In our organization, we would record all sales calls using ClearSlide's online presentation system (and join.me, WebEx, and others have similar functionality - and the modern version of these are Chorus and Gong). This way, at any point, we can pull a recording and listen to it, after the fact. Even that would be time costly, though, so instead we require reps to surface to the team (at standups) when they've had a particularly awesome or particularly heinous call—institutionalizing the practice of sharing. For the awesome calls, we pull the recording and put it in a hall of fame, to be used for future onboarding; for the heinous ones, we discuss them and, if needed, listen to them to see where the wheels came off.

Beyond formal reviews, there are the ambient ones. As a sales manager, you should situate your desk centrally in your org so you can hear what's going on. Or walk around; take your laptop or smart phone and sit in a different part of the office, listening while you work there. Most of the time, you'll just go about your normal tasks. But you'll be attuned to oral distress and pick up any issues, which you can either note for coaching after the fact or address in the moment with a helpful Post-it note dropped on the rep's desk, pointing out a direction they can think about going. (It's important to characterize to reps that these are suggestions, and not mandates, lest they become flustered over including something that isn't relevant if your assumption is wrong.)

These proactive and ambient reviews, coupled with a culture of sharing and learning, will ensure that you catch issues early. Don't risk leaving them hidden (whether from lack of visibility, or actual obfuscation driven by embarrassment.) You'll see that rep confidence ramps quickly through early wins.

KPI Tracking and One-on-Ones

Lastly, as your new hires ramp, you can dial down the amount of high-touch monitoring and coaching and start relying on the core set of KPIs you use to monitor performance across your entire sales team. These would be things like hold rates for demos set by MDRs, win/lost ratios for account executives (although, depending on your sales cycle, this may be a lagging indicator of problems), and signifiers of health or concern at the top of the funnel, like activity levels and stuck opportunities.

While your team cadence should already pick up these indicators of health or distress, take extra time to check in on new reps' KPIs to make sure they are tracking correctly. And always cover these, and get rep feedback on how they are actually feeling, in your standard (ideally every-other-week) one-on-one meetings.

ONGOING LEARNING & DEVELOPMENT

One thing about onboarding is that it can feel like when you're done with it, and a rep or class of reps is up and running and success, you're "done" with the learning and training. While onboarding is the most intensive period of learning and development, ignore ongoing investment in that at your peril. Not only can reps continue to get better with better coaching, it's key for professional development, retention, and promotion. Further, it's unlikely that your product and the market will remain static. As your product changes, and the market in which it operates changes, your reps will need to be updated, and then tested on this new information, so they can be just as sharp as when they exited onboarding, however many months or years ago.

Cadenced Coaching & Professional Development

Just like you had a structured calendar for onboarding reps, whether SDRs, AEs, or AMs, you'll want to do the same for ongoing learning and development. At TalentBin, we had an hour blocked at the end of the day on Friday that was specifically for this. SDRs took the time to do drilling with their management and each other to work on objection handling, messaging review, or demo practice (which wasn't something that was important for their day to day, but was part of professional development, and had the added benefit of making them more confident and competent in their prospect-facing interactions, regardless.) AEs would use this time to work with their managers and teammates on different parts of their sales motions, whether it was discovery, presentation, objection handling, negotiation and so on. But the important part was that the time was on the calendar, and as such, would be prioritized.

Ensuring that this time is well used is particularly important for SDRs. The ability to hire, onboarding, and train up SDRs to the point where they can be revenue-generating AEs is an extremely valuable skill for an organization to have. It's a sort of enterprise value sales alchemy, where through smart recruiting, onboarding, and training, you can turn copper into silver into gold. This also keeps your cost of hire and sales down, in that you'll have a machine manufacturing fully-functional junior reps, rather than having to bid at existing reps at benchmark organizations. And your investment in SDR professional development will pay dividends.

Releases & Market Changes

It's highly unlikely that your product will stay static for very long, which means that it's important that your reps are able to present it and all its latest features in a way that reflects its current state. And the market is continually changing, with competitors making their own moves, and incumbents reacting. All of this means that when something occurs that extends or modifies the information that reps learning in onboarding, you will want.

With new releases, a good way to ensure the sales team is up to date is to embed new product updates into part of a cadenced meeting. For instance, if you have a weekly sales team meeting, having product management or product marketing participate for ten minutes of that meeting to give a review of what just shipped, and what's on deck, can help start that information soaking into your reps' brains. That likely won't be sufficient, so additionally consider having one-off training exercises built around new releases. For instance, if you ship a big new feature, and you've built some new slides for the sales deck, and would like to add some messaging for it to the sales demo, then make sure that you have that information documented, and then you can either schedule a special event—maybe it's during a catered lunch—or choose to "take over" the hour that you have scheduled weekly for training and professional development for this. So too with market changes. If a competitor does something that meaningfully impacts how you position or present your product, treat it like a product release, but instead, it was the market that released new "features" of its own that changes how your product is viewed. The point is these product and market changes won't just naturally be consumed and understood by your reps, and rather than having their understanding of your product and market "frozen in amber" from the point at which they were onboarded, you want them at the vanguard of knowledge both regarding your product, and the market.

As noted at the beginning of this chapter, the biggest cost to a young sales organization that has hit product/market fit and is now scaling is the opportunity cost of missed or delayed sales. Rigorous, thoughtful onboarding will minimize these costs; engender a positive feedback loop, faster time to revenue for new reps, and higher retention (making your recruiters very happy, or minimizing recruiting agency costs); and enhance team cohesion and excellence.

When onboarding is done right, it's just a good scene, all the way around.

CHAPTER 13

Where Do You Go From Here?

CONCLUSION

At the beginning of this book, I told you that your go to market would have two stages: figuring out how to sell your offering (the approaches for which were discussed in the first two-thirds of the book), and then the beginnings of scaling that up (which is what the last third of the book is about.).

If you are now, successfully scaling up, then congratulations! You've moved beyond the province of this book. You are now a bona-fide sales professional, and if you have a set of sellers reporting to you—successfully closing business—then guess what? You are now a "Sales Leader." Way to go!

Am I Ready to Hire a Sales Leader?

However, it's key that before you progress to "professionalizing" your sales organization—by bringing in dedicated sales management—that you're ready to do so, and that you've met the "exit criteria" for moving to the next stage of your company. Remember how the "exit criteria" for knowing that it was time to hire dedicated sales staff (to prove that someone other than you could sell your solution) was that you had successfully sold to a statistically significant number of customers? Well, the exit criteria for knowing that you're ready to hand the reins off to a dedicated sales leader, is that you have a set of sellers who they themselves are successfully selling your solution at least as well as you were.

This isn't to say everything will be humming like a fine-tuned machine, because startups are chaos and that will likely never be the case. However you will want to know that you have successfully gotten one, two, or three sellers to the point of "repeatability." If you have, you should definitely congratulate yourself, in that this is a very powerful thing. SaaS sales organizations "scale up via scale out," which is to say that revenue growth comes from more sellers selling more deals—not by a small number of sellers magically selling bigger and bigger deals more quickly. So proving that you can bring new salespeople into your organization, and that they can generate $30k, $50k, $100k, and up in revenue a month is a momentous occasion in the development of your company, and something that investors will likely be very excited by. Why would investors be excited? Because you've now proven that you can take the money an investor gives you and turn it into sales people who a few months out will start bringing cash into the organization.

If you haven't proven this quite yet, well then you're probably not ready to move on to professionalized sales management just yet. While it's tempting to make it someone else's responsibility to own the management and enablement of your small band of "experimental sellers," it's a rather dangerous exercise to engage in. Namely, having proven the ability to sell this repeatedly yourself, you are now the most expert person in the world at selling your solution. You're the one who cracked the code on the repeated sale, with you as the seller, so you are also the best positioned person to teach others how to sell your solution. Having someone else teach others to sell would be engaging in a high risk game of telephone—with you teaching the new leader, and then them teaching the new reps—and that's a situation that your company likely doesn't have time for. So this is your warning that prematurely adding a sales leader before you've systematized your sales process enough for a handful of reps to be repeatedly successful is likely a losing proposition in all but the rarest of cases.

Who Should I Hire?

If you have indeed met the exit criteria to professionalizing your sales leadership, the next question of course is, what type of person should you be looking for?

Similar to how when you were converging on your hiring profile for your reps, it's important to understand the difference between varying candidate characteristics, and what is stage-appropriate for your organization. People throw around the term "VP of Sales" quite a bit (and boy, people LOVE to spill it all over LinkedIn profiles...), but please be clear about what you're actually hiring for.

For the most part, assuming that you're hiring a sales leader to slide in on top of a handful of existing AEs and SDRs to stabilize that team, and then likely doubling it in the short-term, and then potentially doubling it again shortly thereafter, what you're looking for is a hands-on "tactical sales leader." Someone who is currently probably running a single sales team (i.e., 6 AEs), or perhaps a director who sits on top of a handful of teams (i.e., an 8 person SMB AE team, a 4 person Mid-Market AE team, and a 6 person SDR team). And this tactical sales leader is probably working at a similar organization to the ones we used to target our AE candidate profile—a scaled startup that's in your space, or a tangential space, with a similar sales motion and Average Selling Price, that's scaled up to dozens or maybe low hundreds of sellers, but isn't a doddering dinosaur. If you're a new Business Intelligence (BI) company, then hiring a sales manager or director from Looker, Mode, Domo, etc., is the better bet than hiring one from Tableau, SAP, or Oracle. If you're a new recruiting solution, it's the better bet to hire from Greenhouse, Lever, Workable, etc., than from say Oracle, Taleo, SAP, or SuccessFactors. Whatever your space, you should be able to figure out the set of companies to consider.

I won't get much more into this as this is something that I haven't done enough times to speak authoritatively on (whereas the stuff earlier in the book I've done the hell out of). Suffice it to say, that this is an extremely critical hire, and the key is to reference, and back channel reference, the heck out of any candidates who get down to the finish line. And then once onboard, much like your job when bringing on your first set of AEs was to get out of the business of selling, and into the business of getting those reps to be successful, your job is to help this new sales leader ingest your now well-documented sales process, and quickly get up to speed successfully managing the team. Congratulations! You are now no longer the Sales Manager. You are now the Manager of the Sales Manager.

Further Reading

Founding Sales was written because there wasn't yet a tactical textbook for early stage sales, written specifically for founders and other non-sellers. But there's a whole constellation of high quality sales books for sales professionals, of which my favorites are listed below. I highly recommend you check them out to help further your sales education.

Selling:

The Transparency Sale (Caponi)

The Challenger Sale (Dixon & Adamson)

Triangle Selling (Bray & Sorey)

SPIN Selling (Rackham)

Sales Management:

  Cracking the Sales Management Code (Jordan)

  The Revenue Acceleration Formula (Roberge)

  Blueprints For A SaaS Sales Organization (VanderKooij)

Prospecting & SDR Management:

  The Sales Development Playbook (Bertuzzi)

  Leading Sales Development (Donovan & Homison)

  Fanatical Prospecting (Blount)

Startup Sales:

  David Skok's writing on his blog *forEntrepreneurs.com* is also quite good when it comes to a very clear, tactical early stage go-to-market education.

Acknowledgments

Founding Sales was the culmination of many people's efforts. Thank you to my editor, Christina Bailly, for reducing redundancy and unnecessary loquaciousness. Thank you to my designer, and wife, Tracy Moeller, for laying out the book for print and e-publishing, designing the cover, and building the entire FoundingSales.com website.

Thank you to the First Round Capital portfolio community that supported me at the earliest stages of my journey, specifically Sean Black and Angus Davis for their peer support. And while we're on the topic, thank you to First Round Capital and Charles River Ventures for funding TalentBin, and now Atrium, and providing the initial capital for the companies in which these lessons were learned.

Thank you to my TalentBin team, including my co-founder, Jason Heidema, and engineering leaders, Ignacio Andreu and Rodrigo Leroux, for providing a market-leading product on which I could learn to sell. And thank you to the early TalentBin sales team, including Rob Perez, Brad Snider, Manny Ortega, Akio Aida, Marcus Knight, and Jared McGriff for being the combination guinea pigs/mad scientists with me as we figured this out. Also thank you to Adam Abeles who lead TalentBin's customer success function. And thank you to my extended peer education network of Modern Sales experts, including Jeremey Donovan, Trish Bertuzzi, Jason Jordan, and Jacco vanderKooij for constantly pushing forward the frontier of Modern Sales, and teaching me along the way.

And thank you again to my wife, Tracy Moeller, for being my partner in my entrepreneurial journeys. Last, but not least, thank you to my parents, Cathey and Bob Kazanjy, for instilling in me a lifelong love of learning and critical inquiry without which none of this would be possible.

CPSIA information can be obtained
at www.ICGtesting.com
Printed in the USA
LVHW051649270422
716776LV00005B/12